The Well-Grounded Rubyist

Second Edition

DAVID A. BLACK

MANNING

SHELTER ISLAND

For online information and ordering of this and other Manning books, please visit www.manning.com. The publisher offers discounts on this book when ordered in quantity. For more information, please contact

> Special Sales Department
> Manning Publications Co.
> 20 Baldwin Road
> PO Box 261
> Shelter Island, NY 11964
> Email: orders@manning.com

Manning Publications Co.
20 Baldwin Road
PO Box 261
Shelter Island, NY 11964

Development editor:	Dan Maharry
Technical development editor:	Andrew Gibson
Copyeditor:	Jodie Allen
Proofreader:	Melody Dolab
Technical proofreader:	Deepak Vohra
Typesetter:	Dennis Dalinnik
Cover designer:	Marija Tudor

ISBN: 9781617291692
Printed in the United States of America
1 2 3 4 5 6 7 8 9 10 – EBM – 19 18 17 16 15 14

To Barbara Aronstein Black,
and in memory of Charles L. Black, Jr.
(1915–2001),
with love.
Thanks for the writing genes.

brief contents

contents

preface

Welcome to the second edition of *The Well-Grounded Rubyist*. In the five years since the first edition came out, the Ruby language has changed and evolved—most notably with the release, on Ruby's twentieth birthday (February 24, 2013), of Ruby 2.0. At the end of 2013—Christmas, to be precise—Ruby 2.1 was released; that's the version covered in this edition.

The Well-Grounded Rubyist has been very well-received. It seemed to hit a sweet spot for a lot of readers, including many who were completely new to Ruby, as well as many who had done some Ruby already but wanted to make a thorough pass through the language and make sure they really understood it. I've been particularly pleased by those comments that describe the experience of reading the book as being like working directly with a Ruby teacher. After all, I *am* a Ruby teacher, and though teaching involves wearing a different hat than writing, the two hats aren't all that different after all.

Much hasn't changed in Ruby—but quite a lot has. This second edition includes a lot of new material, along with an extensive review and reworking of the original text. As with the first edition, the book doesn't pretend to be an exhaustive Ruby and standard library reference (those are available elsewhere), but an in-depth examination and explication of the key aspects of Ruby's object model, built-in classes, and important programming facilities.

I'd like to extend a warm welcome to all of the book's readers, including those who read the first edition and those who are entirely new to *The Well-Grounded Rubyist*. I hope and trust that you'll find a great deal to interest and excite you here. Enjoy!

preface to the first edition

In 2006, Manning published my book *Ruby for Rails: Ruby Techniques for Rails Developers*. My goal in writing *Ruby for Rails*—or, as it has come to be known, *R4R*—was to provide Rails developers with both an understanding of the fact that being a Rails developer means being a Ruby developer, and a solid grasp of Ruby. I chose Ruby topics for inclusion (or exclusion) based on my judgment as to their relative importance for people who wanted to learn Ruby mainly in order to use Rails correctly and effectively.

Critical response to *R4R* was very good. The book filled a void: it was neither just a Ruby book nor just a Rails book, but a Ruby book "optimized," so to speak, for the Rails developer. I was pleased by the book's reception—and particularly by the many people who, after reading it, asked me whether I had any plans to write a whole book just about Ruby, and encouraged me to write one.

And that, to make a long story short, is what I have done.

The Well-Grounded Rubyist is a "just Ruby" book, and it's written to be read by anyone interested in Ruby. It's a descendant of *R4R* but not exactly an update. It's more of a repurposing. There's some overlap with *R4R*, but there's also a lot of new material (more than I originally anticipated, in fact); and everything, overlap or not, has been oiled and polished and spiffed up to work with Ruby 1.9.1, the newest version of Ruby (and very new) at the time the book went to press.

Mind you, I don't mean for Rails developers *not* to read *The Well-Grounded Rubyist*. On the contrary: I'm optimistic that in the three years since *R4R* was published, the idea that Rails developers should learn Ruby has become commonplace, and many people who first got into Ruby through Rails have gotten interested in Ruby in its own right. I want this book to be there waiting for them—and for the many people who are discovering Ruby through completely different channels.

So whatever brings you here, I hope you enjoy the book.

acknowledgments

Thanks first of all to everyone whom I thanked in the first edition. This edition would not exist if it were not for that ensemble of editors, production personnel, reviewers, publishers, and colleagues.

For the second edition my thanks go first and foremost to development editor Dan Maharry, whose patience, support, and guidance kept the book on track when it felt like it might otherwise not be. Technical development editor Andrew Gibson cast an expert and expertly critical eye on the entire book, to its great benefit. Copyeditor Jodie Allen contributed greatly to the process of putting an overall polish on the text. Technical proofreader Deepak Vohra meticulously examined the sample code, and spotted some problems in a timely manner. Proofreader Melody Dolab contributed an adept final read-through and correction of the entire text.

In pre-production, Kevin Sullivan kept everything on track and on time. Production manager Mary Piergies once again guided the book to completion with tremendous expertise. Typesetter Dennis Dalinnik did a superb job of making everything look good and flow smoothly. In the QA phase, Katie Tennant contributed numerous valuable insights and suggestions.

Along the way, a number of outside reviewers contributed comments and critiques, all of which helped me greatly in making the second edition even more polished and accessible than the first. Thanks to Jason Brown, Marius Butuc, Hector Sansores, Jeffrey Schwab, Doug Sparling, Andrea Tarocchi, Ted Roche, and William E. Wheeler.

Throughout my work on the second edition, David Williams provided support and encouragement. I owe him much gratitude for his role in keeping me on track and keeping my morale high.

As always, thanks to Yukihiro "Matz" Matsumoto for creating the wonderful Ruby language—which, by the way, recently celebrated its twenty-first birthday (February 24, 2014), as measured from Matz's first public announcement of the project. I'm particularly pleased that the appearance of this second edition coincides, at least roughly, with that wonderful milestone.

about this book

Welcome

... to the second edition of *The Well-Grounded Rubyist*.

Ruby is a general-purpose, object-oriented, interpreted programming language designed by Yukihiro "Matz" Matsumoto. Ruby was first announced in 1993. The first public release appeared in 1995, and the language became very popular in Japan during the 1990s. It's known and admired for its expressiveness—its ability to do a lot with relatively little code—and the elegance and visual smoothness of its syntax and style. Ruby has proven useful and productive in a wide variety of programming contexts, ranging from administrative scripting to device embedding, from web development to PDF document processing. Moreover, and at the risk of sounding non-technical, Ruby programming is fun. It's designed that way. As Matz has said, Ruby is optimized for the programmer experience. Indeed, Ruby started as Matz's pet project and gained attention and traction because so many other programmers got pleasure from the same kind of language design that Matz did.

The first English-language book on Ruby (*Programming Ruby* by Dave Thomas and Andy Hunt [Addison-Wesley]) appeared in late 2000 and ushered in a wave of Ruby enthusiasm outside of Japan. Ruby's popularity in the West has grown steadily since the appearance of the "Pickaxe book" (the nickname of the Thomas-Hunt work, derived from its cover illustration). Four years after the first edition of the Pickaxe, the introduction of the Ruby on Rails web application development framework by David Heinemeier Hansson sparked a massive surge in worldwide interest in Ruby. The years since 2004 have seen exponential growth in the use of Ruby, as well as books about Ruby, Ruby user groups, and Ruby-related conferences and other events.

I'm a Rails developer and devotee. At the same time, I'm firmly convinced that even if Rails had never come along, the world would have "discovered" Ruby eventually on the scale that we're seeing in the Rails era. Ruby is too pleasing and versatile a language to have remained a semi-secret jewel forever. I've loved Ruby for almost 14 years, and it has been my pleasure to introduce a large number of people to the language through my writing and teaching, and to watch the vast majority of those people embrace Ruby with pleasure and satisfaction.

And that's why I wrote this book. The purpose of *The Well-Grounded Rubyist* is to give you a broad and deep understanding of how Ruby works and a considerable toolkit of Ruby techniques and idioms that you can use for real programming.

How this book is organized

The Well-Grounded Rubyist, Second Edition consists of 15 chapters and is divided into 3 parts:

- Part 1: Ruby foundations
- Part 2: Built-in classes and modules
- Part 3: Ruby dynamics

Part 1 (chapters 1 through 6) introduces you to the syntax of Ruby and to a number of the key concepts and semantics on which Ruby programming builds: objects, methods, classes and modules, identifiers, and more. It also covers the Ruby programming lifecycle (how to prepare and execute code files, writing programs that span more than one file), as well as many of the command-line tools that ship with Ruby and that Ruby programmers use frequently, including the interactive Ruby interpreter (irb), the RubyGems package manager (gem), and the Ruby interpreter (ruby).

Part 2 (chapters 7 through 12) surveys the major built-in classes—including strings, arrays, hashes, numerics, ranges, dates and times, and regular expressions—and provides you with insight into what the various built-ins are for, as well as the nuts and bolts of how to use them. It also builds on your general Ruby literacy with exploration of such topics as Boolean logic in Ruby, built-in methods for converting objects from one class to another (for example, converting a string to an integer), Ruby's considerable facilities for engineering collections and their enumeration, and techniques for comparing objects for identity and equality. You'll also learn about file and console I/O as well as issuing system commands from inside Ruby programs.

Part 3 (chapters 13 through 15) addresses the area of Ruby dynamics. Under this heading you'll find a number of subtopics—among them some metaprogramming techniques—including Ruby's facilities for runtime reflection and object introspection; ways to endow objects with individualized behaviors; and the handling of functions, threads, and other runnable and executable objects. This part of the book also introduces you to techniques for issuing system commands from inside a Ruby program and encompasses a number of Ruby's event-triggered runtime hooks and callbacks, such as handlers for calls to non-existent methods and interception of events like class inheritance and method definition.

Ruby is a system, and presenting any system in a strictly linear way is a challenge. I meet the challenge by thinking of the learning process as a kind of widening spiral, building on the familiar but always opening out into the unknown. At times, you'll be shown enough of a future topic to serve as a placeholder, so that you can learn the current topic in depth. Later, with the necessary bootstrapping already done, you'll come back to the placeholder topic and study it in its own right. *The Well-Grounded Rubyist, Second Edition* is engineered to expose you to as much material as possible as efficiently as possible, consistent with its mission of providing you with a solid foundation in Ruby—a real and lasting understanding of how the language works.

Who should read this book

The Well-Grounded Rubyist, Second Edition is optimized for a reader who's done some programming and perhaps even some Ruby and wants to learn more about the Ruby language—not only the specific techniques (although the book includes plenty of those), but also the design principles that make Ruby what it is. I'm a great believer in knowing what you're doing. I also believe that knowing what you're doing doesn't mean you have to compose a treatise in your head every time you write a line of code; it means you know how to make the most out of the language, and understand how to analyze problems when they arise.

I've hedged my bets a little, in terms of targeted readership, in that I've included some introductory remarks about a number of topics and techniques that are possibly familiar to experienced programmers. I ask the indulgence of those readers. The remarks in question go by pretty quickly, and I believe that even a few words of explanation of terms here and there can make a surprisingly big difference in how many people feel at home in, and welcomed by, the book. If you're a more experienced programmer and see passages where I seem to be spoon-feeding, please bear with me. It's for a good cause.

By the same token, if this is your first foray into programming, be prepared to do a little extra self-imposed "homework" to get ramped up into the programming process—but by all means, give *The Well-Grounded Rubyist, Second Edition* a go. The book isn't specifically an introduction to programming, but it does take you through all the practicalities, including the creation and running of program files, as well as explaining Ruby from the ground up.

What this book doesn't include

The Well-Grounded Rubyist, Second Edition is a serious, extensive look at the Ruby language. But it isn't a complete language reference. There are core classes that I say little or nothing about, and I discuss only a modest number of standard library packages. That's by design. You don't need me to spell out for you how to use every standard-library API, and I don't. What you do need, in all likelihood, is someone to explain to you exactly what `class << self` means, or why two instance variables two lines apart aren't the same variable, or the distinction between singleton methods and private methods, or what an enumerator is and how it differs from an iterator. You need to know these things, and you need to see them in operation and to start using them. You must, of course, plunge deeply into the standard library in your work with Ruby, and I'm not encouraging you not to. I'm aiming to impart a particular kind and degree of understanding in this book.

A word on Ruby versions

The Well-Grounded Rubyist, Second Edition covers version 2.1 of the Ruby language, the most recent version at time of writing. Version 1.9 is still in wide use, though I predict it won't be for much longer. If you're still using 1.9, you'll get a lot of value from the book—especially as the odds are that you'll make the transition to some flavor of Ruby 2 in the not-too-distant future.

Code conventions, examples, and downloads

In the text, names of Ruby variables and constants are in monospace. Names of classes and modules are in `monospace` where they represent direct references to existing class or module objects; for example, "Next, we'll reopen the class definition block for `Person`." Where the name of a class or module is used in a more high-level narrative sense, the name appears in regular type; for example, "Now we need an Array instance." In all cases, you'll be able to tell from the context that a class, module, or other Ruby entity is under discussion.

Source code for all of the working examples in this book is available for download from www.manning.com/black3 or www.manning.com/TheWellGroundedRubyist-SecondEdition.

Names of programs, such as `ruby` and `rails`, are in `monospace font` where reference is made directly to the program executable or to command-line usage; otherwise, they appear in regular type.

Italics or an asterisk are used for wildcard expressions; for example, `to_*` might indicate the general category of Ruby methods that includes `to_i` and `to_s`, whereas *position*`_match` might correspond to `post_match` or `pre_match`.

You can run the standalone code samples in the book either by placing them in a text file and running the `ruby` command on them, or by typing them into the Interactive Ruby interpreter irb. In chapter 1, you'll learn these techniques. As the book progresses, it will be assumed that you can do this on your own and that you'll make up names for your sample files if no names are suggested (or if you prefer different names).

A considerable number of examples in the book are presented in the form of irb sessions. What you'll see on the page are cut-and-pasted lines from a live interactive session, where the code was entered into irb and irb responded by running the code. You'll come to recognize this format easily (especially if you start using irb yourself).

This mode of presentation is particularly suitable for short code snippets and expressions; and because irb always prints out the results of executing whatever you type in (rather like a calculator), it lets you see results while economizing on explicit `print` commands.

In other cases, the output from code samples is printed separately after the samples, printed alongside the code (and clearly labeled as output), or embedded in the discussion following the appearance of the code.

Some examples are accompanied by numbered cueballs that appear to the side of the code. These cueballs are linked to specific points in the ensuing discussion and give you a way to refer back quickly to the line under discussion.

Command-line program invocations are shown with a dollar-sign ($) prompt, in the general style of shell prompts in UNIX-like environments. Most of these commands will work on Windows, even though the prompt may be different. (In all environments, the availability of the commands depends, as always, on the setting of the relevant path environment variable.)

The use of *web* rather than *Web* to designate the World Wide Web is a Manning in-house style convention that I have followed here, although in other contexts I follow the W3C's guideline, which is to use *Web*.

Author Online

Purchase of *The Well-Grounded Rubyist, Second Edition* includes free access to a private web forum run by Manning Publications where you can make comments about the book, ask technical questions, and receive help from the author and from other users. To access the forum and subscribe to it, point your web browser to

- www.manning.com/TheWellGroundedRubyistSecondEdition or
- www.manning.com/black3

This page provides information on how to get on the forum once you're registered, what kind of help is available, and the rules of conduct on the forum. Manning's commitment to our readers is to provide a venue where a meaningful dialog between individual readers and between readers and the author can take place. It's not a commitment to any specific amount of participation on the part of the author, whose contribution to the forum remains voluntary (and unpaid). We suggest you try asking the author some challenging questions lest his interest stray!

The Author Online forum and the archives of previous discussions will be accessible from the publisher's website as long as the book is in print.

about the cover illustration

The figure on the cover of *The Well-Grounded Rubyist* is a "Noble Française" or a French noblewoman. The illustration is taken from the 1805 edition of Sylvain Maréchal's four-volume compendium of regional dress customs. This book was first published in Paris in 1788, one year before the French Revolution. Each illustration is colored by hand.

The colorful variety of Maréchal's collection reminds us vividly of how culturally apart the world's towns and regions were just 200 years ago. Isolated from one another, people spoke different dialects and languages. In the streets or in the countryside, it was easy to identify where they lived and what their trade or station in life was just by their dress. Dress codes have changed since then and the diversity by region, so rich at the time, has faded away. Today, it is hard to tell apart the inhabitants of different continents, let alone different towns or regions. Perhaps we have traded cultural diversity for a more varied personal life—certainly a more varied and faster-paced technological life.

At a time when it is hard to tell one computer book from another, Manning celebrates the inventiveness and initiative of the computer business with book covers based on the rich diversity of regional life of two centuries ago, brought back to life by Maréchal's pictures.

Part 1

Ruby foundations

The goal of this part of the book is to give you a broad but practical foundation layer on which to build, and to which to anchor, the further explorations of Ruby that follow in parts 2 and 3. We'll start with a chapter on bootstrapping your Ruby literacy; after working through that first chapter, you'll be able to run Ruby programs comfortably and have a good sense of the layout of a typical Ruby installation. Starting with chapter 2, we'll get into the details of the Ruby language. Ruby is an object-oriented language, and the sooner you dive into how Ruby handles objects, the better. Accordingly, objects will serve both as a way to bootstrap the discussion of the language (and your knowledge of it) and as a golden thread leading us to further topics and techniques.

Objects are created by classes, and in chapter 3 you'll learn how classes work. The discussion of classes is followed by a look at modules in chapter 4. Modules allow you to fine-tune classes and objects by splitting out some of the object design into separate, reusable units of code. To understand Ruby programs—both your own and others'—you need to know about Ruby's notion of a current *default object*, known by the keyword self. Chapter 5 will take you deep into the concept of self, along with a treatment of Ruby's handling of variable visibility and scope.

In chapter 6, the last in this part of the book, you'll learn about control flow in Ruby programs—that is, how to steer the Ruby interpreter through conditional (if) logic, how to loop repeatedly through code, and even how to break away from normal program execution when an error occurs. By the end of chapter 6, you'll be thinking along with Ruby as you write and develop your code.

The title of this part is "Ruby foundations," which obviously suggests that what's here is to be built on later. And that's true. But it doesn't mean that the material in part 1 isn't important in itself. As you'll see once you read them, these six chapters present you with real Ruby techniques, real code, and information you'll use every time you write or execute a Ruby program. It's not the "foundations" because you'll learn it once and then ignore it, but because there's so much *more* about Ruby yet to follow!

Bootstrapping
your Ruby literacy

1

This chapter covers

- A Ruby syntax survival kit
- A basic Ruby programming how-to: writing, saving, running, and error-checking programs
- A tour of the Ruby installation
- The mechanics of Ruby extensions
- Ruby's out-of-the-box command-line tools, including the interactive Ruby interpreter (irb)

This book will give you a foundation in Ruby, and this chapter will give your foundation a foundation. The goal of the chapter is to bootstrap you into the study of Ruby with enough knowledge and skill to proceed comfortably into what lies beyond.

We'll look at basic Ruby syntax and techniques and at how Ruby works: what you do when you write a program, how you get Ruby to run your program, and how you split a program into more than one file. You'll learn several of the switches that alter how the Ruby interpreter (the program with the name ruby, to which you feed your program files for execution) acts, as well as how to use some important auxiliary tools designed to make your life as a Rubyist easier and more productive.

3

The chapter is based on a view of the whole Ruby landscape as being divided into three fundamental levels:

- Core language: design principles, syntax, and semantics
- Extensions and libraries that ship with Ruby, and the facilities for adding extensions of your own
- Command-line tools that come with Ruby, with which you run the interpreter and some other important utilities

It's not always possible to talk about these three levels in isolation—after all, they're interlocking parts of a single system—but we'll discuss them separately as much as possible in this chapter. You can, in any case, use the three level descriptions as pegs to hang subtopics on, wherever they're introduced.

> **Ruby, `ruby`, and ... RUBY?!**
>
> Ruby is a programming language. We talk about things like "learning Ruby," and we ask questions like, "Do you know Ruby?" The lowercase version, `ruby`, is a computer program; specifically, it's the Ruby interpreter, the program that reads your programs and runs them. You'll see this name used in sentences like "I ran `ruby` on my file, but nothing happened," or "What's the full path to your `ruby` executable?" Finally, there's RUBY—or, more precisely, there isn't. Ruby isn't an acronym, and it's never correct to spell it in all capital letters. People do this, as they do (also wrongly) with Perl, perhaps because they're used to seeing language names like BASIC and COBOL. Ruby isn't such a language. It's Ruby for the language, `ruby` for the interpreter.

Nor does this first chapter exist solely in the service of later chapters. It has content in its own right: you'll learn real Ruby techniques and important points about the design of the language. The goal is to bootstrap or jumpstart you, but even that process will involve close examination of some key aspects of the Ruby language.

1.1   *Basic Ruby language literacy*

The goal of this section is to get you going with Ruby. It takes a breadth-first approach: we'll walk through the whole cycle of learning some syntax, writing some code, and running some programs.

At this point, you need to have Ruby installed on your computer.[1] The examples in this book use Ruby 2.1.0. You also need a text editor (you can use any editor you like, as long as it's a plain-text editor and not a word processor) and a directory (a.k.a. a folder) in which to store your Ruby program files. You might name that directory rubycode or rubysamples—any name is fine, as long as it's separate from other work areas so that you can keep track of your practice program files.

---

[1] You can find full up-to-date instructions for installing Ruby at http://ruby-lang.org.

The interactive Ruby console program (irb), your new best friend

The irb utility ships with Ruby and is the most widely used Ruby command-line tool other than the interpreter itself. After starting irb, you type Ruby code into it, and it executes the code and prints out the resulting value.

Type `irb` at the command line and enter sample code as you encounter it in the text. For example:

```
>> 100 + 32
=> 132
```

Having an open irb session means you can test Ruby snippets at any time and in any quantity. Most Ruby developers find irb indispensable, and you'll see a few examples of its use as we proceed through this chapter.

The irb examples you'll see in this book will use a command-line option that makes irb output easier to read:

```
irb --simple-prompt
```

If you want to see the effect of the `--simple-prompt` option, try starting irb with and without it. As you'll see, the simple prompt keeps your screen a lot clearer. The default (nonsimple) prompt displays more information, such as a line-number count for your interactive session; but for the examples we'll look at, the simple prompt is sufficient.

Because irb is one of the command-line tools that ship with Ruby, it's not discussed in detail until section 1.4.2. Feel free to jump to that section and have a look; it's pretty straightforward.

With Ruby installed and your work area created, let's continue to bootstrap your Ruby literacy so we have a shared ground on which to continuing building and exploring. One thing you'll need is enough exposure to basic Ruby syntax to get you started.

1.1.1 A Ruby syntax survival kit

The following three tables summarize some Ruby features that you'll find useful in understanding the examples in this chapter and in starting to experiment with Ruby. You don't have to memorize them, but do look them over and refer back to them later as needed.

Table 1.1 contains some of Ruby's basic operations. Table 1.2 covers retrieving basic input from the keyboard, sending output to the screen, and basic conditional statements. Table 1.3 briefly details Ruby's special objects and syntax for comments.

A few fundamental aspects of Ruby and Ruby syntax are too involved for summary in a table. You need to be able to recognize a handful of different Ruby identifiers and, above all, you need a sense of what an object is in Ruby and what a method call looks like. We'll take a look at both of those aspects of the language next.

Table 1.1 Basic operations in Ruby

Operation	Example(s)	Comments
Arithmetic	2 + 3 (addition) 2 – 3 (subtraction) 2 * 3 (multiplication) 2 / 3 (division) 10.3 + 20.25 103 - 202.5 32.9 * 10 100.0 / 0.23	All these operations work on integers or floating-point numbers (*floats*). Mixing integers and floats together, as some of the examples do, produces a floating-point result. Note that you need to write 0.23 rather than .23.
Assignment	x = 1 string = "Hello"	This operation binds a local variable (on the left) to an object (on the right). For now, you can think of an object as a value represented by the variable.
Compare two values	x == y	Note the two equal signs (not just one, as in assignment).
Convert a numeric string to a number	x = "100".to_i s = "100" x = s.to_i	To perform arithmetic, you have to make sure you have numbers rather than strings of characters. to_i performs string-to-integer conversion.

Table 1.2 Basic input/output methods and flow control in Ruby

Operation	Example(s)	Comments
Print something to the screen	print "Hello" puts "Hello" x = "Hello" puts x x = "Hello" print x x = "Hello" p x	puts adds a newline to the string it outputs if there isn't one at the end already; print doesn't. print prints exactly what it's told to and leaves the cursor at the end. (Note: On some platforms, an extra line is automatically output at the end of a program.) p outputs an inspect string, which may contain extra information about what it's printing.
Get a line of keyboard input	gets string = gets	You can assign the input line directly to a variable (the variable string in the second example).

Conditional execution	if x == y
	  puts "Yes!"
	else
	  puts "No!"
	end
		Conditional statements always end with the word end. More on these in chapter 6.

Table 1.3 Ruby's special objects and comment

Operation	Example(s)	Comments
Special value objects	true false nil	The objects true and false often serve as return values for conditional expressions. The object nil is a kind of "nonobject" indicating the absence of a value or result. false and nil cause a conditional expression to fail; all other objects (including true, of course, but also including 0 and empty strings) cause it to succeed. More on these in chapter 7.

Table 1.3 Ruby's special objects and comment (*continued*)

Operation	Example(s)	Comments
Default object	`self`	The keyword `self` refers to the default object. Self is a role that different objects play, depending on the execution context. Method calls that don't specify a calling object are called on `self`. More on this in chapter 5.
Put comments in code files	`# A comment` `x = 1 # A comment`	Comments are ignored by the interpreter.

1.1.2 *The variety of Ruby identifiers*

Ruby has a small number of identifier types that you'll want to be able to spot and differentiate from each other at a glance. The identifier family tree looks like this:

- Variables:
  - Local
  - Instance
  - Class
  - Global
- Constants
- Keywords
- Method names

It's a small family, and easily learned. We'll survey them here. Keep in mind that this section's purpose is to teach you to recognize the various identifiers. You'll also learn a lot more throughout the book about when and how to use them. This is just the first lesson in identifier literacy.

VARIABLES

Local variables start with a lowercase letter or an underscore and consist of letters, underscores, and/or digits. x, `string`, `abc`, `start_value`, and `firstName` are all valid local variable names. Note, however, that the Ruby convention is to use underscores rather than camel case when composing local variable names from multiple words—for example, `first_name` rather than `firstName`.

Instance variables, which serve the purpose of storing information for individual objects, always start with a single at sign (@) and consist thereafter of the same character set as local variables—for example, `@age` and `@last_name`. Although a local variable can't start with an uppercase letter, an instance variable can have one in the first position after the at sign (though it may not have a digit in this position). But usually the character after the at sign is a lowercase letter.

Class variables, which store information per class hierarchy (again, don't worry about the semantics at this stage), follow the same rules as instance variables, except that they start with two at signs—for example, `@@running_total`.

Global variables are recognizable by their leading dollar sign ($)—for example, `$population`. The segment after the dollar sign doesn't follow local-variable naming conventions; there are global variables called $:, $1, and $/, as well as $stdin and $LOAD_PATH. As long as it begins with a dollar sign, it's a global variable. As for the nonalphanumeric ones, the only such identifiers you're likely to see are predefined, so you don't need to worry about which punctuation marks are legal and which aren't.

Table 1.4 summarizes Ruby's variable naming rules.

Table 1.4   Valid variable names in Ruby by variable type

Type	Ruby convention	Nonconventional
Local	`first_name`	`firstName`, `_firstName`, `__firstName`, `name1`
Instance	`@first_name`	`@First_name`, `@firstName`, `@name1`
Class	`@@first_name`	`@@First_name`, `@@firstName`, `@@name1`
Global	`$FIRST_NAME`	`$first_name`, `$firstName`, `$name1`

CONSTANTS

Constants begin with an uppercase letter. `A`, `String`, `FirstName`, and `STDIN` are all valid constant names. The Ruby convention is to use either camel case (`FirstName`) or underscore-separated all-uppercase words (`FIRST_NAME`) in composing constant names from multiple words.

KEYWORDS

Ruby has numerous keywords: predefined, reserved terms associated with specific programming tasks and contexts. Keywords include `def` (for method definitions), `class` (for class definitions), `if` (conditional execution), and `__FILE__` (the name of the file currently being executed). There are about 40 of them, and they're generally short, single-word (as opposed to underscore-composed) identifiers.

METHOD NAMES

Names of methods in Ruby follow the same rules and conventions as local variables (except that they can end with ?, !, or =, with significance you'll see later). This is by design: methods don't call attention to themselves as methods but rather blend into the texture of a program as, simply, expressions that provide a value. In some contexts you can't tell just by looking at an expression whether you're seeing a local variable or a method name—and that's intentional.

Speaking of methods, now that you've got a roadmap to Ruby identifiers, let's get back to some language semantics—in particular, the all-important role of the object and its methods.

1.1.3   Method calls, messages, and Ruby objects

Ruby sees all data structures and values—from simple scalar (atomic) values like integers and strings, to complex data structures like arrays—as *objects*. Every object is capable of understanding a certain set of *messages*. Each message that an object understands corresponds directly to a *method*—a named, executable routine whose execution the object has the ability to trigger.

Objects are represented either by literal constructors—like quotation marks for strings—or by variables to which they've been bound. Message sending is achieved via the special dot operator: the message to the right of the dot is sent to the object to the left of the dot. (There are other, more specialized ways to send messages to objects, but the dot is the most common and fundamental way.) Consider this example from table 1.1:

```
x = "100".to_i
```

The dot means that the message `to_i` is being sent to the string `"100"`. The string `"100"` is called the *receiver* of the message. We can also say that the method `to_i` is being *called* on the string `"100"`. The result of the method call—the integer 100— serves as the right-hand side of the assignment to the variable x.

Why the double terminology?

Why bother saying both "sending the message `to_i`" and "calling the method `to_i`"? Why have two ways of describing the same operation? Because they aren't quite the same. Most of the time, you send a message to a receiving object, and the object executes the corresponding method. But sometimes there's no corresponding method. You can put anything to the right of the dot, and there's no guarantee that the receiver will have a method that matches the message you send.

If that sounds like chaos, it isn't, because objects can intercept unknown messages and try to make sense of them. The Ruby on Rails web development framework, for example, makes heavy use of the technique of sending unknown messages to objects, intercepting those messages, and making sense of them on the fly based on dynamic conditions like the names of the columns in the tables of the current database.

Methods can take *arguments*, which are also objects. (Almost everything in Ruby is an object, although some syntactic structures that help you create and manipulate objects aren't themselves objects.) Here's a method call with an argument:

```
x = "100".to_i(9)
```

Calling `to_i` on 100 with an argument of 9 generates a decimal integer equivalent to the base-nine number 100: x is now equal to 81 decimal.

This example also shows the use of parentheses around method arguments. These parentheses are usually optional, but in more complex cases they may be required to clear up what may otherwise be ambiguities in the syntax. Many programmers use parentheses in most or all method calls, just to be safe.

The whole universe of a Ruby program consists of objects and the messages that are sent to them. As a Ruby programmer, you spend most of your time either specifying the things you want objects to be able to do (by defining methods) or asking the objects to do those things (by sending them messages).

We'll explore all of this in much greater depth later in the book. Again, this brief sketch is just part of the process of bootstrapping your Ruby literacy. When you see a dot in what would otherwise be an inexplicable position, you should interpret it as a message (on the right) being sent to an object (on the left). Keep in mind, too, that some method calls take the form of *bareword*-style invocations, like the call to puts in this example:

```
puts "Hello."
```

Here, in spite of the lack of a message-sending dot and an explicit receiver for the message, we're sending the message puts with the argument "Hello." to an object: the default object self. There's always a self defined when your program is running, although which object is self changes, according to specific rules. You'll learn much more about self in chapter 5. For now, take note of the fact that a bareword like puts can be a method call.

The most important concept in Ruby is the concept of the object. Closely related, and playing an important supporting role, is the concept of the *class*.

THE ORIGIN OF OBJECTS IN CLASSES

Classes define clusters of behavior or functionality, and every object is an instance of exactly one class. Ruby provides a large number of built-in classes, representing important foundational data types (classes like String, Array, and Fixnum). Every time you create a string object, you've created an instance of the class String.

You can also write your own classes. You can even modify existing Ruby classes; if you don't like the behavior of strings or arrays, you can change it. It's almost always a bad idea to do so, but Ruby allows it. (We'll look at the pros and cons of making changes to built-in classes in chapter 13.)

Although every Ruby object is an instance of a class, the concept of class is less important than the concept of object. That's because objects can change, acquiring methods and behaviors that weren't defined in their class. The class is responsible for launching the object into existence, a process known as *instantiation*; but the object, thereafter, has a life of its own.

The ability of objects to adopt behaviors that their class didn't give them is one of the most central defining principles of the design of Ruby as a language. As you can surmise, we'll come back to it frequently in a variety of contexts. For now, just be aware that although every object has a class, the class of an object isn't the sole determinant of what the object can do.

Armed with some Ruby literacy (and some material to refer back to when in doubt), let's walk through the steps involved in running a program.

1.1.4 *Writing and saving a simple program*

At this point, you can start creating program files in the Ruby sample code directory you created a little while back. Your first program will be a Celsius-to-Fahrenheit temperature converter.

NOTE A real-world temperature converter would, of course, use floating-point numbers. We're sticking to integers in the input and output to keep the focus on matters of program structure and execution.

We'll work through this example several times, adding to it and modifying it as we go. Subsequent iterations will

- Tidy the program's output
- Accept input via the keyboard from the user
- Read a value in from a file
- Write the result of the program to a file

The first version is simple; the focus is on the file-creation and program-running processes, rather than any elaborate program logic.

CREATING A FIRST PROGRAM FILE

Using a plain-text editor, type the code from the following listing into a text file and save it under the filename c2f.rb in your sample code directory.

> **Listing 1.1 Simple, limited-purpose Celsius-to-Fahrenheit converter (c2f.rb)**

```
celsius = 100
fahrenheit = (celsius * 9 / 5) + 32
puts "The result is: "
puts fahrenheit
puts "."
```

NOTE Depending on your operating system, you may be able to run Ruby program files standalone—that is, with just the filename, or with a short name (like c2f) and no file extension. Keep in mind, though, that the .rb filename extension is mandatory in some cases, mainly involving programs that occupy more than one file (which you'll learn about in detail later) and that need a mechanism for the files to find each other. In this book, all Ruby program filenames end in .rb to ensure that the examples work on as many platforms, and with as few administrative digressions, as possible.

You now have a complete (albeit tiny) Ruby program on your disk, and you can run it.

1.1.5 *Feeding the program to Ruby*

Running a Ruby program involves passing the program's source file (or files) to the Ruby interpreter, which is called `ruby`. You'll do that now...sort of. You'll feed the program to `ruby`, but instead of asking Ruby to run the program, you'll ask it to check the program code for syntax errors.

CHECKING FOR SYNTAX ERRORS

If you add 31 instead of 32 in your conversion formula, that's a programming error. Ruby will still happily run your program and give you the flawed result. But if you accidentally leave out the closing parenthesis in the second line of the program, that's a syntax error, and Ruby won't run the program:

```
$ ruby broken_c2f.rb
broken_c2f.rb:5: syntax error, unexpected end-of-input, expecting ')'
```

(The error is reported on line 5—the last line of the program—because Ruby waits patiently to see whether you're ever going to close the parenthesis before concluding that you're not.)

Conveniently, the Ruby interpreter can check programs for syntax errors without running the programs. It reads through the file and tells you whether the syntax is okay. To run a syntax check on your file, do this:

```
$ ruby -cw c2f.rb
```

The -cw command-line flag is shorthand for two flags: -c and -w. The -c flag means *check for syntax errors*. The -w flag activates a higher level of warning: Ruby will fuss at you if you've done things that are legal Ruby but are questionable on grounds other than syntax.

Assuming you've typed the file correctly, you should see the message

```
Syntax OK
```

printed on your screen.

RUNNING THE PROGRAM

To run the program, pass the file once more to the interpreter, but this time without the combined -c and -w flags:

```
$ ruby c2f.rb
```

If all goes well, you'll see the output of the calculation:

```
The result is
212
.
```

The result of the calculation is correct, but the output spread over three lines looks bad.

SECOND CONVERTER ITERATION

The problem can be traced to the difference between the puts command and the print command. puts adds a newline to the end of the string it prints out, if the string doesn't end with one already. print, on the other hand, prints out the string you ask it to and then stops; it doesn't automatically jump to the next line.

To fix the problem, change the first two puts commands to print:

```
print "The result is "
print fahrenheit
puts "."
```

(Note the blank space after is, which ensures that a space appears between is and the number.) Now the output is

```
The result is 212.
```

puts is short for *put* (that is, print) *string*. Although *put* may not intuitively invoke the notion of skipping down to the next line, that's what puts does: like print, it prints what you tell it to, but then it also automatically goes to the next line. If you ask puts to print a line that already ends with a newline, it doesn't bother adding one.

If you're used to print facilities in languages that don't automatically add a newline, such as Perl's print function, you may find yourself writing code like this in Ruby when you want to print a value followed by a newline:

```
print fahrenheit, "\n"
```

You almost never have to do this, though, because puts adds a newline for you. You'll pick up the puts habit, along with other Ruby idioms and conventions, as you go along.

> **WARNING** On some platforms (Windows, in particular), an extra newline character is printed out at the end of the run of a program. This means a print that should really be a puts will be hard to detect, because it will act like a puts. Being aware of the difference between the two and using the one you want based on the usual behavior should be sufficient to ensure you get the desired results.

Having looked a little at screen output, let's widen the I/O field a bit to include keyboard input and file operations.

1.1.6 Keyboard and file I/O

Ruby offers lots of techniques for reading data during the course of program execution, both from the keyboard and from disk files. You'll find uses for them—if not in the course of writing every application, then almost certainly while writing Ruby code to maintain, convert, housekeep, or otherwise manipulate the environment in which you work. We'll look at some of these input techniques here; an expanded look at I/O operations can be found in chapter 12.

KEYBOARD INPUT

A program that tells you over and over again that 100° Celsius equals 212° Fahrenheit has limited value. A more valuable program lets you specify a Celsius temperature and tells you the Fahrenheit equivalent.

Modifying the program to allow for this functionality involves adding a couple of steps and using one method each from tables 1.1 and 1.2: gets (get a line of keyboard input) and to_i (convert to an integer), one of which you're familiar with already. Because this is a new program, not just a correction, put the version from the following listing in a new file: c2fi.rb (the *i* stands for interactive).

> **Listing 1.2   Interactive temperature converter (c2fi.rb)**

```
print "Hello. Please enter a Celsius value: "
celsius = gets
fahrenheit = (celsius.to_i * 9 / 5) + 32
```

```
print "The Fahrenheit equivalent is "
print fahrenheit
puts "."
```

A couple of sample runs demonstrate the new program in action:

```
$ ruby c2fi.rb
Hello. Please enter a Celsius value: 100
The Fahrenheit equivalent is 212.
$ ruby c2fi.rb
Hello. Please enter a Celsius value: 23
The Fahrenheit equivalent is 73.
```

Shortening the code

You can shorten the code in listing 1.2 considerably by consolidating the operations of input, calculation, and output. A compressed rewrite looks like this:

```
print "Hello. Please enter a Celsius value: "
print "The Fahrenheit equivalent is ", gets.to_i * 9 / 5 + 32, ".\n"
```

This version economizes on variables—there aren't any—but requires anyone reading it to follow a somewhat denser (but shorter!) set of expressions. Any given program usually has several or many spots where you have to decide between longer (but maybe clearer?) and shorter (but perhaps a bit cryptic). And sometimes, shorter can be clearer. It's all part of developing a Ruby coding style.

We now have a generalized, if not terribly nuanced, solution to the problem of converting from Celsius to Fahrenheit. Let's widen the circle to include file input.

READING FROM A FILE

Reading a file from a Ruby program isn't much more difficult, at least in many cases, than reading a line of keyboard input. The next version of our temperature converter will read one number from a file and convert it from Celsius to Fahrenheit.

First, create a new file called temp.dat (temperature data), containing one line with one number on it:

```
100
```

Now create a third program file, called c2fin.rb (*in* for [file] input), as shown in the next listing.

Listing 1.3   Temperature converter using file input (c2fin.rb)

```
puts "Reading Celsius temperature value from data file..."
num = File.read("temp.dat")
celsius = num.to_i
fahrenheit = (celsius * 9 / 5) + 32
puts "The number is " + num
print "Result: "
puts fahrenheit
```

This time, the sample run and its output look like this:

```
$ ruby c2fin.rb
Reading Celsius temperature value from data file...
The number is 100
Result: 212
```

Naturally, if you change the number in the file, the result will be different.

What about writing the result of the calculation to a file?

WRITING TO A FILE

The simplest file-writing operation is just a little more elaborate than the simplest file-reading operation. As you can see from the following listing, the main extra step when you write to a file is the specification of a file *mode*—in this case, w (for *write*). Save the version of the program from this listing to c2fout.rb and run it.

> **Listing 1.4   Temperature converter with file output (c2fout.rb)**

```
print "Hello. Please enter a Celsius value: "
celsius = gets.to_i
fahrenheit = (celsius * 9 / 5) + 32
puts "Saving result to output file 'temp.out'"
fh = File.new("temp.out", "w")
fh.puts fahrenheit
fh.close
```

The method call fh.puts fahrenheit has the effect of printing the value of fahrenheit to the file for which fh is a write handle. If you inspect the file temp.out, you should see that it contains the Fahrenheit equivalent of whatever number you typed in.

As an exercise, you might try to combine the previous examples into a Ruby program that reads a number from a file and writes the Fahrenheit conversion to a different file. Meanwhile, with some basic Ruby syntax in place, our next stop will be an examination of the Ruby installation. This, in turn, will equip you for a look at how Ruby manages extensions and libraries.

1.2   Anatomy of the Ruby installation

Having Ruby installed on your system means having several disk directories' worth of Ruby-language libraries and support files. Most of the time, Ruby knows how to find what it needs without being prompted. But knowing your way around the Ruby installation is part of a good Ruby grounding.

> **Looking at the Ruby source code**
>
> In addition to the Ruby installation directory tree, you may also have the Ruby source code tree on your machine; if not, you can download it from the Ruby homepage. The source code tree contains a lot of Ruby files that end up in the eventual installation and a lot of C-language files that get compiled into object files that are then installed. In addition, the source tree contains informational files like the ChangeLog and software licenses.

Ruby can tell you where its installation files are located. To get the information while in an irb session, you need to preload a Ruby library package called `rbconfig` into your irb session. `rbconfig` is an interface to a lot of compiled-in configuration information about your Ruby installation, and you can get irb to load it by using irb's `-r` command-line flag and the name of the package:

```
$ irb --simple-prompt -rrbconfig
```

Now you can request information. For example, you can find out where the Ruby executable files (including ruby and irb) have been installed:

```
>> RbConfig::CONFIG["bindir"]
```

`RbConfig::CONFIG` is a *constant* referring to the *hash* (a kind of data structure) where Ruby keeps its configuration knowledge. The string `"bindir"` is a hash *key*. Querying the hash with the `"bindir"` key gives you the corresponding hash *value*, which is the name of the binary-file installation directory.

The rest of the configuration information is made available the same way: as values inside the configuration data structure that you can access with specific hash keys. To get additional installation information, you need to replace `bindir` in the irb command with other terms. But each time you use the same basic formula: `RbConfig::CONFIG["term"]`. Table 1.5 outlines the terms and the directories they refer to.

Table 1.5 Key Ruby directories and their `RbConfig` terms

Term	Directory contents
rubylibdir	Ruby standard library
bindir	Ruby command-line tools
archdir	Architecture-specific extensions and libraries (compiled, binary files)
sitedir	Your own or third-party extensions and libraries (written in Ruby)
vendordir	Third-party extensions and libraries (written in Ruby)
sitelibdir	Your own Ruby language extensions (written in Ruby)
sitearchdir	Your own Ruby language extensions (written in C)

Here's a rundown of the major installation directories and what they contain. You don't have to memorize them, but you should be aware of how to find them if you need them (or if you're curious to look through them and check out some examples of Ruby code!).

1.2.1 *The Ruby standard library subdirectory (RbConfig::CONFIG[rubylibdir])*

In rubylibdir, you'll find program files written in Ruby. These files provide standard library facilities, which you can require from your own programs if you need the functionality they provide.

Here's a sampling of the files you'll find in this directory:

- *cgi.rb*—Tools to facilitate CGI programming
- *fileutils.rb*—Utilities for manipulating files easily from Ruby programs
- *tempfile.rb*—A mechanism for automating the creation of temporary files
- *drb.rb*—A facility for distributed programming with Ruby

Some of the standard libraries, such as the drb library (the last item on the previous list), span more than one file; you'll see both a drb.rb file and a whole drb subdirectory containing components of the drb library.

Browsing your rubylibdir directory will give you a good (if perhaps initially overwhelming) sense of the many tasks for which Ruby provides programming facilities. Most programmers use only a subset of these capabilities, but even a subset of such a large collection of programming libraries gives you a lot to work with.

1.2.2 *The C extensions directory (RbConfig::CONFIG[archdir])*

Usually located one level down from rubylibdir, archdir contains architecture-specific extensions and libraries. The files in this directory typically have names ending in .so, .dll, or .bundle (depending on your hardware and operating system). These files are C extensions: binary, runtime-loadable files generated from Ruby's C-language extension code, compiled into binary form as part of the Ruby installation process.

Like the Ruby-language program files in rubylibdir, the files in archdir contain standard library components that you can load into your own programs. (Among others, you'll see the file for the rbconfig extension—the extension you're using with irb to uncover the directory names.) These files aren't human-readable, but the Ruby interpreter knows how to load them when asked to do so. From the perspective of the Ruby programmer, all standard libraries are equally useable, whether written in Ruby or written in C and compiled to binary format.

The files installed in archdir vary from one installation to another, depending on which extensions were compiled—which, in turn, depends on a mixture of what the person doing the compiling asked for and which extensions Ruby was able to compile.

1.2.3 *The site_ruby (RbConfig::CONFIG[sitedir]) and vendor_ruby (RbConfig::CONFIG[vendordir]) directories*

Your Ruby installation includes a subdirectory called site_ruby, where you and/or your system administrator store third-party extensions and libraries. Some of these may be code you write, while others are tools you download from other people's sites and archives of Ruby libraries.

The site_ruby directory parallels the main Ruby installation directory, in the sense that it has its own subdirectories for Ruby-language and C-language extensions (sitelibdir and sitearchdir, respectively, in `RbConfig::CONFIG` terms). When you require an extension, the Ruby interpreter checks for it in these subdirectories of site_ruby, as well as in both the main rubylibdir and the main archdir.

Alongside site_ruby you'll find the directory vendor_ruby. Some third-party extensions install themselves here. The vendor_ruby directory was new as of Ruby 1.9, and standard practice as to which of the two areas gets which packages is still developing.

1.2.4   *The gems directory*

The RubyGems utility is the standard way to package and distribute Ruby libraries. When you install *gems* (as the packages are called), the unbundled library files land in the gems directory. This directory isn't listed in the config data structure, but it's usually at the same level as site_ruby; if you've found site_ruby, look at what else is installed next to it. You'll learn more about using gems in section 1.4.5.

Let's look now at the mechanics and semantics of how Ruby uses its own extensions as well as those you may write or install.

1.3   *Ruby extensions and programming libraries*

The first major point to take on board as you read this section is that it isn't a Ruby standard library reference. As explained in the introduction, this book doesn't aim to document the Ruby language; it aims to teach you the language and to confer Ruby citizenship upon you so that you can keep widening your horizons.

The purpose of this section, accordingly, is to show you how extensions work: how you get Ruby to run its extensions, the difference among techniques for doing so, and the extension architecture that lets you write your own extensions and libraries.

The extensions that ship with Ruby are usually referred to collectively as the *standard library*. The standard library includes extensions for a wide variety of projects and tasks: database management, networking, specialized mathematics, XML processing, and many more. The exact makeup of the standard library usually changes, at least a little, with every new release of Ruby. But most of the more widely used libraries tend to stay, once they've proven their worth.

The key to using extensions and libraries is the `require` method, along with its near relation `load`. These methods allow you to load extensions at runtime, including extensions you write yourself. We'll look at them in their own right and then expand our scope to take in their use in loading built-in extensions.

1.3.1   *Loading external files and extensions*

Storing a program in a single file can be handy, but it starts to be a liability rather than an asset when you've got hundreds or thousands—or hundreds *of* thousands—of lines of code. Somewhere along the line, breaking your program into separate files starts to make lots of sense. Ruby facilitates this process with the `require` and `load` methods. We'll start with `load`, which is the more simply engineered of the two.

> **Feature, extension, or library?**
>
> Things you load into your program at runtime get called by several different names. *Feature* is the most abstract and is rarely heard outside of the specialized usage "requiring a feature" (that is, with `require`). *Library* is more concrete and more common. It connotes the actual code as well as the basic fact that a set of programming facilities exists and can be loaded. *Extension* can refer to any loadable add-on library but is often used to mean a library for Ruby that has been written in the C programming language, rather than in Ruby. If you tell people you've written a Ruby extension, they'll probably assume you mean that it's in C.

To try the examples that follow, you'll need a program that's split over two files. The first file, loaddemo.rb, should contain the following Ruby code:

```
puts "This is the first (master) program file."
load "loadee.rb"
puts "And back again to the first file."
```

When it encounters the `load` method call, Ruby reads in the second file. That file, loadee.rb, should look like this:

```
puts "> This is the second file."
```

The two files should be in the same directory (presumably your sample code directory). When you run loaddemo.rb from the command line, you'll see this output:

```
This is the first (master) program file.
> This is the second file.
And back again to the first file.
```

The output gives you a trace of which lines from which files are being executed, and in what order.

The call to `load` in loaddemo.rb provides a filename, loadee.rb, as its argument:

```
load "loadee.rb"
```

If the file you're loading is in your current working directory, Ruby will be able to find it by name. If it isn't, Ruby will look for it in the *load path*.

1.3.2 *"Load"-ing a file in the default load path*

The Ruby interpreter's load path is a list of directories in which it searches for files you ask it to load. You can see the names of these directories by examining the contents of the special global variable `$:` (dollar-colon). What you see depends on what platform you're on. A typical load-path inspection on Mac OS X looks like the following (an example that includes the .rvm directory, where the Ruby Version Manager keeps a selection of Ruby versions):

```
$ ruby -e 'puts $:'                                          ← -e signals
/Users/dblack/.rvm/rubies/ruby-2.1.0/lib/ruby/site_ruby/2.1.0     that you're
/Users/dblack/.rvm/rubies/ruby-2.1.0/lib/ruby/site_ruby/2.1.0/x86_64-   providing an
    darwin12.0                                                   inline script
                                                                 to interpreter
```

```
/Users/dblack/.rvm/rubies/ruby-2.1.0/lib/ruby/site_ruby
/Users/dblack/.rvm/rubies/ruby-2.1.0/lib/ruby/vendor_ruby/2.1.0
/Users/dblack/.rvm/rubies/ruby-2.1.0/lib/ruby/vendor_ruby/2.1.0/x86_64-
    darwin12.0
/Users/dblack/.rvm/rubies/ruby-2.1.0/lib/ruby/vendor_ruby
/Users/dblack/.rvm/rubies/ruby-2.1.0/lib/ruby/2.1.0
/Users/dblack/.rvm/rubies/ruby-2.1.0/lib/ruby/2.1.0/x86_64-darwin12.0
```

On your machine, the part to the left of "ruby-2.1.0" may say something different, like "/usr/local/lib/," but the basic pattern of subdirectories will be the same. When you load a file, Ruby looks for it in each of the listed directories, in order from top to bottom.

> **NOTE** The current working directory, usually represented by a single dot (.), is actually not included in the load path. The load command acts as if it is, but that's a specially engineered case.

You can navigate relative directories in your `load` commands with the conventional double-dot "directory up" symbol:

```
load "../extras.rb"
```

Note that if you change the current directory during a program run, relative directory references will change, too.

> **NOTE** Keep in mind that `load` is a method, and it's executed at the point where Ruby encounters it in your file. Ruby doesn't search the whole file looking for load directives; it finds them when it finds them. This means you can load files whose names are determined dynamically during the run of the program. You can even wrap a `load` call in a conditional statement, in which case the call will be executed only if the condition is true.

You can also force `load` to find a file, regardless of the contents of the load path, by giving it the fully qualified path to the file:

```
load "/home/users/dblack/book/code/loadee.rb"
```

This is, of course, less portable than the use of the load path or relative directories, but it can be useful, particularly if you have an absolute path stored as a string in a variable and want to load the file it represents.

A call to `load` always loads the file you ask for, whether you've loaded it already or not. If a file changes between loadings, then anything in the new version of the file that rewrites or overrides anything in the original version takes priority. This can be useful, especially if you're in an irb session while you're modifying a file in an editor at the same time and want to examine the effect of your changes immediately.

The other file-loading method, `require`, also searches the directories that lie in the default load path. But `require` has some features that `load` doesn't have.

1.3.3 *"Require"-ing a feature*

One major difference between `load` and `require` is that `require`, if called more than once with the same arguments, doesn't reload files it's already loaded. Ruby keeps track of which files you've required and doesn't duplicate the effort.

`require` is more abstract than `load`. *Strictly speaking, you don't require a file; you require a feature.* And typically, you do so without even specifying the extension on the filename. To see how this works, change this line in loaddemo.rb,

```
load "loadee.rb"
```

to this:

```
require "./loadee.rb"
```

When you run loaddemo.rb, you get the same result as before, even though you haven't supplied the full name of the file you want loaded.

By viewing loadee as a "feature" rather than a file, `require` allows you to treat extensions written in Ruby the same way you treat extensions written in C—or, to put it another way, to treat files ending in .rb the same way as files ending in .so, .dll, or .bundle.

> ### Specifying the working directory
>
> `require` doesn't know about the current working directory (`.`). You can specify it explicitly
>
> ```
> require "./loadee.rb"
> ```
>
> or you can append it to the load path using the array append operator,
>
> ```
> $: << "."
> ```
>
> so you don't need to specify it in calls to require:
>
> ```
> require "loadee.rb"
> ```

You can also feed a fully qualified path to `require`, as you can to `load`, and it will pull in the file/feature. And you can mix and match; the following syntax works, for example, even though it mixes the static path specification with the more abstract syntax of the feature at the end of the path:

```
require "/home/users/dblack/book/code/loadee.rb"
```

Although `load` is useful, particularly when you want to load a file more than once, `require` is the day-to-day technique you'll use to load Ruby extensions and libraries—standard and otherwise. Loading standard library features isn't any harder than loading loadee. You just require what you want. After you do, and of course depending on what the extension is, you'll have new classes and methods available to you. Here's a before-and-after example in an irb session:

```
>> "David Black".scanf("%s%s")
NoMethodError: undefined method `scanf' for "David Black":String    ①
>> require "scanf"                                                   ②
```

```
=> true
>> "David Black".scanf("%s%s")                ❸
=> ["David", "Black"]                          ←┘
```

The first call to scanf fails with an error ❶. But after the require call ❷, and with no further programmer intervention, string objects like "David Black" respond to the scanf message. (In this example ❸, we're asking for two consecutive strings to be extracted from the original string, with whitespace as an implied separator.)

1.3.4 *require_relative*

There's a third way to load files: require_relative. This command loads features by searching relative to the directory in which the file from which it's called resides. Thus in the previous example you could do this

```
require_relative "loadee"
```

without manipulating the load path to include the current directory. require_relative is convenient when you want to navigate a local directory hierarchy—for example:

```
require_relative "lib/music/sonata"
```

We'll conclude this chapter with an examination of the command-line tools that ship with Ruby.

1.4 *Out-of-the-box Ruby tools and applications*

When you install Ruby, you get a handful of important command-line tools, which are installed in whatever directory is configured as bindir—usually /usr/local/bin, /usr/bin, or the /opt equivalents. (You can require "rbconfig" and examine RbConfig::CONFIG["bindir"] to check.) These tools are

- ruby—The interpreter
- irb—The interactive Ruby interpreter
- rdoc and ri—Ruby documentation tools
- rake—Ruby make, a task-management utility
- gem—A Ruby library and application package-management utility
- erb—A templating system
- testrb—A high-level tool for use with the Ruby test framework

In this section we'll look at all of these tools except erb and testrb. They're both useful in certain situations but not an immediate priority as you get your bearings and grounding in Ruby.

You don't need to memorize all the techniques in this section on the spot. Rather, read through it and get a sense of what's here. You'll use some of the material soon and often (especially some of the command-line switches and the ri utility) and some of it increasingly as you get more deeply into Ruby.

1.4.1   *Interpreter command-line switches*

When you start the Ruby interpreter from the command line, you can provide not only the name of a program file, but also one or more command-line switches, as you've already seen in the chapter. The switches you choose instruct the interpreter to behave in particular ways and/or take particular actions.

Ruby has more than 20 command-line switches. Some of them are used rarely, while others are used every day by many Ruby programmers. Table 1.6 summarizes the most commonly used ones.

Table 1.6   Summary of commonly used Ruby command-line switches

Switch	Description	Example of usage
`-c`	Check the syntax of a program file without executing the program	`ruby -c c2f.rb`
`-w`	Give warning messages during program execution	`ruby -w c2f.rb`
`-e`	Execute the code provided in quotation marks on the command line	`ruby -e 'puts "Code demo!"'`
`-l`	Line mode: print a newline after every line of output	`ruby -le 'print "+ newline!"'`
`-rname`	Require the named feature	`ruby -rprofile`
`-v`	Show Ruby version information and execute the program in verbose mode	`ruby -v`
`--version`	Show Ruby version information	`ruby --version`
`-h`	Show information about all command-line switches for the interpreter	`ruby -h`

Let's look at each of these switches in more detail.

CHECK SYNTAX (-C)
The `-c` switch tells Ruby to check the code in one or more files for syntactical accuracy without executing the code. It's usually used in conjunction with the `-w` flag.

TURN ON WARNINGS (-W)
Running your program with `-w` causes the interpreter to run in warning mode. This means you see more warnings printed to the screen than you otherwise would, drawing your attention to places in your program that, although not syntax errors, are stylistically or logically suspect. It's Ruby's way of saying, "What you've done is syntactically correct, but it's weird. Are you sure you meant to do that?" Even without this switch, Ruby issues certain warnings, but fewer than it does in full warning mode.

EXECUTE LITERAL SCRIPT (-E)
The `-e` switch tells the interpreter that the command line includes Ruby code in quotation marks, and that it should execute that actual code rather than execute the code

contained in a file. This can be handy for quick scripting jobs where entering your code into a file and running `ruby` on the file may not be worth the trouble.

For example, let's say you want to see your name printed out backward. Here's how you can do this quickly in one command-line command, using the execute switch:

```
$ ruby -e 'puts "David A. Black".reverse'
kcalB .A divaD
```

What lies inside the single quotation marks is an entire (although short) Ruby program. If you want to feed a program with more than one line to the -e switch, you can use literal line breaks (press Enter) inside the mini-program:

```
$ ruby -e 'print "Enter a name: "
puts gets.reverse'
Enter a name: David A. Black

kcalB .A divaD
```

Or you can separate the lines with semicolons:

```
$ ruby -e 'print "Enter a name: "; print gets.reverse'
```

> **NOTE** Why is there a blank line between the program code and the output in the two-line reverse example? Because the line you enter on the keyboard ends with a newline character, so when you reverse the input, the new string starts with a newline! Ruby takes you very literally when you ask it to manipulate and print data.

RUN IN LINE MODE (-L)

The -l switch produces the effect that every string output by the program is placed on a line of its own, even if it normally wouldn't be. Usually this means that lines that are output using `print`, rather than `puts`, and that therefore don't automatically end with a newline character, now end with a newline.

We made use of the `print` versus `puts` distinction to ensure that the temperature-converter programs didn't insert extra newlines in the middle of their output (see section 1.1.5). You can use the -l switch to reverse the effect; it causes even `print`ed lines to appear on a line of their own. Here's the difference:

```
$ ruby c2f-2.rb
The result is 212.
$ ruby -l c2f-2.rb
The result is
212
.
```

The result with -l is, in this case, exactly what you don't want. But the example illustrates the effect of the switch.

If a line ends with a newline character already, running it through -l adds another newline. In general, the -l switch isn't commonly used or seen, largely because of the availability of `puts` to achieve the "add a newline only if needed" behavior, but it's good to know -l is there and to be able to recognize it.

REQUIRE NAMED FILE OR EXTENSION (-RNAME)

The `-r` switch calls `require` on its argument; `ruby -rscanf` will require `scanf` when the interpreter starts up. You can put more than one `-r` switch on a single command line.

RUN IN VERBOSE MODE (-V, --VERBOSE)

Running with `-v` does two things: it prints out information about the version of Ruby you're using, and then it turns on the same warning mechanism as the `-w` flag. The most common use of `-v` is to find out the Ruby version number:

```
$ ruby -v
ruby 2.1.0p0 (2013-12-25 revision 44422) [x86_64-darwin12.0]
```

In this case, we're using Ruby 2.1.0 (patchlevel 0), released on December 25, 2013, and compiled for an i686-based machine running Mac OS X. Because there's no program or code to run, Ruby exits as soon as it has printed the version information.

PRINT RUBY VERSION (--VERSION)

This flag causes Ruby to print a version information string and then exit. It doesn't execute any code, even if you provide code or a filename. You'll recall that `-v` prints version information and then runs your code (if any) in verbose mode. You might say that `-v` is slyly standing for both *version* and *verbose*, whereas `--version` is just *version*.

PRINT SOME HELP INFORMATION (-H, --HELP)

These switches give you a table listing all the command-line switches available to you, and summarizing what they do.

In addition to using single switches, you can also combine two or more in a single invocation of Ruby.

COMBINING SWITCHES (-CW)

You've already seen the `-cw` combination, which checks the syntax of the file without executing it, while also giving you warnings:

```
$ ruby -cw filename
```

Another combination of switches you'll often see is `-v` and `-e`, which shows you the version of Ruby you're running and then runs the code provided in quotation marks. You'll see this combination a lot in discussions of Ruby, on mailing lists, and elsewhere; people use it to demonstrate how the same code might work differently in different versions of Ruby. For example, if you want to show clearly that a string method called `start_with?` wasn't present in Ruby 1.8.6 but is present in Ruby 2.1.0, you can run a sample program using first one version of Ruby and then the other:

```
$ ruby-1.8.6-p399 -ve "puts 'abc'.start_with?('a')"
ruby 1.8.6 (2010-02-05 patchlevel 399) [x86_64-linux]              ❶
-e:1: undefined method `start_with?' for "abc":String (NoMethodError)  ←┘
$ ruby-2.1.0p0 -ve "puts 'abc'.start_with?('a')"
ruby 2.1.0p0 (2013-12-25 revision 44422) [x86_64-linux]            ❷
true                                                               ←┘
```

(Of course, you must have both versions of Ruby installed on your system.) The `undefined method 'start_with?'` message ❶ on the first run (the one using version 1.8.6) means that you've tried to perform a nonexistent named operation. But when you run the same Ruby snippet using Ruby 2.1.0, it works ❷: Ruby prints `true`. This is a convenient way to share information and formulate questions about changes in Ruby's behavior from one release to another.

At this point, we'll go back and look more closely at the interactive Ruby interpreter, irb. You may have looked at this section already, when it was mentioned near the beginning of the chapter. If not, you can take this opportunity to learn more about this exceptionally useful Ruby tool.

> **Specifying switches**
>
> You can feed Ruby the switches separately, like this
>
> ```
> $ ruby -c -w
> ```
>
> or
>
> ```
> $ ruby -v -e "puts 'abc'.start_with?('a')"
> ```
>
> But it's common to type them together, as in the examples in the main text.

1.4.2 A closer look at interactive Ruby interpretation with irb

As you've seen, irb is an interactive Ruby interpreter, which means that instead of processing a file, it processes what you type in during a session. irb is a great tool for testing Ruby code and a great tool for learning Ruby.

To start an irb session, you use the command `irb`. irb prints out its prompt:

```
$ irb
2.1.0 :001 >
```

As you've seen, you can also use the `--simple-prompt` option to keep irb's output shorter:

```
$ irb --simple-prompt
>>
```

Once irb starts, you can enter Ruby commands. You can even run a one-shot version of the Celsius-to-Fahrenheit conversion program. As you'll see in this example, irb behaves like a pocket calculator: it evaluates whatever you type in and prints the result. You don't have to use a `print` or `puts` command:

```
>> 100 * 9 / 5 + 32
=> 212
```

To find out how many minutes there are in a year (if you don't have a CD of the relevant hit song from the musical *Rent* handy), type in the appropriate multiplication expression:

```
>> 365 * 24 * 60
=> 525600
```

irb will also, of course, process any Ruby instructions you enter. For example, if you want to assign the day, hour, and minute counts to variables, and then multiply those variables, you can do that in irb:

```
>> days = 365
=> 365
>> hours = 24
=> 24
>> minutes = 60
=> 60
>> days * hours * minutes
=> 525600
```

The last calculation is what you'd expect. But look at the first three lines of entry. When you type days = 365, irb responds by printing 365. Why?

The expression days = 365 is an assignment expression: you're assigning the value 365 to a variable called days. The main business of an assignment expression is to assign a value to a variable so that you can use the variable later. But the assignment expression (the entire line days = 365) has a value. The value of an assignment expression is its right-hand side. When irb sees any expression, it prints out the value of that expression. So, when irb sees days = 365, it prints out 365. This may seem like over-zealous printing, but it comes with the territory; it's the same behavior that lets you type 2 + 2 into irb and see the result without having to use an explicit print statement.

Similarly, even a call to the puts method has a return value—namely, nil. If you type a puts statement in irb, irb will obediently execute it, and will also print out the return value of puts:

```
$ irb --simple-prompt
>> puts "Hello"
Hello
=> nil
```

There's a way to get irb not to be quite so talkative: the --noecho flag. Here's how it works:

```
$ irb --simple-prompt --noecho
>> 2 + 2
>> puts "Hi"
Hi
```

Thanks to --noecho, the addition expression doesn't report back its result. The puts command does get executed (so you see "Hi"), but the return value of puts (nil) is suppressed.

Interrupting irb

It's possible to get stuck in a loop in irb, or for the session to feel like it's not responding (which often means you've typed an opening quotation mark but not a closing one, or something along those lines). How you get control back is somewhat system-dependent. On most systems, Ctrl-C will do the trick. On others, you may need

> **(continued)**
>
> to use Ctrl-Z. It's best to apply whatever general program-interrupting information you have about your system directly to irb. Of course, if things get really frozen, you can go to your process or task-management tools and kill the irb process.
>
> To exit from irb normally, you can type `exit`. On many systems, Ctrl-D works too.
>
> Occasionally, irb may blow up on you (that is, hit a fatal error and terminate itself). Most of the time, though, it catches its own errors and lets you continue.

Once you get the hang of irb's approach to printing out the value of everything, and how to shut it up if you want to, you'll find it an immensely useful tool (and toy).

Ruby's source code is marked up in such a way as to provide for automatic generation of documentation; and the tools needed to interpret and display that documentation are `ri` and RDoc, which we'll look at now.

1.4.3   *ri and RDoc*

`ri` (Ruby Index) and RDoc (Ruby Documentation), originally written by Dave Thomas, are a closely related pair of tools for providing documentation about Ruby programs. `ri` is a command-line tool; the RDoc system includes the command-line tool `rdoc`. `ri` and `rdoc` are standalone programs; you run them from the command line. (You can also use the facilities they provide from within your Ruby programs, although we're not going to look at that aspect of them here.)

RDoc is a documentation system. If you put comments in your program files (Ruby or C) in the prescribed RDoc format, `rdoc` scans your files, extracts the comments, organizes them intelligently (indexed according to what they comment on), and creates nicely formatted documentation from them. You can see RDoc markup in many of the source files, in both Ruby and C, in the Ruby source tree, and in many of the Ruby files in the Ruby installation.

`ri` dovetails with RDoc: it gives you a way to view the information that RDoc has extracted and organized. Specifically (although not exclusively, if you customize it), `ri` is configured to display the RDoc information from the Ruby source files. Thus on any system that has Ruby fully installed, you can get detailed information about Ruby with a simple command-line invocation of `ri`.

For example, here's how you request information about the `upcase` method of string objects:

```
$ ri String#upcase
```

And here's what you get back:

```
= String#upcase

(from ruby core)
------------------------------------------------------------------------------
  str.upcase   -> new_str
```

```
Returns a copy of str with all lowercase letters replaced with their
uppercase counterparts. The operation is locale insensitive---only characters
``a'' to ``z'' are affected. Note: case replacement is effective only in
ASCII region.

    "hEllO".upcase    #=> "HELLO"
```

The hash mark (#) between `String` and `upcase` in the `ri` command indicates that you're looking for an instance method, as distinct from a class method. In the case of a class method, you'd use the separator `::` instead of #. We'll get to the class method/instance method distinction in chapter 3. The main point for the moment is that you have lots of documentation at your disposal from the command line.

> **TIP** By default, `ri` runs its output through a pager (such as `more` on Unix). It may pause at the end of output, waiting for you to hit the spacebar or some other key to show the next screen of information or to exit entirely if all the information has been shown. Exactly what you have to press in this case varies from one operating system, and one pager, to another. Spacebar, Enter, Escape, Ctrl-C, Ctrl-D, and Ctrl-Z are all good bets. If you want `ri` to write the output without filtering it through a pager, you can use the `-T` command-line switch (`ri -T topic`).

Next among the Ruby command-line tools is `rake`.

1.4.4 The rake task-management utility

As its name suggests (it comes from "Ruby `make`"), `rake` is a `make`-inspired task-management utility. It was written by the late Jim Weirich. Like `make`, `rake` reads and executes tasks defined in a file—a Rakefile. Unlike `make`, however, `rake` uses Ruby syntax to define its tasks.

Listing 1.5 shows a Rakefile. If you save the listing as a file called Rakefile, you can then issue this command at the command line:

```
$ rake admin:clean_tmp
```

`rake` executes the `clean_tmp` task defined inside the `admin` namespace.

> **Listing 1.5 Rakefile defining `clean_tmp` tasks inside the `admin` namespace**

```
namespace :admin do
  desc "Interactively delete all files in /tmp"          Declares
  task :clean_tmp do                                     clean_tmp task
    Dir["/tmp/*"].each do |f|                        ← ❶
      next unless File.file?(f)                       ←
      print "Delete #{f}? "                          ← ❷
      answer = $stdin.gets
                                                       ❸
      case answer
      when /^y/
        File.unlink(f)                   ← ❹
      when /^q/                                ❺
        break                          ←
```

```
        end
      end
    end
end
```

The `rake` task defined here uses several Ruby techniques that you haven't seen yet, but the basic algorithm is pretty simple:

1 Loop through each directory entry in the /tmp directory **❶**.
2 Skip the current loop iteration unless this entry is a file. Note that hidden files aren't deleted either, because the directory listing operation doesn't include them **❷**.
3 Prompt for the deletion of the file **❸**.
4 If the user types y (or anything beginning with y), delete the file **❹**.
5 If the user types q, break out of the loop; the task stops **❺**.

The main programming logic comes from looping through the list of directory entries (see the sidebar "Using `each` to loop through a collection") and from the `case` statement, a conditional execution structure. (You'll see both of these techniques in detail later in chapter 6.)

Using `each` to loop through a collection

The expression `Dir["/tmp/*"].each do |f|` is a call to the `each` method of the array of all the directory entry names. The entire block of code starting with `do` and ending with `end` (the `end` that lines up with `Dir` in the indentation) gets executed once for each item in the array. Each time through, the current item is bound to the parameter `f`; that's the significance of the `|f|` part. You'll see `each` several times in the coming chapters, and we'll examine it in detail when we look at *iterators* (methods that automatically traverse collections) in chapter 9.

The `desc` command above the task definition provides a description of the task. This comes in handy not only when you're perusing the file, but also if you want to see all the tasks that `rake` can execute at a given time. If you're in the directory containing the Rakefile in listing 1.5 and you give the command

```
$ rake --tasks
```

you'll see a listing of all defined tasks:

```
$ rake --tasks
(in /Users/ruby/hacking)
rake admin:clean_tmp  # Interactively delete all files in /tmp
```

You can use any names you want for your `rake` namespaces and tasks. You don't even need a namespace; you can define a task at the top-level namespace,

```
task :clean_tmp do
  # etc.
end
```

and then invoke it using the simple name:

```
$ rake clean_tmp
```

But namespacing your tasks is a good idea, particularly if and when the number of tasks you define grows significantly. You can namespace to any depth; this structure, for example, is legitimate:

```
namespace :admin do
  namespace :clean do
    task :tmp do
      # etc.
    end
  end
end
```

The task defined here is invoked like this:

```
$ rake admin:clean:tmp
```

As the directory-cleaning example shows, rake tasks don't have to be confined to actions related to Ruby programming. With rake, you get the whole Ruby language at your disposal, for the purpose of writing whatever tasks you need.

The next tool on the tour is the gem command, which makes installation of third-party Ruby packages very easy.

1.4.5 *Installing packages with the gem command*

The RubyGems library and utility collection includes facilities for packaging and installing Ruby libraries and applications. We're not going to cover gem creation here, but we'll look at gem installation and usage.

Installing a Ruby gem can be, and usually is, as easy as issuing a simple install command:

```
$ gem install prawn
```

Such a command gives you output something like the following (depending on which gems you already have installed and which dependencies have to be met by installing new gems):

```
Fetching: Ascii85-1.0.2.gem (100%)
Fetching: ruby-rc4-0.1.5.gem (100%)
Fetching: hashery-2.1.0.gem (100%)
Fetching: ttfunk-1.0.3.gem (100%)
Fetching: afm-0.2.0.gem (100%)
Fetching: pdf-reader-1.3.3.gem (100%)
Fetching: prawn-0.12.0.gem (100%)
Successfully installed Ascii85-1.0.2
Successfully installed ruby-rc4-0.1.5
Successfully installed hashery-2.1.0
Successfully installed ttfunk-1.0.3
Successfully installed afm-0.2.0
Successfully installed pdf-reader-1.3.3
Successfully installed prawn-0.12.0
7 gems installed
```

These status reports are followed by several lines indicating that ri and RDoc documentation for the various gems are being installed. (The installation of the documentation involves processing the gem source files through RDoc, so be patient; this is often the longest phase of gem installation.)

During the gem installation process, gem downloads gem files as needed from rubygems.org (www.rubygems.org). Those files, which are in .gem format, are saved in the cache subdirectory of your gems directory. You can also install a gem from a gem file residing locally on your hard disk or other storage medium. Give the name of the file to the installer:

```
$ gem install /home/me/mygems/ruport-1.4.0.gem
```

If you name a gem without the entire filename (for example, ruport), gem looks for it in the current directory and in the local cache maintained by the RubyGems system. Local installations still search remotely for dependencies, unless you provide the -l (local) command-line flag to the gem command; that flag restricts all operations to the local domain. If you want only remote gems installed, including dependencies, then you can use the -r (remote) flag. In most cases, the simple gem install gemname command will give you what you need. (To uninstall a gem, use the gem uninstall gemname command.)

Once you've got a gem installed, you can use it via the require method.

LOADING AND USING GEMS

While you won't see gems in your initial load path ($:), you can still "require" them and they'll load. Here's how you'd require "hoe" (a utility that helps you package your own gems), assuming you've installed the Hoe gem:

```
>> require "hoe"
=> true
```

At this point, the relevant hoe directory will appear in the load path, as you can see if you print out the value of $: and grep (select by pattern match) for the pattern "hoe":

```
>> puts $:.grep(/hoe/)
/Users/dblack/.rvm/gems/ruby-2.1.0/gems/hoe-3.8.1/lib
```

If you have more than one gem installed for a particular library and want to force the use of a gem other than the most recent, you can do so using the gem method. (Note that this method isn't the same as the command-line tool called gem.) Here, for example, is how you'd force the use of a not-quite-current version of Hoe:

```
>> gem "hoe", "3.8.0"
=> true
>> puts $:.grep(/hoe/)
/Users/dblack/.rvm/gems/ruby-2.1.0/gems/hoe-3.8.0/lib
```

No need for require if you use gem method

Most of the time, of course, you'll want to use the most recent gems. But the gem system gives you tools for fine-tuning your gem usage, should you need to do so.

With the subject of RubyGems on the map, we're now finished with our current business—the bin/ directory—and we'll move next to a close study of the core language.

1.5 Summary

In this chapter, we've looked at a number of important foundational Ruby topics, including

- The difference between Ruby (the language) and `ruby` (the Ruby interpreter)
- The typography of Ruby variables (all of which you'll meet again and study in more depth)
- Basic Ruby operators and built-in constructs
- Writing, storing, and running a Ruby program file
- Keyboard input and screen output
- Manipulating Ruby libraries with `require` and `load`
- The anatomy of the Ruby installation
- The command-line tools shipped with Ruby

You now have a good blueprint of how Ruby works and what tools the Ruby programming environment provides, and you've seen and practiced some important Ruby techniques. You're now prepared to start exploring Ruby systematically.

Objects, methods, and local variables

This chapter covers

- Objects and object orientation
- Innate versus learned object capabilities
- Method parameter, argument, and calling syntax
- Local variable assignment and usage
- Object references

In this chapter, we'll begin exploring the details of the Ruby programming language. We'll look first and foremost at the concept of the object, around which almost every line of Ruby code you'll write will revolve. What you do with objects, broadly speaking, is send them messages, most of which correspond to names of methods that you're asking the object to execute. We'll look in considerable detail at the combined processes of message sending and method calling.

Ruby objects are often (perhaps most often) handled via variables that represent them, and in this chapter, we'll get deeper technically than we have so far into the nature and behavior of variables in Ruby. Once you've worked through this chapter, you'll have a firm foothold in the landscape of Ruby objects and their manipulation.

As always, you can type the code samples into irb, and/or store them in a file that you then run using the Ruby interpreter. Whichever approach you lean toward, it's not a bad idea to keep an irb session open as you proceed—just in case.

2.1 Talking to objects

In any Ruby program, the bulk of the design, logic, and action revolves around objects. When you write Ruby programs, your main activities are creating objects, endowing them with abilities, and asking them to perform actions. Objects are your handle on the universe of your program. When you want something done—a calculation, an output operation, a data comparison—you ask an object to do it. Rather than ask in the abstract whether *a* equals *b*, you ask *a* whether it considers itself equal to *b*. If you want to know whether a given student is taking a class from a given teacher, you ask the student, "Are you a student of this teacher?" Exactly how this kind of querying plays out, in terms of data structures and syntax, depends on the specifics of your program design. But throughout, writing a Ruby program is largely a matter of engineering your objects so that each object plays a clear role and can perform actions related to that role.

2.1.1 Ruby and object orientation

Ruby comes to the idea of manipulating data through objects via the program-language design principle *object orientation*. Many extremely popular programming languages are object-oriented (such as Java, C++, and Python, as well as Ruby), and some languages that aren't fully object-oriented have facilities for writing object-oriented code (for example, Perl, as described in *Object-Oriented Perl* by Damian Conway [Manning, 1999]). In object-oriented programming (OOP), you perform calculations, data manipulation, and input/output operations by creating objects and asking them to perform actions and provide you with information.

In most object-oriented languages, including Ruby, every object is an example or instance of a particular class, and the behavior of individual objects is determined at least to some extent by the method definitions present in the object's class. We'll explore classes in depth in chapter 3. Here, we'll focus directly on objects.

> **The real world**
>
> The term *real world* gets thrown around a lot in discussions of programming. There's room for debate (and there *is* debate) as to whether this or that programming language, or even this or that kind of programming language, corresponds more closely than others to the shape of the real world. A lot depends on how you perceive the world. Do you perceive it as peopled with things, each of which has tasks to do and waits for someone to request the task? If so, you may conclude that object-oriented languages model the world best. Do you see life as a series of to-do items on a checklist, to be gone through in order? If so, you may see a strictly procedural programming language as having closer ties to the characteristics of the real world.

(continued)

In short, there's no one answer to the question of what the real world is—so there's no answer to the question of what it means for a programming language to model the real world. Nor is it necessarily as important an issue as it may seem. The world you construct in a computer program is at heart an imaginary world, and limiting yourself to making it seem otherwise can be overly constrictive.

Designing object-oriented software is largely a matter of figuring out what you want your objects to be: what they should do, how they'll interact with each other, how many of each there should be (for example, many students, one registrar), and other such questions. As you'll see, Ruby provides a complete set of tools for naming, creating, addressing, and manipulating objects—and, through the manipulation of those objects, the data they operate on.

2.1.2 Creating a generic object

At first, the concept of OOP tends to come across as both simple (you write programs that have books and bottles and cars and houses, and you orchestrate a kind of conversation among those things) and abstract (*Object? What does that mean? What do I type into my program file to create a "house" object?*). OOP does have a component of simplicity; it lets you draw on objects, entities, roles, and behaviors as a source for how you design your programs, and that can be a help. At the same time, to create and use objects in your programs, you have to learn how it's done in a given language.

> **NOTE** Depending on your background and expectations, you may be wondering why we're not starting our exploration of objects with a close look at classes rather than objects. Classes are important in Ruby; they're a way to bundle and label behaviors (you can have a `Person` class, a `Task` class, and so on) and to create multiple objects with similar behaviors easily. But—and in this respect, Ruby differs from some other object-oriented languages—the real action is with the individual objects: every object has the potential to "learn" behaviors (methods) that its class didn't teach it. The class concept fits on top of the object concept, not the other way around. In fact, a class in Ruby is itself an object! More later … but that's the basics of why we're starting with objects.

Seeing a language-specific explanation of OOP can make the abstract parts easier to grasp. We'll therefore proceed to some Ruby code. We'll create a new object. It won't represent or model anything specific, like a house or a book or a teacher; it will be a generic object:

```
obj = Object.new
```

Now you have an object and a variable through which you can address it.

All Ruby objects are created with certain innate abilities—certain methods that they know how to execute because they're Ruby objects. Those abilities, although

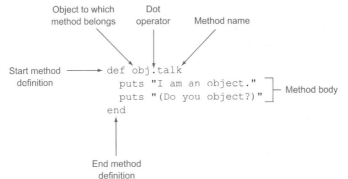

Figure 2.1 Anatomy of a method definition

important, aren't that exciting, so we'll keep them to the side for the moment. More exciting is what happens when you teach your object how to do the things you want it to do.

DEFINING AN OBJECT'S BEHAVIOR

Let's say you've created an object and you want it to do something interesting: you want it to talk. To get it to talk, you have to ask it to talk. But before you ask it to talk, you have to teach it how to talk.

Specifically, and more technically, you have to define a *method* for your object. You do this using a special term—a *keyword*—namely, the keyword def.

Here's how to define the method talk for the object obj:

```
def obj.talk
  puts "I am an object."
  puts "(Do you object?)"
end
```

Figure 2.1 shows an analysis of that chunk of code.

Now obj knows how to talk, and you can ask it to do so.

SENDING MESSAGES TO OBJECTS

To ask obj to talk, use the message-sending or method-calling syntax you encountered in chapter 1:

```
obj.talk
```

And it talks:

```
I am an object.
(Do you object?)
```

The object obj understands, or *responds to*, the message talk. An object is said to respond to a message if the object has a method defined whose name corresponds to the message.

A few things to consider about the dot-based message-sending syntax:

- The dot (.) is the message-sending operator. The message on the right is sent to the object (or *receiver*, as it's often called in this role) on the left.

- The receiver can be, and often is, represented by a variable that stands in for an object. But a receiver can also be a literal object construct—for example, a string in quotation marks.
- In practice, the message being sent is almost always the name of a method (like talk, the method defined earlier). The object always tries to act on the assumption that the message is the name of a method. If there's no method by that name, error-handling measures are taken.

The semantics of method calls let you go further than the relatively one-dimensional "talk" case, particularly when you start calling methods with arguments.

2.1.3   *Methods that take arguments*

Methods in Ruby are much like mathematical functions: input goes in, the wheels turn, and a result comes out. To feed input to a Ruby method, you call the method with one or more arguments.

In a method definition, you indicate the arguments by means of a list of variables in parentheses after the method name. (Arguments can be required or optional. We'll look at required arguments here and optional arguments a little later.) When you call the method, you provide values corresponding to these variables in your method call. More precisely, the variables listed in the method definition are the method's *formal parameters*, and the values you supply to the method when you call it are the corresponding *arguments*. (It's common to use the word *arguments*, informally, to refer to a method's parameters as well as a method call's arguments, but it's useful to know the technical distinction.)

Let's say you want your object to function as a Celsius-to-Fahrenheit converter. You can teach it how to do the conversion by defining a method:

```
def obj.c2f(c)
  c * 9.0 / 5 + 32
end
```

(This time 9 has become 9.0 in the conversion formula. That will force the result to be a float, which is more precise than an integer.) The method obj.c2f has one formal parameter, which means it takes one argument. When you call the method, you provide an argument:

```
puts obj.c2f(100)
```

The result is

```
212.0
```

As you can see, there's a direct correspondence between the syntax of the parameter list in a method definition and the syntax of the argument list when the method is called. The parentheses are optional in both cases; you could do this

```
def obj.c2f c
```

and this:

```
obj.c2f 100
```

They're not always optional, though, particularly when you're stringing multiple method calls together, so it's good to lean toward using them rather than leaving them out. You can make an exception for common or conventional cases where parentheses are usually excluded, like calls to `puts`. But when in doubt, use the parentheses.

At the other end of the process, every method call hands back—*returns*—a value.

2.1.4 *The return value of a method*

Ruby code is made up of expressions, each of which evaluates to a particular value. Table 2.1 shows some examples of expressions and their values (along with explanatory comments).

Table 2.1 **Examples of Ruby expressions and the values to which they evaluate**

Expression	Value	Comments
`2 + 2`	`4`	Arithmetic expressions evaluate to their results.
`"Hello"`	`"Hello"`	A simple, literal string (in quotation marks) evaluates to itself.
`"Hello" + " there"`	`"Hello there"`	Strings can be "added" to each other (concatenated) with the plus sign.
`c = 100`	`100`	When you assign to a variable, the whole assignment evaluates to the value you've assigned.
`c * 9/5 + 32`	`212`	The usual rules of precedence apply: multiplication and division bind more tightly than addition and are performed first.
`obj.c2f(100)`	`212`	A method call is an expression.

Look at the last entry in table 2.1: it's a call to `obj.c2f`. Every method call is an expression. When you call a method, the method call evaluates to something. This result of calling a method is the method's *return value.*

The return value of any method is the same as the value of the last expression evaluated during execution of the method. In the case of the temperature-conversion method, the last expression evaluated is the only line of the method body:

```
c * 9.0 / 5 + 32
```

Thus the result of that calculation provides the return value of the method.

Ruby gives you a keyword for making return values explicit: `return`. The use of this keyword is usually optional, but many programmers like to use it because it makes explicit what is otherwise implicit:

```
def obj.c2f(c)
  return c * 9.0 / 5 + 32
end
```

This is equivalent to the earlier version of the method, but it's more expressive about what it's doing. On the other hand, it's wordier. You have to decide, as a matter of your own style, whether you want to use `return`. You have to use it if you return multiple values, which will be automatically wrapped up in an array: `return a,b,c` rather than just `a,b,c` (though you can also return multiple values in an explicit array, like `[a,b,c]`, without `return`). You also have to use `return` if you want to return from somewhere in the middle of a method. But whether you use `return` or not, *something* will be returned from every method call. Even a call to an empty method body, consisting of just the `def` and `end` statements, returns `nil`.

At this point, the object is doing what we need it to do: listening to messages and acting on them. That's a good illustration of how Ruby works, but it's a scrappy one. We started with a generic object and taught it to talk and convert temperatures. That shows you the mechanics of defining and calling methods, but it results in a rather odd object. Let's look at an object that models something a little more structured. We'll handcraft a generic object so that it understands the behavior and business logic of a ticket to an event.

2.2   *Crafting an object: The behavior of a ticket*

A ticket is a familiar object, with a known set of properties and behaviors. Let's take a high-level view at what we expect a ticket-like Ruby object to do and to know about itself.

2.2.1   *The ticket object, behavior first*

A ticket object should be able to provide data about itself. It should field requests for information about the event it's for: when, where, name of event, performer, which seat, and how much it costs.

When asked, the ticket will provide the following information, based on an imaginary public reading by Mark Twain in 1903:

```
01/02/03
Town Hall
Author's reading
Mark Twain
Second Balcony, row J, seat 12
$5.50
```

The goal is to create an object from which we can easily get all this information.

CREATING THE TICKET OBJECT
A generic object will serve as the basis for the ticket:

```
ticket = Object.new
```

Once it exists, we can start to endow the object `ticket` with properties and data by defining methods, each returning the appropriate value:

```
def ticket.date
  "01/02/03"
end
```

```
def ticket.venue
  "Town Hall"
end
def ticket.event
  "Author's reading"
end
def ticket.performer
  "Mark Twain"
end
def ticket.seat
  "Second Balcony, row J, seat 12"
end
def ticket.price                    ◄—❶
  5.50
end
```

The majority of the methods defined here return string values. You can see this at a glance: they hand back a value inside quotation marks. The `price` method returns a floating-point number ❶. Now that the `ticket` object knows a little about itself, let's ask it to share the information.

2.2.2 *Querying the ticket object*

Rather than produce a raw list of items, let's generate a reader-friendly summary of the details of the ticket. The use of `print` and `puts` can help get the information into more or less narrative form:

```
print "This ticket is for: "
print ticket.event + ", at "        Print event
print ticket.venue + ", on "        information
puts ticket.date + "."
print "The performer is "           Print performer
puts ticket.performer + "."         information
print "The seat is "                Print seat
print ticket.seat + ", "            information
print "and it costs $"                        Print floating-point number
puts "%.2f." % ticket.price    ◄—                to two decimal places
```

Save all the code, starting with `ticket = Object.new`, to a file called ticket.rb, and run it. You'll see the following:

```
This ticket is for: Author's reading, at Town Hall, on 01/02/03.
The performer is Mark Twain.
The seat is Second Balcony, row J, seat 12, and it costs $5.50.
```

The code for this example consists of a series of calls to the methods defined earlier: `ticket.event`, `ticket.venue`, and so forth. The printing code embeds those calls—in other words, it embeds the return values of those methods (`"Author's reading"`, `"Town Hall"`, and so on)—in a succession of output commands, and adds connectors (`", at"`, `", on"`, and so on) to make the text read well and look nice.

The Twain ticket is a simple example, but it encompasses some vital Ruby procedures and principles. The most important lesson is that *the knowledge necessary for the program to do anything useful resides in the object.* The ticket object has the knowledge; you tap into that knowledge by asking the ticket for it, via method calls. Nothing is more central to Ruby programming than this. It's all about asking objects to do things and tell you things.

The ticket code works, and it embodies useful lessons; but it's wordy. Ruby has a reputation as a powerful, high-level language. You're supposed to be able to get a lot done with relatively little code. But the ticket example takes ten lines of `print` and `puts` instructions to generate three lines of output.

Let's improve that ratio a bit.

2.2.3   *Shortening the ticket code via string interpolation*

One of the most useful programming techniques available in Ruby is *string interpolation.* The string-interpolation operator gives you a way to drop anything into a string: a variable, for example, or the return value of a method. This can save you a lot of back-and-forth between `print` and `puts`.

Moreover, strings can be concatenated with the plus sign (+). Here's how the printing code looks, using string interpolation to insert the values of expressions into the string and using string addition to consolidate multiple `puts` calls into one:

```
puts "This ticket is for: #{ticket.event}, at #{ticket.venue}." +
  "The performer is #{ticket.performer}." +
  "The seat is #{ticket.seat}, " +
  "and it costs $#{"%.2f." % ticket.price}"
```

Whatever's inside the interpolation operator #{...} gets calculated separately, and the results of the calculation are inserted into the string. When you run these lines, you won't see the #{...} operator on your screen; instead, you'll see the results of calculating or evaluating what was between the curly braces. Interpolation helped eliminate 6 of 10 lines of code and also made the code look a lot more like the eventual format of the output, rather than something that works but doesn't convey much visual information.

So far, we've been asking the ticket for information in the form of strings and numbers. Tickets also have some true/false—Boolean—information about themselves.

2.2.4   *Ticket availability: Expressing Boolean state in a method*

By way of Boolean information, consider the matter of whether a ticket has been sold or is still available. One way to endow a ticket with knowledge of its own availability status is this:

```
def ticket.availability_status
  "sold"
end
```

Another way is to ask the ticket whether it's available and have it report back true or false:

```
def ticket.available?
  false
end
```

false is a special term in Ruby, as is the term true. true and false are objects. Ruby uses them to represent results of, among other things, comparison operations (like x > y), and you can use them to represent truth and falsehood in your own methods. You may have noticed that the method name available? ends with a question mark. Ruby lets you do this so you can write methods that evaluate to true or false and make the method calls look like questions:

```
if ticket.available?
  puts "You're in luck!"
else
  puts "Sorry--that seat has been sold."
end
```

But there's more to truth and falsehood than the true and false objects. Every expression in Ruby evaluates to an object, and every object in Ruby has a truth value. The truth value of almost every object in Ruby is true. The only objects whose truth value (or Boolean value) is false are the object false and the special nonentity object nil. You'll see Boolean values and nil in more detail in chapter 7. For the moment, you can think of both false and nil as functionally equivalent indicators of a negative test outcome.

Playing around with if expressions in irb is a good way to get a feel for how conditional logic plays out in Ruby. Try some examples like these:

```
>> if "abc"
>>   puts "Strings are 'true' in Ruby!"
>> end
Strings are 'true' in Ruby!
=> nil
>> if 123
>>   puts "So are numbers!"
>> end
So are numbers!
=> nil
>> if 0
>>   puts "Even 0 is true, which it isn't in some languages."
>> end
Even 0 is true, which it isn't in some languages.
=> nil
>> if 1 == 2
>>   puts "One doesn't equal two, so this won't appear."
>> end
=> nil
```

❶
❷
❸

(The first of these examples, if "abc", will generate a warning about string literals in conditions. You can ignore the warning for our present purposes.)

Notice how irb not only obeys the puts method calls ❶ but also, on its own initiative, outputs the value of the entire expression ❷. In the cases where the puts happens, the whole expression evaluates to nil—because the return value of puts is always nil. In the last case, where the string isn't printed (because the condition fails), the value of the expression is also nil—because an if statement that fails (and has no else branch to salvage it) also evaluates to nil ❸.

Remembering that `nil` has a Boolean value of `false`, you can, if you wish, get into acrobatics with irb. A call to `puts` returns `nil` and is therefore false, even though the string gets printed. If you put `puts` in an `if` clause, the clause will be false. But it will still be evaluated. So,

```
>> if puts "You'll see this"
>>   puts "but not this"
>> end
You'll see this
=> nil
```

The first `puts` is executed, but the value it returns, namely `nil`, isn't true in the Boolean sense—so the second `puts` isn't executed.

This is a contrived example, but it's a good idea to get used to the fact that *everything in Ruby has a Boolean value*, and sometimes it's not what you might expect. As is often the case, irb can be a great help in getting a handle on this concept.

Now that the `ticket` object has some handcrafted behaviors, let's circle back and consider the matter of what behaviors every object in Ruby is endowed with at its creation.

2.3 *The innate behaviors of an object*

Even a newly created object isn't a blank slate. As soon as an object comes into existence, it responds to a number of messages. Every object is "born" with certain innate abilities.

To see a list of innate methods, you can call the `methods` method (and throw in a `sort` operation, to make it easier to browse visually):

```
p Object.new.methods.sort
```

The result is a list of all the messages (methods) this newly minted object comes bundled with. (Warning: The output looks cluttered. This is how Ruby displays arrays—and the `methods` method gives you an array of method names. If you want a list of the methods one per line, use `puts` instead of `p` in the command.)

```
[:!, :!=, :!~, :<=>, :==, :===, :=~, :__id__, :__send__, :class, :clone,
:define_singleton_method, :display, :dup, :enum_for, :eql?, :equal?, :extend,
:freeze, :frozen?, :hash, :inspect, :instance_eval, :instance_exec,
:instance_of?, :instance_variable_defined?, :instance_variable_get,
:instance_variable_set, :instance_variables, :is_a?, :kind_of?, :method,
:methods, :nil?, :object_id, :private_methods, :protected_methods,
:public_method, :public_methods, :public_send, :remove_instance_variable,
:respond_to?, :send, :singleton_class, :singleton_methods, :taint, :tainted?,
:tap, :to_enum, :to_s, :trust, :untaint, :untrust, :untrusted?]
```

Don't worry if most of these methods make no sense to you right now. You can try them in irb, if you're curious to see what they do (and if you're not afraid of getting some error messages).

But a few of these innate methods are common enough—and helpful enough, even in the early phases of acquaintance with Ruby—that we'll look at them in detail here. The following methods fit this description:

- `object_id`
- `respond_to?`
- `send` (synonym: `__send__`)

Adding these to your Ruby toolbox won't be amiss, because of what they do and because they serve as examples of innate methods.

> **Generic objects vs. basic objects**
>
> Asking Ruby to create a new object for you with the `Object.new` command produces what we're calling here, informally, a *generic* object. Ruby also has *basic* objects—and that's a more formal name. If you call `BasicObject.new`, you get a kind of proto-object that can do very little. You can't even ask a basic object to show you its methods, because it has no `methods` method! In fact, it has only seven methods—enough for the object to exist and be identifiable, and not much more. You'll learn more about these basic objects in chapters 3 and 13.

2.3.1 *Identifying objects uniquely with the object_id method*

Every object in Ruby has a unique ID number associated with it. You can see an object's ID by asking the object to show you its `object_id`, using this or similar code:

```
obj = Object.new
puts "The id of obj is #{obj.object_id}."
str = "Strings are objects too, and this is a string!"
puts "The id of the string object str is #{str.object_id}."
puts "And the id of the integer 100 is #{100.object_id}."
```

Having a unique ID number for every object can come in handy when you're trying to determine whether two objects are the same as each other. How can two objects be the same? Well, the integer object `100` is the same as … the integer object `100`. (Ask 100 for its object ID twice, and the result will be the same.) And here's another case:

```
a = Object.new
b = a
puts "a's id is #{a.object_id} and b's id is #{b.object_id}."
```

Even though the variables `a` and `b` are different, the object they both refer to is the same. (See section 2.5.1 for more on the concept of object references.) The opposite scenario can happen too: sometimes two objects appear to be the same, but they're not. This happens a lot with strings. Consider the following example:

```
string_1 = "Hello"
string_2 = "Hello"
puts "string_1's id is #{string_1.object_id}."      string_1 id:
puts "string_2's id is #{string_2.object_id}."      287090      string_2 id:
                                                                 279110
```

Even though these two strings contain the same text, they aren't, technically, the same object. If you printed them out, you'd see the same result both times (`"Hello"`). But the string objects themselves are different. It's like having two copies of the same book: they contain the same text, but they aren't the same thing as each other. You could destroy one, and the other would be unaffected.

ID NUMBERS AND EQUALITY OF OBJECTS

As in the case of human institutions, one of the points of giving objects ID numbers in Ruby is to be able to make unique identifications—and, in particular, to be able to determine when two objects are the same object.

Ruby provides a variety of ways to compare objects for different types of equality. If you have two strings, you can test to see whether they contain the same characters. You can also test to see whether they're the same object (which, as you've just seen, isn't necessarily the case, even if they contain the same characters). The same holds true, with slight variations, for other objects and other types of objects.

Comparing ID numbers for equality is just one way of measuring object equality. We'll get into more detail about these comparisons a little later. Right now, we'll turn to the next innate method on our list: `respond_to?`.

2.3.2 *Querying an object's abilities with the respond_to? method*

Ruby objects respond to messages. At different times during a program run, depending on the object and what sorts of methods have been defined for it, an object may or may not respond to a given message. For example, the following code results in an error:

```
obj = Object.new
obj.talk
```

Ruby is only too glad to notify you of the problem:

```
NoMethodError: undefined method `talk' for #<Object:0x00000102836550>
```

You can determine in advance (before you ask the object to do something) whether the object knows how to handle the message you want to send it, by using the `respond_to?` method. This method exists for all objects; you can ask any object whether it responds to any message. `respond_to?` usually appears in connection with conditional (`if`) logic:

```
obj = Object.new
if obj.respond_to?("talk")
  obj.talk
else
  puts "Sorry, the object doesn't understand the 'talk' message."
end
```

`respond_to?` is an example of *introspection* or *reflection*, two terms that refer to examining the state of a program while it's running. Ruby offers a number of facilities for introspection. Examining an object's methods with the `methods` method, as we did earlier, is another introspective or reflective technique. (You'll see many more such techniques in part 3 of the book.)

Up to now, we've used the dot operator (.) to send messages to objects. Nothing wrong with that. But what if you don't know which message you want to send?

2.3.3   *Sending messages to objects with the send method*

Suppose you want to let a user get information from the ticket object by entering an appropriate query term (venue, performer, and so on) at the keyboard. Here's what you'd add to the existing program:

```
print "Information desired: "
request = gets.chomp
```

The second line of code gets a line of keyboard input, "chomps" off the trailing newline character, and saves the resulting string in the variable request.

At this point, you could test the input for one value after another by using the double equal sign comparison operator (==), which compares strings based on their content, and calling the method whose value provides a match:

```
if request == "venue"
  puts ticket.venue
elsif request == "performer"
  puts ticket.performer
...
```

To be thorough, though, you'd have to continue through the whole list of ticket properties. That's going to get lengthy.

There's an alternative: you can send the word directly to the ticket object. Instead of the previous code, you'd do the following:

```
if ticket.respond_to?(request)
  puts ticket.send(request)        ◁──┐
else                                  ❶
  puts "No such information available"
end
```

This version uses the send method as an all-purpose way of getting a message to the ticket object. It relieves you of having to march through the whole list of possible requests. Instead, having checked that the ticket object knows what to do ❶, you hand the ticket the message and let it do its thing.

Using __send__ or public_send instead of send

Sending is a broad concept: email is sent, data gets sent to I/O sockets, and so forth. It's not uncommon for programs to define a method called send that conflicts with Ruby's built-in send method. Therefore, Ruby gives you an alternative way to call send: __send__. By convention, no one ever writes a method with that name, so the built-in Ruby version is always available and never comes into conflict with newly written methods. It looks strange, but it's safer than the plain send version from the point of view of method-name clashes.

> **(continued)**
>
> In addition, there's a safe—but in a different way—version of `send` (or `__send__`) called `public_send`. The difference between plain `send` and `public_send` is that `send` can call an object's private methods, and `public_send` can't. We cover private methods later in the book, but in case you're curious what `public_send` was doing in the method list, that's the gist.

Most of the time, you'll use the dot operator to send messages to objects. But the `send` alternative can be useful and powerful—powerful enough, and error-prone enough, that it almost always merits at least the level of safety-netting represented by a call to `respond_to?`. In some cases, `respond_to?` might even be too broad to be safe; you might only `send` a message to an object if the message is included in a predetermined message "whitelist." The guiding principle is care: be careful about sending arbitrary messages to objects, especially if those messages are based on user choice or input.

Next, we'll put method argument syntax and semantics under the microscope.

2.4   A close look at method arguments

Methods you write in Ruby can take zero or more arguments. They can also allow a variable number of arguments. We'll examine argument semantics in several different ways in this section:

- The difference between required and optional arguments
- How to assign default values to arguments
- The rules governing the order in which you have to arrange the parameters in the method signature so that Ruby can make sense of argument lists in method calls and bind the parameters correctly
- What you can't do with arguments in Ruby

Table 2.2 will summarize these at the end of this section.

NOTE   There's more to argument list semantics than we'll cover here. Specifically, there's such a thing in Ruby as keyword arguments (or named parameters). That feature is strongly connected to the use of hashes as method arguments—which is why you won't see a full explanation of it until we've talked about hashes in depth in chapter 9.

2.4.1   Required and optional arguments

When you call a Ruby method, you have to supply the correct number of arguments. If you don't, Ruby tells you there's a problem. For example, calling a one-argument method with three arguments

```
obj = Object.new
def obj.one_arg(x)
  puts "I require one and only one argument!"
end
obj.one_arg(1,2,3)
```

results in

```
ArgumentError: wrong number of arguments (3 for 1)
```

It's possible to write a method that allows any number of arguments. To do this, put a star (an asterisk, *) in front of a single argument name:

```
def obj.multi_args(*x)
  puts "I can take zero or more arguments!"
end
```

The *x notation means that when you call the method, you can supply any number of arguments (or none). In this case, the variable x is assigned an array of values corresponding to whatever arguments were sent. You can then examine the values one at a time by traversing the array. (We'll look more closely at arrays in chapter 9.)

You can fine-tune the number of arguments by mixing required and optional arguments:

```
def two_or_more(a,b,*c)
  puts "I require two or more arguments!"
  puts "And sure enough, I got: "
  p a, b, c
end
```

In this example, a and b are required arguments. The final *c will sponge up any other arguments that you may send and put them into an array in the variable c. If you call two_or_more(1,2,3,4,5), you'll get the following report of what got assigned to a, b, and c:

```
I require two or more arguments!
And sure enough, I got:
1
2
[3, 4, 5]
```

(Using p rather than print or puts results in the array being printed out in array notation. Otherwise, each array element would appear on a separate line, making it harder to see that an array is involved at all.)

You can also make an argument optional by giving it a default value.

2.4.2 *Default values for arguments*

When you supply a default value for an argument, the result is that if that argument isn't supplied, the variable corresponding to the argument receives the default value.

Default arguments are indicated with an equal sign and a value. Here's an example:

```
def default_args(a,b,c=1)
  puts "Values of variables: ",a,b,c
end
```

If you make a call like this

```
default_args(3,2)
```

you'll see this result:

```
Values of variables:
3
2
1
```

No value was supplied in the method call for c, so c was set to the default value provided for it in the parameter list: 1. If you do supply a third argument, that value overrides the default assignment of 1. The following call

```
default_args(4,5,6)
```

produces this result:

```
Values of variables:
4
5
6
```

The real fun starts when you mix and match the different elements of argument syntax and have to figure out what order to put everything in.

2.4.3   *Order of parameters and arguments*

What output would you expect from the following code snippet?

```
def mixed_args(a,b,*c,d)
  puts "Arguments:"
  p a,b,c,d
end
mixed_args(1,2,3,4,5)
```

You've seen that a starred parameter, like *c, sponges up the remaining arguments—at least, it did so in the method two_or_more, where *c occurred last in the parameter list. What happens when another argument follows it?

Basically, Ruby tries to assign values to as many variables as possible. And the sponge parameters get the lowest priority: if the method runs out of arguments after it's performed the assignments of required arguments, then a catch-all parameter like *c ends up as an empty array. The required arguments both before *c and after *c get taken care of before *c does.

The output of the previous snippet is this:

```
Arguments:
1
2
[3, 4]
5
```

The parameters a and b get the first two arguments, 1 and 2. Because the parameter at the end of the list, d, represents a required argument, it grabs the first available value from the right-hand end of the argument list—namely, 5. Whatever's left in the middle (3, 4) gets sponged up by c.

If you only give enough arguments to match the required arguments of the method, then the sponge array will be empty. The method call

```
mixed_args(1,2,3)
```

results in this output:

```
1
2
[]
3
```

In this example, c is out of luck; there's nothing left.

You can get reasonably fancy with parameter syntax. Here's a method that takes a required argument; an optional argument that defaults to 1; two more required arguments taken from the right; and, somewhere in the middle, everything else:

```
def args_unleashed(a,b=1,*c,d,e)
  puts "Arguments:"
  p a,b,c,d,e
end
```

And here's an irb session that puts this method through its paces. Note that the return value of the method call, in every case, is an array consisting of all the values. That's the return value of the call to p. It's an array representation of the same values that you see printed out as individual values on separate lines:

```
>> args_unleashed(1,2,3,4,5)              <──┐
1                                            ①
2
[3]
4
5
=> [1, 2, [3], 4, 5]
>> args_unleashed(1,2,3,4)            <──②
1
2
[]
3
4
=> [1, 2, [], 3, 4]
>> args_unleashed(1,2,3)              <──③
1
1
[]
2
3
=> [1, 1, [], 2, 3]
>> args_unleashed(1,2,3,4,5,6,7,8)        <──④
1
2
[3, 4, 5, 6]
7
8
```

```
=> [1, 2, [3, 4, 5, 6], 7, 8]
>> args_unleashed(1,2)                                          ⊲──❺
ArgumentError: wrong number of arguments (2 for 3+)
```

The first call to `args_unleashed` has five arguments ❶. That means there are enough to go around: b gets its default overridden, and the array c gets one element. The second call is stingier ❷, and c loses out: b gets to override its default, leaving c empty (because the last two arguments are spoken for by the required arguments d and e).

The third call tightens its belt even further ❸. This time, there are only enough arguments to satisfy the basic requirements—that is, something to assign to a, d, and e. The parameter b falls back on its default, and c is empty.

The fourth call goes the other way ❹: this time, there are more arguments than the method requires and more than enough to populate the optional and default-valued parameters. It's a bonanza for c, which does its job of sponging up all the arguments that aren't needed elsewhere and ends up containing four elements.

The fifth call, on the other hand, doesn't send enough arguments to satisfy the basic requirements ❺. The variable bindings can't be made, so you get an argument error.

Along with the nuts and bolts of argument syntax, the most important thing to take away from these examples is the perhaps obvious point that, no matter what you do, every parameter ends up bound to some value. There's no such thing as a parameter that just sort of floats away into nothingness. If it's in the list, it ends up as a local variable inside the method—even if it's just bound to an empty array, like c sometimes is. You may or may not use every such variable, but the bindings are always made.

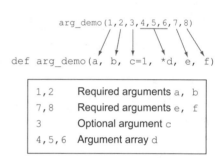

Figure 2.2   Argument assignment logic in action

Figure 2.2 offers a graphic representation of the basic logic of argument assignment. The listing of assignments in the box shows the order of priority: required arguments are handled first, then the default-valued optional argument, and then the sponge.

If you have complex argument needs, you must follow the rules carefully—and also keep in mind what you can't do.

2.4.4   *What you can't do in argument lists*

Parameters have a pecking order. Required ones get priority, whether they occur at the left or at the right of the list. All the optional ones have to occur in the middle. The middle may be the middle of nothing:

```
def all_optional(*args)                ⊲──┤  Zero left- or right-side
                                           required arguments
```

And you can have required arguments on the left only or on the right only—or both.

What you can't do is put the argument sponge to the left of any default-valued arguments. If you do this,

```
def broken_args(x,*y,z=1)
end
```

it's a syntax error, because there's no way it could be correct. Once you've given x its argument and sponged up all the remaining arguments in the array y, nothing can ever be left for z. And if z gets the right-hand argument, leaving the rest for y, it makes no sense to describe z as "optional" or "default-valued." The situation gets even thornier if you try to do something like the equally illegal (x, *y, z=1, a, b). Fortunately, Ruby doesn't allow for more than one sponge argument in a parameter list. Make sure you order your arguments sensibly and, when possible, keep your argument lists reasonably simple!

Table 2.2 summarizes what you've learned so far about argument syntax and semantics. You can treat this table more as a reference than as something you need to commit to memory and quiz yourself on—as long as you follow the basic reasoning of why each example works as it does.

Table 2.2 Sample method signatures with required, optional, and default-valued arguments

Argument type(s)	Method signature	Sample call(s)	Variable assignments
Required (R)	def m(a,b,c)	m(1,2,3)	a = 1, b = 2, c = 3
Optional (O)	def m(*a)	m(1,2,3)	a = [1,2,3]
Default-valued (D)	def m(a=1)	m m(2)	a = 1 a = 2
R/O	def m(a,*b)	m(1)	a = 1, b = [ ]
R/D	def m(a,b=1)	m(2) m(2,3)	a = 2, b = 1 a = 2, b = 3
D/O	def m(a=1,*b)	m m(2)	a = 1, b = [ ] a = 2, b = [ ]
R/D/O	def m(a,b=2,*c)	m(1) m(1,3) m(1,3,5,7)	a = 1, b = 2, c = [ ] a = 1, b = 3, c = [ ] a = 1, b = 3, c = [5,7]
R/D/O/R	def m(a,b=2,*c,d)	m(1,3) m(1,3,5) m(1,3,5,7) m(1,3,5,7,9)	a = 1, b = 2, c = [ ], d = 3 a = 1, b = 3, c = [ ], d = 5 a = 1, b = 3, c = [5], d = 7 a = 1, b = 3, c = [5,7], d = 9

As you can see from table 2.2, the arguments you send to methods are assigned to variables—specifically, local variables, visible and usable for the duration of the method. Assignment of local variables through method argument binding is just one case of the general process of local variable assignment, a process that we'll look at in detail next.

2.5   *Local variables and variable assignment*

Local variable names start with a lowercase letter or an underscore and are made up of alphanumeric characters and underscores. All of these are valid local variable names, including the lone underscore:

```
x
_x
name
first_name
plan9
user_ID
_
```

The *local* in *local variables* pertains to the fact that they have limited *scope*: a local variable is only visible in a limited part of a program, such as a method definition. Local variable names can be reused in different scopes. You can use, say, the variable name x in more than one place, and as long as those places have different scopes, the two x variables are treated as completely separate. (Remember that conventional Ruby style prefers under_score names over camelCase names for local variables.)

Scope is an important topic in its own right, and we'll get deeply into it in chapter 5. You can start getting familiar with some key aspects of it now, though, as you examine how local variables come and go. The classic case of local scope is a method definition. Watch what happens with x in this example:

```
def say_goodbye                                          ❶
  x = "Goodbye"
  puts x
end
def start_here                                           ❷
  x = "Hello"
  puts x
  say_goodbye                                            ❸
  puts "Let's check whether x remained the same:"        ❹
  puts x
end                                                      ❺
start_here
```

The output from this program is as follows:

```
Hello
Goodbye
Let's check whether x remained the same:
Hello
```

When you call start_here ❺, the method start_here is executed. Inside that method, the string Hello is assigned to x ❷—that is, to *this* x, the x in scope inside the method.

start_here prints out its x (Hello) and then calls the method say_goodbye ❸. In say_goodbye, something similar happens: a string (Goodbye) is assigned to x ❶. But this is a different x—as you see when the call to say_goodbye is finished and control returns to start_here: Ruby prints out this x, and the value is still Hello ❹. Using x as a local variable name in the scope of one method didn't affect its value in the scope of the other.

The local variables in this last example are created through explicit assignment. (Local variables can come into being, as you've seen, through the binding of method arguments to method parameters.) But what happens when the assignment or initialization takes place? What exactly is the relation between a variable and the object that it represents?

2.5.1 *Variables, objects, and references*

Variable assignments give the appearance, and have the apparent effect, of causing the variable on the left to be set equal to the object on the right. After this assignment, for example,

```
str = "Hello"
```

statements like puts str will deliver the string "Hello" for printing and processing.

Now, look at this example:

```
str = "Hello"
abc = str
puts abc
```

This, too, prints "Hello". Apparently the variable abc also contains "Hello", thanks to having had str assigned to it.

But there's more to it. The next example involves a method called replace, which does an in-place replacement of a string's content with new text:

```
str = "Hello"
abc = str
str.replace("Goodbye")
puts str
puts abc
def say_goodbye
  str = "Hello"
abc = str
str.replace("Goodbye")
puts str
puts abc

end
say_goodbye
```

Look closely at the output:

```
Goodbye
Goodbye
```

The first "Goodbye" is str; the second is abc. But we only replaced str. How did the string in abc get replaced?

ENTER REFERENCES

The answer is that variables in Ruby (with a few exceptions, most notably variables bound to integers) don't hold object values. `str` doesn't contain `"Hello"`. Rather, `str` contains a reference to a string object. It's the string object that has the characteristic of containing the letters that make up `"Hello"`.

In an assignment with a variable name on the left and an object on the right, the variable receives a reference to the object. In an assignment from one variable to another (`abc = str`), the variable on the left receives a copy of the reference stored in the variable on the right, with the result that both variables now contain references to the same object.

The fact that variables hold references to objects has implications for operations that change objects. The string-replace operation

```
str.replace("Goodbye")
```

replaces the characters of the string to which `str` is a reference with the text `"Goodbye"`. The variable `abc` contains another reference to the same string object. Even though the `replace` message goes to `str`, it causes a change to the object to which the reference in `abc` refers. When you print out `abc`, you see the result: the contents of the string have changed.

The un-reference: Immediate values

Some objects in Ruby are stored in variables as immediate values. These include integers, symbols (which look like `:this`), and the special objects `true`, `false`, and `nil`. When you assign one of these values to a variable (`x = 1`), the variable holds the value itself, rather than a reference to it.

In practical terms, this doesn't matter (and it will often be left as implied, rather than spelled out repeatedly, in discussions of references and related topics in this book). Ruby handles the dereferencing of object references automatically; you don't have to do any extra work to send a message to an object that contains, say, a reference to a string, as opposed to an object that contains an immediate integer value.

But the immediate-value representation rule has a couple of interesting ramifications, especially when it comes to integers. For one thing, any object that's represented as an immediate value is always exactly the same object, no matter how many variables it's assigned to. There's only one object `100`, only one object `false`, and so on.

The immediate, unique nature of integer-bound variables is behind Ruby's lack of pre- and post-increment operators—which is to say, you can't do this in Ruby:

```
x = 1
x++    # No such operator
```

The reason is that due to the immediate presence of `1` in `x`, `x++` would be like `1++`, which means you'd be changing the number 1 to the number 2—and that makes no sense.

For every object in Ruby, there can and must be one or more references to that object. If there are no references, the object is considered defunct, and its memory space is released and reused.

If you have two or more variables containing references to a single object, you can use any of them, on an equal basis, to send messages to the object. References have a many-to-one relationship to their objects. But if you assign a completely new object to a variable that's already referring to an object, things change.

2.5.2 References in variable assignment and reassignment

Every time you assign to a variable—every time you put a variable name to the left of an equal sign and something else on the right—you start from scratch: the variable is wiped clean, and a new assignment is made.

Here's a new version of our earlier example, illustrating this point:

```
str = "Hello"
abc = str
str = "Goodbye"
puts str
puts abc
```

This time the output is

```
Goodbye
Hello
```

The second assignment to `str` gives `str` a reference to a different string object. `str` and `abc` part company at that point. `abc` still refers to the old string (the one whose contents are `"Hello"`), but `str` now refers to a different string (a string whose contents are `"Goodbye"`).

The first version of the program changed a single string, but the second version has two separate strings. After it's reused, the variable `str` has nothing further to do with the object it referred to previously. But reusing `str` has no effect on `abc`, which still contains a reference to the original string.

> **NOTE** The examples use local variables to demonstrate what does and doesn't happen when you assign to a variable that's already been assigned to. But the rules and behaviors you're seeing here aren't just for local variables. Class, global, and instance variables follow the same rules. (So do so-called constants, which you can assign to more than once, oddly enough!) All of these categories of identifier are *l-values*: they can serve as the left-hand side, or target, of an assignment. (Compare with, say, `100 = 10`, which fails because `100` isn't an l-value.) And they all behave the same with respect to how they bind to their right-hand side and what happens when you use a given one more than once.

Ruby variables are often described as labels or names for objects. It's a useful comparison. Say you have two names for your dog. "I'm taking Fido to the vet" and "I'm taking

Rover to the vet" refer to the same animal. But if you get a new dog and transfer the name Fido to him, then the name-to-dog bindings have changed. Fido and Rover no longer refer to the same animal, and the name Fido has no further connection with the first dog.

And the new Fido doesn't even have to be a dog; you could stop calling your dog Fido and start using the name for your car instead. It's the same when you do x = 1 followed by x = "A string". You're reusing the identifier x for a completely new class of object (String rather than Fixnum). Unlike some languages, Ruby doesn't have typed variables. Any variable can be bound to any object of any class at any time.

The semantics of references and (re)assignment have important implications for how things play out when you call a method with arguments. What does the method receive? And what can the method do with it?

2.5.3   *References and method arguments*

Let's stick with a string-based example, because strings are easy to change and track. Here's a method that takes one argument:

```
def change_string(str)
  str.replace("New string content!")
end
```

Next, create a string and send it to change_string:

```
s = "Original string content!"
change_string(s)
```

Now, examine s:

```
puts s
```

The examination reveals that the contents of the string to which s refers have changed:

```
New string content!
```

This tells you that inside the change_string method, the variable str is assigned a reference to the string also referred to by s. When you call a method with arguments, you're really trafficking in object references. And once the method has hold of a reference, any changes it makes to the object through the reference are visible when you examine the object through any of its references.

Ruby gives you some techniques for protecting objects from being changed, should you wish or need to do so.

DUPING AND FREEZING OBJECTS

If you want to protect objects from being changed inside methods to which you send them, you can use the dup method, which duplicates an object:

```
s = "Original string content!"
change_string(s.dup)          ⟵┐  Prints "Original
puts s                           │  string content!"
```

You can also freeze an object, which prevents it from undergoing further change:

```
s = "Original string content!"
s.freeze
change_string(s)
```

RuntimeError: can't modify frozen string

Note that there's no corresponding unfreeze method. Freezing is forever.

To complete the picture, there's also a method called clone. It's a lot like dup. The difference is that if you clone a frozen object, the clone is also frozen—whereas if you dup a frozen object, the duplicate isn't frozen.

With these tools in hand—dup, clone, and freeze—you can protect your objects against most rogue change operations. Some dangers still lurk, though. Even if you freeze an array, it's still possible to change the objects *inside* the array (assuming they're not frozen):

```
>> numbers = ["one", "two", "three"]
=> ["one", "two", "three"]
>> numbers.freeze
=> ["one", "two", "three"]
>> numbers[2] = "four"                              ❶
RuntimeError: can't modify frozen array             ❷
>> numbers[2].replace("four")
=> "four"
>> numbers                                          ❸
=> ["one", "two", "four"]
```

In this example, the fact that the numbers array is frozen means you can't change the array ❶. But the strings inside the array aren't frozen. If you do a replace operation on the string "three", mischievously turning it into "four" ❷, the new contents of the string are revealed when you reexamine the (still frozen!) array ❸.

Be careful with references, and remember that a reference to an object inside a collection isn't the same as a reference to the collection. (You'll get a strong feel for collections as objects in their own right when we look at them in detail in chapter 9.)

A final point about variables—local variables in particular—involves their physical resemblance to method calls, and how Ruby figures out what you mean when you throw a plain, unadorned identifier at it.

2.5.4 Local variables and the things that look like them

When Ruby sees a plain word sitting there—a bareword identifier, like s, ticket, puts, or user_name—it interprets it as one of three things:

- A local variable
- A keyword
- A method call

Keywords are special reserved words that you can't use as variable names. def is a keyword; the only thing you can use it for is to start a method definition. (Strictly speaking, you can trick Ruby into naming a method def. But...well...don't.) if is also a keyword; lots of Ruby code involves conditional clauses that start with if, so it would be confusing to also allow the use of `if` as a variable name. A sequence like `if = 3` would be difficult for Ruby to parse.

Like local variables, method calls can be plain words. You've seen several examples, including `puts` and `print`. If the method call includes arguments in parentheses—or even empty parentheses—then it's clear that it's not a local variable. In other cases, there may be some ambiguity, and Ruby has to figure it out.

Here's how Ruby decides what it's seeing when it encounters a plain identifier:

1 If the identifier is a keyword, it's a keyword (Ruby has an internal list of these and recognizes them).

2 If there's an equal sign (=) to the right of the identifier, it's a local variable undergoing an assignment.

3 Otherwise, the identifier is assumed to be a method call.

If you use an identifier that isn't any of these three things, then Ruby will complain and halt execution with a fatal error. The error message you get when this happens is instructive:

```
$ ruby -e "x"
-e:1:in `<main>': undefined local variable or method 'x' for main:Object
    (NameError)
```

Note that Ruby can't tell whether you thought x was a variable or a method. It knows that x isn't a keyword, but it could be either of the other two. So the error message includes both.

At this point, you've got a large, growing store of knowledge about objects and variables and how they're related. We'll turn next in chapter 3 to the topic of how to create objects in a structured, scalable way with classes.

2.6   Summary

We've covered a lot of ground in chapter 2. In this chapter you saw

- How to create a new object and define methods for it
- The basics of the message-sending mechanism by which you send requests to objects for information or action
- Several of the important built-in methods that every Ruby object comes with: `object_id`, `respond_to?`, and `send`
- Details of the syntax for method argument lists, including the use of required, optional, and default-valued arguments
- How local variables and variable assignment work
- Ruby's use of references to objects and how references play out when multiple variables refer to the same object

Writing a Ruby program can involve thinking about how you might map elements of a domain (even a modest one-entity domain like "a ticket to an event") onto a system of objects so that those objects can store information and perform tasks. At the same time, it's important not to think too rigidly about the relation between objects and the real world. Object-oriented languages certainly offer a strong component of real-world modeling; but Ruby, at the same time, is extremely elastic in its modeling facilities—as you can see from how easy it is to enhance a given object's behavior. The chief goal in designing a program and the objects inside it is to come up with a system that works and that has internal consistency.

And, of course, the language offers lots of facilities for developing program structure. Creating objects one by one, as we've done in this chapter, is little more than the tip of the iceberg. We'll expand the discussion exponentially next, by looking at how to create objects on a multiple, more automated basis using Ruby classes.

Organizing objects with classes 3

This chapter covers

- Creating multiple objects with classes
- Setting and reading object state
- Automating creation of attribute read and write methods
- Class inheritance mechanics
- Syntax and semantics of Ruby constants

Creating a new object with `Object.new`—and equipping that object with its own methods, one method at a time—is a great way to get a feel for the object-centeredness of Ruby programming. But this approach doesn't exactly scale; if you're running an online box office and your database has to process records for tickets by the hundreds, you've got to find another way to create and manipulate ticket-like objects in your Ruby programs.

Sure enough, Ruby gives you a full suite of programming techniques for creating objects on a batch basis. You don't have to define a separate `price` method for every ticket. Instead, you can define a ticket *class*, engineered in such a way that every individual ticket object automatically has the `price` method.

Defining a class lets you group behaviors (methods) into convenient bundles, so that you can quickly create many objects that behave essentially the same way. You can also add methods to individual objects, if that's appropriate for what you're trying to do in your program. But you don't have to do that with every object if you model your domain into classes.

Everything you handle in Ruby is either an object or a construct that evaluates to an object, and every object is an instance of some class. This fact holds true even where it might at first seem a little odd. Integers are instances of a class, and classes themselves are objects. You'll learn in this chapter how this pervasive aspect of the design of Ruby operates.

Talking about classes doesn't mean you're not talking about objects; that's why this chapter has the title it has, rather than, say, "Ruby classes." Much of what we'll look at here pertains to objects and methods—but that's because classes are, at heart, a way to organize objects and methods. We'll look at the kinds of things you can and will do inside classes, as well as what classes themselves are.

3.1 Classes and instances

A typical class consists of a collection of method definitions. Classes usually exist for the purpose of being *instantiated*—that is, of having objects created that are instances of the class.

You've already seen instantiation in action. It's our old signature tune:

```
obj = Object.new
```

Object is a built-in Ruby class. When you use the dot notation on a class, you send a message to the class. Classes can respond to messages, just like objects; in fact, as you'll have reason to be aware of in any number of situations, classes are objects. The new method is a *constructor*: a method whose purpose is to manufacture and return to you a new instance of the class, a newly minted object.

You define a class with the class keyword. Classes are named with *constants*, a special type of identifier recognizable by the fact that it begins with a capital letter. Constants are used to store information and values that don't change over the course of a program run.

> **WARNING** Constants can change—they're not as constant as their name implies. But if you assign a new value to a constant, Ruby prints a warning. The best practice is to avoid assigning new values to constants that you've already assigned a value to. (See section 3.7.2 for more information about reassignment to constants.)

Let's define a Ticket class. Inside the class definition, we define a single, simple method:

```
class Ticket
  def event
    "Can't really be specified yet..."
  end
end
```

Define event method
for Ticket class

Now we can create a new `ticket` object and ask it (pointlessly, but to see the process) to describe its event:

```
ticket = Ticket.new
puts ticket.event
```

The method call `ticket.event` results in the execution of our `event` method and, consequently, the printing out of the (rather uninformative) string specified inside that method:

```
Can't really be specified yet...
```

The information is vague, but the process is fully operational: we've written and executed an instance method.

Meaning what, exactly?

3.1.1 *Instance methods*

The examples of method definitions in chapter 2 involved defining methods directly on individual objects:

```
def ticket.event
```

The `event` method in the previous example, however, is defined in a general way, inside the `Ticket` class:

```
def event
```

That's because this `event` method will be shared by all tickets—that is, by all instances of `Ticket`. Methods of this kind, defined inside a class and intended for use by all instances of the class, are called *instance methods*. They don't belong only to one object. Instead, any instance of the class can call them.

> **NOTE** Methods that you define for one particular object—as in `def ticket .price`—are called *singleton methods*. You've already seen examples, and we'll look in more depth at how singleton methods work in chapter 13. An object that has a `price` method doesn't care whether it's calling a singleton method or an instance method of its class. But the distinction is important from the programmer's perspective.

Once you've defined an instance method in a class, nothing stops you from defining it again—that is, overriding the first definition with a new one.

3.1.2 *Overriding methods*

Here's an example of defining the same method twice in one class:

```
class C
  def m
    puts "First definition of method m"
  end
```

```
def m
    puts "Second definition of method m"
  end
end
```

Given these two definitions, what happens when we call `m` on an instance of `C`? Let's ask the object:

```
C.new.m
```

The printed result is `Second definition of method m`. The second definition has prevailed: we see the output from that definition, not from the first. When you override a method, the new version takes precedence.

(The preceding example is deliberately minimalist, because it's illustrating something that you wouldn't normally do in exactly this form. When you override a method, it's usually because you've written a class that inherits from the original class, and you want it to behave differently. We'll look at inheritance soon.)

You can also add to a class's methods, or override them, by reopening the class definition.

3.1.3   *Reopening classes*

In most cases, when you're defining a class, you create a single class definition block:

```
class C
  # class code here
end
```

But it's possible to reopen a class and make additions or changes. Here's an example:

```
class C
  def x
  end
end
class C
  def y
  end
end
```

We open the class definition body, add one method (`x`), and close the definition body. Then, we reopen the definition body, add a second method (`y`), and close the definition body. The result is the same as if we'd done this:

```
class C
  def x
  end
  def y
  end
end
```

Here we open the class only once and add both methods. Of course, you're not going to break your class definitions into separate blocks just for fun. There has to be a reason—and it should be a good reason, because separating class definitions can make it harder for people reading or using your code to follow what's going on.

One reason to break up class definitions is to spread them across multiple files. If you require a file that contains a class definition (perhaps you load it from the disk at runtime from another file, and you also have a partial definition of the same class in the file from which the second file is required), the two definitions are merged. This isn't something you'd do arbitrarily: it must be a case where the program's design demands that a class be defined partially in one place and partially in another.

Here's a real-life example. Ruby has a `Time` class. It lets you manipulate times, format them for timestamp purposes, and so forth. You can use UNIX-style date-format strings to get the format you want. For example, the command

```
puts Time.new.strftime("%m-%d-%y")
```

prints the string `"02-09-14"`, representing the date on which the method call was made.

In addition to the built-in `Time` class, Ruby also has a program file called time.rb, inside of which are various enhancements of, and additions to, the `Time` class. time.rb achieves its goal of enhancing the `Time` class by reopening that class. If you look for the file time.rb either in the lib subdirectory of the Ruby source tree or in your Ruby installation, you'll see this on or near line 87:

```
class Time
```

That's a reopening of the `Time` class, done for the purpose of adding new methods.

You can see the effect best by trying it in irb. irb lets you call a nonexistent method without causing the session to terminate, so you can see the effects of the `require` command all in one session:

```
>> t = Time.new
=> 2014-02-09 09:41:29 -0500
>> t.xmlschema
NoMethodError: undefined method 'xmlschema' for 2014-02-09 09:41:29 -
    0500:Time
    from (irb):2
    from /Users/dblack/.rvm/rubies/ruby-2.1.0/bin/irb:11:in `<main>'
>> require 'time'
=> true
>> t.xmlschema
=> "2014-02-09T09:41:29-05:00"
```

❶
❷

Here we send the unrecognized message `xmlschema` to our `Time` object, and it doesn't work ❶. Then, we load the time.rb file ❷ and, sure enough, the `Time` object now has an `xmlschema` method. (That method, according to its documentation, "returns a string that represents the time as dateTime defined by XML Schema.")

You can spread code for a single class over multiple files or over multiple locations in the same file. But be aware that it's considered better practice not to do so, when possible. In the case of the `Time` extensions, people often suggest the possibility of unification: giving `Time` objects all the extension methods in the first place, and not separating those methods into a separate library. It's possible that such unification will take place in a later release of Ruby.

Ruby is about objects, and objects are instances of classes. We'll look next at instance variables, a special language feature designed to allow every instance of every class in Ruby to set and maintain its own private stash of information.

3.2 *Instance variables and object state*

When we created individual objects and wrote methods for each action or value we needed, we hard-coded the value into the object through the methods. With this technique, if a ticket costs $117.50, then it has a method called `price` that returns precisely that amount:

```
ticket = Object.new
def ticket.price
  117.50
end
```

But now we're moving away from one-at-a-time object creation with `Object.new` and setting our sights on the practice of designing classes and creating many objects from them.

This means we're changing the rules of the game when it comes to information like the price of a ticket. If you create a `Ticket` class, you can't give it a `price` method that returns $117.50, for the simple reason that not every ticket costs $117.50. Similarly, you can't give every ticket the event-name Benefit Concert, nor can every ticket think that it's for Row G, Seat 33.

Instead of hard-coding values into every object, we need a way to tell different objects that they have different values. We need to be able to create a new `Ticket` object and store with that object the information about the event, price, and other properties. When we create another ticket object, we need to store different information with that object. And we want to be able to do this without having to handcraft a method with the property hard-coded into it.

Information and data associated with a particular object embodies the *state* of the object. We need to be able to do the following:

- Set, or reset, the state of an object (say to a ticket, "You cost $11.99.").
- Read back the state (ask a ticket, "How much do you cost?").

Conveniently, Ruby objects come with their own storage and retrieval mechanism for values: *instance variables*.

The instance variable enables individual objects to remember state. Instance variables work much like other variables: you assign values to them, and you read those values back; you can add them together, print them out, and so on. But instance variables have a few differences:

- Instance variable names always start with a single @ (at sign). This enables you to recognize an instance variable at a glance.
- Instance variables are only visible to the object to which they belong. (Being "visible to an object" has a technical definition having to do with the default object `self`, which you'll see more about in chapter 5.)

- An instance variable initialized in one method inside a class can be used by any method defined within that class.

The following listing shows a simple example illustrating the way the assigned value of an instance variable stays alive from one method call to another.

> **Listing 3.1   An instance variable maintaining its value between method calls**

```
class Person
  def set_name(string)
    puts "Setting person's name..."          ❶
    @name = string
  end

  def get_name
    puts "Returning the person's name..."
    @name
  end
end

joe = Person.new                              ❷
joe.set_name("Joe")
puts joe.get_name                             ❸
```

Thanks to the assignment ❶ that happens as a result of the call to set_name ❷, when you ask for the person's name ❸, you get back what you put in: "Joe". Unlike a local variable, the instance variable @name retains the value assigned to it even after the method in which it was initialized has terminated. This property of instance variables—their survival across method calls—makes them suitable for maintaining state in an object.

You'll see better, more idiomatic ways to store and retrieve values in objects shortly. But they're all based on setting and retrieving the values of instance variables, so it pays to get a good feel for how instance variables behave.

The scene is set to do something close to useful with our Ticket class. The missing step, which we'll now fill in, is the object initialization process.

3.2.1   Initializing an object with state

When you write a class (like Ticket), you can, if you wish, define a special method called initialize. If you do so, that method will be executed every time you create a new instance of the class.

For example, given an initialize method that prints a message

```
class Ticket
  def initialize
    puts "Creating a new ticket!"
  end
end
```

you'll see the message "Creating a new ticket!" every time you create a new ticket object by calling Ticket.new.

You can employ this automatic initialization process to set an object's state at the time of the object's creation. Let's say we want to give each ticket object a venue and date when it's created. We can send the correct values as arguments to `Ticket.new`, and those same arguments will be sent to `initialize` automatically. Inside `initialize`, we'll have access to the venue and date information, and can save that information by means of instance variables:

```
class Ticket
  def initialize(venue,date)
    @venue = venue
    @date = date
  end
```

Before closing the class definition with `end`, we should add something else: a way to read back the venue and date. Let's drop the `get_` formula that we used with `get_name` (in listing 3.1) and instead name the get methods after the instance variables whose values they return. Add this code (which includes the end directive for the class definition) to the previous lines:

```
  def venue
    @venue
  end
  def date
    @date
  end
end
```

Each of these methods hands back the value of an instance variable. In each case, that variable is the last (and only) expression in the method and therefore also serves as the method's return value.

NOTE The names of the instance variables, methods, and arguments to `initialize` don't have to match. You could use `@v` instead of `@venue`, for example, to store the value passed in the argument venue. You could call the second method `event_date` and still use `@date` inside it. Still, it's usually good practice to match the names to make it clear what goes with what.

Now we're ready to create some tickets with dynamically set values for venue and date, rather than the hard-coded values of our earlier examples:

```
th = Ticket.new("Town Hall", "11/12/13")
cc = Ticket.new("Convention Center", "12/13/14")
puts "We've created two tickets."
puts "The first is for a #{th.venue} event on #{th.date}."
puts "The second is for an event on #{cc.date} at #{cc.venue}."
```

Run this code, along with the previous class definition of `Ticket`, and you'll see the following:

```
We've created two tickets.
The first is for a Town Hall event on 11/12/13.
The second is for an event on 12/13/14 at Convention Center.
```

The phrase at Convention Center is a bit stilted, but the process of saving and retrieving information for individual objects courtesy of instance variables operates perfectly. Each ticket has its own state (saved information), thanks to what our initialize method does; and each ticket lets us query it for the venue and date, thanks to the two methods with those names.

This opens up our prospects immensely. We can create, manipulate, compare, and examine any number of tickets at the same time, without having to write separate methods for each of them. All the tickets share the resources of the Ticket class. At the same time, each ticket has its own set of instance variables to store state information.

So far, we've arranged things in such a way that we set the values of the instance variables at the point where the object is created and can then retrieve those values at any point during the life of the object. That arrangement is often adequate, but it's not symmetrical. What if you want to set values for the instance variables at some point other than object-creation time? What if you want to change an object's state after it's already been set once?

3.3   *Setter methods*

When you need to set or change an object's state at some point in your program other than the initialize method, the heart of the matter is assigning (or reassigning) values to instance variables. You can, of course, change any instance variable's value in any method. For example, if we wanted tickets to have the ability to discount themselves, we could write an instance method like this inside the Ticket class definition:

```
def discount(percent)
  @price = @price * (100 - percent) / 100.0
end
```

But the most common case is the simplest: calling a setter method with an argument and setting the appropriate instance variable to the argument. That's what set_name does in the Person class example.

There's more to it, though. Ruby has some specialized method-naming conventions that let you write setter methods in a way that's more elegant than sticking set_ in front of a descriptive word like *name*. We'll make another pass at Ticket, this time with an eye on setter methods and the techniques available for streamlining them.

3.3.1   *The equal sign (=) in method names*

Let's say we want a way to set the price of a ticket. As a starting point, price can be set along with everything else at object-creation time:

```
class Ticket
  def initialize(venue,date,price)
    @venue = venue
    @date = date
    @price = price
  end
  # etc.
```

```
    def price
      @price
    end
    # etc.
end
th = Ticket.new("Town Hall", "11/12/13", 63.00)
```

The initialization command is getting awfully long, though, and requires that we remember what order to put the many arguments in so we don't end up with a ticket whose price is "Town Hall". And we still don't have a way to change a ticket's price later.

Let's solve the problem, initially, with a set_price method that allows us to set, or reset, the price of an existing ticket. We'll also rewrite the initialize method so that it doesn't expect a price figure:

```
class Ticket
  def initialize(venue, date)
    @venue = venue
    @date = date
  end
  def set_price(amount)
    @price = amount
  end
  def price
    @price
  end
end
```

Here's some price manipulation in action:

```
ticket = Ticket.new("Town Hall", "11/12/13")
ticket.set_price(63.00)
puts "The ticket costs $#{"%.2f" % ticket.price}."      ◁──┐ Format price to
ticket.set_price(72.50)                                      two decimal places
puts "Whoops -- it just went up. It now costs $#{"%.2f" % ticket.price}."
```

The output is

```
The ticket costs $63.00.
Whoops -- it just went up. It now costs $72.50.
```

This technique works: you can write all the set_property methods you need, and the instance variable–based retrieval methods to go with them. But there's a nicer way.

TIP The percent sign technique you saw in the last example allows you to format strings using sprintf-like syntax. Ruby also has a sprintf method (also available with the name format); we could rewrite the ticket price example as sprintf("%.2f", ticket.price). Possible format specifiers (the % things inside the pattern string) include %d for decimal numbers, %s for strings, %f for floats, and %x for hexadecimal numbers. Run ri sprintf for full documentation.

Ruby allows you to define methods that end with an equal sign (=). Let's replace set_price with a method called price= ("price" plus an equal sign):

```
def price=(amount)
  @price = amount
end
```

price= does exactly what set_price did, and in spite of the slightly odd method name, you can call it just like any other method:

```
ticket.price=(63.00)
```

The equal sign gives you that familiar "assigning a value to something" feeling, so you know you're dealing with a setter method. It still looks odd, though; but Ruby takes care of that, too.

3.3.2 *Syntactic sugar for assignment-like methods*

Programmers use the term *syntactic sugar* to refer to special rules that let you write your code in a way that doesn't correspond to the normal rules but that's easier to remember how to do and looks better.

Ruby gives you some syntactic sugar for calling setter methods. Instead of

```
ticket.price=(63.00)
```

you're allowed to do this:

```
ticket.price = 63.00
```

When the interpreter sees this sequence of code, it automatically ignores the space before the equal sign and reads price = as the single message price= (a call to the method whose name is price=, which we've defined). As for the right-hand side, parentheses are optional for method arguments, as long as there's no ambiguity. So you can put 63.00 there, and it will be picked up as the argument to the price= method.

The intent behind the inclusion of this special syntax is to allow you to write method calls that look like assignments. If you just saw ticket.price = 63.00 in a program, you might assume that ticket.price is some kind of l-value to which the value 63.00 is being assigned. But it isn't. The whole thing is a method call. The receiver is ticket, the method is price=, and the single argument is 63.00.

The more you use this setter style of method, the more you'll appreciate how much better the sugared version looks. This kind of attention to appearance is typical of Ruby.

Keep in mind, too, that setter methods can do more than simple variable assignment.

3.3.3 *Setter methods unleashed*

The ability to write your own =-terminated methods and the fact that Ruby provides the syntactic sugar way of calling those methods open up some interesting possibilities.

One possibility is abuse. It's possible to write =-terminated methods that look like they're going to do something involving assignment but don't:

```ruby
class Silly
  def price=(x)
    puts "The current time is #{Time.now}"
  end
end
s = Silly.new
s.price = 111.22
```

This example discards the argument it receives (111.22) and prints out an unrelated message:

```
The current time is 2014-02-09 09:53:31 -0500
```

This example is a deliberate caricature. But the point is important: Ruby checks your syntax but doesn't police your semantics. You're allowed to write methods with names that end with =, and you'll always get the assignment-syntax sugar. Whether the method's name makes any sense in relation to what the method does is in your hands.

Equal sign methods can also serve as filters or gatekeepers. Let's say we want to set the price of a ticket only if the price makes sense as a dollar-and-cents amount. We can add intelligence to the price= method to ensure the correctness of the data. Here, we'll multiply the number by 100, lop off any remaining decimal-place numbers with the to_i (convert to integer) operation, and compare the result with the original number multiplied by 100. This should expose any extra decimal digits beyond the hundredths column:

```ruby
class Ticket
  def price=(amount)
    if (amount * 100).to_i == amount * 100
      @price = amount
    else
      puts "The price seems to be malformed"
    end
  end
  def price
    @price
  end
end
```

You can also use this kind of filtering technique to *normalize* data—that is, to make sure certain data always takes a certain form. For example, let's say you have a travel agent website where the user needs to type in the desired date of departure. You want to allow both mm/dd/yy and mm/dd/yyyy.

If you have, say, a Ruby CGI script that's processing the incoming data, you might normalize the year by writing a setter method like this:

```ruby
class TravelAgentSession
  def year=(y)
    @year = y.to_i
```

```
    if @year < 100
       @year = @year + 2000
    end
  end
end
```

Handle one- or two-digit number by adding century to it

Then, assuming you have a variable called date in which you've stored the date field from the form (using Ruby's CGI library), you can get at the components of the date like this:

```
month, day, year = date.split('/')
self.year = year
```

The idea is to split the date string into three strings using the slash character (/) as a divider, courtesy of the built-in split method, and then to store the year value in the TravelAgentSession object using that object's year= method.

> **WARNING**   Setter methods don't return what you might think. When you use the syntactic sugar that lets you make calls to = methods that look like assignments, Ruby takes the assignment semantics seriously. Assignments (like x = 1) evaluate to whatever's on their right-hand side. Methods usually return the value of the last expression evaluated during execution. But = method calls behave like assignments: the value of the expression ticket.price = 63.00 is 63.00, even if the ticket= method returns the string "Ha ha!". The idea is to keep the semantics consistent. Under the hood, it's a method call; but it looks like an assignment and behaves like an assignment with respect to its value as an expression.

You'll write complex getter and setter methods sometimes, but the simple get and set operations, wrapped around instance variables, are the most common—so common, in fact, that Ruby gives you some shortcuts for writing them.

3.4   *Attributes and the attr_* method family*

An *attribute* is a property of an object whose value can be read and/or written through the object. In the case of ticket objects, we'd say that each ticket has a price attribute as well as a date attribute and a venue attribute. Our price= method can be described as an *attribute writer* method. date, venue, and price (without the equal sign) are *attribute reader* methods. (The write/read terminology is equivalent to the set/get terminology used earlier, but write/read is more common in Ruby discussions.)

The attributes of Ruby objects are implemented as reader and/or writer methods wrapped around instance variables—or, if you prefer, instance variables wrapped up in reader and/or writer methods. There's no separate "attribute" construct at the language level. *Attribute* is a high-level term for a particular configuration of methods and instance variables. But it's a useful term, and Ruby does embed the concept of attributes in the language, in the form of shortcuts that help you write the methods that implement them.

3.4.1   *Automating the creation of attributes*

Consider the following listing's full picture of what we have, by way of attribute reader and/or writer methods, in our `Ticket` class. (There's nothing new here; the code is just being pulled together in one place.)

Listing 3.2   `Ticket` class, with the attribute reader/writer methods spelled out

```
class Ticket
  def initialize(venue, date)
    @venue = venue
    @date = date
  end
  def price=(price)
    @price = price
  end
  def venue
    @venue
  end
  def date
    @date
  end
  def price
    @price
  end
end
```

There's one read/write attribute (`price`) and two read attributes (`venue` and `date`). It works, but the code is repetitive. Three methods look like this:

```
def something
  @something
end
```

And there's repetition on top of repetition: not only are there three such methods, but each of those three methods repeats its name in the name of the instance variable it uses.

Any time you see repetition on that scale, you should try to trim it—not by reducing what your program does, but by finding a way to express the same thing more concisely. In pursuit of this conciseness, Ruby is one step ahead: it provides a built-in shortcut that automatically creates a method that reads and returns the value of the instance variable with the same name as the method (give or take an `@`). It works like this:

```
class Ticket
  attr_reader :venue, :date, :price
end
```

The elements that start with colons (`:venue`, and so on) are *symbols*. Symbols are a kind of naming or labeling facility. They're a cousin of strings, although not quite the same thing. We'll look at symbols in more depth in chapter 8. For our present purposes, you can think of them as functionally equivalent to strings.

> **`self` as default receiver**
>
> You're seeing more method calls without an explicit receiver; there's no left-hand object and no dot in `attr_reader`, for example. In the absence of an explicit receiver, messages go to `self`, the default object. In the topmost level of a class definition body, `self` is the class object itself. So the object receiving the `attr_reader` message is the actual class object `Ticket`. We'll go into more depth about classes as objects and thus as message receivers later in this chapter, and into more depth about `self` in chapter 5.

The `attr_reader` (attribute reader) method automatically writes for you the kind of method we've just been looking at. And there's an `attr_writer` method, too:

```
class Ticket
  attr_writer :price
end
```

With that single line, we wrote (or, rather, Ruby wrote for us) our `price=` setter method. One line takes the place of three. In the case of the reader methods, one line took the place of nine!

The whole program now looks like the following listing.

Listing 3.3　`Ticket` class, with getter and setter methods defined via `attr_*` calls

```
class Ticket
  attr_reader :venue, :date, :price
  attr_writer :price
  def initialize(venue, date)
    @venue = venue
    @date = date
  end
end
```

Not only is the code in listing 3.3 shorter, it's also more informative—self-documenting, even. You can see at a glance that each ticket object has a `venue`, `date`, and `price`. The first two are readable attributes, and `price` can be read or written.

You can even create reader and writer methods with one command.

CREATING READER/WRITER ATTRIBUTES WITH ATTR_ACCESSOR

In the realm of object attributes, combination reader/writer attributes like `price` are common. Ruby provides a single method, `attr_accessor`, for creating both a reader and a writer method for an attribute. `attr_accessor` is the equivalent of `attr_reader` plus `attr_writer`. We can use this combined technique for `price`, because we want both operations:

```
class Ticket
  attr_reader :venue, :date
  attr_accessor :price
  # ... etc.
end
```

Alternately, you can achieve `attr_accessor` functionality with the plain `attr` method, as follows:

```
attr :price, true
```

Calling `attr` with `true` as the second argument triggers the creation of both reader and writer attributes, like `attr_accessor`. But `attr_accessor` is clearer in its intention—the word "accessor" tells you what's going on—and it also has the advantage that you can give it more than one accessor name at a time (whereas `attr` takes only one, plus the optional `true` argument). Without the second argument of `true`, `attr` just provides a reader attribute.

3.4.2 Summary of attr_* methods

The `attr_*` family of methods is summarized in table 3.1.

Table 3.1 Summary of the `attr_*` family of getter/setter creation methods

Method name	Effect	Example	Equivalent code

`attr_reader`	Creates a reader method	`attr_reader :venue`	<pre>def venue
			  @venue
			end</pre>

`attr_writer`	Creates a writer method	`attr_writer :price`	<pre>def price=(price)
			  @price = price
			end</pre>

`attr_accessor`	Creates reader and writer methods	`attr_accessor :price`	<pre>def price=(price)
			  @price = price
			end</pre>
			<pre>def price
			  @price
			end</pre>

`attr`	Creates a reader and optionally a writer method (if the second argument is `true`)	1. `attr :venue` 2. `attr :price, true`	1. See `attr_reader` 2. See `attr_accessor`

In all cases, the `attr_` techniques have the effect of writing one or more get and/or set methods for you. They're a powerful set of coding shortcuts.

Let's zoom back out to a broader view of classes—specifically, to the matter of class *inheritance*.

3.5 Inheritance and the Ruby class hierarchy

Inheritance is a kind of downward-chaining relationship between two classes (the superclass and the subclass), whereby one class "inherits" from another and the instances of the subclass acquire the behaviors—the methods—defined in the superclass.

In this example, `Magazine` inherits from `Publication`. Note the syntax in `Magazine`'s class definition:

```
class Publication
  attr_accessor :publisher
end
class Magazine < Publication
  attr_accessor :editor
end
```

The symbol < designates `Magazine` as a subclass of `Publication`. Because every publication object has `publisher` and `publisher=` methods (thanks to `attr_accessor :publisher`), every magazine object has those methods too. In addition, magazine objects have `editor` and `editor=` methods:

```
mag = Magazine.new
mag.publisher = "David A. Black"
mag.editor = "Joe Smith"
puts "Mag is published by #{mag.publisher}, and edited by #{mag.editor}."
```

We can continue the cascade downward:

```
class Ezine < Magazine
end
```

Instances of `Ezine` have both `publisher` and `editor` attributes, as defined in the superclass and super-superclass of `Ezine`. Note that it's not mandatory to add new methods to every subclass. You might want to create an `Ezine` class just for the sake of being able to call `Ezine.new` rather than `Magazine.new`, to make your code more expressive.

Of course it's not all about attribute accessor methods. Any instance method you define in a given class can be called by instances of that class, and also by instances of any subclasses of that class:

```
class Person                    ❶
  def species
    "Homo sapiens"
  end
end
class Rubyist < Person          ❷
end
david = Rubyist.new
puts david.species                 Output: Homo
                                   sapiens
```

In this example, the `Rubyist` class descends from `Person` ❷. That means a given `Rubyist` instance, such as `david`, can call the `species` method that was defined in the `Person` class ❶. As always in Ruby, it's about objects: what a given object can and can't do at a given point in the program. Objects get their behaviors from their classes, from their individual or singleton methods, and also from the ancestors (superclass, super-superclass, and so on) of their classes (and from one or two places we haven't looked at yet). All in all, Ruby objects lead interesting and dynamic lives. Inheritance is part of that picture.

Inheritance has an important limitation, though.

3.5.1 *Single inheritance: One to a customer*

In some object-oriented languages, it's possible for a given class to inherit from more than one class. You might, for example, have a `Teacher` class that inherits from a `Person` class and also inherits from an `Employee` class, or a `Car` class that inherits from `Machine`, `Powered`, and `Driveable`. Ruby doesn't allow multiple inheritance; every Ruby class can have only one superclass, in keeping with the principle of *single inheritance.*

Despite what might be your first impression, Ruby's single inheritance doesn't restrict you: Ruby provides *modules*, which are bundles of programming functionality similar to classes (except that they don't have instances), that you can easily graft onto your class's family tree to provide as many methods for your objects as you need. (Chapter 4 will focus on modules.) There's no limit to how richly you can model your objects—it just can't be done strictly with classes and inheritance.

The single inheritance principle means that you can't just draw a big tree of entities and then translate the tree directly into a class hierarchy. Inheritance often functions more as a convenient way to get two or more classes to share method definitions than as a definitive statement of how real-world objects relate to each other in terms of generality and specificity. There's some of that involved; every class in Ruby, for example, ultimately descends (as subclass or sub-subclass, and so on) from the `Object` class, and obviously `Object` is a more general class than, say, `String` or `Ticket`. But the single-inheritance limitation means that you can't bank on designing a hierarchy of classes that cascade downward in strict tree-graph fashion.

Again, modules play a key role here, and they'll get their due in chapter 4. For now, though, we'll follow the thread of inheritance upward, so to speak, and look at the classes that appear at the top of the inheritance tree of every Ruby object: the `Object` and `BasicObject` classes.

3.5.2 *Object ancestry and the not-so-missing link: The Object class*

You've seen the standard technique for creating a generic object:

```
obj = Object.new
```

You're now in a position to understand more deeply what's going on in this snippet.

The class `Object` is almost at the top of the inheritance chart. Every class is either a subclass of `Object`, a sub-subclass of `Object`, or, at some distance, a direct descendant of `Object`:

```
class C
end
class D < C
end
puts D.superclass
puts D.superclass.superclass
```

The output is

```
C
Object
```

because `C` is `D`'s superclass (that's our doing) and `Object` is `C`'s superclass (that's Ruby's doing).

If you go up the chain far enough from any class, you hit `Object`. Any method available to a bare instance of `Object` is available to every object; that is, if you can do

```
obj = Object.new
obj.some_method
```

then you can call `some_method` on any object.

There's that "almost," though. There is, as it turns out, another generation at the top.

3.5.3   *El Viejo's older brother: BasicObject*

My father's younger brother, now an 85-year-old great-grandfather, is known to his descendants as El Viejo: The Old Man. This presented my cousin with a conundrum: namely, how to explain to his little daughter—El Viejo's granddaughter—exactly who my father was, the first time she met him. In the end, he took the bull by the horns and introduced my father to his great-niece as "El Viejo's older brother."

The `BasicObject` class, like my late father in his time, is older than old: it comes before `Object` in the Ruby class family tree. The idea behind `BasicObject` is to offer a kind of blank-slate object—an object with almost no methods. (Indeed, the precedent for `BasicObject` was a library by Jim Weirich called `BlankSlate`.) `BasicObject`s have so few methods that you'll run into trouble if you create a `BasicObject` instance in irb:

```
>> BasicObject.new
(Object doesn't support #inspect)
```

The object gets created, but irb can't display the customary string representation of it because it has no `inspect` method!

A newly created `BasicObject` instance has only 8 instance methods—whereas a new instance of `Object` has 55. (These numbers may change a little among different versions or releases of Ruby, but they're accurate enough to make the point about `BasicObject` having few methods.) You're not likely to need to instantiate or subclass `BasicObject` on a regular basis, if ever. It's mainly handy for situations where you're modeling objects closely to some particular domain, almost to the point of writing a kind of Ruby dialect, and you don't want any false positives when you send messages to those objects. The 55 methods can get in the way, if you have your own ideas about whether your objects should play dumb when you send them messages like `display`, `extend`, or `clone`. (There'll be more to say about this when we take up the topic thread of `BasicObject` in chapter 13.)

Having put inheritance into the mix and looked at some of the key components of the lineage of Ruby objects, let's return to the subject of classes—specifically, to one of the most striking aspects of classes: the fact that they are objects and can therefore serve as receivers of messages, just like other objects.

3.6 Classes as objects and message receivers

Classes are special objects: they're the only kind of object that has the power to spawn new objects (instances). Nonetheless, they're objects. When you create a class, like Ticket, you can send messages to it, add methods to it, pass it around to other objects as a method argument, and generally do anything to it you would to another object.

Like other objects, classes can be created—indeed, in more than one way.

3.6.1 Creating class objects

Every class—Object, Person, Ticket—is an instance of a class called Class. As you've already seen, you can create a class object with the special class keyword formula:

```
class Ticket
  # your code here
end
```

That formula is a special provision by Ruby—a way to make a nice-looking, easily accessible class-definition block. But you can also create a class the same way you create most other objects, by sending the message new to the class object Class:

```
my_class = Class.new
```

In this case, the variable my_class is assigned a new class object.

Class.new corresponds precisely to other constructor calls like Object.new and Ticket.new. When you instantiate the class Class, you create a class. That class, in turn, can create instances of its own:

```
instance_of_my_class = my_class.new
```

In section 3.1, you saw that class objects are usually represented by constants (like Ticket or Object). In the preceding scenario, the class object is bound to a regular local variable (my_class). Calling the new method sends the message new to the class through that variable.

Defining instance methods in connection with Class.new

If you want to create an anonymous class using Class.new, and you also want to add instance methods at the time you create it, you can do so by appending a code block after the call to new. A *code block* is a fragment of code that you supply as part of a method call, which can be executed from the method. You'll see much more about code blocks when we look at iterators in chapter 6. Meanwhile, here's a small example of Class.new with a block:

```
c = Class.new do
  def say_hello
    puts "Hello!"
  end
end
```

If you now create an instance of the class (with c.new), you'll be able to call the method say_hello on that instance.

And yes, there's a paradox here...

THE CLASS/OBJECT CHICKEN-OR-EGG PARADOX
The class `Class` is an instance of itself—that is, it's a `Class` object. And there's more. Remember the class `Object`? Well, `Object` is a class—but classes are objects. So, `Object` is an object. And `Class` is a class. And `Object` is a class, and `Class` is an object.

Which came first? How can the class `Class` be created unless the class `Object` already exists? But how can there be a class `Object` (or any other class) until there's a class `Class` of which there can be instances?

The best way to deal with this paradox, at least for now, is to ignore it. Ruby has to do some of this chicken-or-egg stuff to get the class and object system up and running—and then the circularity and paradoxes don't matter. In the course of programming, you just need to know that classes are objects, instances of the class called `Class`. (If you want to know in brief how it works, it's like this: every object has an internal record of what class it's an instance of, and the internal record inside the object `Class` points back to `Class` itself.)

Classes are objects, and objects receive messages and execute methods. How exactly does the method-calling process play out in the case of class objects?

3.6.2 *How class objects call methods*

When you send a message to a class object, it looks like this:

```
Ticket.some_message
```

Or, if you're inside a class-definition body and the class is playing the role of the default object `self`, it looks like this:

```
class Ticket
  some_message
```

Such as "attr_accessor"!

That's how the class object gets messages. But where do the methods come from to which the messages correspond?

To understand where classes get their methods, think about where objects in general get their methods (minus modules, which we haven't explored yet):

- From their class
- From the superclass and earlier ancestors of their class
- From their own store of singleton methods (the "talk" in `def obj.talk`)

The situation is basically the same for classes. There are some, but very few, special cases or bells and whistles for class objects. Mostly they behave like other objects.

Let's look at the three scenarios for method calling just listed, in the case of class objects.

Instances of `Class` can call methods that are defined as instance methods in their class. `Ticket`, for example, is an instance of `Class`, and `Class` defines an instance method called new. That's why we can write

```
Ticket.new
```

That takes care of scenario 1. Now, scenario 2.

The superclass of Class is Module. Instances of Class therefore have access to the instance methods defined in Module; among these are the attr_accessor family of methods. That's why we can write

```
class Ticket
  attr_reader :venue, :date
  attr_accessor :price
```

Those method calls go directly to the class object Ticket, which is in the role of the default object self at the point when the calls are made.

That leaves just scenario 3: calling a singleton method of a class object.

3.6.3 *A singleton method by any other name...*

Here's an example. Let's say we've created our Ticket class. At this point, Ticket isn't only a class from which objects (ticket instances) can arise. Ticket (the class) is also an object in its own right. As we've done with other objects, let's add a singleton method to it. Our method will tell us which ticket, from a list of ticket objects, is the most expensive. There's some black-box code here. Don't worry about the details; the basic idea is that the max_by operation will find the ticket whose price is highest:

```
def Ticket.most_expensive(*tickets)
  tickets.max_by(&:price)
end
```

Now we can use the Ticket.most_expensive method to tell which of several tickets is the most expensive. (We'll avoid having two tickets with the same price, because our method doesn't deal gracefully with that situation.)

```
th = Ticket.new("Town Hall","11/12/13")
cc = Ticket.new("Convention Center","12/13/14/")
fg = Ticket.new("Fairgrounds", "13/14/15/")
th.price = 12.55
cc.price = 10.00
fg.price = 18.00
highest = Ticket.most_expensive(th,cc,fg)
puts "The highest-priced ticket is the one for #{highest.venue}."
```

The output is

```
The highest-priced ticket is the one for Fairgrounds.
```

The method most_expensive is defined directly on the class object Ticket, in singleton-method style. A singleton method defined on a class object is commonly referred to as a *class method* of the class on which it's defined. The idea of a class method is that you send a message to the object that's the class rather than to one of the class's instances. The message most_expensive goes to the class Ticket, not to a particular ticket.

The term *class method*: More trouble than it's worth?

Ruby lets objects have singleton methods, and classes are objects. So when you do `def Ticket.most_expensive`, you're basically creating a singleton method for `Ticket`. On the calling side, when you see a method called on a class object—like `Ticket.new`—you can't tell just by looking whether you're dealing with a singleton method defined directly on this class (`def Ticket.new`) or an instance method of the class `Class`.

Just to make it even more fun, the class `Class` has both a class-method version of `new` and an instance-method version; the former is called when you write `Class.new` and the latter when you write `Ticket.new`. Unless, of course, you override it by defining `new` for `Ticket` yourself...

Admittedly, `new` is a particularly thorny case. But in general, the term *class method* isn't necessarily a great fit for Ruby. It's a concept shared with other object-oriented languages, but in those languages there's a greater difference between class methods and instance methods. In Ruby, when you send a message to a class object, you can't tell where and how the corresponding method was defined.

So *class method* has a fuzzy meaning and a sharp meaning. Fuzzily, any method that gets called directly on a `Class` object is a class method. Sharply, a class method is defined, not just called, directly on a `Class` object. You'll hear it used both ways, and as long as you're aware of the underlying engineering and can make the sharp distinctions when you need to, you'll be fine.

Why would you want to do that? Doesn't it mess up the underlying order—that is, the creation of ticket objects and the sending of messages to those objects?

3.6.4   *When, and why, to write a class method*

Class methods serve a purpose. Some operations pertaining to a class can't be performed by individual instances of that class. The `new` method is an excellent example. We call `Ticket.new` because, until we've created an individual ticket, we can't send it any messages! Besides, the job of spawning a new object logically belongs to the class. It doesn't make sense for instances of `Ticket` to spawn each other. But it does make sense for the instance-creation process to be centralized as an activity of the class `Ticket`.

Another similar case is the built-in Ruby method `File.open`—a method that, as you saw in chapter 1, opens a file for reading and/or writing. The `open` operation is a bit like `new`; it initiates file input and/or output and returns a `File` object. It makes sense for `open` to be a class method of `File`: you're requesting the creation of an individual object from the class. The class is acting as a point of departure for the objects it creates.

`Ticket.most_expensive` is a different case, in that it doesn't create a new object—but it's still a method that belongs logically to the class. Finding the most expensive ticket in a list of tickets can be viewed as an operation from above, something that's done collectively with respect to tickets, rather than something that's done by an individual ticket object. Writing `most_expensive` as a class method of `Ticket` lets us keep the method in the ticket family, so to speak, while assigning it to the abstract, supervisory level represented by the class.

It's not unheard of to create a class only for the purpose of giving it class methods. Our earlier temperature-conversion exercises offer an opportunity for using this approach.

CONVERTING THE CONVERTER

Let's convert the converter to a converter class, adding class methods for conversion in both directions:

```
class Temperature
  def Temperature.c2f(celsius)
    celsius * 9.0 / 5 + 32
  end
  def Temperature.f2c(fahrenheit)
    (fahrenheit - 32) * 5 / 9.0
  end
end
```

And let's try it out:

```
puts Temperature.c2f(100)
```
⟵┘ **Outputs 212.0**

The idea is that we have temperature-related utility methods—methods pertaining to temperature as a concept but not to a specific temperature. The `Temperature` class is a good choice of object to own those methods. We could get fancier and have `Temperature` instances that knew whether they were Celsius or Fahrenheit and could convert themselves; but practically speaking, having a `Temperature` class with class methods to perform the conversions is adequate and is an acceptable design. (Even better, because we don't need instances of `Temperature` at all, would be to use a module—a kind of "instanceless" class, which you'll learn about in detail in chapter 4.)

Class methods and instance methods aren't radically different from each other; they're all methods, and their execution is always triggered by sending a message to an object. It's just that the object getting the message may be a class object. Still, there are differences and important points to keep in mind as you start writing methods at various levels.

3.6.5 *Class methods vs. instance methods*

By defining `Ticket.most_expensive`, we've defined a method that we can access through the class object `Ticket` but not through its instances. Individual ticket objects (instances of the class `Ticket`) don't have this method. You can test this easily. Try adding this to the code from section 3.6.3, where the variable `fg` referred to a `Ticket` object (for an event at the fairgrounds):

```
puts "Testing the response of a ticket instance...."
wrong = fg.most_expensive
```

You get an error message, because fg has no method called most_expensive. The class of fg, namely Ticket, has such a method. But fg, which is an instance of Ticket, doesn't. Remember:

- Classes are objects.
- Instances of classes are objects, too.
- A class object (like Ticket) has its own methods, its own state, and its own identity. *It doesn't share these things with instances of itself.* Sending a message to Ticket isn't the same thing as sending a message to fg or cc or any other instance of Ticket.

If you ever get tangled up over what's a class method and what's an instance method, you can usually sort out the confusion by going back to these three principles.

A note on method notation

In writing about and referring to Ruby methods (outside of code, that is), it's customary to refer to instance methods by naming the class (or module, as the case may be) in which they're defined, followed by a hash mark (#) and the name of the method; and to refer to class methods with a similar construct but using a period instead of the hash mark. Sometimes you'll see a double colon (::) instead of a period in the class-method case.

Here are some examples of this notation and what they refer to:

- Ticket#price refers to the instance method price in the class Ticket.
- Ticket.most_expensive refers to the class method most_expensive in the class Ticket.
- Ticket::most_expensive also refers to the class method most_expensive in the class Ticket.

From now on, when you see this notation (in this book or elsewhere), you'll know what it means. (The second example—class-method reference using a dot—looks the same as a call to the method, but you'll know from the context whether it's a method call or a reference to the method in a discussion.)

Discussion of classes always entails the use of a lot of constants—and so will the upcoming discussion of modules in chapter 4. So let's take a deeper look than we have so far at what constants are and how they work.

3.7   *Constants up close*

Many classes consist principally of instance methods and/or class methods. But constants are an important and common third ingredient in many classes. You've already seen constants used as the names of classes. Constants can also be used to set and preserve important data values in classes.

Later, we'll look at the scope of constants and techniques for nesting them inside multilevel classes and modules. For now, we'll focus on the basics of how to use them—and the question of how constant these constants really are.

3.7.1 Basic use of constants

The name of every constant begins with a capital letter. You assign to constants much as you do to variables.

Let's say we decide to establish a list of predefined venues for the Ticket class—a list that every ticket object can refer to and select from. We can assign the list to a constant. Constant definitions usually go at or near the top of a class definition:

```
class Ticket
  VENUES = ["Convention Center", "Fairgrounds", "Town Hall"]
```

A constant defined in a class can be referred to from inside the class's instance or class methods. Let's say you wanted to make sure that every ticket was for a legitimate venue. You could rewrite the initialize method like this:

```
def initialize(venue, date)
  if VENUES.include?(venue)         ◁——  Is this one of the
    @venue = venue                        known venues?
  else
    raise ArgumentError, "Unknown venue #{venue}"   ◁——  Raise an exception
  end                                                     (fatal error—see
  @date = date                                            chapter 6)
end
```

It's also possible to refer to a constant from outside the class definition entirely, using a special constant lookup notation: a double colon (::). Here's an example of setting a constant inside a class and then referring to that constant from outside the class:

```
class Ticket
  VENUES = ["Convention Center", "Fairgrounds", "Town Hall"]   ◁——  Stores venues as
end                                                                  array of strings
puts "We've closed the class definition."
puts "So we have to use the path notation to reach the constant."
puts "The venues are:"
puts Ticket::VENUES
```

The double-colon notation pinpoints the constant VENUES inside the class known by the constant Ticket, and the list of venues is printed out.

Ruby comes with some predefined constants that you can access this way and that you may find useful.

RUBY'S PREDEFINED CONSTANTS
Try typing this into irb:

```
Math::PI
```

Math is a module (the subject of chapter 4), but the principle is the same as in the case of a constant defined inside a class: you use the :: connector to do a lookup on the constant PI defined in the Math module. You can look up E the same way.

Many of the predefined constants you can examine when you start up Ruby (or irb) are the names of the built-in classes: String, Array, Symbol, and so forth. Some are informational; even without loading the `rbconfig` package (which you saw in chapter 1), you can get the interpreter to tell you a fair amount about its settings. Here are some examples:

```
>> RUBY_VERSION
=> "2.1.0"
>> RUBY_PATCHLEVEL
=> 0
>> RUBY_RELEASE_DATE
=> "2013-12-25"
>> RUBY_REVISION
=> 44422
>> RUBY_COPYRIGHT
=> "ruby - Copyright (C) 1993-2013 Yukihiro Matsumoto"
```

As you can see, the information stored in these constants corresponds to the information you get with the -v switch:

```
$ ruby -v
ruby 2.1.0p0 (2013-12-25 revision 44422) [x86_64-darwin12.0]
```

One peculiarity of Ruby constants is that they aren't constant. You can change them, in two senses of the word *change*—and therein lies an instructive lesson.

3.7.2 *Reassigning vs. modifying constants*

It's possible to perform an assignment on a constant to which you've already assigned something—that is, to reassign to the constant. But you get a warning if you do this (even if you're not running with the -w command-line switch). Try this in irb:

```
A = 1
A = 2
```

You'll receive the following message:

```
(irb):2: warning: already initialized constant A
(irb):1: warning: previous definition of A was here
```

The fact that constant names are reusable while the practice of reusing them is a warnable offense represents a compromise. On the one hand, it's useful for the language to have a separate category for constants, as a way of storing data that remains visible over a longer stretch of the program than a regular variable. On the other hand, Ruby is a dynamic language, in the sense that anything can change during runtime. Engineering constants to be an exception to this would theoretically be possible, but would introduce an anomaly into the language.

In addition, because you can reload program files you've already loaded, and program files can include constant assignments, forbidding reassignment of constants would mean that many file-reloading operations would fail with a fatal error.

So you can reassign to a constant, but doing so isn't considered good practice. If you want a reusable identifier, you should use a variable.

The other sense in which it's possible to "change" a constant is by making changes to the object to which the constant refers. For example, adding a venue to the `Ticket` class's venue list is easy:

```
venues = Ticket::VENUES
venues << "High School Gym"
```
Uses << to add new element
to an existing array

There's no warning, because there's no redefinition of a constant. Rather, we're modifying an array—and that array has no particular knowledge that it has been assigned to a constant. It just does what you ask it to.

The difference between reassigning a constant name and modifying the object referenced by the constant is important, and it provides a useful lesson in two kinds of change in Ruby: changing the mapping of identifiers to objects (assignment) and changing the state or contents of an object. With regular variable names, you aren't warned when you do a reassignment; but reassignment is still different from making changes to an object, for any category of identifier.

If you put together the topics in this chapter with some of the examples you've seen previously, you start to get a good overall picture of how Ruby objects are engineered: they derive their functionality from the instance methods defined in their classes and the ancestors of those classes, but they're also capable of "learning" specific, individualized behaviors in the form of singleton methods. This is what makes Ruby so fascinating. The life of a Ruby object is, at least potentially, a mixture of the circumstances of its "birth" and the traits it acquires across its lifetime. We'll wrap up this chapter with some further exploration along these important lines.

3.8 *Nature vs. nurture in Ruby objects*

The relation between classes and their instances is essentially a relation between the general and the specific—a familiar pattern from the world at large. We're used to seeing the animal kingdom in general/specific terms, and likewise everything from musical instruments to university departments to libraries' shelving systems to pantheons of gods.

To the extent that a programming language helps you model the real world (or, conversely, that the real world supplies you with ways to organize your programs), you could do worse than to rely heavily on the general-to-specific relationship. As you can see, inheritance—the superclass-to-subclass relationship—mirrors the general/specific ratio closely. Moreover, if you hang out in object-oriented circles you'll pick up some shorthand for this relationship: the phrase *is a*. If, say, `Ezine` inherits from `Magazine`, we say that "an ezine is a magazine." Similarly, a `Magazine` object is a `Publication`, if `Magazine` inherits from `Publication`.

Ruby lets you model this way. You can get a lot of mileage out of thinking through your domain as a cascaded, inheritance-based chart of objects. Ruby even provides an `is_a?` method that tells you whether an object has a given class either as its class or as one of its class's ancestral classes:

```
>> mag = Magazine.new
=> #<Magazine:0x36289c>
>> mag.is_a?(Magazine)
=> true
>> mag.is_a?(Publication)
=> true
```

Organizing classes into family trees of related entities, with each generation a little more specific than the last, can confer a pleasing sense of order and determinism on your program's landscape.

But Ruby objects (unlike objects in some other object-oriented languages) can be individually modified. An instance of a given class isn't stuck with only the behaviors and traits that its class has conferred upon it. You can always add methods on a per-object basis, as you've seen in numerous examples. Furthermore, classes can change. It's possible for an object to gain capabilities—methods—during its lifetime, if its class or an ancestral class acquires new instance methods.

In languages where you can't add methods to individual objects or to classes that have already been written, an object's class (and the superclass of that class, and so forth) tells you everything you need to know about the object. If the object is an instance of `Magazine`, and you're familiar with the methods provided by the class `Magazine` for the use of its instances, you know exactly how the object behaves.

But in Ruby the behavior or capabilities of an object can deviate from those supplied by its class. We can make a magazine sprout wings:

```
mag = Magazine.new
def mag.wings
  puts "Look! I can fly!"
end
mag.wings
```

Output: Look! I can fly!

This demonstrates that the capabilities the object was born with aren't necessarily the whole story.

Thus the inheritance tree—the upward cascade of class to superclass and super-superclass—isn't the only determinant of an object's behavior. If you want to know what a brand-new magazine object does, look at the methods in the `Magazine` class and its ancestors. If you want to know what a magazine object can do later, you have to know what's happened to the object since its creation. (And `respond_to?`—the method that lets you determine in advance whether an object knows how to handle a particular method—can come in handy.)

Ruby objects are tremendously flexible and dynamic. That flexibility translates into programmer power: you can make magazines fly, make cows tell you who published them, and all the rest of it. As these silly examples make clear, the power implies responsibility. When you make changes to an individual object—when you add methods to that object, and that object alone—you must have a good reason.

Most Ruby programmers are conservative in this area. You'll see less adding of methods to individual objects than you might expect. The most common use case for adding methods directly to objects is the adding of class methods to class objects. The vast majority of singleton-style method definitions you'll see (def some_object.some _method) will be class-method definitions. Adding methods to other objects (magazines, tickets, cows, and so on) is also possible—but you have to do it carefully and selectively, and with the design of the program in mind.

In most cases, object individuation (the subject of the entirety of chapter 13, by the way) has to do with dynamically determined conditions at runtime; for example, you might add accessor methods to objects to match the names of database columns that you don't know until the program is running and you've queried the database. Or you might have a library of special methods that you've written for string objects, and that you want only certain strings to have access to. Ruby frees you to do these things, because an object's class is only part of the story—its nature, you might say, as opposed to its nurture.

And there's another piece to the puzzle: modules, a Ruby construct you've seen mentioned here several times in passing, which you'll meet up close and in depth in the next chapter.

3.9 *Summary*

In this chapter, you've learned the basics of Ruby classes:

- How writing a class and then creating instances of that class allow you to share behaviors among numerous objects.
- How to use setter and getter methods, either written out or automatically created with the attr_* family of methods, to create object attributes, which store an object's state in instance variables.
- As objects, classes can have methods added to them on a per-object basis—such methods being commonly known as class methods, and providing general utility functionality connected with the class.
- Ruby constants are a special kind of identifier usually residing inside class (or module) definitions.
- Inheritance is a class-to-class relationship between a superclass and one or more subclasses, and all Ruby objects have a common ancestry in the Object and BasicObject classes.
- The superclass/subclass structure can lend itself to modeling entities in a strictly hierarchical, taxonomical way, but the dynamic qualities of Ruby objects (including class objects!) can offer less strictly determined ways of thinking about objects and how their behaviors might unfold over the course of their lives.

This look at classes gives you a firm foundation for understanding how objects come into being and relate to each other in Ruby. Next, we'll build on that foundation by looking at modules, the other important building block of the object system.

Modules and
program organization
4

This chapter covers

- Encapsulation of behavior in modules
- Modular extension of classes
- The object method-lookup path
- Handling method-lookup failure
- Establishing namespaces with modules
  and nesting

This chapter will introduce you to a Ruby construct that's closely related to classes: modules. As their name suggests, modules encourage modular design: program design that breaks large components into smaller ones and lets you mix and match object behaviors.

Like classes, modules are bundles of methods and constants. Unlike classes, modules don't have instances; instead, you specify that you want to add the functionality of a particular module to that of a class or of a specific object.

It's no accident that modules are similar in many respects to classes: the Class class is a subclass of the Module class, so every class object is also a module object. We discussed classes first because Ruby is object-centric and objects are instances of classes. But you could say that modules are the more basic structure, and classes are just a specialization. The bottom line is that they're both part of Ruby, and both are available to you as you design your programs and model your data.

Looking at modules takes us further along some paths we partially walked in the previous chapter:

- You saw that all objects descend from Object; here, you'll meet the Kernel module that contains the majority of the methods common to all objects.
- You learned that objects seek their methods in both class and superclass, all the way up the inheritance tree; in this chapter, we'll look in considerable detail at how this method-lookup process works when both classes and modules are involved.

4.1   *Basics of module creation and use*

Writing a module is similar to writing a class, except you start your definition with the module keyword instead of the class keyword:

```
module MyFirstModule
  def say_hello
    puts "Hello"
  end
end
```

When you write a class, you then create instances of the class. Those instances can execute the class's instance methods. In contrast, modules don't have instances. Instead, modules get *mixed in* to classes, using either the include method or the prepend method.

> **NOTE** prepend is new in Ruby 2.0, whereas include has been part of Ruby since the beginning.

A module "mixed in" in this manner is sometimes referred to as a "mix-in." The result of mixing in a module is that instances of the class have access to the instance methods defined in the module.

For example, using the little module from the previous example, you can go on to do this:

```
class ModuleTester
  include MyFirstModule
end
mt = ModuleTester.new
mt.say_hello
```

The ModuleTester object calls the appropriate method (say_hello) and outputs Hello. Notice that say_hello isn't defined in the class of which the object is an instance. Instead, it's defined in a module that the class mixes in.

The mix-in operation in this example is achieved with the call to include. Mixing in a module bears a strong resemblance to inheriting from a superclass. If, say, class B inherits from class A, instances of class B can call instance methods of class A. And if, say, class C mixes in module M, instances of class C can call instance methods of module M.

In both cases, the instances of the class at the bottom of the list reap the benefits: they get to call not only their own class's instances methods, but also those of (in one case) a superclass or (in the other case) a mixed-in module.

The main difference between inheriting from a class and mixing in a module is that you can mix in more than one module. No class can inherit from more than one class. In cases where you want numerous extra behaviors for a class's instances—and you don't want to stash them all in the class's superclass and its ancestral classes—you can use modules to organize your code in a more granular way. Each module can add something different to the methods available through the class. (We'll explore the mix-in versus inheritance choice further in section 4.4.1.)

Modules open up lots of possibilities—particularly for sharing code among more than one class, because any number of classes can mix in the same module. We'll look next at some further examples, and you'll get a sense of the possibilities.

4.1.1   *A module encapsulating "stacklikeness"*

Modules give you a way to collect and encapsulate behaviors. A typical module contains methods connected to a particular subset of what will be, eventually, the full capabilities of an object.

By way of fleshing out this statement, we'll write a module that encapsulates the characteristic of being like a stack, or *stacklikeness*. We'll then use that module to impart stacklike behaviors to objects, via the process of mixing the stacklike module into one or more classes.

As you may know from previous studies, a *stack* is a data structure that operates on the last in, first out (LIFO) principle. The classic example is a (physical) stack of plates. The first plate to be used is the last one placed on the stack. Stacks are usually discussed paired with queues, which exhibit first in, first out (FIFO) behavior. Think of a cafeteria: the plates are in a stack; the customers are in a queue.

Numerous items behave in a stacklike, LIFO manner. The last sheet of printer paper you put in the tray is the first one printed on. Double-parked cars have to leave in an order that's the opposite of the order of their arrival. The quality of being stacklike can manifest itself in a wide variety of collections and aggregations of entities.

That's where modules come in. When you're designing a program and you identify a behavior or set of behaviors that may be exhibited by more than one kind of entity or object, you've found a good candidate for a module. Stacklikeness fits the bill: more than one entity, and therefore imaginably more than one class, exhibit stacklike behavior. By creating a module that defines methods that all stacklike objects have in common, you give yourself a way to summon stacklikeness into any and all classes that need it.

The following listing shows a simple implementation of stacklikeness in Ruby module form. Save this listing to a file called stacklike.rb; you'll load this file in later examples.

Listing 4.1 `Stacklike` **module, encapsulating stacklike structure and behavior**

```
module Stacklike
  def stack
    @stack ||= []                    ❶
  end
  def add_to_stack(obj)             ❷
    stack.push(obj)
  end                               ❸
  def take_from_stack
    stack.pop
  end
end
```

The `Stacklike` module in this listing uses an *array* (an ordered collection of objects) to represent the stack. The array is preserved in the instance variable `@stack` and made accessible through the method `stack` ❶. That method uses a common technique for conditionally setting a variable: the `||=` (or-equals) operator. The effect of this operator is to set the variable to the specified value—which in this case is a new, empty array—if and only if the variable isn't already set to something other than `nil` or `false`. In practical terms, this means that the first time `stack` is called, it will set `@stack` to an empty array, whereas on subsequent calls it will see that `@stack` already has a value and will simply return that value (the array).

Ruby's shortcut operators

In addition to or-equals, Ruby has another family of shortcut operators, similar in appearance to `||=` but engineered a little differently. These operators expand to calls to an underlying method. A common one is the `+=` operator; the expression `a += 1` is equivalent to `a = a + 1`. Other members of this shortcut family include `-=, *=, /=, **=` (raise to a power), `&=` (bitwise AND), `|=` (bitwise OR), `^=` (bitwise EXCLUSIVE OR), `%=` (modulo), and a (rarely used) and-equals operator (`&&=`) that works similarly to or-equals. Thus `a -= 1` means `a = a - 1`, `a *= 10` means `a = a * 10`, and so forth.

Each of these method-wrapping operators works with any object that has the relevant underlying method, including instances of your own classes. If you define a `+` method, for example, you can use the `x += y` syntax on an instance of your class (`x`), and the expression will be automatically expanded to `x = x + y`. And that, in turn, is just syntactic sugar for `x = x.+(y)`, a call to the `+` method.

You'll meet these shortcut techniques "officially" in chapter 7. Meanwhile, by all means try them out in irb.

When an object is added to the stack ❷, the operation is handled by pushing the object onto the `@stack` array—that is, adding it to the end. (`@stack` is accessed through a call to the `stack` method, which ensures that it will be initialized to an empty array the first time an object is added.) Removing an object from the stack ❸ involves popping an element from the array—that is, removing it from the end. (`push` and `pop` are instance methods of the `Array` class. You'll see them again when we look at container objects, including arrays, in chapter 10.)

The module `Stacklike` thus implements stacklikeness by selectively deploying behaviors that already exist for `Array` objects: add an element to the end of the array, take an element off the end. Arrays are more versatile than stacks; a stack can't do everything an array can. For example, you can remove elements from an array in any order, whereas by definition the only element you can remove from a stack is the one that was added most recently. But an array can do everything a stack can. As long as we don't ask it to do anything unstacklike, using an array as a kind of agent or proxy for the specifically stacklike add/remove actions makes sense.

We now have a module that implements stacklike behavior: maintaining a list of items, such that new ones can be added to the end and the most recently added one can be removed. The next question is this: What can we do with this module?

4.1.2 *Mixing a module into a class*

As you've seen, modules don't have instances, so you can't do this:

```
s = Stacklike.new          ⟵── Wrong! No such method.
```

To create instances (objects), you need a class, and to make those objects stacklike, you'll need to mix the `Stacklike` module into that class. But what class? The most obviously stacklike thing is probably a `Stack`. Save the code in the following listing to stack.rb, in the same directory as stacklike.rb.

> **Listing 4.2   Mixing the `Stacklike` module into the `Stack` class**

```
require_relative "stacklike"
class Stack
  include Stacklike          ⟵──❶
end
```

The business end of the `Stack` class in this listing is the `include` statement ❶, which has the effect of mixing in the `Stacklike` module. It ensures that instances of `Stack` exhibit the behaviors defined in `Stacklike`.

Syntax of `require`/`load` vs. syntax of `include`

You may have noticed that when you use `require` or `load`, you put the name of the item you're requiring or loading in quotation marks; but with `include` (and `prepend`), you don't. That's because `require` and `load` take strings as their arguments, whereas `include` takes the name of a module in the form of a constant. More fundamentally, it's because `require` and `load` are locating and loading disk files, whereas `include` and `prepend` perform a program-space, in-memory operation that has nothing to do with files. It's a common sequence to `require` a feature and then `include` a module that the feature defines. The two operations thus often go together, but they're completely different from each other.

Notice that our class's name is a noun, whereas the module's name is an adjective. Neither of these practices is mandatory, but they're both common. What we end up with, expressed in everyday language, is a kind of predicate on the class: *Stack objects are stacklike*. That's English for

```
class Stack
  include Stacklike
end
```

To see the whole thing in action, let's create a `Stack` object and put it through its paces. The code in the next listing creates a `Stack` object and performs some operations on it; you can enter this code at the end of your stack.rb file.

Listing 4.3 Creating and using an instance of class `Stack`

```
s = Stack.new                               ◁── ❶
s.add_to_stack("item one")
s.add_to_stack("item two")                  ❷
s.add_to_stack("item three")
puts "Objects currently on the stack:"
puts s.stack                                ◁── Calling puts on an array
taken = s.take_from_stack       ◁──             calls puts on each array
puts "Removed this object:"                     element in turn
puts taken                          ❸
puts "Now on stack:"
puts s.stack
```

This listing starts with the innocent-looking (but powerful) instantiation ❶ of a new `Stack` object, which is assigned to the variable s. That `Stack` object is born with the knowledge of what to do when we ask it to perform stack-related actions, thanks to the fact that its class mixed in the `Stacklike` module. The rest of the code involves asking it to jump through some stacklike hoops: adding items (strings) to itself ❷ and popping the last one off itself ❸. Along the way, we ask the object to report on its state.

Now, let's run the program. Here's an invocation of stack.rb, together with the output from the run:

```
$ ruby stack.rb
Objects currently on the stack:
item one
item two
item three
Removed this object:
item three
Now on stack:
item one
item two
```

Sure enough, our little `Stack` object knows what to do. It is, as advertised, stacklike.

The `Stack` class is fine as far as it goes. But it may leave you wondering: why did we bother writing a module? It would be possible, after all, to pack all the functionality of the `Stacklike` module directly in the `Stack` class without writing a module. The following listing shows what the class would look like.

Listing 4.4   Nonmodular rewrite of the `Stack` **class**

```ruby
class Stack
  attr_reader :stack
  def initialize
    @stack = []
  end
  def add_to_stack(obj)
    @stack.push(obj)
  end
  def take_from_stack
    @stack.pop
  end
end
```

Constructor method:
@stack cannot yet have
been initialized, so it's set
using = rather than ||=

As you'll see if you add the code in listing 4.3 to listing 4.4 and run it all through Ruby, it produces the same results as the implementation that uses a module.

Before you conclude that modules are pointless, remember what the modularization buys you: it lets you apply a general concept like stacklikeness to several cases, not just one.

So what else is stacklike?

4.1.3   *Using the module further*

A few examples came up earlier: plates, printer paper, and so forth. Let's use a new one, borrowed from the world of urban legend.

Lots of people believe that if you're the first passenger to check in for a flight, your luggage will be the last off the plane. Real-world experience suggests that it doesn't work this way. Still, for stack practice, let's see what a Ruby model of an urban-legendly-correct cargo hold would look like.

To model it reasonably closely, we'll define the following:

- A barebones `Suitcase` class: a placeholder (or stub) that lets us create suitcase objects to fling into the cargo hold.
- A `CargoHold` class with two methods: `load_and_report` and `unload`.
  - `load_and_report` prints a message reporting that it's adding a suitcase to the cargo hold, and it gives us the suitcase object's ID number, which will help us trace what happens to each suitcase.
  - `unload` calls `take_from_stack`. We could call `take_from_stack` directly, but *unload* sounds more like a term you might use to describe removing a suitcase from a cargo hold.

Put the code in the next listing into cargohold.rb, and run it.

Listing 4.5   Using the `Stacklike` **module a second time, for a different class**

```ruby
require_relative "stacklike"
class Suitcase
end
```

```
class CargoHold
  include Stacklike                    ←—❶
  def load_and_report(obj)             ←┐
    print "Loading object "            ❷
    puts obj.object_id

    add_to_stack(obj)                  ←—❸
  end
  def unload
    take_from_stack                    ←—❹
  end
end
ch = CargoHold.new                     ←—❺
sc1 = Suitcase.new
sc2 = Suitcase.new
sc3 = Suitcase.new
ch.load_and_report(sc1)
ch.load_and_report(sc2)
ch.load_and_report(sc3)
first_unloaded = ch.unload
print "The first suitcase off the plane is...."
puts first_unloaded.object_id
```

At its heart, the program in this listing isn't that different from those in listings 4.2 and 4.3 (which you saved incrementally to stack.rb). It follows much the same procedure: mixing `Stacklike` into a class ❶, creating an instance of that class ❺, and adding items to ❸ and removing them from ❹ that instance (the stacklike thing—the cargo hold, in this case). It also does some reporting of the current state of the stack ❷, as the other program did.

The output from the cargo-hold program looks like this (remember that suitcases are referred to by their object ID numbers, which may be different on your system):

```
Loading object 1001880
Loading object 1001860
Loading object 1001850
The first suitcase off the plane is....1001850
```

The cargo-hold example shows how you can use an existing module for a new class. Sometimes it pays to wrap the methods in new methods with better names for the new domain (like `unload` instead of `take_from_stack`), although if you find yourself changing too much, it may be a sign that the module isn't a good fit.

In the next section, we'll put together several of the pieces we've looked at more or less separately: method calls (message sending), objects and their status as instances of classes, and the mixing of modules into classes. All these concepts come together in the process by which an object, upon being sent a message, looks for and finds (or fails to find) a method to execute whose name matches the message.

4.2 Modules, classes, and method lookup

You already know that when an object receives a message, the intended (and usual) result is the execution of a method with the same name as the message in the object's class or that class's superclass—and onward, up to the `Object` or even `BasicObject` class—or in a module that has been mixed into any of those classes. But how does this come about? And what happens in ambiguous cases—for example, if a class and a mixed-in module both define a method with a given name? Which one does the object choose to execute?

It pays to answer these questions precisely. Imprecise accounts of what happens are easy to come by. Sometimes they're even adequate: if you say, "This object has a `push` method," you may succeed in communicating what you're trying to communicate, even though objects don't "have" methods but, rather, find them by searching classes and modules.

But an imprecise account won't scale. It won't help you understand what's going on in more complex cases, and it won't support you when you're designing your own code. Your best course of action is to learn what really happens when you send messages to objects.

Fortunately, the way it works turns out to be straightforward.

4.2.1 *Illustrating the basics of method lookup*

In the interest of working toward a clear understanding of how objects find methods, let's backpedal on the real-world references and, instead, write some classes and modules with simple names like C and M. Doing so will help you concentrate on the logic and mechanics of method lookup without having to think simultaneously about modeling a real-world domain. We'll also write some methods that don't do anything except print a message announcing that they've been called. This will help track the order of method lookup.

Look at the program in the following listing.

> **Listing 4.6 Demonstration of module inclusion and inheritance**

```
module M
  def report
    puts "'report' method in module M"
  end
end
class C
  include M
end
class D < C
end
obj = D.new
obj.report
```

The instance method `report` is defined in module M. Module M is mixed into class C. Class D is a subclass of C, and `obj` is an instance of D. Through this cascade, the object (`obj`) gets access to the `report` method.

Still, *gets access to* a method, like *has* a method, is a vague way to put it. Let's try to get more of a fix on the process by considering an object's-eye view of it.

AN OBJECT'S-EYE VIEW OF METHOD LOOKUP

You're the object, and someone sends you a message. You have to figure out how to respond to it—or whether you even *can* respond to it. Here's a bit of object stream-of-consciousness:

> I'm a Ruby object, and I've been sent the message `'report'`. I have to try to find a method called `report` in my method lookup path. `report`, if it exists, resides in a class or module.

> I'm an instance of a class called D. Does class D define an instance method `report`?
> *No.*
> Does D mix in any modules?
> *No.*
> Does D's superclass, C, define a `report` instance method?
> *No.*
> Does C mix in any modules?
> *Yes*, M.
> Does M define a `report` method?
> *Yes.*
> Good! I'll execute that method.

The search ends when the method being searched for is found, or with an error condition if it isn't found. The error condition is triggered by a special method called `method_missing`, which gets called as a last resort for otherwise unmatched messages. You can override `method_missing` (that is, define it anew in one of your own classes or modules) to define custom behavior for such messages, as you'll see in detail in section 4.3.

Let's move now from object stream-of-consciousness to specifics about the method-lookup scenario, and in particular the question of how far it can go.

HOW FAR DOES THE METHOD SEARCH GO?

Ultimately, every object in Ruby is an instance of some class descended from the big class in the sky: `BasicObject`. However many classes and modules it may cross along the way, the search for a method can always go as far up as `BasicObject`. But recall that the whole point of `BasicObject` is that it has few instance methods. Getting to know `BasicObject` doesn't tell you much about the bulk of the methods that all Ruby objects share.

If you want to understand the common behavior and functionality of all Ruby objects, you have to descend from the clouds and look at `Object` rather than `BasicObject`. More precisely, you have to look at `Kernel`, a module that `Object` mixes in. It's in `Kernel` (as its name suggests) that most of Ruby's fundamental methods objects are defined. And because `Object` mixes in `Kernel`, all instances of `Object` and all descendants of `Object` have access to the instance methods in `Kernel`.

Suppose you're an object, and you're trying to find a method to execute based on a message you've received. If you've looked in `Kernel` and `BasicObject` and you

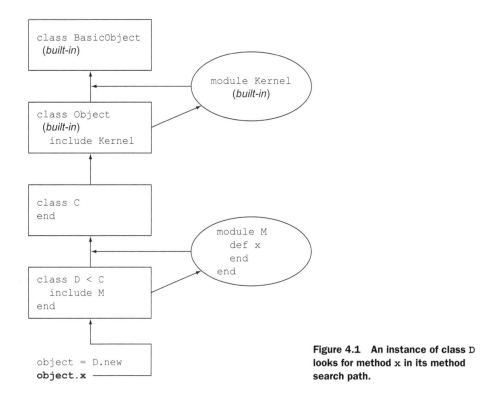

Figure 4.1 An instance of class D **looks for method** x **in its method search path.**

haven't found it, you're not going to. (It's possible to mix modules into BasicObject, thus providing all objects with a further potential source of methods. It's hard to think of a case where you'd do this, though.)

Figure 4.1 illustrates the method search path from our earlier example (the class D object) all the way up the ladder. In the example, the search for the method succeeds at module M; the figure shows how far the object would look if it didn't find the method there. When the message x is sent to the object, the method search begins, hitting the various classes and mix-ins (modules) as shown by the arrows.

The internal definitions of BasicObject, Object, and Kernel are written in the C language. But you can get a reasonable handle on how they interact by looking at a Ruby mockup of their relations:

```
class BasicObject
  # a scant seven method definitions go here
end
module Kernel
  # over 100 method definitions go here!
end
class Object < BasicObject
  # one or two private methods go here,
  # but the main point is to mix in the Kernel module
  include Kernel
end
```

`Object` is a subclass of `BasicObject`. Every class that doesn't have an explicit super-class is a subclass of `Object`. You can see evidence of this default in irb:

```
>> class C
>> end
=> nil
>> C.superclass
=> Object
```

Every class has `Object`—and therefore `Kernel` and `BasicObject`—among its ancestors. Of course, there's still the paradox that `BasicObject` is an `Object`, and `Object` is a `Class`, and `Class` is an `Object`. But as you saw earlier, a bit of circularity in the class model serves to jump-start the hierarchy; and once set in motion, it operates logically and cleanly.

4.2.2 *Defining the same method more than once*

You learned in chapter 3 that if you define a method twice inside the same class, the second definition takes precedence over the first. The same is true of modules. The rule comes down to this: there can be only one method of a given name per class or module at any given time. If you have a method called `calculate_interest` in your `BankAccount` class and you write a second method called `calculate_interest` in the same class, the class forgets all about the first version of the method.

That's how classes and modules keep house. But when we flip to an object's-eye view, the question of having access to two or more methods with the same name becomes more involved.

An object's methods can come from any number of classes and modules. True, any one class or module can have only one `calculate_interest` method (to use that name as an example). But an object can have multiple `calculate_interest` methods in its method-lookup path, because the method-lookup path passes through multiple classes or modules.

Still, the rule for objects is analogous to the rule for classes and modules: an object can see only one version of a method with a given name at any given time. If the object's method-lookup path includes two or more same-named methods, the first one encountered is the "winner" and is executed.

The next listing shows a case where two versions of a method lie on an object's method-lookup path: one in the object's class, and one in a module mixed in by that class.

Listing 4.7 Two same-named methods on a single search path

```
module InterestBearing
  def calculate_interest
    puts "Placeholder! We're in module InterestBearing."
  end
end
class BankAccount
  include InterestBearing
```

```
  def calculate_interest
    puts "Placeholder! We're in class BankAccount."
    puts "And we're overriding the calculate_interest method..."
    puts "which was defined in the InterestBearing module."
  end
end
account = BankAccount.new
account.calculate_interest
```

When you run this listing, you get the following output:

```
Placeholder! We're in class BankAccount.
And we're overriding the calculate_interest method...
which was defined in the InterestBearing module.
```

Two `calculate_interest` methods lie on the method-lookup path of object c. But the lookup hits the class `BankAccount` (account's class) before it hits the module `Interest-Bearing` (a mix-in of class `BankAccount`). Therefore, the report method it executes is the one defined in `BankAccount`.

An object may have two methods with the same name on its method-lookup path in another circumstance: when a class mixes in two or more modules, more than one implements the method being searched for. In such a case, the modules are searched in reverse order of inclusion—that is, the most recently mixed-in module is searched first. If the most recently mixed-in module happens to contain a method with the same name as a method in a module that was mixed in earlier, the version of the method in the newly mixed-in module takes precedence because the newer module is closer on the object's method-lookup path.

For example, consider a case where two modules, M and N (we'll keep this example relatively schematic), both define a `report` method and are both mixed into a class, C, as in the following listing.

> **Listing 4.8   Mixing in two modules with a same-named method defined**

```
module M
  def report
    puts "'report' method in module M"
  end
end
module N
  def report
    puts "'report' method in module N"
  end
end
class C
  include M
  include N
end
```

What does an instance of this class do when you send it the "report" message and it walks the lookup path, looking for a matching method? Let's ask it:

```
c = C.new
c.report
```

The answer is `"'report' method in module N"`. The first `report` method encountered in c's method lookup path is the one in *the most recently mixed-in module.* In this case, that means N—so N's `report` method wins over M's method of the same name.

To this should be added the observation that including a module more than once has no effect.

INCLUDING A MODULE MORE THAN ONCE

Look at this example, which is based on the previous example—but this time we include M a second time, after N:

```
class C
  include M
  include N
  include M
end
```

You might expect that when you run the `report` method, you'll get M's version, because M was the most recently included module. But re-including a module doesn't do anything. Because M already lies on the search path, the second `include M` instruction has no effect. N is still considered the most recently included module:

```
c = C.new
c.report
```
    ◁──┘   **Output: 'report' method in module N**

In short, you can manipulate the method-lookup paths of your objects, but only up to a point.

In all the examples so far, we've been using `include` to mix in modules. It's time to bring `prepend` back into the discussion.

4.2.3   *How prepend works*

Every time you `include` a module in a class, you're affecting what happens when instances of that class have to resolve messages into method names. The same is true of `prepend`. The difference is that if you `prepend` a module to a class, the object looks in that module first, before it looks in the class.

Here's an example:

```
module MeFirst
  def report
    puts "Hello from module!"
  end
end

class Person
  prepend MeFirst
  def report
    puts "Hello from class!"
  end
end

p = Person.new
p.report
```

The output is "Hello from module!" Why? Because we have prepended the MeFirst module to the class. That means that the instance of the class will look in the module first when it's trying to find a method called report. If we'd used include, the class would be searched before the module and the class's version of report would "win."

You can see the difference between include and prepend reflected both in figure 4.2 and in the list of a class's ancestors—which means all the classes and modules where an instance of the class will search for methods, listed in order. Here are the ancestors of the Person class from the last example, in irb:

```
> Person.ancestors
=> [MeFirst, Person, Object, Readline, Kernel, BasicObject]
```

Now modify the example to use include instead of prepend. Two things happen. First, the output changes:

```
Hello from class!
```

Second, the order of the ancestors changes:

```
> Person.ancestors
=> [Person, MeFirst, Object, Readline, Kernel, BasicObject]
```

(Of course, the name MeFirst ceases to make sense, but you get the general idea.)

You can use prepend when you want a module's version of one or more methods to take precedence over the versions defined in a given class. As mentioned earlier, prepend is new in Ruby 2.0. You won't see it used much, at least not yet. But it's useful to know it's there, both so that you can use it if you need it and so that you'll know what it means if you encounter it in someone else's code.

4.2.4   *The rules of method lookup summarized*

The basic rules governing method lookup and the ordering of the method search path in Ruby 2 are illustrated in figure 4.2.

To resolve a message into a method, an object looks for the method in

1 Modules prepended to its class, in reverse order of prepending
2 Its class
3 Modules included in its class, in reverse order of inclusion
4 Modules prepended to its superclass
5 Its class's superclass
6 Modules included in its superclass
7 Likewise, up to Object (and its mix-in Kernel) and BasicObject

Note in particular the point that modules are searched for methods in reverse order of prepending or inclusion. That ensures predictable behavior in the event that a class mixes in two modules that define the same method.

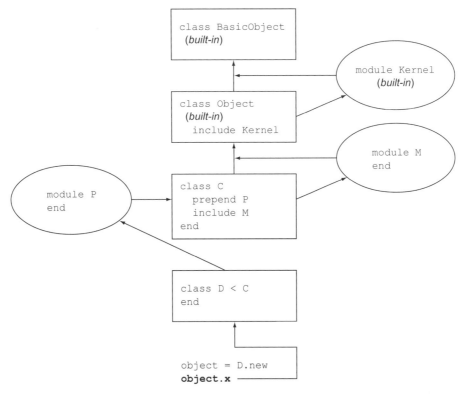

Figure 4.2 An instance of class D looks for method x in its method search path across both included and prepended modules.

What about singleton methods?

You're familiar from chapter 3 with the *singleton method*—a method defined directly on an object (def obj.talk)—and you may wonder where in the method-lookup path singleton methods lie. The answer is that they lie in a special class, created for the sole purpose of containing them: the object's singleton class. We'll look at singleton classes in detail later in the book, at which point we'll slot them into the method-lookup model.

A somewhat specialized but useful and common technique is available for navigating the lookup path explicitly: the keyword super.

4.2.5 *Going up the method search path with super*

Inside the body of a method definition, you can use the super keyword to jump up to the next-highest definition in the method-lookup path of the method you're currently executing.

The following listing shows a basic example (after which we'll get to the "Why would you do that?" aspect).

Listing 4.9 Using the `super` keyword to reach up one level in the lookup path

```
module M
  def report                                  ◁—①
    puts "'report' method in module M"
  end
end
class C
  include M
                                        ②
  def report                                  ◁—┐
    puts "'report' method in class C"
    puts "About to trigger the next higher-up report method..."
    super                                          ◁—┐
    puts "Back from the 'super' call."                │
  end                                              ③
end
c = C.new                        ④
c.report                         ◁—┘
```

The output from running listing 4.9 is as follows:

```
'report' method in class C
About to trigger the next higher-up report method...
'report' method in module M
Back from the 'super' call.
```

An instance of `C` (namely, `c`) receives the `'report'` message ④. The method-lookup process starts with `c`'s class (`C`)—and, sure enough, there's a `report` method ②. That method is executed.

Inside the method is a call to `super` ③. That means even though the object found a method corresponding to the message (`'report'`), it must keep looking and find the next match. The next match for `report`, in this case, is the `report` method defined in module `M` ①.

Note that `M#report` would have been the first match in a search for a `report` method if `C#report` didn't exist. The `super` keyword gives you a way to call what would have been the applicable version of a method in cases where that method has been overridden later in the lookup path. Why would you want to do this?

Sometimes, particularly when you're writing a subclass, a method in an existing class does almost but not quite what you want. With `super`, you can have the best of both worlds by hooking into or wrapping the original method, as the next listing illustrates.

Listing 4.10 Using `super` to wrap a method in a subclass

```
class Bicycle
  attr_reader :gears, :wheels, :seats
  def initialize(gears = 1)                  ◁—①
    @wheels = 2
    @seats = 1
    @gears = gears
  end
end
```

```
class Tandem < Bicycle
  def initialize(gears)
    super
    @seats = 2            ◁──❷
  end
end
```

super provides a clean way to make a tandem almost like a bicycle. We change only what needs to be changed (the number of seats ❷), and super triggers the earlier initialize method ❶, which sets bicycle-like default values for the other properties of the tandem.

When we call super, we don't explicitly forward the gears argument that's passed to initialize. Yet when the original initialize method in Bicycle is called, any arguments provided to the Tandem version are visible. This is a special behavior of super. The way super handles arguments is as follows:

- Called with no argument list (empty or otherwise), super automatically forwards the arguments that were passed to the method from which it's called.
- Called with an empty argument list—super()—super sends no arguments to the higher-up method, even if arguments were passed to the current method.
- Called with specific arguments—super(a,b,c)—super sends exactly those arguments.

This unusual treatment of arguments exists because the most common case is the first one, where you want to bump up to the next-higher method with the same arguments as those received by the method from which super is being called. That case is given the simplest syntax—you just type super. (And because super is a keyword rather than a method, it can be engineered to provide this special behavior.)

Now that you've seen how method lookup works, let's consider what happens when method lookup fails.

4.3 The method_missing method

The Kernel module provides an instance method called method_missing. This method is executed whenever an object receives a message that it doesn't know how to respond to—that is, a message that doesn't match a method anywhere in the object's method-lookup path:

```
>> o = Object.new
=> #<Object:0x0000010141bbb0>
>> o.blah
NoMethodError: undefined method `blah' for #<Object:0x0000010141bbb0>
```

It's easy to intercept calls to missing methods. You override method_missing, either on a singleton basis for the object you're calling the method on, or in the object's class or one of that class's ancestors:

```
>> def o.method_missing(m, *args)            ◁──❶
>>   puts "You can't call #{m} on this object; please try again."
>> end
```

```
=> nil
>> o.blah
You can't call blah on this object; please try again.
```

When you override `method_missing`, you need to imitate the method signature of the original ❶. The first argument is the name of the missing method—the message that you sent the object and that it didn't understand. The `*args` parameter sponges up any remaining arguments. (You can also add a special argument to bind to a code block, but let's not worry about that until we've looked at code blocks in more detail.) The first argument comes to you in the form of a symbol object. If you want to examine or parse it, you need to convert it to a string.

Even if you override `method_missing`, the previous definition is still available to you via `super`.

4.3.1 Combining method_missing and super

It's common to want to intercept an unrecognized message and decide, on the spot, whether to handle it or pass it along to the original `method_missing` (or possibly an intermediate version, if another one is defined). You can do this easily by using `super`. Here's an example of the typical pattern:

```
class Student
  def method_missing(m, *args)                    Convert symbol to string,
    if m.to_s.start_with?("grade_for_")    ◄──    with to_s, before testing
      # return the appropriate grade, based on parsing the method name
    else
      super
    end
  end
end
```

Given this code, a call to, say, `grade_for_english` on an instance of `student` leads to the true branch of the `if` test. If the missing method name doesn't start with `grade_for`, the `false` branch is taken, resulting in a call to `super`. That call will take you to whatever the next `method_missing` implementation is along the object's method-lookup path. If you haven't overridden `method_missing` anywhere else along the line, super will find `Kernel`'s `method_missing` and execute that.

Let's look at a more extensive example of these techniques. We'll write a `Person` class. Let's start at the top with some code that exemplifies how we want the class to be used. We'll then implement the class in such a way that the code works.

The following listing shows some usage code for the `Person` class.

Listing 4.11   Sample usage of the `Person` class

```
j = Person.new("John")
p = Person.new("Paul")
g = Person.new("George")
r = Person.new("Ringo")
j.has_friend(p)
j.has_friend(g)
```

```
g.has_friend(p)
r.has_hobby("rings")
Person.all_with_friends(p).each do |person|
  puts "#{person.name} is friends with #{p.name}"
end
Person.all_with_hobbies("rings").each do |person|
  puts "#{person.name} is into rings"
end
```

We'd like the output of this code to be

```
John is friends with Paul
George is friends with Paul
Ringo is into rings
```

The overall idea is that a person can have friends and/or hobbies. Furthermore, the Person class lets us look up all people who have a given friend, or all people who have a given hobby. The searches are accomplished with the all_with_friends and all_with_hobbies class methods.

The all_with_* method-name formula looks like a good candidate for handling via method_missing. Although we're using only two variants of it (friends and hobbies), it's the kind of pattern that could extend to any number of method names. Let's intercept method_missing in the Person class.

In this case, the method_missing we're dealing with is the class method: we need to intercept missing methods called on Person. Somewhere along the line, therefore, we need a definition like this:

```
class Person
  def self.method_missing(m, *args)      ◁──┐  Define method directly on self,
  # code here                                 which is the Person class object
  end
end
```

The method name, m, may or may not start with the substring all_with_. If it does, we want it; if it doesn't, we toss it back—or up—courtesy of super, and let Kernel #method_missing handle it. (Remember: classes are objects, so the class object Person has access to all of Kernel's instance methods, including method_missing.)

Here's a slightly more elaborate (but still schematic) view of method_missing:

```
class Person
  def self.method_missing(m, *args)                    ❶
    method = m.to_s                          ◁──────┘
    if method.start_with?("all_with_")       ◁──────┐
      # Handle request here                          ❷
    else
      super                       ◁──❸
    end
  end
end
```

The reason for the call to to_s ❶ is that the method name (the message) gets handed off to method_missing in the form of a symbol. Symbols don't have a start_with? method, so we have to convert the symbol to a string before testing its contents.

The conditional logic ❷ branches on whether we're handling an `all_with_*` message. If we are, we handle it. If not, we punt with `super` ❸.

With at least a blueprint of `method_missing` in place, let's develop the rest of the `Person` class. A few requirements are clear from the top-level calling code listed earlier:

- `Person` objects keep track of their friends and hobbies.
- The `Person` class keeps track of all existing people.
- Every person has a name.

The second point is implied by the fact that we've already been asking the `Person` class for lists of people who have certain hobbies and/or certain friends.

The following listing contains an implementation of the parts of the `Person` class that pertain to these requirements.

Listing 4.12   Implementation of the main logic of the `Person` class

```
class Person                                        ❶
  PEOPLE = []
  attr_reader :name, :hobbies, :friends             ❷
  def initialize(name)
    @name = name                                    ❸
    @hobbies = []
    @friends = []
    PEOPLE << self                                  ❹
  end
  def has_hobby(hobby)
    @hobbies << hobby                               ❺
  end
  def has_friend(friend)
    @friends << friend
  end
```

We stash all existing people in an array, held in the constant PEOPLE ❶. When a new person is instantiated, that person is added to the people array, courtesy of the array append method `<<` ❹. Meanwhile, we need some reader attributes: `name`, `hobbies`, and `friends` ❷. Providing these attributes lets the outside world see important aspects of the `Person` objects; `hobbies` and `friends` will also come in handy in the full implementation of `method_missing`.

The `initialize` method takes a name as its sole argument and saves it to `@name`. It also initializes the `hobbies` and `friends` arrays ❸. These arrays come back into play in the `has_hobby` and `has_friend` methods ❺, which are really just user-friendly wrappers around those arrays.

We now have enough code to finish the implementation of `Person.method_missing`. Listing 4.13 shows what it looks like (including the final `end` delimiter for the whole class). We use a convenient built-in query method, `public_method_defined?`, which tells us whether `Person` (represented in the method by the keyword `self`) has a method with the same name as the one at the end of the `all_with_` string.

```
def self.method_missing(m, *args)
  method = m.to_s
  if method.start_with?("all_with_")
    attr = method[9..-1]
    if self.public_method_defined?(attr)
      PEOPLE.find_all do |person|
        person.send(attr).include?(args[0])
      end
    else
      raise ArgumentError, "Can't find #{attr}"
    end
  else
    super
  end
end
end
```

❶   **❷**   **❸**   **❹**   **❺**   **❻**

If we have an `all_with_` message ❶, we want to ignore that part and capture the rest of the string, which we can do by taking the substring that lies in the ninth through last character positions; that's what indexing the string with `9..-1` achieves ❷. (This means starting at the tenth character, because string indexing starts at zero.) Now we want to know whether the resulting substring corresponds to one of `Person`'s instance methods—specifically, `hobbies` or `friends`. Rather than hard-code those two names, we keep things flexible and scalable by checking whether the `Person` class defines a method with our substring as its name ❸.

What happens next depends on whether the search for the symbol succeeds. To start with the second branch first, if the requested attribute doesn't exist, we raise an error with an appropriate message ❺. If it does succeed—which it will if the message is `friends` or `hobbies` or any other attribute we added later—we get to the heart of the matter.

In addition to the `all_with_*` method name, the method call includes an argument containing the thing we're looking for (the name of a friend or hobby, for example). That argument is found in `args[0]`, the first element of the argument "sponge" array designated as `*args` in the argument list; the business end of the whole `method_missing` method is to find all people whose `attr` includes `args[0]` ❹. That formula translates into, say, all people whose hobbies include music, or all people whose friends include some particular friend.

Note that this version of `method_missing` includes two conditional structures. That's because two things can go wrong: first, we may be handling a message that doesn't conform to the `all_with_*` pattern (`"blah"`, for example); and second, we may have an `all_with_*` request where the `*` part doesn't correspond to anything that the `Person` class knows about (`all_with_children`, for example). We treat the second as a fatal condition and raise an error ❺. If the first condition fails, it means this particular message isn't what this particular `method_missing` is looking for. We hand control upward to the next-highest definition of `method_missing` by calling `super` ❻.

Called with no arguments, super automatically gets all the arguments that came to the current method; thus the bare call to super is, in this case, equivalent to super(m, *args) (but shorter and more convenient).

> **NOTE** We'll look again at method_missing in chapter 15, as part of a broader look at Ruby's runtime hooks and callbacks, of which method_missing is only one. (There's also one called respond_to_missing?, which as its name implies is a sort of hybrid; you'll meet it in chapter 15.) It's worth having introduced method_missing here, though, because it's probably the most commonly used member of the callback family, and one that you're likely to see and hear discussed sooner rather than later in your Ruby explorations.

You now have a good grasp of both classes and modules, as well as how individual objects, on receiving messages, look for a matching method by traversing their class/ module family tree, and how they handle lookup failure. Next, we'll look at what you can do with this system—specifically, the kinds of decisions you can and should make as to the design and naming of your classes and modules, in the interest of writing clear and comprehensible programs.

4.4   *Class/module design and naming*

The fact that Ruby has classes and modules—along with the fact that from an object's perspective, all that matters is whether a given method exists, not what class or module the method's definition is in—means you have a lot of choice when it comes to your programs' design and structure. This richness of design choice raises some considerations you should be aware of.

We've already looked at one case (the Stack class) where it would have been possible to put all the necessary method definitions into one class, but it was advantageous to yank some of them out, put them in a module (Stacklike), and then mix the module into the class. There's no rule for deciding when to do which. It depends on your present and—to the extent you can predict them—future needs. It's sometimes tempting to break everything out into separate modules, because modules you write for one program may be useful in another ("I just know I'm going to need that ThreePronged module again someday!" says the packrat voice in your head). But there's such a thing as overmodularization. It depends on the situation. You've got a couple of powerful tools available to you—mix-ins and inheritance—and you need to consider in each case how to balance them.

4.4.1   *Mix-ins and/or inheritance*

Module mix-ins are closely related to class inheritance. In both cases, one entity (class or module) is establishing a close connection with another by becoming neighbors on a method-lookup path. In some cases, you may find that you can design part of your program either with modules or with inheritance.

Our CargoHold class is an example. We implemented it by having it mix in the Stacklike module. But had we gone the route of writing a Stack class instead of a

`Stacklike` module, we still could have had a `CargoHold`. It would have been a subclass of `Stack`, as illustrated in the next listing.

```
class Stack
  attr_reader :stack
  def initialize
    @stack = []
  end
  def add_to_stack(obj)
    @stack.push(obj)
  end
  def take_from_stack
    @stack.pop
  end
end
class Suitcase
end
class CargoHold < Stack
  def load_and_report(obj)
    print "Loading object "
    puts obj.object_id
    add_to_stack(obj)
  end
  def unload
    take_from_stack
  end
end
```

From the point of view of an individual `CargoHold` object, the process works in this listing exactly as it worked in the earlier implementation, where `CargoHold` mixed in the `Stacklike` module. The object is concerned with finding and executing methods that correspond to the messages it receives. It either finds such methods on its method-lookup path, or it doesn't. It doesn't care whether the methods were defined in a module or a class. It's like searching a house for a screwdriver: you don't care which room you find it in, and which room you find it in makes no difference to what happens when you subsequently employ the screwdriver for a task.

There's nothing wrong with this inheritance-based approach to implementing `CargoHold`, except that it eats up the one inheritance opportunity `CargoHold` has. If another class might be more suitable than `Stack` to serve as `CargoHold`'s superclass (like, hypothetically, `StorageSpace` or `AirplaneSection`), we might end up needing the flexibility we'd gain by turning at least one of those classes into a module.

No single rule or formula always results in the right design. But it's useful to keep a couple of considerations in mind when you're making class-versus-module decisions:

- *Modules don't have instances.* It follows that entities or things are generally best modeled in classes, and characteristics or properties of entities or things are best encapsulated in modules. Correspondingly, as noted in section 4.1.1, class names tend to be nouns, whereas module names are often adjectives (Stack versus Stacklike).

- *A class can have only one superclass, but it can mix in as many modules as it wants.* If you're using inheritance, give priority to creating a sensible superclass/subclass relationship. Don't use up a class's one and only superclass relationship to endow the class with what might turn out to be just one of several sets of characteristics.

Summing up these rules in one example, here is what you should *not* do:

```
module Vehicle
...
class SelfPropelling
...
class Truck < SelfPropelling
  include Vehicle
...
```

Rather, you should do this:

```
module SelfPropelling
...
class Vehicle
  include SelfPropelling
...
class Truck < Vehicle
...
```

The second version models the entities and properties much more neatly. Truck descends from Vehicle (which makes sense), whereas SelfPropelling is a characteristic of vehicles (at least, all those we care about in this model of the world)—a characteristic that's passed on to trucks by virtue of Truck being a descendant, or specialized form, of Vehicle.

Another important consideration in class/module design is the nesting of modules and/or classes inside each other.

4.4.2   *Nesting modules and classes*

You can nest a class definition inside a module definition like this:

```
module Tools
  class Hammer
  end
end
```

To create an instance of the Hammer class defined inside the Tools module, you use the double-colon constant lookup token (::) to point the way to the name of the class:

```
h = Tools::Hammer.new
```

Nested module/class chains like Tools::Hammer are sometimes used to create separate namespaces for classes, modules, and methods. This technique can help if two classes have a similar name but aren't the same class. For example, if you have a

`Tools::Hammer` class, you can also have a `Piano::Hammer` class, and the two `Hammer` classes won't conflict with each other because each is nested in its own namespace (`Tools` in one case, `Piano` in the other).

(An alternative way to achieve this separation would be to have a `ToolsHammer` class and a `PianoHammer` class, without bothering to nest them in modules. But stringing names together like that can quickly lead to visual clutter, especially when elements are nested deeper than two levels.)

Class or module?

When you see a construct like `Tools::Hammer`, you can't tell solely from that construct what's a class and what's a module—nor, for that matter, whether `Hammer` is a plain, old constant. (`Tools` has to be a class or module, because it's got `Hammer` nested inside it.) In many cases, the fact that you can't tell classes from modules in this kind of context doesn't matter; what matters is the nesting or chaining of names in a way that makes sense. That's just as well, because you can't tell what's what without looking at the source code or the documentation. This is a consequence of the fact that classes are modules—the class `Class` is a subclass of the class `Module`—and in many respects (with the most notable exception that classes can be instantiated), their behavior is similar. Of course, normally you'd know what `Tools::Hammer` represents, either because you wrote the code or because you've seen documentation. Still, it pays to realize that the notation itself doesn't tell you everything.

We'll look further at nested classes, modules, and other constants in the next chapter, when we talk in more detail about the subject of scope. Meanwhile, note that this ability to nest modules and classes inside each other (to any depth, in any order) gives you yet another axis along which you can plan your program's design and structure.

4.5   Summary

Chapter 4 has been both a companion to and a continuation of the previous chapter on classes. In this chapter you've seen

- Modules, up close and in detail
- Similarities and differences between modules and classes (both can bundle methods and constants together, but modules can't be instantiated)
- Examples of how you might use modules to express the design of a program
- An object's-eye view of the process of finding and executing a method in response to a message, or handling failure with `method_missing` in cases where the message doesn't match a method
- How to nest classes and modules inside each other, with the benefit of keeping namespaces separate and clear

It's particularly important to take on board the way that objects resolve messages into methods: they go on a search through a succession of classes and modules. Objects don't themselves have methods, even though phrasing it that way is sometimes a handy shortcut. Classes and modules have methods; objects have the ability to traverse classes and modules in search of methods.

Now that we're nesting elements inside each other, the next topic we should and will examine in detail is scope: what happens to data and variables when your program moves from one code context to another. We'll look at scope in conjunction with the related, often interwoven topic of self, the default object.

5

The default object (self), scope, and visibility

This chapter covers

- The role of the current or default object, self
- Scoping rules for local, global, and class variables
- Constant lookup and visibility
- Method-access rules

In describing and discussing computer programs, we often use spatial and, sometimes, human metaphors. We talk about being "in" a class definition or returning "from" a method call. We address objects in the second person, as in `obj.respond_to?("x")` (that is, "Hey obj, do you respond to 'x'?"). As a program runs, the question of which objects are being addressed, and where in the imaginary space of the program they stand, constantly shifts.

And the shifts aren't just metaphorical. The meanings of identifiers shift too. A few elements mean the same thing everywhere. Integers, for example, mean what they mean wherever you see them. The same is true for keywords: you can't use keywords like `def` and `class` as variable names, so when you see them, you can easily glean what they're doing. But most elements depend on context for their meaning.

Most words and tokens—most identifiers—can mean different things at different places and times.

This chapter is about orienting yourself in Ruby code: knowing how the identifiers you're using are going to resolve, following the shifts in context, and making sense of the use and reuse of identifiers and terms. If you understand what can change from one context to another, and also what triggers a change in context (for example, entering a method-definition block), you can always get your bearings in a Ruby program. And it's not just a matter of passive Ruby literacy: you also need to know about contexts and how they affect the meaning of what you're doing when you're writing Ruby.

This chapter focuses initially on two topics: *self* and *scope. Self* is the "current" or "default" object, a role typically assigned to many objects in sequence (though only one at a time) as a program runs. The self object in Ruby is like the first person or *I* of the program. As in a book with multiple first-person narrators, the *I* role can get passed around. There's always one self, but what object it is will vary. The rules of scope govern the visibility of variables (and other elements, but largely variables). It's important to know what scope you're in, so that you can tell what the variables refer to and not confuse them with variables from different scopes that have the same name, nor with similarly named methods.

Between them, self and scope are the master keys to orienting yourself in a Ruby program. If you know what scope you're in and know what object is self, you'll be able to tell what's going on, and you'll be able to analyze errors quickly.

The third main topic of this chapter is *method access.* Ruby provides mechanisms for making distinctions among access levels of methods. Basically, this means rules limiting the calling of methods depending on what self is. Method access is therefore a meta-topic, grounded in the study of self and scope.

Finally, we'll also discuss a topic that pulls together several of these threads: *top-level methods,* which are written outside of any class or module definition.

Let's start with self.

5.1   *Understanding self, the current/default object*

One of the cornerstones of Ruby programming—the backbone, in some respects—is the default object or current object, accessible to you in your program through the keyword `self`. At every point when your program is running, there's one and only one self. Being self has certain privileges, as you'll see. In this section, we'll look at how Ruby determines which object is self at a given point and what privileges are granted to the object that is self.

5.1.1   *Who gets to be self, and where*

There's always one (and only one) current object or self. You can tell which object it is by following the small set of rules summarized in table 5.1. The table's contents will be explained and illustrated as we go along.

Table 5.1 How the current object (self) is determined

Context	Example	Which object is self?
Top level of program	Any code outside of other blocks	`main` (built-in top-level default object)
Class definition	`class C` `  self`	The class object `C`
Module definition	`module M` `  self`	The module object `M`

Method definitions	**1** Top level (outside any definition block):
	`def method_name`
	`  self`
		Whatever object is self when the method is called; top-level methods are available as private methods to all objects

	2 Instance-method definition in a class:
	`class C`
	`  def method_name`
	`    self`
		An instance of `C`, responding to `method_name`

	3 Instance-method definition in a module:
	`module M`
	`  def method_name`
	`    self`
		▪ Individual object extended by `M`
		▪ Instance of class that mixes in `M`

	4 Singleton method on a specific object:
	`def obj.method_name`
	`  self`
		`Obj`

To know which object is self, you need to know what context you're in. In practice, there aren't many contexts to worry about. There's the top level (before you've entered any other context, such as a class definition). There are class-definition blocks, module-definition blocks, and method-definition blocks. Aside from a few subtleties in the way these contexts interact, that's about it. As shown in table 5.1, self is determined by which of these contexts you're in (class and module definitions are similar and closely related).

Figure 5.1 gives you a diagrammatic view of most of the cases in table 5.1. Both show you that some object is always self and that which object is self depends on where you are in the program.

The most basic program context, and in some respects a unique one, is the top level: the context of the program before any class or module definition has been opened, or after they've all been closed. We'll look next at the top level's ideas about self.

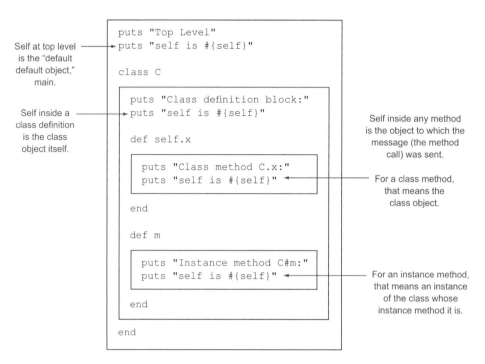

Figure 5.1　The determination of self in different contexts

5.1.2　*The top-level self object*

The term *top-level* refers to program code written outside of any class- or module-definition block. If you open a brand-new text file and type

```
x = 1
```

you've created a top-level local variable x. If you type

```
def m
end
```

you've created a top-level method. (We'll look at top-level methods in much more detail in section 5.4; they're relevant here just as pointers to the existence of a top-level self.) A number of our examples, particularly in the early chapters (for example, those in chapter 2 demonstrating argument semantics) involved top-level code. Once we started writing class and module definitions, more of our code began to appear inside those definitions. The way self shifts in class, module, and method definitions is uniform: the keyword (class, module, or def) marks a switch to a new self. But what's self when you haven't yet entered any definition block?

The answer is that Ruby provides you with a start-up self at the top level. If you ask it to identify itself with

```
ruby -e 'puts self'
```

it will tell you that it's called main.

main is a special term that the default self object uses to refer to itself. You can't refer to it as main; Ruby will interpret your use of main as a regular variable or method name. If you want to grab main for any reason, you need to assign it to a variable at the top level:

```
m = self
```

It's not likely that you'd need to do this, but that's how it's done. More commonly, you'll feel the need for a fairly fine-grained sense of what self is in your class, module, and method definitions, where most of your programming will take place.

5.1.3   *Self inside class, module, and method definitions*

It pays to keep a close eye on self as you write classes, modules, and methods. There aren't that many rules to learn, and they're applied consistently. But they're worth learning well up front, so you're clear on why the various techniques you use that depend on the value of self play out the way they do.

It's all about self switching from one object to another, which it does when you enter a class or module definition, an instance-method definition, or a singleton-method (including class-method) definition.

SELF IN CLASS AND MODULE DEFINITIONS

In a class or module definition, self is the class or module object. This innocent-sounding rule is important. If you master it, you'll save yourself from several of the most common mistakes that people make when they're learning Ruby.

You can see what self is at various levels of class and/or module definition by using puts explicitly, as shown in the following listing.

> **Listing 5.1   Examining self via calls to puts in class and module definitions**

```
class C
  puts "Just started class C:"
  puts self                              ⟵── Output: C
  module M
    puts "Nested module C::M:"
    puts self                            ⟵── Output: C::M
  end
  puts "Back in the outer level of C:"
  puts self                              ⟵── Output: C
end
```

As soon as you cross a class or module keyword boundary, the class or module whose definition block you've entered—the Class or Module object—becomes self. Listing 5.1 shows two cases: entering C, and then entering C::M. When you leave C::M but are still in C, self is once again C.

Of course, class- and module-definition blocks do more than just begin and end. They also contain method definitions, which, for both instance methods and class methods, have rules determining self.

SELF IN INSTANCE-METHOD DEFINITIONS

The notion of self inside an instance-method definition is subtle, for the following reason: when the interpreter encounters a def/end block, it defines the method immediately. But the code inside the method definition isn't executed until later, when an object capable of triggering its execution receives the appropriate message.

When you're looking at a method definition on paper or on the screen, you can only know in principle that, when the method is called, self will be the object that called it (the receiver of the message). At the time the method gets defined, the most you can say is that self inside this method will be some future object that calls the method.

You can rig a method to show you self as it runs:

```
class C
  def x
    puts "Class C, method x:"
    puts self
  end
end
c = C.new
c.x
puts "That was a call to x by: #{c}"
```

This snippet outputs

```
Class C, method x:
#<C:0x00000101b381a0>
That was a call to x by: #<C:0x00000101b381a0>
```

The weird-looking item in the output (#<C:0x00000101b381a0>) is Ruby's way of saying "an instance of C." (The hexadecimal number after the colon is a memory-location reference. When you run the code on your system, you'll probably get a different number.) As you can see, the receiver of the "x" message, namely c, takes on the role of self during execution of x.

SELF IN SINGLETON-METHOD AND CLASS-METHOD DEFINITIONS

As you might expect, when a singleton method is executed, self is the object that owns the method, as an object will readily tell you:

```
obj = Object.new
def obj.show_me
  puts "Inside singleton method show_me of #{self}"
end
obj.show_me
puts "Back from call to show_me by #{obj}"
```

The output of this example is as follows:

```
Inside singleton method show_me of #<Object:0x00000101b19840>
Back from call to show_me by #<Object:0x00000101b19840>
```

It makes sense that if a method is written to be called by only one object, that object gets to be self. Moreover, this is a good time to remember class methods—which are, essentially, singleton methods attached to class objects. The following example reports on self from inside a class method of C:

```
class C
  def C.x
    puts "Class method of class C"
    puts "self: #{self}"
  end
end
C.x
```

Here's what it reports:

```
Class method of class C
self: C
```

Sure enough, self inside a singleton method (a class method, in this case) is the object whose singleton method it is.

Using self instead of hard-coded class names

By way of a little programming tip, here's a variation on the last example:

```
class C
  def self.x                       ◁——❶
    puts "Class method of class C"
    puts "self: #{self}"
  end
end
```

Note the use of `self.x` ❶ rather than `C.x`. This way of writing a class method takes advantage of the fact that in the class definition, self is C. So `def self.x` is the same as `def C.x`.

The `self.x` version offers a slight advantage: if you ever decide to rename the class, `self.x` will adjust automatically to the new name. If you hard-code `C.x`, you'll have to change C to your class's new name. But you do have to be careful. Remember that self inside a method is always the object on which the method was called. You can get into a situation where it feels like self should be one class object, but is actually another:

```
class D < C
end
D.x
```

D gets to call `x`, because subclasses get to call the class methods of their super-classes. As you'll see if you run the code, the method `C.x` reports self—correctly—as being D, because it's D on which the method is called.

Being self at a given point in the program comes with some privileges. The chief privilege enjoyed by self is that of serving as the default receiver of messages, as you'll see next.

5.1.4   *Self as the default receiver of messages*

Calling methods (that is, sending messages to objects) usually involves the dot notation:

```
obj.talk
ticket.venue
"abc".capitalize
```

That's the normal, full form of the method-calling syntax in Ruby. But a special rule governs method calls: if the receiver of the message is self, you can omit the receiver and the dot. Ruby will use self as the default receiver, meaning the message you send will be sent to self, as the following equivalencies show:

```
talk                            Same as self.talk
venue                           Same as self.venue
capitalize                      Same as self.capitalize
```

> **WARNING** You can give a method and a local variable the same name, but it's rarely if ever a good idea. If both a method and a variable of a given name exist, and you use the bare identifier (like talk), the variable takes precedence. To force Ruby to see the identifier as a method name, you'd have to use self.talk or call the method with an empty argument list: talk(). Because variables don't take arguments, the parentheses establish that you mean the method rather than the variable. Again, it's best to avoid these name clashes if you can.

Let's see this concept in action by inducing a situation where we know what self is and then testing the dotless form of method calling. In the top level of a class-definition block, self is the class object. And we know how to add methods directly to class objects. So we have the ingredients to do a default receiver demo:

```
class C
  def C.no_dot
    puts "As long as self is C, you can call this method with no dot"
  end
  no_dot            ①
end                          ②
C.no_dot
```

The first call to no_dot ① doesn't have an explicit receiver; it's a bareword. When Ruby sees this (and determines that it's a method call rather than a variable or keyword), it figures that you mean it as shorthand for

```
self.no_dot
```

and the message gets printed. In the case of our example, self.no_dot would be the same as C.no_dot, because we're inside C's definition block and, therefore, self is C. The result is that the method C.no_dot is called, and we see the output.

The second time we call the method ② we're back outside the class-definition block, so C is no longer self. Therefore, to call no_dot, we need to specify the receiver: C.

The result is a second call to `no_dot` (albeit with a dot) and another printing of the output from that method.

The most common use of the dotless method call occurs when you're calling one instance method from another. Here's an example:

```
class C
  def x
    puts "This is method 'x'"
  end
  def y
    puts "This is method 'y', about to call x without a dot."
    x
  end
end
c = C.new
c.y
```

The output is

```
This is method 'y', about to call x without a dot.
This is method 'x'.
```

Upon calling `c.y`, the method `y` is executed, with self set to `c` (which is an instance of C). Inside `y`, the bareword reference to `x` is interpreted as a message to be sent to self. That, in turn, means the method `x` is executed.

There's one situation where you can't omit the object-plus-dot part of a method call: when the method name ends with an equal sign—a *setter* method, in other words. You have to do `self.venue = "Town Hall"` rather than `venue = "Town Hall"` if you want to call the method `venue=` on self. The reason is that Ruby always interprets the sequence *identifier = value* as an assignment to a local variable. To call the method `venue=` on the current object, you need to include the explicit self. Otherwise, you end up with a variable called `venue` and no call to the setter method.

The default to self as receiver for dotless method invocations allows you to streamline your code nicely in cases where one method makes use of another. A common case is composing a whole name from its components: first, optional middle, and last. The following listing shows a technique for doing this, using attributes for the three name values and conditional logic to include the middle name, plus a trailing space, if and only if there's a middle name.

> **Listing 5.2   Composing whole name from values, using method calls on implicit self**

```
class Person
  attr_accessor :first_name, :middle_name, :last_name
  def whole_name
    n = first_name + " "
    n << "#{middle_name} " if middle_name
    n << last_name                              ←———❶
  end
end
david = Person.new
david.first_name = "David"
```

```
david.last_name = "Black"
puts "David's whole name: #{david.whole_name}"
david.middle_name = "Alan"
puts "David's new whole name: #{david.whole_name}"
```

The output from the calling code in this listing is as follows:

```
David's whole name: David Black
David's new whole name: David Alan Black
```

The definition of whole_name depends on the bareword method calls to first_name, middle_name, and last_name being sent to self—self being the Person instance (david in the example). The variable n serves as a string accumulator, with the components of the name added to it one by one. The return value of the entire method is n, because the expression n << last_name ❶ has the effect of appending last_name to n and returning the result of that operation.

In addition to serving automatically as the receiver for bareword messages, self also enjoys the privilege of being the owner of instance variables.

5.1.5 *Resolving instance variables through self*

A simple rule governs instance variables and their resolution: every instance variable you'll ever see in a Ruby program belongs to whatever object is the current object (self) at that point in the program.

Here's a classic case where this knowledge comes in handy. See if you can figure out what this code will print, before you run it:

```
class C
  def show_var
    @v = "I am an instance variable initialized to a string."    ◄─❶
    puts @v
  end
  @v = "Instance variables can appear anywhere...."              ◄─❷
end
C.new.show_var
```

The code prints the following:

```
I am an instance variable initialized to a string.
```

The trap is that you may think it will print "Instance variables can appear anywhere...." The code prints what it does because the @v in the method definition ❶ and the @v outside it ❷ are completely unrelated to each other. They're both instance variables, and both are named @v, but they aren't the same variable. They belong to different objects.

Whose are they?

The first @v ❶ lies inside the definition block of an instance method of C. That fact has implications not for a single object, but for instances of C in general: each instance of C that calls this method will have its own instance variable @v.

The second @v ❷ belongs to the class object C. This is one of the many occasions where it pays to remember that classes are objects. Any object may have its own instance variables—its own private stash of information and object state. Class objects enjoy this privilege as much as any other object.

Again, the logic required to figure out what object owns a given instance variable is simple and consistent: every instance variable belongs to whatever object is playing the role of self at the moment the code containing the instance variable is executed.

Let's do a quick rewrite of the example, this time making it a little chattier about what's going on. The following listing shows the rewrite.

Listing 5.3 Demonstrating the relationship between instance variables and self

```
class C
  puts "Just inside class definition block. Here's self:"
  p self
  @v = "I am an instance variable at the top level of a class body."
  puts "And here's the instance variable @v, belonging to #{self}:"
  p @v
  def show_var
    puts "Inside an instance method definition block. Here's self:"
    p self
    puts "And here's the instance variable @v, belonging to #{self}:"
    p @v
  end
end
c = C.new
c.show_var
```

The output from this version is as follows:

```
Just inside class definition block. Here's self:
C
And here's the instance variable @v, belonging to C:
"I am an instance variable at the top level of a class body."
Inside an instance method definition block. Here's self:
#<C:0x00000101a77338>
And here's the instance variable @v, belonging to #<C:0x00000101a77338>:
nil
```

Sure enough, each of these two different objects (the class object C and the instance of C, c) has its own instance variable @v. The fact that the instance's @v is nil demonstrates that the assignment to the class's @v had nothing to do with the instance's @v.

Understanding self—both the basic fact that such a role is being played by some object at every point in a program and knowing how to tell which object is self—is one of the most vital aspects of understanding Ruby. Another equally vital aspect is understanding scope, to which we'll turn now.

5.2 *Determining scope*

Scope refers to the reach or visibility of identifiers, specifically variables and constants. Different types of identifiers have different scoping rules; using, say, the identifier x for a local variable in each of two method definitions has a different effect than using the global variable $x in the same two places, because local and global variables differ as to scope. In this section, we'll consider three types of variables: global, local, and class variables. (As you've just seen, instance variables are self-bound, rather than scope-bound.) We'll also look at the rules for resolving constants.

Self and scope are similar in that they both change over the course of a program, and in that you can deduce what's going on with them by reading the program as well as running it. But scope and self aren't the same thing. You can start a new local scope without self changing—but sometimes scope and self change together. They have in common the fact that they're both necessary to make sense of what your code is going to do. Like knowing which object self is, knowing what scope you're in tells you the significance of the code.

Let's start with global variables—not the most commonly used construct, but an important one to grasp.

5.2.1   *Global scope and global variables*

Global scope is scope that covers the entire program. Global scope is enjoyed by global variables, which are recognizable by their initial dollar-sign ($) character. They're available everywhere. They walk through walls: even if you start a new class or method definition, even if the identity of self changes, the global variables you've initialized are still available to you.

In other words, global variables never go out of scope. (An exception to this is "thread-local globals," which you'll meet in chapter 14.) In this example, a method defined inside a class-definition body (two scopes removed from the outer- or top-level scope of the program) has access to a global variable initialized at the top:

```
$gvar = "I'm a global!"
class C
  def examine_global
    puts $gvar
  end
end
c = C.new                    Output:
c.examine_global   ←─┘       "I'm a global!"
```

You'll be told by $gvar, in no uncertain terms, "I'm a global!" If you change all the occurrences of $gvar to a non-global variable, such as `local_var`, you'll see that the top-level `local_var` isn't in scope inside the method-definition block.

BUILT-IN GLOBAL VARIABLES

The Ruby interpreter starts up with a fairly large number of global variables already initialized. These variables store information that's of potential use anywhere and everywhere in your program. For example, the global variable $0 contains the name of the startup file for the currently running program. The global $: (dollar sign followed by a colon) contains the directories that make up the path Ruby searches when you load an external file. $$ contains the process ID of the Ruby process. And there are more.

TIP A good place to see descriptions of all the built-in global variables you're likely to need—and then some—is the file English.rb in your Ruby installation. This file provides less-cryptic names for the notoriously cryptic global variable set. (Don't blame Ruby for the names—most of them come from shell languages and/or Perl and awk.) If you want to use the slightly friendlier names in your programs, you can do `require "English"`, after which you can refer to `$IGNORECASE` instead of `$=`, `$PID` instead of `$$`, and so forth. A few globals have their English-language names preloaded; you can say `$LOAD_PATH` instead of `$:` even without loading English.rb.

Creating your own global variables can be tempting, especially for beginning programmers and people learning a new language (not just Ruby, either). But that's rarely a good or appropriate choice.

PROS AND CONS OF GLOBAL VARIABLES

Globals appear to solve lots of design problems: you don't have to worry about scope, and multiple classes can share information by stashing it in globals rather than designing objects that have to be queried with method calls. Without doubt, global variables have a certain allure.

But they're used very little by experienced programmers. The reasons for avoiding them are similar to the reasons they're tempting. Using global variables tends to end up being a substitute for solid, flexible program design, rather than contributing to it. One of the main points of object-oriented programming is that data and actions are encapsulated in objects. You're *supposed* to have to query objects for information and to request that they perform actions.

And objects are supposed to have a certain privacy. When you ask an object to do something, you're not supposed to care what the object does internally to get the job done. Even if you yourself wrote the code for the object's methods, when you send the object a message, you treat the object as a black box that works behind the scenes and provides a response.

Global variables distort the landscape by providing a layer of information shared by every object in every context. The result is that objects stop talking to each other and, instead, share information by setting global variables.

Here's a small example—a rewrite of our earlier `Person` class (the one with the first, optional middle, and last names). This time, instead of attributes on the object, we'll generate the whole name from globals:

```
class Person
  def whole_name
    n = $first_name + " "
    n << "#{$middle_name} " if $middle_name
    n << $last_name
  end
end
```

To use this class and to get a whole name from an instance of it, you'd have to do this:

```
david = Person.new
$first_name = "David"
$middle_name = "Alan"
$last_name = "Black"      Output: David
puts david.whole_name  ◁───┘ Alan Black
```

This version still derives the whole name, from outside, by querying the object. But the components of the name are handed around over the heads of the objects, so to speak, in a separate network of global variables. It's concise and easy, but it's also drastically limited. What would happen if you had lots of Person objects, or if you wanted to save a Person object, including its various names, to a database? Your code would quickly become tangled, to say the least.

Globally scoped data is fundamentally in conflict with the object-oriented philosophy of endowing objects with abilities and then getting things done by sending requests to those objects. Some Ruby programmers work for years and never use a single global variable (except perhaps a few of the built-in ones). That may or may not end up being your experience, but it's not a bad target to aim for.

Now that we've finished with the "try not to do this" part, let's move on to a detailed consideration of local scope.

5.2.2   *Local scope*

Local scope is a basic layer of the fabric of every Ruby program. At any given moment, your program is in a particular local scope. The main thing that changes from one local scope to another is your supply of local variables. When you leave a local scope—by returning from a method call, or by doing something that triggers a new local scope—you get a new supply. Even if you've assigned to a local variable x in one scope, you can assign to a new x in a new scope, and the two x's won't interfere with each other.

You can tell by looking at a Ruby program where the local scopes begin and end, based on a few rules:

- The top level (outside of all definition blocks) has its own local scope.
- Every class or module-definition block (class, module) has its own local scope, even nested class-/module-definition blocks.
- Every method definition (def) has its own local scope; more precisely, every call to a method generates a new local scope, with all local variables reset to an undefined state.

Exceptions and additions to these rules exist, but they're fairly few and don't concern us right now.

Figure 5.2 illustrates the creation of a number of local scopes.

Every time you cross into a class-, module-, or method-definition block—every time you step over a class, module, or def keyword—you start a new local scope. Local

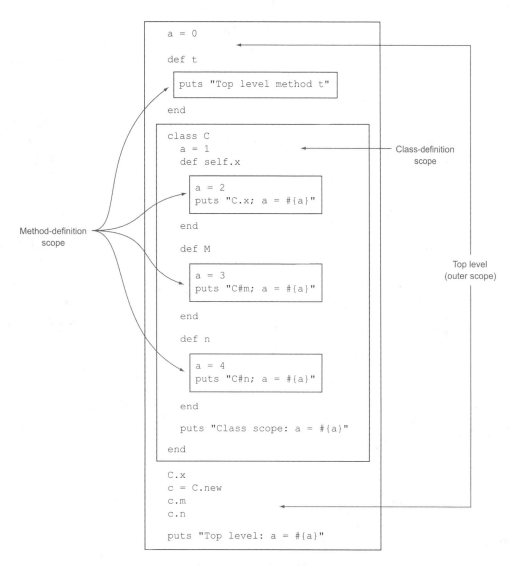

Figure 5.2 Schematic view of local scopes at the top level, the class-definition level, and the method-definition level

variables that lie very close to each other physically may in fact have nothing whatso-ever to do with each other, as this example shows:

```
class C
  a = 1                        ⟵─❶
  def local_a
    a = 2                      ⟵─❷
    puts a
  end
  puts a                       ⟵─❸
end
```

```
c = C.new
c.local_a          ◁——④
```

This code produces the following output:

```
1
2
```

The variable a that gets initialized in the local scope of the class definition ❶ is in a different scope than the variable a inside the method definition ❷. When you get to the `puts a` statement after the method definition ❸, you're back in the class-definition local scope; the a that gets printed is the a you initialized back at the top ❶, not the a that's in scope in the method definition ❷. Meanwhile, the second a isn't printed until later, when you've created the instance c and sent the message `local_a` to it ❹.

When you nest classes and modules, every crossing into a new definition block creates a new local scope. The following listing shows some deep nesting of classes and modules, with a number of variables called a being initialized and printed out along the way.

Listing 5.4   Reusing a variable name in nested local scopes

```
class C
  a = 5
  module M
    a = 4
    module N
      a = 3
      class D
        a = 2
        def show_a
          a = 1
          puts a
        end
        puts a              ◁—— Output: 2
      end
      puts a                ◁—— Output: 3
    end
    puts a                  ◁—— Output: 4
  end
  puts a                    ◁—— Output: 5
end
d = C::M::N::D.new
d.show_a                    ◁—— Output: 1
```

Every definition block—whether for a class, a module, or a method—starts a new local scope—a new local-variable scratchpad—and gets its own variable a. This example also illustrates the fact that all the code in class- and module-definition blocks gets executed when it's first encountered, whereas methods aren't executed until an object is sent the appropriate message. That's why the value of a that's set inside the `show_a` method is displayed last among the five values that the program prints; the other four are executed as they're encountered in the class or module definitions, but the last one isn't executed until show_a is executed by the object d.

Local scope changes often, as you can see. So does the identity of self. Sometimes, but only sometimes, they vary together. Let's look a little closer at the relationship between scope and self.

5.2.3 *The interaction between local scope and self*

When you start a definition block (method, class, module), you start a new local scope, and you also create a block of code with a particular self. But local scope and self don't operate entirely in parallel, not only because they're not the same thing, but also because they're not the same *kind* of thing.

Consider the following listing. This program uses *recursion*: the instance method x calls itself. The point is to demonstrate that every time a method is called—even if a previous call to the method is still in the process of running—a new local scope is generated.

Listing 5.5 Demonstrating the generation of a new local scope per method call

```
class C
  def x(value_for_a,recurse=false)        1  2
    a = value_for_a
    print "Here's the inspect-string for 'self':"
    p self                                        3
    puts "And here's a:"
    puts a
    if recurse
      puts "Calling myself (recursion)..."       4
      x("Second value for a")
      puts "Back after recursion; here's a:"   5
      puts a                                   6
    end
  end
end
c = C.new                                       7
c.x("First value for a", true)
```

The instance method C#x takes two arguments: a value to assign to the variable a and a flag telling the method whether to call itself **1**. (The use of the flag provides a way to prevent infinite recursion.) The first line of the method initializes a **2**, and the next several lines of the method print out the string representation of self and the value of a **3**.

Now comes the decision: to recurse, or not to recurse. It depends on the value of the recurse variable **4**. If the recursion happens, it calls x without specifying a value for the recurse parameter **5**; that parameter will default to false, and recursion won't happen the second time through.

The recursive call uses a different value for the value_for_a argument; therefore, different information will be printed out during that call. But upon returning from the recursive call, we find that the value of a in this run of x hasn't changed **6**. In short, every call to x generates a new local scope, even though self doesn't change.

The output from calling x on an instance of C and setting the recurse flag to true **7** looks like this:

```
Here's the inspect-string for 'self': #<C:0x00000101b25be0>
And here's a:
First value for a
Calling myself (recursion)...
Here's the inspect-string for 'self': #<C:0x00000101b25be0>
And here's a:
Second value for a
Back after recursion; here's a:
First value for a
```

There's no change to self, but the local variables are reset.

> **TIP** Instead of printing out the default string representation of an object, you can also use the object_id method to identify the object uniquely. Try changing p self to puts self.object_id, and puts a to puts a.object_id in the previous example.

If this listing seems like the long way around to making the point that every method call has its own local scope, think of it as a template or model for the kinds of demonstrations you might try yourself as you develop an increasingly fine-grained sense of how scope and self work, separately and together.

> **NOTE** It's also possible to do the opposite of what listing 5.5 demonstrates— namely, to change self without entering a new local scope. This is accomplished with the instance_eval and instance_exec methods, which we'll look at later.

Like variables, constants are governed by rules of scope. We'll look next at how those rules work.

5.2.4 *Scope and resolution of constants*

As you've seen, constants can be defined inside class- and method-definition blocks. If you know the chain of nested definitions, you can access a constant from anywhere. Consider this nest:

```
module M
  class C
    class D
      module N
        X = 1
      end
    end
  end
end
```

You can refer to the module M, the class M::C, and so forth, down to the simple constant M::C::D::N::X (which is equal to 1).

Constants have a kind of global visibility or reachability: as long as you know the path to a constant through the classes and/or modules in which it's nested, you can get to that constant. Stripped of their nesting, however, constants definitely aren't globals. The constant X in one scope isn't the constant X in another:

```
module M
  class C
    X = 2
    class D
      module N
        X = 1
      end
    end
  end
end
puts M::C::D::N::X       ❶
puts M::C::X             ❷
```

As per the nesting, the first puts ❶ gives you 1; the second ❷ gives you 2. A particular constant identifier (like X) doesn't have an absolute meaning the way a global variable (like $x) does.

Constant lookup—the process of resolving a constant identifier, or finding the right match for it—bears a close resemblance to searching a file system for a file in a particular directory. For one thing, constants are identified relative to the point of execution. Another variant of our example illustrates this:

```
module M
  class C
    class D
      module N
        X = 1
      end
    end
    puts D::N::X        ⟵— Output: 1
  end
end
```

Here the identifier D::N::X is interpreted relative to where it occurs: inside the definition block of the class M::C. From M::C's perspective, D is just one level away. There's no need to do M::C::D::N::X, when just D::N::X points the way down the path to the right constant. Sure enough, we get what we want: a printout of the number 1.

Forcing an absolute constant path

Sometimes you don't want a relative path. Sometimes you really want to start the constant-lookup process at the top level—just as you sometimes need to use an absolute path for a file.

This may happen if you create a class or module with a name that's similar to the name of a Ruby built-in class or module. For example, Ruby comes with a `String` class. But if you create a `Violin` class, you may also have `Strings`:

```
class Violin
  class String
    attr_accessor :pitch
    def initialize(pitch)
      @pitch = pitch
    end
  end
  def initialize
    @e = String.new("E")          <──❶
    @a = String.new("A")
    ...etc....
```

The constant `String` in this context ❶ resolves to `Violin::String`, as defined. Now let's say that elsewhere in the overall `Violin` class definition, you need to refer to Ruby's built-in `String` class. If you have a plain reference to `String`, it resolves to `Violin::String`. To make sure you're referring to the built-in, original `String` class, you need to put the constant path separator `::` (double colon) at the beginning of the class name:

```
def history
  ::String.new(maker + ", " + date)
end
```

This way, you get a Ruby `String` object instead of a `Violin::String` object. Like the slash at the beginning of a pathname, the `::` in front of a constant means "start the search for this at the top level." (Yes, you could just piece the string together inside double quotes, using interpolation, and bypass `String.new`. But then we wouldn't have such a vivid name-clash example!)

In addition to constants and local, instance, and global variables, Ruby also features *class variables*, a category of identifier with some idiosyncratic scoping rules.

5.2.5 *Class variable syntax, scope, and visibility*

Class variables begin with two at signs—for example, `@@var`. Despite their name, class variables aren't class scoped. Rather, they're class-hierarchy scoped, except...sometimes. Don't worry; we'll go through the details. After a look at how class variables work, we'll evaluate how well they fill the role of maintaining state for a class.

CLASS VARIABLES ACROSS CLASSES AND INSTANCES

At its simplest, the idea behind a class variable is that it provides a storage mechanism that's shared between a class and instances of that class, and that's not visible to any other objects. No other entity can fill this role. Local variables don't survive the scope change between class definitions and their inner method definitions. Globals do, but they're also visible and mutable everywhere else in the program, not just in one class. Constants likewise: instance methods can see the constants defined in the class in which they're defined, but the rest of the program can see those constants, too. Instance variables, of course, are visible strictly per object. A class isn't the same object as any of its instances, and no two of its instances are the same as each other. Therefore it's impossible, by definition, for a class to share instance variables with its instances.

So class variables have a niche to fill: visibility to a class and its instances, and to no one else. Typically, this means being visible in class-method definitions and instance-method definitions, and sometimes at the top level of the class definition.

Here's an example: a little tracker for cars. Let's start with a trial run and the output; then, we'll look at how the program works. Let's say we want to register the makes (manufacturer names) of cars, which we'll do using the class method `Car.add_make(make)`. Once a make has been registered, we can create cars of that make, using `Car.new(make)`. We'll register Honda and Ford, and create two Hondas and one Ford:

```
Car.add_make("Honda")
Car.add_make("Ford")
h = Car.new("Honda")
f = Car.new("Ford")
h2 = Car.new("Honda")
```

The program tells us which cars are being created:

```
Creating a new Honda!
Creating a new Ford!
Creating a new Honda!
```

At this point, we can get back some information. How many cars are there of the same make as h2? We'll use the instance method `make_mates` to find out, interpolating the result into a string:

```
puts "Counting cars of same make as h2..."
puts "There are #{h2.make_mates}."
```

As expected, there are two cars of the same make as h2 (namely, Honda).

How many cars are there altogether? Knowledge of this kind resides in the class, not in the individual cars, so we ask the class:

```
puts "Counting total cars..."
puts "There are #{Car.total_count}."
```

The output is

```
Counting total cars...
There are 3.
```

Finally, we try to create a car of a nonexistent make:

```
x = Car.new("Brand X")
```

The program doesn't like it, and we get a fatal error:

```
car.rb:21:in `initialize': No such make: Brand X. (RuntimeError)
```

The main action here is in the creation of cars and the ability of both individual cars and the Car class to store and return statistics about the cars that have been created. The next listing shows the program. If you save this listing and then add the previous sample code to the end of the file, you can run the whole file and see the output of the code.

Listing 5.6   Keeping track of car manufacturing statistics with class variables

```
class Car
  @@makes = []
  @@cars = {}                                    ❶
  @@total_count = 0
  attr_reader :make                              ❷
  def self.total_count                ◁──❸
    @@total_count
  end
  def self.add_make(make)             ◁──❹
    unless @@makes.include?(make)
      @@makes << make
      @@cars[make] = 0
    end
  end
  def initialize(make)
    if @@makes.include?(make)
      puts "Creating a new #{make}!"              ❺
      @make = make                    ◁──
      @@cars[make] += 1               ◁──❻
      @@total_count += 1
    else      raise "No such make: #{make}."  ◁──❼
    end
  end
  def make_mates                      ◁──❽
    @@cars[self.make]
  end
end
```

The key to the program is the presence of the three class variables defined at the top of the class definition ❶. @@makes is an array and stores the names of makes. @@cars is a *hash*: a keyed structure whose keys are makes of cars and whose corresponding values are counts of how many of each make there are. Finally, @@total_count is a running tally of how many cars have been created overall.

The Car class also has a make reader attribute ❷, which enables us to ask every car what its make is. The value of the make attribute must be set when the car is created. There's no writer attribute for makes of cars, because we don't want code outside the class changing the makes of cars that already exist.

To provide access to the @@total_count class variable, the Car class defines a total_count method ❸, which returns the current value of the class variable. There's also a class method called add_make ❹; this method takes a single argument and adds it to the array of known makes of cars, using the << array-append operator. It first takes the precaution of making sure the array of makes doesn't already include this particular make. Assuming all is well, it adds the make and also sets the counter for this make's car tally to zero. Thus when we register the make Honda, we also establish the fact that zero Hondas exist.

Now we get to the `initialize` method, where new cars are created. Each new car needs a make. If the make doesn't exist (that is, if it isn't in the `@@makes` array), then we raise a fatal error **❼**. If the make does exist, then we set this car's `make` attribute to the appropriate value **❺**, increment by one the number of cars of this make that are recorded in the `@@cars` hash **❻**, and also increment by one the total number of existing cars stored in `@@total_count`. (You may have surmised that `@@total_count` represents the total of all the values in `@@cars`. Storing the total separately saves us the trouble of adding up all the values every time we want to see the total.) There's also an implementation of the instance method `make_mates` **❽**, which returns a list of all cars of a given car's make.

The `initialize` method makes heavy use of the class variables defined at the top, outer level of the class definition—a totally different local scope from the inside of `initialize`, but not different for purposes of class-variable visibility. Those class variables were also used in the class methods `Car.total_count` and `Car.add_make`—each of which also has its own local scope. You can see that class variables follow their own rules: their visibility and scope don't line up with those of local variables, and they cut across multiple values of self. (Remember that at the outer level of a class definition and inside the class methods, self is the class object—`Car`—whereas in the instance methods, self is the instance of `Car` that's calling the method.)

So far, you've seen the simplest aspects of class variables. Even at this level, opinions differ as to whether, or at least how often, it's a good idea to create variables that cut this path across multiple self objects. Does the fact that a car is an instance of `Car` really mean that the `car` object and the `Car` class object need to share data? Or should they be treated throughout like the two separate objects they are?

There's no single (or simple) answer. But there's a little more to how class variables work; and at the very least, you'll probably conclude that they should be handled with care.

CLASS VARIABLES AND THE CLASS HIERARCHY

As noted earlier, class variables aren't class-scoped variables. They're class-hierarchy-scoped variables.

Here's an example. What would you expect the following code to print?

```
class Parent
  @@value = 100          ◁─┐  Sets class variable
end                          │  in class Parent
class Child < Parent
  @@value = 200          ◁─┐  Sets class variable in class
end                          │  Child, a subclass of Parent
class Parent
  puts @@value          ◁─┐  Back in Parent class:
end                          │  what's the output?
```

What gets printed is 200. The Child class is a subclass of Parent, and that means Parent and Child share the same class variables—not different class variables with the same names, but the same actual variables. When you assign to @@value in Child, you're setting the one and only @@value variable that's shared throughout the hierarchy—that is, by Parent and Child and any other descendant classes of either of them. The term *class variable* becomes a bit difficult to reconcile with the fact that two (and potentially a lot more) classes share exactly the same ones.

As promised, we'll end this section with a consideration of the pros and cons of using class variables as a way to maintain state in a class.

EVALUATING THE PROS AND CONS OF CLASS VARIABLES

The bread-and-butter way to maintain state in an object is the instance variable. Class variables come in handy because they break down the dam between a class object and instances of that class. But by so doing, and especially because of their hierarchy-based scope, they take on a kind of quasi-global quality: a class variable isn't global, but it sure is visible to a lot of objects, once you add up all the subclasses and all the instances of those subclasses.

The issue at hand is that it's useful to have a way to maintain state in a class. You saw this even in the simple Car class example. We wanted somewhere to stash class-relevant information, like the makes of cars and the total number of cars manufactured. We also wanted to get at that information, both from class methods and from instance methods. Class variables are popular because they're the easiest way to distribute data in that configuration.

But they're also leaky. Too many objects can get hold of them. Let's say we wanted to create a subclass of Car called Hybrid to keep a count of manufactured (partly) electric vehicles. We couldn't do this:

```
class Hybrid < Car
end
hy = Hybrid.new("Honda")
puts "There are #{Hybrid.total_count} hybrids in existence!"
```

because Hybrid.total_count is the same method as Car.total_count, and it wraps the same variable. Class variables aren't reissued freshly for every subclass, the way instance variables are for every object.

To track hybrids separately, we'd have to do something like this:

```
class Hybrid < Car
  @@total_hybrid_count = 0
  # etc.
end
```

Although there are ways to abstract and semi-automate this kind of splitting out of code by class namespace, it's not the easiest or most transparent technique in the world.

What's the alternative?

MAINTAINING PER-CLASS STATE WITH INSTANCE VARIABLES OF CLASS OBJECTS

The alternative is to go back to basics. We need a slot where we can put a value (the total count), and it should be a different slot for every class. In other words, we need to maintain state on a per-class basis; and because classes are objects, that means on a per-object basis (for a certain group of objects, namely, class objects). And per-object state, whether the object in question is a class or something else, suggests instance variables.

The following listing shows a rewrite of the Car class in listing 5.6. Two of the class variables are still there, but @@total_count has been transformed into an instance variable.

Listing 5.7   Car with @@total_count replaced by instance variable @total_count

```
class Car
  @@makes = []
  @@cars = {}
  attr_reader :make
  def self.total_count
    @total_count ||= 0                          ← ❶
  end
  def self.total_count=(n)
    @total_count = n                            ← ❷
  end
  def self.add_make(make)
    unless @@makes.include?(make)
      @@makes << make
      @@cars[make] = 0
    end
  end
  def initialize(make)
    if @@makes.include?(make)
      puts "Creating a new #{make}!"
      @make = make
      @@cars[make] += 1
      self.class.total_count += 1               ← ❸
    else
      raise "No such make: #{make}."
    end
  end
  def make_mates
    @@cars[self.make]
  end
end
```

The key here is storing the counter in an instance variable belonging to the class object Car, and wrapping that instance variable in accessor methods—manually written ones, but accessor methods nonetheless. The accessor methods are Car.total_count and Car.total_count=. The first of these performs the task of initializing @total_count to zero ❶. It does the initialization conditionally, using the or-equals operator, so that on the second and subsequent calls to total_count, the value of the instance variable is simply returned.

The total_count= method is an attribute-writer method, likewise written as a class method so that the object whose instance variable is in use is the class object ❷. With these methods in place, we can now increment the total count from inside the instance method `initialize` by calling `self.class.total_count=` **③**.

The payoff comes when we subclass `Car`. Let's have another look at `Hybrid` and some sample code that uses it:

```
class Hybrid < Car
end
h3 = Hybrid.new("Honda")
f2 = Hybrid.new("Ford")
puts "There are #{Hybrid.total_count} hybrids on the road!"
```

Output: There are 2 hybrids on the road!

`Hybrid` is a new class object. It isn't the same object as `Car`. Therefore, it has its own instance variables. When we create a new `Hybrid` instance, the `initialize` method from `Car` is executed. But this time, the expression

```
self.class.total_count += 1
```

has a different meaning. The receiver of the "total_count=" message is `Hybrid`, not `Car`. That means when the `total_count=` class method is executed, the instance variable `@total_count` belongs to `Hybrid`. (Instance variables always belong to self.) Adding to `Hybrid`'s total count therefore won't affect `Car`'s total count.

We've made it so that a subclass of `Car` can maintain its own state, because we've shifted from a class variable to an instance variable. Every time `total_count` or `total_count=` is called, the `@total_count` to which it refers is the one belonging to self at that point in execution. Once again, we're back in business using instance variables to maintain state per object (class objects, in this case).

The biggest obstacle to understanding these examples is understanding the fact that classes are objects—and that every object, whether it's a car, a person, *or a class*, gets to have its own stash of instance variables. `Car` and `Hybrid` can keep track of manufacturing numbers separately, thanks to the way instance variables are quarantined per object.

We've reached the limit of our identifier scope journey. You've seen much of what variables and constants can do (and what they can't do) and how these abilities are pegged to the rules governing scope and self. In the interest of fulfilling the chapter's goal of showing you how to orient yourself regarding who gets to do what, and where, in Ruby code, we'll look at one more major subtopic: Ruby's system of method-access rules.

5.3   *Deploying method-access rules*

As you've seen, the main business of a Ruby program is to send messages to objects. And the main business of an object is to respond to messages. Sometimes, an object wants to be able to send itself messages that it doesn't want anyone else to be able to send it. For this scenario, Ruby provides the ability to make a method private.

There are two access levels other than private: protected, which is a slight variation on private, and public. Public is the default access level; if you don't specify that a method is protected or private, it's public. Public instance methods are the common currency of Ruby programming. Most of the messages you send to objects are calling public methods.

We'll focus here on methods that aren't public, starting with private methods.

5.3.1 Private methods

Think of an object as someone you ask to perform a task for you. Let's say you ask someone to bake you a cake. In the course of baking you a cake, the baker will presumably perform a lot of small tasks: measure sugar, crack an egg, stir batter, and so forth.

The baker does all these things, but not all of them have equal status when it comes to what the baker is willing to do in response to requests from other people. It would be weird if you called a baker and said, "Please stir some batter" or "Please crack an egg." What you say is "Please bake me a cake," and you let the baker deal with the details.

Let's model the baking scenario. We'll use minimal, placeholder classes for some of the objects in our domain, but we'll develop the `Baker` class in more detail.

Save the code in the following listing to a file called baker.rb.

Listing 5.8 `Baker` and other baking-domain classes

```
class Cake
  def initialize(batter)
    @batter = batter
    @baked = true
  end
end
class Egg
end
class Flour
end
class Baker
  def bake_cake
    @batter = []                        Implements @batter as array
    pour_flour                          of objects (ingredients)
    add_egg
    stir_batter
    return Cake.new(@batter)            Returns new
  end                                   Cake object
  def pour_flour
    @batter.push(Flour.new)
  end                                   Adds element (ingredient)
  def add_egg                           to @batter
    @batter.push(Egg.new)
  end
  def stir_batter
  end
  private :pour_flour, :add_egg, :stir_batter    ←—❶
end
```

There's something new in this code: the `private` method ❶, which takes as arguments a list of the methods you want to make private. (If you don't supply any arguments, the call to `private` acts like an on switch: all the instance methods you define below it, until you reverse the effect by calling `public` or `protected`, will be private.)

Private means that the method can't be called with an explicit receiver. You can't say

```
b = Baker.new
b.add_egg
```

As you'll see if you try it, calling `add_egg` this way results in a fatal error:

```
`<main>': private method `add_egg' called for #<Baker:0x00000002aeae50>
    (NoMethodError)
```

`add_egg` is a private method, but you've specified the receiving object, b, explicitly. That's not allowed.

Okay; let's go along with the rules. We won't specify a receiver. We'll just say

```
add_egg
```

But wait. Can we call `add_egg` in isolation? Where will the message go? How can a method be called if there's no object handling the message?

A little detective work will answer this question.

If you don't use an explicit receiver for a method call, Ruby assumes that you want to send the message to the current object, self. Thinking logically, you can conclude that the message `add_egg` has an object to go to only if self is an object that responds to `add_egg`. In other words, you can only call the `add_egg` instance method of `Baker` when self is an instance of `Baker`.

And when is self an instance of `Baker`?

When any instance method of `Baker` is being executed. Inside the definition of `bake_cake`, for example, you can call `add_egg`, and Ruby will know what to do. Whenever Ruby hits that call to `add_egg` inside that method definition, it sends the message `add_egg` to self, and self is a `Baker` object.

Private and singleton are different

It's important to note the difference between a private method and a singleton method. A singleton method is "private" in the loose, informal sense that it belongs to only one object, but it isn't private in the technical sense. (You can make a singleton method private, but by default it isn't.) A private, non-singleton instance method, on the other hand, may be shared by any number of objects but can only be called under the right circumstances. What determines whether you can call a private method isn't the object you're sending the message to, but which object is self at the time you send the message.

It comes down to this: by tagging `add_egg` as private, you're saying the `Baker` object gets to send this message to itself (the baker can tell himself or herself to add an egg to the batter), but no one else can send the message to the baker (you, as an outsider, can't tell the baker to add an egg to the batter). Ruby enforces this privacy through the mechanism of forbidding an explicit receiver. And the only circumstances under which you can omit the receiver are precisely the circumstances in which it's okay to call a private method.

It's all elegantly engineered. There's one small fly in the ointment, though.

PRIVATE SETTER (=) METHODS

The implementation of private access through the "no explicit receiver" rule runs into a hitch when it comes to methods that end with equal signs. As you'll recall, when you call a setter method, you have to specify the receiver. You can't do this

```
dog_years = age * 7
```

because Ruby will think that dog_years is a local variable. You have to do this:

```
self.dog_years = age * 7
```

But the need for an explicit receiver makes it hard to declare the method dog_years= private, at least by the logic of the "no explicit receiver" requirement for calling private methods.

The way out of this conundrum is that Ruby doesn't apply the rule to setter methods. If you declare dog_years= private, you can call it with a receiver—as long as the receiver is self. It can't be another reference to self; it has to be the keyword self.

Here's an implementation of a dog-years-aware Dog:

```
class Dog
  attr_reader :age, :dog_years
  def dog_years=(years)
    @dog_years = years
  end
  def age=(years)
    @age = years
    self.dog_years = years * 7
  end
  private :dog_years=
end
```

You indicate how old a dog is, and the dog automatically knows its age in dog years:

```
rover = Dog.new
rover.age = 10
puts "Rover is #{rover.dog_years} in dog years."
```
Output: Rover is 70 in dog years

The setter method age= performs the service of setting the dog years, which it does by calling the private method dog_years=. In doing so, it uses the explicit receiver self. If you do it any other way, it won't work. With no receiver, you'd be setting a local variable. And if you use the same object, but under a different name, like this

```
def age=(years)
  @age = years
  dog = self
  dog.dog_years = years * 7
end
```

execution is halted by a fatal error:

```
NoMethodError: private method 'dog_years=' called for
#<Dog:0x00000101b0d1a8 @age=10>
```

Ruby's policy is that it's okay to use an explicit receiver for private setter methods, but you have to thread the needle by making sure the receiver is exactly `self`.

The third method-access level, along with public and private, is protected.

5.3.2   Protected methods

A protected method is like a slightly kinder, gentler private method. The rule for protected methods is as follows: you can call a protected method on an object x, as long as the default object (self) is an instance of the same class as x or of an ancestor or descendant class of x's class.

This rule sounds convoluted. But it's generally used for a particular reason: you want one instance of a certain class to do something with another instance of its class. The following listing shows such a case.

Listing 5.9   Example of a protected method and its use

```
class C
  def initialize(n)
    @n = n
  end
  def n
    @n
  end
  def compare(c)
    if c.n > n
      puts "The other object's n is bigger."
    else
      puts "The other object's n is the same or smaller."
    end
  end
  protected :n
end
c1 = C.new(100)
c2 = C.new(101)              Output: The other
c1.compare(c2)              object's n is bigger.
```

The goal in this listing is to compare one C instance with another C instance. The comparison depends on the result of a call to the method n. The object doing the comparing (c1, in the example) has to ask the other object (c2) to execute its n method. Therefore, n can't be private.

That's where the protected level comes in. With n protected rather than private, c1 can ask c2 to execute n, because c1 and c2 are both instances of the same class. But if you try to call the n method of a C object when self is anything other than an instance of C (or of one of C's ancestors or descendants), the method fails.

A protected method is thus like a private method, but with an exemption for cases where the class of self (c1) and the class of the object having the method called on it (c2) are the same or related by inheritance.

Inheritance and method access

Subclasses inherit the method-access rules of their superclasses. Given a class C with a set of access rules, and a class D that's a subclass of C, instances of D exhibit the same access behavior as instances of C. But you can set up new rules inside the class definition of D, in which case the new rules take precedence for instances of D over the rules inherited from C.

The last topic we'll cover in this chapter is top-level methods. As you'll see, top-level methods enjoy a special case status. But even this status meshes logically with the aspects of Ruby's design you've encountered in this chapter.

5.4 Writing and using top-level methods

The most natural thing to do with Ruby is to design classes and modules and instantiate your classes. But sometimes you just want to write a quick script—a few commands stuffed in a file and executed. It's sometimes more convenient to write method definitions at the top level of your script and then call them on top-level objects than to wrap everything in class definitions. When you do this, you're coding in the context of the top-level default object, main, which is an instance of Object brought into being automatically for the sole reason that *something* has to be self, even at the top level.

But you're not inside a class or module definition, so what exactly happens when you define a method?

5.4.1 Defining a top-level method

Suppose you define a method at the top level:

```
def talk
  puts "Hello"
end
```

It's not inside a class- or module-definition block, so it doesn't appear to be an instance method of a class or module. So what is it?

A method that you define at the top level is stored as a private instance method of the Object class. The previous code is equivalent to this:

```
class Object
  private
  def talk
    puts "Hello"
  end
end
```

Defining private instance methods of `Object` has some interesting implications.

First, these methods not only can but *must* be called in bareword style. Why? Because they're private. You can only call them on self, and only without an explicit receiver (with the usual exemption of private setter methods, which must be called with `self` as the receiver).

Second, private instance methods of `Object` can be called from anywhere in your code, because `Object` lies in the method lookup path of every class (except `Basic-Object`, but that's too special a case to worry about). So a top-level method is always available. No matter what self is, it will be able to recognize the message you send it if that message resolves to a private instance method of `Object`.

To illustrate, let's extend the `talk` example. Here it is again, with some code that exercises it:

```
def talk
  puts "Hello"
end
puts "Trying 'talk' with no receiver..."
talk                                                    ←──❶
puts "Trying 'talk' with an explicit receiver..."
obj = Object.new                                            ❷
obj.talk                                                ←──┘
```

The first call to `talk` succeeds ❶; the second fails with a fatal error ❷, because it tries to call a private method with an explicit receiver.

What's nice about the way top-level methods work is that they provide a useful functionality (simple, script-friendly, procedural-style bareword commands), but they do so in complete conformity with the rules of Ruby: private methods have to default to self as the receiver, and methods defined in `Object` are visible to all objects. No extra language-level constructs are involved, just an elegant and powerful combination of the ones that already exist.

The rules concerning definition and use of top-level methods bring us all the way back to some of the bareword methods we've been using since as early as chapter 1. You're now in a position to understand how those methods work.

5.4.2 *Predefined (built-in) top-level methods*

From our earliest examples onward, we've been making bareword-style calls to `puts` and `print`, like this one:

```
puts "Hello"
```

`puts` and `print` are built-in private instance methods of `Kernel`—not, like the ones you write, of `Object`, but of `Kernel`. The upshot is similar, though (because `Object` mixes in `Kernel`): you can call such methods at any time, and you must call them without a receiver. The `Kernel` module thus provides a substantial toolkit of imperative methods, like `puts` and `print`, that increases the power of Ruby as a scripting language. You can get a lot done with Ruby scripts that don't have any class, module, or method definitions, because you can do so much (read and write, run system commands, exit your program, and so on) with Ruby's top-level methods.

If you want to see all of the private instance methods that `Kernel` provides, try this:

```
$ ruby -e 'p Kernel.private_instance_methods.sort'
```

The `private_instance_methods` method gives you an array of all the relevant methods, and `sort` sorts the array of method names for easier reading. As you can see, these methods, although often useful in imperative, script-style programming, aren't restricted in their usefulness to that style; they include commands like `require`, `load`, `raise` (raise an exception), and others, that are among the most common techniques in all Ruby programs, whatever style of program design they exhibit.

5.5 Summary

This chapter covered

- The rotating role of self (the current or default object)
- Self as the receiver for method calls with no explicit receiver
- Self as the owner of instance variables
- Implications of the "classes are objects too" rule
- Variable scope and visibility for local, global, and class variables
- The rules for looking up and referencing constants
- Ruby's method-access levels (public, private, protected)
- Writing and working with top-level method definitions

The techniques in this chapter are of great importance to Ruby. Concepts like the difference between instance variables in a class definition and instance variables in an instance-method definition are crucial. It's easy to look at a Ruby program and get a general sense of what's going on. But to understand a program in depth—and to write well-organized, robust programs—you need to know how to detect where the various local scopes begin and end; how constants, instance variables, and other identifiers are resolved; and how to evaluate the impact of the ever-shifting role of self.

This chapter has shown you how to get your bearings in a Ruby program. It's also shown you some techniques you can use more accurately and effectively in your code by virtue of having your bearings. But there's more to explore, relating to what you can do in the landscape of a program, beyond understanding it. The next chapter, on the subject of control flow, will address some of these techniques.

Control-flow techniques

As you've already seen in the case of method calls—where control of the program jumps from the spot where the call is made to the body of the method definition—programs don't run in a straight line. Instead, execution order is determined by a variety of rules and programming constructs collectively referred to as *control-flow* techniques.

Ruby's control-flow techniques include the following:

- *Conditional execution*—Execution depends on the truth of an expression.
- *Looping*—A single segment of code is executed repeatedly.
- *Iteration*—A call to a method is supplemented with a segment of code that the method can call one or more times during its own execution.
- *Exceptions*—Error conditions are handled by special control-flow rules.

We'll look at each of these in turn. They're all indispensable to both the understanding and the practice of Ruby. The first, conditional execution (if and friends), is a fundamental and straightforward programming tool in almost any programming language. Looping is a more specialized but closely related technique, and Ruby provides you with several ways to do it. When we get to iteration, we'll be in true Ruby hallmark territory. The technique isn't unique to Ruby, but it's a relatively rare programming language feature that figures prominently in Ruby. Finally, we'll look at Ruby's extensive mechanism for handling error conditions through exceptions. Exceptions stop the flow of a program, either completely or until the error condition has been dealt with. Exceptions are objects, and you can create your own exception classes, inheriting from the ones built in to Ruby, for specialized handling of error conditions in your programs.

6.1 Conditional code execution

Allow a user access to a site if the password is correct. Print an error message unless the requested item exists. Concede defeat if the king is checkmated. The list of uses for controlling the flow of a program conditionally—executing specific lines or segments of code only if certain conditions are met—is endless. Without getting too philosophical, we might even say that decision making based on unpredictable but discernible conditions is as common in programming as it is in life.

Ruby gives you a number of ways to control program flow on a conditional basis. The most important ones fall into two categories:

- if and related keywords
- Case statements

We'll look at both in this section.

6.1.1 The if keyword and friends

The workhorse of conditional execution, not surprisingly, is the if keyword. if clauses can take several forms. The simplest is the following:

```
if condition
  # code here, executed if condition is true
end
```

The code inside the conditional can be any length and can include nested conditional blocks.

You can also put an entire if clause on a single line, using the then keyword after the condition:

```
if x > 10 then puts x end
```

You can also use semicolons to mimic the line breaks, and to set off the end keyword:

```
if x > 10; puts x; end
```

Conditional execution often involves more than one branch; you may want to do one thing if the condition succeeds and another if it doesn't. For example, *if the password is correct, let the user in; otherwise, print an error message.* Ruby makes full provisions for multiple conditional branches, using else and elsif.

THE ELSE AND ELSIF KEYWORDS

You can provide an else branch in your if statement as follows:

```
if condition
  # code executed if condition is true
else
  # code executed if condition is false
end
```

There's also an elsif keyword (spelled like that, with no second *e*). elsif lets you cascade your conditional logic to more levels than you can with just if and else:

```
if condition1
  # code executed if condition1 is true
elsif condition2
  # code executed if condition1 is false
  # and condition2 is true
elsif condition3
  # code executed if neither condition1
  # nor condition2 is true, but condition3 is
end
```

You can have any number of elsif clauses in a given if statement. The code segment corresponding to the first successful if or elsif is executed, and the rest of the statement is ignored:

```
print "Enter an integer: "
n = gets.to_i
if n > 0
  puts "Your number is positive."
elsif n < 0
  puts "Your number is negative."
else
  puts "Your number is zero."
end
```

Note that you can use a final else even if you already have one or more elsifs. The else clause is executed if none of the previous tests for truth has succeeded. If none of the conditions is true and there's no else clause, the whole if statement terminates with no action.

Sometimes you want an if condition to be negative: *if something isn't true, then execute a given segment of code.* You can do this in several ways.

NEGATING CONDITIONS WITH NOT AND !

One way to negate a condition is to use the not keyword:

```
if not (x == 1)
```

You can also use the negating ! (exclamation point, or *bang*) operator:

```
if !(x == 1)
```

Both of these examples use parentheses to set apart the expression being tested. You don't need them in the first example; you can do this:

```
if not x == 1
```

But you *do* need the parentheses in the second example, because the negating ! operator has higher precedence than the == operator. In other words, if you do this

```
if !x == 1
```

you're really, in effect, comparing the negation of x with the integer 1:

```
if (!x) == 1
```

The best practice is to use parentheses most or even all of the time when writing constructs like this. Even if they're not strictly necessary, they can make it easier for you and others to understand your code and to modify it later if necessary.

A third way to express a negative condition is with unless.

THE UNLESS KEYWORD

The unless keyword provides a more natural-sounding way to express the same semantics as if not or if !:

```
unless x == 1
```

But take "natural-sounding" with a grain of salt. Ruby programs are written in Ruby, not English, and you should aim for good Ruby style without worrying unduly about how your code reads as English prose. Not that English can't occasionally guide you; for instance, the unless/else sequence, which does a flip back from a negative to a positive not normally associated with the use of the word *unless*, can be a bit hard to follow:

```
unless x > 100
  puts "Small number!"
else
  puts "Big number!"
end
```

In general, if/else reads better than unless/else—and by flipping the logic of the condition, you can always replace the latter with the former:

```
if x <= 100
  puts "Small number!"
else
  puts "Big number!"
end
```

If you come across a case where negating the logic seems more awkward than pairing unless with else, then keep unless. Otherwise, if you have an else clause, if is generally a better choice than unless.

Life without the dangling `else` ambiguity

In some languages, you can't tell which `else` clause goes with which `if` clause without a special rule. In C, for example, an `if` statement might look like this:

```
if (x)
    if (y) { execute this code }
    else   { execute this code };
```
x is true,
but y isn't

But wait: Does the code behave the way the indentation indicates (the `else` belongs to the second `if`)? Or does it work like this?

```
if (x)
    if (y) { execute this code }
else { execute this code };
```
x isn't true

All that's changed is the indentation of the third line (which doesn't matter to the C compiler; the indentation just makes the ambiguity visually obvious). Which `if` does the `else` belong to? And how do you tell?

You tell by knowing the rule in C: a dangling `else` goes with the last unmatched `if` (the first of the two behaviors in this example). But in Ruby, you have `end` to help you out:

```
if x > 50
  if x > 100
    puts "Big number"
  else
    puts "Medium number"
  end
end
```

The single `else` in this statement has to belong to the second `if`, because that `if` hasn't yet hit its end. The first `if` and the last `end` always belong together, the second `if` and the second-to-last `end` always belong together, and so forth. The `if`/`end` pairs encircle what belongs to them, including `else`. Of course, this means you have to place your `end` keywords correctly.

You can also put conditional tests in *modifier* position, directly after a statement.

CONDITIONAL MODIFIERS

It's not uncommon to see a conditional modifier at the end of a statement in a case like this one:

```
puts "Big number!" if x > 100
```

This is the same as

```
if x > 100
  puts "Big number!"
end
```

You can also do this with `unless`:

```
puts "Big number!" unless x <= 100
```

Conditional modifiers have a conversational tone. There's no end to worry about. You can't do as much with them (no else or elsif branching, for example), but when you need a simple conditional, they're often a good fit. Try to avoid really long statements that end with conditional modifiers, though; they can be hard to read, and hard to keep in your head while waiting for the modifier at the end:

```
puts "done" && return (x > y && a < b) unless c == 0
```
◁─ **Potentially confusing tacking on of an unless to an already-long line**

Like other statements in Ruby, every if statement evaluates to an object. Let's look at how that plays out.

THE VALUE OF IF STATEMENTS

If an if statement succeeds, the entire statement evaluates to whatever is represented by the code in the successful branch. Type this code into irb and you'll see this principle in action:

```
x = 1
if x < 0
  "negative"
elsif x > 0
  "positive"
else
  "zero"
end
```

As irb will tell you, the value of that entire if statement is the string "positive".

An if statement that doesn't succeed anywhere returns nil. Here's a full irb example of such a case:

```
>> x = 1
=> 1
>> if x == 2
>>   "it's 2!"
>> elsif x == 3
>>   "it's 3!"
>> end
=> nil
```
◁─ **Entire if statement evaluates to nil because it fails**

Conditional statements interact with other aspects of Ruby syntax in a couple of ways that you need to be aware of—in particular, with assignment syntax. It's worth looking in some detail at how conditionals behave in assignments, because it involves some interesting points about how Ruby parses code.

6.1.2 Assignment syntax in condition bodies and tests

Assignment syntax and conditional expressions cross paths at two points: in the bodies of conditional expressions, where the assignments may or may not happen at all, and in the conditional tests themselves:

```
if x = 1
   y = 2                                          Assignment in
end            Assignment in                      conditional test
               conditional body
```

What happens (or doesn't) when you use these idioms? We'll look at both, starting with variable assignment in the body of the conditional—specifically, local variable assignment, which displays some perhaps unexpected behavior in this context.

LOCAL VARIABLE ASSIGNMENT IN A CONDITIONAL BODY

Ruby doesn't draw as clear a line as compiled languages do between "compile time" and "runtime," but the interpreter does parse your code before running it, and certain decisions are made during that process. An important one is the recognition and allocation of local variables.

When the Ruby parser sees the sequence *identifier, equal-sign,* and *value,* as in this expression,

```
x = 1
```

it allocates space for a local variable called x. The creation of the variable—not the assignment of a value to it, but the internal creation of a variable—always takes place as a result of this kind of expression, even if the code isn't executed!

Consider this example:

```
if false
   x = 1
end                   Output: nil
p x                                     Fatal error:
p y                                     y is unknown
```

The assignment to x isn't executed, because it's wrapped in a failing conditional test. But the Ruby parser sees the sequence x = 1, from which it deduces that the program involves a local variable x. The parser doesn't care whether x is ever assigned a value. Its job is just to scour the code for local variables for which space needs to be allocated.

The result is that x inhabits a strange kind of variable limbo. It has been brought into being and initialized to `nil`. In that respect, it differs from a variable that has no existence at all; as you can see in the example, examining x gives you the value `nil`, whereas trying to inspect the nonexistent variable y results in a fatal error. But although x exists, it hasn't played any role in the program. It exists only as an artifact of the parsing process.

None of this happens with class, instance, or global variables. All three of those variable types are recognizable by their appearance (@@x, @x, $x). But local variables look just like method calls. Ruby needs to apply some logic at parse time to figure out what's what, to as great an extent as it can.

You also have to keep your wits about you when using assignment syntax in the test part of a conditional.

ASSIGNMENT IN A CONDITIONAL TEST

In this example, note that the conditional test is an assignment (x = 1) and not an equality test (which would be x==1):

```
if x = 1
  puts "Hi!"
end
```

The assignment works as assignments generally do: x gets set to 1. The test, therefore, reduces to if 1, which is true. Therefore, the body of the conditional is executed, and the string "Hi!" is printed.

But you also get a warning:

```
warning: found = in conditional, should be ==
```

Ruby's thinking in a case like this is as follows. The test expression if x = 1 will always succeed, and the conditional body will always be executed. That means there's no conceivable reason for a programmer ever to type if x = 1. Therefore, Ruby concludes that you almost certainly meant to type something else and issues the warning to alert you to the probable mistake. Specifically, the warning suggests the == operator, which produces a real test (that is, a test that isn't necessarily always true).

What's particularly nice about this warning mechanism is that Ruby is smart enough not to warn you in cases where it's not certain that the condition will be true. If the right-hand side of the assignment is itself a variable or method call, then you don't get the warning:

```
if x = y                    ◁── No warning
```

Unlike x = 1, the assignment expression x = y may or may not succeed as a conditional test. (It will be false if y is false.) Therefore, it's not implausible that you'd test that expression, so Ruby doesn't warn you.

Why would you want to use an assignment in a conditional test? You certainly never have to; you can always do this:

```
x = y
if x
# etc.
```

But sometimes it's handy to do the assigning and testing at the same time, particularly when you're using a method that returns nil on failure and some other value on success. A common example is pattern matching with the match method. This method, which you'll see a lot more of in chapter 11, tests a string against a regular expression, returning nil if there's no match and an instance of MatchData if there is one. The MatchData object can be queried for information about the specifics of the match. Note the use of a literal regular expression, /la/, in the course of testing for a match against the string name:

```
name = "David A. Black"
if m = /la/.match(name)                              ←——❶
  puts "Found a match!"
  print "Here's the unmatched start of the string: "
  puts m.pre_match
  print "Here's the unmatched end of the string: "
  puts m.post_match
else
  puts "No match"
end
```

The output from this snippet is

```
Found a match!
Here's the unmatched start of the string: David A. B
Here's the unmatched end of the string: ck
```

The match method looks for the pattern la in the string "David A. Black". The variable m is assigned in the conditional ❶ and will be nil if there's no match. The deck is stacked in the example, of course: there's a match, so m is a MatchData object and can be queried. In the example, we ask it about the parts of the string that occurred before and after the matched part of the string, and it gives us the relevant substrings.

As always, you could rewrite the assignment and the conditional test like this:

```
m = /la/.match(name)
if m
  # etc.
```

You don't have to combine them into one expression. But at least in this case there's some semantic weight to doing so: the expression may or may not pass the conditional test, so it's reasonable to test it.

Although if and friends are Ruby's bread-and-butter conditional keywords, they're not the only ones. We'll look next at case statements.

6.1.3   *case statements*

A case statement starts with an expression—usually a single object or variable, but any expression can be used—and walks it through a list of possible matches. Each possible match is contained in a when statement consisting of one or more possible matching objects and a segment of code. When one of the terms in a given when clause matches, that when is considered to have "won," and its code segment is executed. Only one match, at most, can win.

case statements are easier to grasp by example than by description. The following listing shows a case statement that tests a line of keyboard input and branches based on its value.

Listing 6.1   Interpreting user input with a case statement

```
print "Exit the program? (yes or no): "
answer = gets.chomp                      ←┐   Chomps off trailing newline
case answer                              ←——❶   character on input string
```

```
when "yes"
  puts "Good-bye!"                   ◄─┐
  exit                                 ❷
when "no"
  puts "OK, we'll continue"
else                                            ◄──❸
  puts "That's an unknown answer -- assuming you meant 'no'"
end                                             ◄──❹
puts "Continuing with program...."
```

The case statement begins with the case keyword ❶, continues through all the when blocks ❷ and an (optional) else clause ❸, and ends with the end keyword ❹. At most, one match will succeed and have its code executed. If it's the one belonging to "yes", then the program exits. Any other input is either "no" or some other value, which this particular program interprets as equivalent to "no", causing the program to continue running.

You can put more than one possible match in a single when, as this snippet shows:

```
case answer
when "y", "yes"
  puts "Good-bye!"
  exit
    # etc.
```

The comma between multiple conditions in a when clause is a kind of "or" operator; this code will say "Good-bye!" and exit if answer is either "y" or "yes".

Let's look next at how when clauses work under the hood. You won't be surprised to learn that some message sending is involved.

HOW WHEN WORKS

The basic idea of the case/when structure is that you take an object and cascade through a series of tests for a match, taking action based on the test that succeeds. But what does *match* mean in this context? What does it mean, in our example, to say that answer matches the word *yes*, or the word *no*, or neither?

Ruby has a concrete definition of *match* when it comes to when statements.

Every Ruby object has a *case equality* method called === (three equal signs, sometimes called the *threequal operator*). The outcome of calling the === method determines whether a when clause has matched.

You can see this clearly if you look first at a case statement and then at a translation of this statement into threequal terms. Look again at the case statement in listing 6.1. Here's the same thing rewritten to use the threequal operator explicitly:

```
if "yes" === answer
  puts "Good-bye!"
  exit
elsif "no" === answer
  puts "OK, we'll continue"
else
  puts "That's an unknown answer—assuming you meant 'no'"
end
```

The === in infix operator position (that is, between a left-hand term and a right-hand term) is really syntactic sugar for a method call:

```
if "yes".===(answer)
```

A when statement wraps that method call in yet more sugar: you don't have to use === explicitly in either operator or method position. It's done for you.

That's the logic of the syntax. But why does

```
"yes" === answer
```

return true when answer contains "yes"?

The method call returns true because of how the threequal method is defined for strings. When you ask a string to threequal itself against another string (string1 === string2), you're asking it to compare its own contents character by character against the other string and report back true for a perfect match, or false otherwise.

The most important point in this explanation is the phrase "for strings." Every class (and, in theory, every individual object, although it's usually handled at the class level) can define its own === method and thus its own case-equality logic. For strings and, indeed, for any object that doesn't override it, === works the same as == (the basic string-equals-some-other-string test method). But other classes can define the threequal test any way they want.

case/when logic is thus really object === other_object logic in disguise; and object === other_object is really object.===(other_object) in disguise. By defining the threequal method however you wish for your own classes, you can exercise complete control over the way your objects behave inside a case statement.

PROGRAMMING OBJECTS' CASE STATEMENT BEHAVIOR

Let's say we decide that a Ticket object should match a when clause in a case statement based on its venue. We can bring this about by writing the appropriate threequal method. The following listing shows such a method, bundled with enough ticket functionality to make a complete working example.

Listing 6.2 Implementing case statement behavior for the Ticket class

```
class Ticket
  attr_accessor :venue, :date
  def initialize(venue, date)
    self.venue = venue
    self.date = date
  end
  def ===(other_ticket)                      ⬅—❶
    self.venue == other_ticket.venue
  end
end
ticket1 = Ticket.new("Town Hall", "07/08/13")
ticket2 = Ticket.new("Conference Center", "07/08/13")
ticket3 = Ticket.new("Town Hall", "08/09/13")
puts "ticket1 is for an event at: #{ticket1.venue}."
case ticket1
```

```
when ticket2
  puts "Same location as ticket2!"
when ticket3
  puts "Same location as ticket3!"
else
  puts "No match"
end
```

❷
❸

The output from this listing is as follows:

```
ticket1 is for an event at: Town Hall.
Same location as ticket3!
```

The match is found through the implicit use of the `===` instance method of the Ticket class ❶. Inside the case statement, the first when expression ❷ triggers a hidden call to `===`, equivalent to doing this:

```
if ticket2 === ticket1
```

Because the `===` method returns `true` or `false` based on a comparison of venues, and ticket2's venue isn't the same as ticket1's, the comparison between the two tickets returns `false`. Therefore, the body of the corresponding when clause isn't executed.

The next test is then performed: another threequal comparison between ticket1 and ticket3 ❸. This test returns `true`; the when expression succeeds, and the code in its body is executed.

This kind of interflow between method definitions (`===`) and code that doesn't look like it's calling methods (case/when) is typical of Ruby. The case/when structure provides an elegant way to perform cascaded conditional tests; and the fact that it's a bunch of `===` calls means you can make it do what you need by defining the `===` method in your classes.

The case statement also comes in a slightly abbreviated form, which lets you test directly for a truth value: case without a case expression.

THE SIMPLE CASE TRUTH TEST

If you start a case statement with the case keyword by itself—that is, with no test expression—followed by some when clauses, the first when clause whose condition is true will be the winner. Assuming an object user with first_name and last_name methods, you could imaginably write a case statement like this:

```
case
when user.first_name == "David", user.last_name == "Black"
  puts "You might be David Black."
when Time.now.wday == 5
  puts "You're not David Black, but at least it's Friday!"
else
  puts "You're not David Black, and it's not Friday."
end
```

Ordinal number for day of week (Sunday is 0)

The simple case keyword in this manner is an alternate way of writing an if statement. In fact, any case statement can be written as an if statement. case statements with explicit arguments to case are often considerably shorter than their if counterparts, which have to resort to calling === or other comparison methods. Those without explicit test arguments are usually no shorter than the equivalent if statements; for instance, the previous example would be written like this using if:

```
if user.first_name == "David" or user.last_name == "Black"
  puts "You might be David Black."
elsif Time.now.wday == 5
  puts "You're not David Black, but at least it's Friday!"
else
  puts "You're not David Black, and it's not Friday."
end
```

The advantage of the testless case statement is that it doesn't limit you to what you can test with === on a given object. When you have a choice between a testless case or an if, your choice will be based on your sense of what looks and reads best.

THE RETURN VALUE OF CASE STATEMENTS

An important final point to keep in mind about case statements is that every case statement evaluates to a single object. If there's a successful when or else clause, the return value of the entire case statement is the value returned by the code in that clause. Otherwise, if the case statement fails to find a match, the entire statement evaluates to nil, similar to if statements that fail.

Thus you could, for example, rewrite the conditionless example like this:

```
puts case
     when user.first_name == "David", user.last_name == "Black"
       "You might be David Black."
     when Time.now.wday == 5
       "You're not David Black, but at least it's Friday!"
     else
       "You're not David Black, and it's not Friday."
     end
```

In this version, the calls to puts have been extracted out of the when clauses; the whole case statement is dedicated to finding an argument to the single puts call on the left. That argument will be whichever of the three strings the case statement returns.

Conditionals like if and case/when let you control program flow by doing one thing instead of another. But sometimes you need to perform a single task again and again. This kind of repetition can be accomplished with loops, which we'll look at next.

6.2   *Repeating actions with loops*

Ruby's facilities for looping repeatedly through code also allow you to incorporate conditional logic: you can loop *while* a given condition is true (such as a variable being equal to a given value), and you can loop *until* a given condition is true. You can also break out of a loop *unconditionally*, terminating the loop at a certain point, and resume execution of the program after the loop.

We'll look at several ways to loop—starting, appropriately, with a method called loop.

6.2.1 *Unconditional looping with the loop method*

The `loop` method doesn't take any normal arguments: you just call it. It does, however, take a code block—that is, a delimited set of program instructions, written as part of the method call (the call to `loop`) and available to be executed *from* the method. (We'll look at code blocks in much more detail later in this chapter. You can get by with just the placeholder level of knowledge here.) The anatomy of a call to `loop`, then, looks like this:

```
loop codeblock
```

Code blocks can be written in one of two ways: either in curly braces ({ }) or with the keywords do and end. The following two snippets are equivalent:

```
loop { puts "Looping forever!" }

loop do
  puts "Looping forever!"
end
```

A loose convention holds that one-line code blocks use the curly braces, and multiline blocks use do/end. But Ruby doesn't enforce this convention. (The braces and the do/end pair do, in fact, differ from each other slightly, in terms of precedence. You don't have to worry about that now.)

Generally, you don't want a loop to loop forever; you want it to stop at some point. You can usually stop by pressing Ctrl-C, but there are other, more programmatic ways, too.

CONTROLLING THE LOOP

One way to stop a loop is with the `break` keyword, as in this admittedly verbose approach to setting n to 10:

```
n = 1
loop do
  n = n + 1
  break if n > 9
end
```

Another technique skips to the next iteration of the loop without finishing the current iteration. To do this, you use the keyword next:

```
n = 1
loop do
  n = n + 1
  next unless n == 10
  break
end
```

Here, control falls through to the break statement only if n == 10 is true. If n == 10 is *not* true (unless n == 10), the next is executed, and control jumps back to the beginning of the loop before it reaches break.

You can also loop conditionally: *while* a given condition is true or *until* a condition becomes true.

6.2.2   *Conditional looping with the while and until keywords*

Conditional looping is achieved via the keywords while and until. These keywords can be used in any of several ways, depending on exactly how you want the looping to play out.

THE WHILE KEYWORD

The while keyword allows you to run a loop while a given condition is true. A block starting with while has to end with end. The code between while and end is the body of the while loop. Here's an example:

```
n = 1
while n < 11
  puts n
  n = n + 1
end
puts "Done!"
```

This code prints the following:

```
1
2
3
4
5
6
7
8
9
10
Done!
```

As long as the condition n < 11 is true, the loop executes. With each iteration of the loop, n is incremented by 1. The eleventh time the condition is tested, it's false (n is no longer less than 11), and the execution of the loop terminates.

You can also place while at the end of a loop. In this case, you need to use the keyword pair begin/end to mark where the loop is (otherwise, Ruby won't know how many of the lines previous to the while you want to include in the loop):

```
n = 1
begin
  puts n
  n = n + 1
end while n < 11
puts "Done!"
```

The output from this example is the same as the output from the previous example.

There's a difference between putting while at the beginning and putting it at the end. If you put while at the beginning, and if the while condition is false, the code isn't executed:

```
n = 10
while n < 10
  puts n
end
```

Because n is already greater than 10 when the test n < 10 is performed the first time, the body of the statement isn't executed. But if you put the while test at the end,

```
n = 10
begin
  puts n
end while n < 10
```

the number 10 is printed. Obviously, n isn't less than 10 at any point. But because the while test is positioned at the end of the statement, the body is executed once before the test is performed.

Like if and unless, the conditional loop keywords come as a pair: while and until.

THE UNTIL KEYWORD

The until keyword is used the same way as while but with reverse logic. Here's another labor-intensive way to print out the integers from 1 to 10, this time illustrating the use of until:

```
n = 1
until n > 10
  puts n
  n = n + 1
end
```

The body of the loop (the printing and incrementing of n, in this example) is executed repeatedly until the condition is true.

You can also use until in the post-block position, in conjunction with a begin/end pairing. As with while, the block will execute once before the until condition is tested.

Like their cousins if and unless, while and until can be used in a modifier position in one-line statements.

THE WHILE AND UNTIL MODIFIERS

Here's a slightly shorter way to count to 10, using until in a modifier position:

```
n = 1
n = n + 1 until n == 10
puts "We've reached 10!"
```

In place of the until statement, you could also use while n < 10.

Note that the one-line modifier versions of while and until don't behave the same way as the post-positioned while and until you use with a begin/end block. In other words, in a case like this

```
a = 1
a += 1 until true
```

a will still be 1; the a += 1 statement won't be executed, because true is already true. But in this case

```
a = 1
begin
  a += 1
end until true
```

the body of the begin/end block does get executed once.

In addition to looping unconditionally (loop) and conditionally (while, until), you can loop through a list of values, running the loop once for each value. Ruby offers several ways to do this, one of which is the keyword for.

6.2.3 Looping based on a list of values

Let's say you want to print a chart of Fahrenheit equivalents of Celsius values. You can do this by putting the Celsius values in an array and then looping through the array using the for/in keyword pair. The loop runs once for each value in the array; each time through, that value is assigned to a variable you specify:

```
celsius = [0, 10, 20, 30, 40, 50, 60, 70, 80, 90, 100]
puts "Celsius\tFahrenheit"                                    ◁───┐  Header for chart
for c in celsius                                                   │  (\t prints a tab)
  puts "#{c}\t#{Temperature.c2f(c)}"
end
```

The body of the loop (the puts statement) runs 11 times. The first time through, the value of c is 0. The second time, c is 10; the third time, it's 20; and so forth.

for is a powerful tool. Oddly enough, though, on closer inspection it turns out that for is just an alternate way of doing something even more powerful.

6.3 Iterators and code blocks

The control-flow techniques we've looked at so far involve controlling how many times, or under what conditions, a segment of code gets executed. In this section, we'll examine a different kind of control-flow facility. The techniques we'll discuss here don't just perform an execute-or-skip operation on a segment of code; they bounce control of the program from one scope to another and back again, through *iteration.*

6.3.1 The ingredients of iteration

In focusing on movement between local scopes, it may sound like we've gone back to talking about method calls. After all, when you call a method on an object, control is passed to the body of the method (a different scope); and when the method has finished executing, control returns to the point right after the point where the method call took place.

We are indeed back in method-call territory, but we're exploring new aspects of it, not just revisiting the old. We're talking about a new construct called a *code block* and a keyword by the name of yield.

In section 6.2.1, you saw a code sample that looked like this:

```
loop { puts "Looping forever!" }
```

The word loop and the message in the string clue you in as to what you get if you run it: that message, printed forever. But what *exactly* is going on? Why does that puts statement get executed at all—and why does it get executed in a loop?

The answer is that `loop` is an *iterator*. An iterator is a Ruby method that has an extra ingredient in its calling syntax: it expects you to provide it with a code block. The curly braces in the loop example delimit the block; the code in the block consists of the `puts` statement.

The `loop` method has access to the code inside the block: the method can *call* (execute) the block. To do this from an iterator of your own, you use the keyword `yield`. Together, the code block (supplied by the calling code) and `yield` (invoked from within the method) are the chief ingredients of iteration.

`loop` itself is written in C (and uses a C function to achieve the same effect as `yield`). But the whole idea of looping suggests an interesting exercise: reimplementing `loop` in pure Ruby. This exercise will give you a first glimpse at `yield` in action.

6.3.2 *Iteration, home-style*

The job of `loop` is to yield control to the code block, again and again, forever. Here's how you might write your own version of `loop`:

```
def my_loop
  while true
    yield
  end
end
```

Or, even shorter:

```
def my_loop
  yield while true
end
```

Then you'd call it just like you call `loop`

```
my_loop { puts "My-looping forever!" }
```

and the message would be printed over and over.

By providing a code block, you're giving `my_loop` something—a chunk of code—to which it can yield control. When the method yields to the block, the code in the block runs, and then control returns to the method. Yielding isn't the same as returning from a method. Yielding takes place while the method is still running. After the code block executes, control returns to the method at the statement immediately following the call to `yield`.

The code block is part of the method call—that is, part of its syntax. This is an important point: a code block isn't an argument. The arguments to methods are the arguments. The code block is the code block. They're two separate constructs. You can see the logic behind the distinction if you look at the full picture of how method calls are put together.

6.3.3   *The anatomy of a method call*

Every method call in Ruby has the following syntax:

- A receiver object or variable (defaulting to `self` if absent)
- A dot (required if there's an explicit receiver; disallowed otherwise)
- A method name (required)
- An argument list (optional; defaults to `()`)
- A code block (optional; no default)

Note in particular that the argument list and the code block are separate. Their existence varies independently. All of these are syntactically legitimate Ruby method calls:

```
loop { puts "Hi" }
loop() { puts "Hi" }
string.scan(/[^,]+/)
string.scan(/[^,]+/) {|word| puts word }
```

(The last example shows a block parameter, `word`. We'll get back to block parameters presently.) The difference between a method call with a block and a method call without a block comes down to whether or not the method can yield. If there's a block, then it can; if not, it can't, because there's nothing to yield to.

Furthermore, some methods are written so they'll at least do *something*, whether you pass them a code block or not. `String#split`, for example, splits its receiver (a string, of course) on the delimiter you pass in and returns an array of the split elements. If you pass it a block, `split` also yields the split elements to the block, one at a time. Your block can then do whatever it wants with each substring: print it out, stash it in a database column, and so forth.

If you learn to think of the code block as a syntactic element of the method call, rather than as one of the arguments, you'll be able to keep things straight as you see more variations on the basic iteration theme.

Earlier you saw, in brief, that code blocks can be delimited either by curly braces or by the do/end keyword pair. Let's look more closely now at how these two delimiter options differ from each other.

6.3.4   *Curly braces vs. do/end in code block syntax*

The difference between the two ways of delimiting a code block is a difference in precedence. Look at this example, and you'll start to see how this plays out:

```
>> array = [1,2,3]
=> [1, 2, 3]
>> array.map {|n| n * 10 }                    ❶
=> [10, 20, 30]
>> array.map do |n| n * 10 end                ❷
=> [10, 20, 30]
>> puts array.map {|n| n * 10 }               ❸
10
20
30
```

```
=> nil
>> puts array.map do |n| n * 10 end          <——4
   #<Enumerator:0x00000101132048>
=> nil
```

The map method works through an array one item at a time, calling the code block once for each item and creating a new array consisting of the results of all of those calls to the block. Mapping our [1,2,3] array through a block that multiplies each item by 10 results in the new array [10,20,30]. Furthermore, for a simple map operation, it doesn't matter whether we use curly braces ❶ or do/end ❷. The results are the same.

But look at what happens when we use the outcome of the map operation as an argument to puts. The curly-brace version prints out the [10,20,30] array (one item per line, in keeping with how puts handles arrays) ❸. But the do/end version returns an enumerator—which is precisely what map does when it's called with *no* code block ❹. (You'll learn more about enumerators in chapter 10. The relevant point here is that the two block syntaxes produce different results.)

The reason is that the precedence is different. The first puts statement is interpreted like this:

```
puts(array.map {|n| n * 10 })
```

The second is interpreted like this:

```
puts(array.map) do |n| n * 10 end
```

In the second case, the code block is interpreted as being part of the call to puts, not the call to map. And if you call puts with a block, it ignores the block. So the do/end version is really equivalent to

```
puts array.map
```

And that's why we get an enumerator.

The call to map using a do/end–style code block illustrates the fact that if you supply a code block but the method you call doesn't see it (or doesn't look for it), no error occurs: methods aren't obliged to yield, and many methods (including map) have well-defined behaviors for cases where there's a code block and cases where there isn't. If a method seems to be ignoring a block that you expect it to yield to, look closely at the precedence rules and make sure the block really is available to the method.

We'll continue looking at iterators and iteration by doing with several built-in Ruby iterators what we did with loop: examining the method and then implementing our own. We'll start with a method that's a slight refinement of loop: times.

6.3.5 *Implementing times*

The times method is an instance method of the Integer class, which means you call it as a method on integers. It runs the code block *n* times, for any integer *n*, and at the end of the method the return value is *n*.

You can see both the output and the return value if you run a `times` example in irb:

```
>> 5.times { puts "Writing this 5 times!" }            ◄─┐
Writing this 5 times!                                    ❶
Writing this 5 times!
Writing this 5 times!
Writing this 5 times!
Writing this 5 times!          ❷
=> 5                           ◄─┘
```

The call to the method includes a code block ❶ that gets executed five times. The return value of the *whole* method is the object we started with: the integer 5 ❷.

The behavior of `times` illustrates nicely the fact that yielding to a block and returning from a method are two different things. A method may yield to its block any number of times, from zero to infinity (the latter in the case of `loop`). But every method returns exactly once (assuming no fatal errors) when it's finished doing everything it's going to do. It's a bit like a jump in figure skating. You take off, execute some rotations in the air, and land. And no matter how many rotations you execute, you only take off once and only land once. Similarly, a method call causes the method to run once and to return once. But in between, like rotations in the air, the method can yield control back to the block (if there is one) zero or more times.

Before we implement `times`, let's look at another of its features. Each time `times` yields to its block, it yields something. Sure enough, code blocks, like methods, can take arguments. When a method yields, it can yield one or more values.

The block picks up the argument through its parameters. In the case of `times`, you can supply a single parameter, and that parameter will be bound to whatever value gets yielded to the block on each iteration. As you might guess, the values yielded by times are the integers 0 through $n - 1$:

```
>> 5.times {|i| puts "I'm on iteration #{i}!" }
I'm on iteration 0!
I'm on iteration 1!
I'm on iteration 2!
I'm on iteration 3!
I'm on iteration 4!
=> 5
```

Each time through—that is, each time `times` yields to the code block—it yields the next value, and that value is placed in the variable `i`.

We're ready to implement `times`—or, rather, `my_times`—and here's what it looks like:

```
class Integer
  def my_times
    c = 0
    until c == self
      yield(c)
      c += 1
    end
    self
  end
end
```

If you want to try an example in irb, you can either type the previous code into your irb session or put it in a file—say, my_times.rb—and then issue the command require "./my_times.rb" in irb. You can then see the results of trying it:

```
>> 5.my_times {|i| puts "I'm on iteration #{i}!" }
I'm on iteration 0!
I'm on iteration 1!
I'm on iteration 2!
I'm on iteration 3!
I'm on iteration 4!
=> 5
```

It works just like times. The implementation of my_times is by no means the most concise implementation possible, but it works. You'll learn plenty more iteration and collection-manipulation techniques that you can use to make your method definitions both concise and clear.

Speaking of which, our next stop is the each method. As you'll see here, and in even greater depth in the later chapters where we explore collection objects extensively, each is a busy, pivotal method.

6.3.6 *The importance of being each*

The idea of each is simple: you run the each method on a collection object, and each yields each item in the collection to your code block, one at a time. Ruby has several collection classes, and even more classes that are sufficiently collection-like to support an each method. You'll see two chapters devoted to Ruby collections. Here, we'll recruit the humble array for our examples.

Here's a simple each operation:

```
array = [1,2,3,4,5]
array.each {|e| puts "The block just got handed #{e}." }
```

The output of the each call looks like this in an irb session:

```
>> array.each {|e| puts "The block just got handed #{e}." }
The block just got handed 1.
The block just got handed 2.
The block just got handed 3.
The block just got handed 4.
The block just got handed 5.
=> [1, 2, 3, 4, 5]
```

The last line isn't method output; it's the return value of each, echoed back by irb. The return value of each, when it's given a block, is its receiver, the original array. (When it isn't given a block, it returns an enumerator; you'll learn about those in chapter 10.) Like times, each doesn't have an exciting return value. All the interest lies in the fact that it yields values to the block.

To implement my_each, we'll take another step along the lines of iteration refinement. With my_loop, we iterated forever. With my_times, we iterated n times. With my_each, the number of iterations—the number of times the method yields—depends on the size of the array.

We need a counter to keep track of where we are in the array and to keep yielding until we're finished. Conveniently, arrays have a size method, which makes it easy to determine how many iterations (how many "rotations in the air") need to be performed. As a return value for the method, we'll use the original array object:

```
class Array
  def my_each
    c = 0
    until c == size
      yield(self[c])          Use [ ] to get current
      c += 1                  array element
    end
    self
  end
end
```

A trial run of my_each produces the result we're aiming for:

```
>> array = [1,2,3,4,5]
>> array.my_each {|e| puts "The block just got handed #{e}." }
The block just got handed 1.
The block just got handed 2.
The block just got handed 3.
The block just got handed 4.
The block just got handed 5.
=> [1, 2, 3, 4, 5]
```

We've successfully implemented at least a simple version of each. The nice thing about each is that it's so vanilla: all it does is toss values at the code block, one at a time, until it runs out. One important implication of this is that it's possible to build any number of more complex, semantically rich iterators *on top of* each. We'll finish this reimplementation exercise with one such method: map, which you saw briefly in section 6.3.4. Learning a bit about map will also take us into some further nuances of code block writing and usage.

Extra credit: Define my_each in terms of my_times

An interesting exercise is to define my_each using the existing definition of my_times. You can use the size method to determine how many iterations you need and then perform them courtesy of my_times, like so:

```
class Array
  def my_each
    size.my_times do |i|
      yield self[i]
    end
    self
  end
end
```

(continued)

Using `my_times` saves you the trouble of writing loop-counter code in `my_each`. But it's a bit backward: many of Ruby's iterators are built on top of `each`, not the other way around. Given the definition of `my_each` in the main text, how would you use it in an implementation of `my_times`?

Unlike the first exercise, this one really will be left to you to try on your own!

6.3.7 *From each to map*

Like `each`, `map` walks through an array one element at a time and yields each element to the code block. The difference between `each` and `map` lies in the return value: `each` returns its receiver, but `map` returns a new array. The new array is always the same size as the original array, but instead of the original elements, the new array contains the accumulated return values of the code block from the iterations.

Here's a `map` example. Notice that the return value contains new elements; it's not just the array we started with:

```
>> names = ["David", "Alan", "Black"]
=> ["David", "Alan", "Black"]
>> names.map {|name| name.upcase }
=> ["DAVID", "ALAN", "BLACK"]
```

The mapping results in a new array, each of whose elements corresponds to the element in the same position in the original array but processed through the code block. The piece of the puzzle that `map` adds to our analysis of iteration is the idea of the code block returning a value *to* the method that yielded to it. And indeed it does: just as the method can yield a value, so too can the block return a value. The return value comes back as the value of the call to `yield`.

To implement `my_map`, then, we have to arrange for an accumulator array, into which we'll drop the return values of the successive calls to the code block. We'll then return the accumulator array as the result of the entire call to `my_map`.

Let's start with a preliminary, but not final, implementation, in which we don't build on `my_each` but write `my_map` from scratch. The purpose is to illustrate exactly how mapping differs from simple iteration. We'll then refine the implementation.

The first implementation looks like this:

```
class Array
  def my_map
    c = 0
    acc = []                    ◁── Initializes accumulator array
    until c == size
      acc << yield(self[c])     ◁── Captures return value from
      c += 1                         block in accumulator array
    end
    acc            ◁── Returns
  end                 accumulator array
end
```

We now get the same results from my_map that we did from map:

```
>> names.my_map {|name| name.upcase }
=> ["DAVID", "ALAN", "BLACK"]
```

Like my_each, my_map yields each element of the array in turn. Unlike my_each, my_map stores the value that comes back from the block. That's how it accumulates the mapping of the old values to the new values: the new values are based on the old values, processed through the block.

But our implementation of my_map fails to deliver on the promise of my_each—the promise being that each serves as the vanilla iterator on top of which the more complex iterators can be built. Let's reimplement map. This time, we'll write my_map in terms of my_each.

BUILDING MAP ON TOP OF EACH

Building map on top of each is almost startlingly simple:

```
class Array
  # Put the definition of my_each here
  def my_map
    acc = []
    my_each {|e| acc << yield(e) }
    acc
  end
end
```

We piggyback on the vanilla iterator, allowing my_each to do the walk-through of the array. There's no need to maintain an explicit counter or to write an until loop. We've already got that logic; it's embodied in my_each. In writing my_map, it makes sense to take advantage of it.

There's much, much more to say about iterators and, in particular, the ways Ruby builds on each to provide an extremely rich toolkit of collection-processing methods. We'll go down that avenue in chapter 10. Here, meanwhile, let's delve a bit more deeply into some of the nuts and bolts of iterators—starting with the assignment and scoping rules that govern their use of parameters and variables.

6.3.8   *Block parameters and variable scope*

You've seen that block parameters are surrounded by pipes, rather than parentheses as method parameters are. But you can use what you've learned about method arguments to create block parameter lists. Remember the args_unleashed method from chapter 2?

```
def args_unleashed(a,b=1,*c,d,e)
  puts "Arguments:"
  p a,b,c,d,e
end
```

Here's a block-based version of the method:

```
def block_args_unleashed
  yield(1,2,3,4,5)
end
```

```
block_args_unleashed do |a,b=1,*c,d,e|
  puts "Arguments:"
  p a,b,c,d,e
end
```

The parameter bindings and program output are the same as they were with the original version:

```
Arguments:
1
2
[3]
4
5
```

What about scope? A method definition, as you know, starts a new local scope. Blocks are a little more complicated.

Let's start with a simple case: inside a block, you refer to a variable (not a block parameter; just a variable) called x, and you've already got a variable called x in scope before you write the block:

```
def block_scope_demo
  x = 100
  1.times do          ◁──┐  Single iteration serves to
    puts x               │  create code block context
  end
end
```

When you run the method (which includes a handy `puts` statement), you'll see that the x inside the block is the same as the x that existed already:

```
block_scope_demo        ◁──  Output: 100
```

Now, what about assigning to the variable inside a block? Again, it turns out that the variable inside the block is the same as the one that existed prior to the block, as you can see by changing it inside the block and then printing it out after the block is finished:

```
def block_scope_demo_2
  x = 100
  1.times do
    x = 200
  end
  puts x
end                            ┐  Output: 200
block_scope_demo_2      ◁──────┘
```

Blocks, in other words, have direct access to variables that already exist (such as x in the example). However, block parameters (the variable names between the pipes) behave differently from non-parameter variables. If you have a variable of a given name in scope and also use that name as one of your block parameters, then the two variables—the one that exists already and the one in the parameter list—are *not* the same as each other.

NOTE   Although it's important in its own right, the fact that blocks share local scope with the code that precedes them will take on further significance when we look at Proc objects and *closures* in chapter 14. You'll learn that blocks can serve as the bodies of anonymous function objects, and those objects preserve the local variables that are in scope at the time of their creation—even if the function objects get handed around other local scopes.

Look at the variables named x in this example:

```
def block_local_parameter                    Outer x
  x = 100                                     (before block)      Block
  [1,2,3].each do |x|                                            parameter x
    puts "Parameter x is #{x}"
    x = x + 10                                        Assignment to
    puts "Reassigned to x in block; it's now #{x}"    x inside block
  end
  puts "Outer x is still #{x}"
end
```

The output from a call to this method is

```
Parameter x is 1
Reassigned to x in block; it's now 11
Parameter x is 2
Reassigned to x in block; it's now 12
Parameter x is 3
Reassigned to x in block; it's now 13
Outer x is still 100
```

The x inside the block isn't the same as the x outside the block, because x is used as a block parameter. Even reassigning to x inside the block doesn't overwrite the "outer" x. This behavior enables you to use any variable name you want for your block parameters without having to worry about whether a variable of the same name is already in scope.

Sometimes you may want to use a temporary variable inside a block, even if it isn't one of the parameters being assigned to when the block is called. And when you do this, it's nice not to have to worry that you're accidentally reusing a variable from outside the block. Ruby provides a special notation indicating that you want one or more variables to be local to the block, even if variables with the same name already exist: a semicolon in the block parameter list.

Here's an example. Note the semicolon in the parameter list:

```
def block_local_variable
  x = "Original x!"
  3.times do |i;x|
    x = i
    puts "x in the block is now #{x}"
  end
  puts "x after the block ended is #{x}"
end
block_local_variable
```

The semicolon, followed by x, indicates that the block needs its own x, unrelated to any x that may have been created already in the scope outside the block. In the example, we assign to x inside the block, but these assignments don't affect the x that existed already. The output shows that the original x survives:

```
x in the block is now 0
x in the block is now 1
x in the block is now 2
x after the block ended is Original x!
```

Sure enough, the original x has been protected from change.

The variables listed after the semicolon aren't considered block parameters; they don't get bound to anything when the block is called. They're *reserved names*—names you want to be able to use as temporary variables inside the block without having to check for name collisions from outside the block.

In sum, three basic "flavors" of block variable are available to you:

- Local variables that exist already when the block is created
- Block parameters, which are always block-local
- True block-locals, which are listed after the semicolon and aren't assigned to but do protect any same-named variables from the outer scope

With these tools at hand, you should be able to engineer your blocks so they do what you need them to with respect to variables and scope, and so you don't "clobber" any variables from the outer scope that you don't want to clobber.

Ruby's iterators and code blocks allow you to write and use methods that are engineered to share their own functionality with their callers. The method contains some logic and procedure, but when you call the method, you supply additional code that fills out the logic and individualizes the particular call you're making. It's an elegant feature with endless applications. We'll come back to iterators when we examine collection objects in detail in chapters 10 and 11.

But now we'll look at another control-flow mechanism. So far, we've been operating in a cooperative, efficient landscape. It doesn't always work that way, though; and one of the most important aspects of control flow that you need to understand is the matter of what happens when things go wrong.

6.4 *Error handling and exceptions*

Way back in chapter 1, we looked at how to test code for syntax errors:

```
$ ruby -cw filename.rb
```

Passing the -cw test means Ruby can run your program. But it doesn't mean nothing will go wrong while your program is running. You can write a syntactically correct program—a program that the interpreter will accept and execute—that does all sorts of unacceptable things. Ruby handles unacceptable behavior at runtime by *raising an exception.*

6.4.1 *Raising and rescuing exceptions*

An *exception* is a special kind of object, an instance of the class Exception or a descendant of that class. *Raising* an exception means stopping normal execution of the program and either dealing with the problem that's been encountered or exiting the program completely.

Which of these happens—dealing with the problem or aborting the program—depends on whether you've provided a rescue clause. If you haven't provided such a clause, the program terminates; if you have, control flows to the rescue clause.

To see exceptions in action, try dividing by zero:

```
$ ruby -e '1/0'
```

Ruby raises an exception:

```
-e:1:in `/': divided by 0 (ZeroDivisionError)
    from -e:1:in `<main>'
```

ZeroDivisionError is the name of this particular exception. More technically, it's the name of a class—a descendant class of the class Exception. Ruby has a whole family tree of exceptions classes, all of them going back eventually to Exception.

SOME COMMON EXCEPTIONS

Table 6.1 shows some common exceptions (each of which is a class, descended from Exception) along with common reasons they're raised and an example of code that will raise each one.

Table 6.1 Common exceptions

Exception name	Common reason(s)	How to raise it
RuntimeError	The default exception raised by the raise method.	Raise
NoMethodError	An object is sent a message it can't resolve to a method name; the default method_missing raises this exception.	a = Object.new a.some_unknown_method_name
NameError	The interpreter hits an identifier it can't resolve as a variable or method name.	a = some_random_identifier
IOError	Caused by reading a closed stream, writing to a read-only stream, and similar operations.	STDIN.puts("Don't write to STDIN!")
Errno::*error*	A family of errors relates to file I/O.	File.open(-12)
TypeError	A method receives an argument it can't handle.	a = 3 + "can't add a string to a number!"
ArgumentError	Caused by using the wrong number of arguments.	def m(x); end; m(1,2,3,4,5)

You can try these examples in irb; you'll get an error message, but the session shouldn't terminate. irb is good about making potentially fatal errors nonfatal—and you can do something similar in your programs, too.

6.4.2 *The rescue keyword to the rescue!*

Having an exception raised doesn't have to mean your program terminates. You can handle exceptions—deal with the problem and keep the program running—by means of the rescue keyword. Rescuing involves a rescue block, which is delimited with the begin and end keywords and has a rescue clause in the middle:

```
print "Enter a number: "
n = gets.to_i
begin
  result = 100 / n
rescue
  puts "Your number didn't work. Was it zero???"
  exit
end
puts "100/#{n} is #{result}."
```

If you run this program and enter 0 as your number, the division operation (100/n) raises a ZeroDivisionError. Because you've done this inside a begin/end block with a rescue clause, control is passed to the rescue clause. An error message is printed out, and the program exits.

If you enter something other than 0 and the division succeeds, program control skips over the rescue statement and block, and execution resumes thereafter (with the call to puts).

You can refine this technique by pinpointing the exception you want to trap. Instead of a generic rescue instruction, which rescues any error that's a descendant class of StandardError, you tell rescue what to rescue:

```
rescue ZeroDivisionError
```

This traps a single type of exception but not others. The advantage is that you're no longer running the risk of inadvertently covering up some other problem by rescuing too eagerly.

Rescuing exceptions inside a method body or code block has a couple of distinct features worth noting.

USING RESCUE INSIDE METHODS AND CODE BLOCKS

The beginning of a method or code block provides an implicit begin/end context. Therefore, if you use the rescue keyword inside a method or code block, you don't have to say begin explicitly—assuming that you want the rescue clause to govern the entire method or block:

```
def open_user_file
  print "File to open: "
  filename = gets.chomp
  fh = File.open(filename)
```

```
    yield fh
    fh.close
  rescue                              <--❷
    puts "Couldn't open your file!"
end
```

If the file-opening operation ❶ triggers an exception, control jumps directly to the rescue clause ❷. The def/end keywords serve to delimit the scope of the rescue operation.

But you may want to get a little more fine-grained about which lines your rescue clause applies to. In the previous example, the rescue clause is triggered even if an exception is raised for reasons having nothing to do with trying to open the file. For example, if the call to gets raises an exception for any reason, the rescue clause executes.

To get more fine-grained, you have to go back to using an explicit begin/end wrapper:

```
def open_user_file
  print "File to open: "
  filename = gets.chomp
  begin                              <--❶
    fh = File.open(filename)
  rescue                             <--❷
    puts "Couldn't open your file!"
    return                           <--❸
  end
  yield fh
  fh.close
end
```

In this version, the rescue clause only governs what comes between the begin keyword ❶ and rescue ❷. Moreover, it's necessary to give an explicit return command inside the rescue clause ❸ because otherwise the method will continue to execute.

So far, we've been looking at how to trap exceptions raised by Ruby—and you'll learn more exception-trapping techniques. But let's turn now to the other side of the coin: how to raise exceptions yourself.

6.4.3   *Raising exceptions explicitly*

When it comes to Ruby's traditional flexibility and compact coding power, exceptions are, so to speak, no exception. You can raise exceptions in your own code, and you can create new exceptions to raise.

To raise an exception, you use raise plus the name of the exception you wish to raise. If you don't provide an exception name (and if you're not re-raising a different kind of exception, as described in section 6.4.4), Ruby raises the rather generic RuntimeError. You can also give raise a second argument, which is used as the message string when the exception is raised:

```
def fussy_method(x)
  raise ArgumentError, "I need a number under 10" unless x < 10
end
fussy_method(20)
```

If run from a file called fussy.rb, this code prints out the following:

```
fussy.rb:2:in `fussy_method': I need a number under 10 (ArgumentError)
    from fussy.rb:5:in `<main>'
```

You can also use `rescue` in such a case:

```
begin
  fussy_method(20)
rescue ArgumentError
  puts "That was not an acceptable number!"
end
```

A nice tweak is that if you give `raise` a message as the only argument, rather than as the second argument where an exception class is the first argument, `raise` figures out that you want it to raise a `RuntimeError` using the message provided. These two lines are equivalent:

```
raise "Problem!"
raise RuntimeError, "Problem!"
```

In your `rescue` clauses, it's possible to capture the exception object in a variable and query it for possibly useful information.

6.4.4 *Capturing an exception in a rescue clause*

To assign the exception object to a variable, you use the special operator `=>` along with the `rescue` command. The exception object, like any object, responds to messages. Particularly useful are the `backtrace` and `message` methods. `backtrace` returns an array of strings representing the call stack at the time the exception was raised: method names, filenames, and line numbers, showing a full roadmap of the code that was executed along the way to the exception. `message` returns the message string provided to `raise`, if any.

To see these facilities in action, put the preceding definition of `fussy_method` in the file fussy.rb (if you haven't already), and then add the following `begin`/`end` block:

```
begin
  fussy_method(20)
rescue ArgumentError => e                                  ⇐──❶
  puts "That was not an acceptable number!"
  puts "Here's the backtrace for this exception:"
  puts e.backtrace                                         ⇐──❷
  puts "And here's the exception object's message:"
  puts e.message                                           ⇐──❸
end
```

In the `rescue` clause, we assign the exception object to the variable e ❶ and then ask the exception object to display its backtrace ❷ and its message ❸. Assuming you've got one blank line between `fussy_method` and the `begin` keyword, you'll see the following output (and, in any case, you'll see something almost identical, although the line numbers may differ) when you run fussy.rb:

```
That was not an acceptable number!
Here's the backtrace for this exception:
fussy.rb:2:in `fussy_method'
fussy.rb:6:in `<main>'
And here's the exception object's message:
I need a number under 10
```

The backtrace shows you that we were in the `fussy_method` method on line 2 of fussy.rb when the exception was raised, and that we were previously on line 6 of the same file in the `<main>` context—in other words, at the top level of the program (outside of any class, module, or method definition). The message, "I need a number under 10" comes from the call to `raise` inside `fussy_method`.

Your `rescue` clause can also re-raise the exception that triggered it.

What gets raised: An exception or an exception class?

The language of exception raising is class-based: `raise ZeroDivisionError` rather than `raise ZeroDivisionError.new`. But really, instances of the exception classes are raised. The syntax lets you raise a class because that looks better and abstracts away the fact that instantiation is involved.

You can see the class/instance switch-off if you examine the object that you capture in the `rescue` clause:

```
begin
raise ArgumentError
rescue => e
p e.class              <—    ArgumentError
end
```

The object's class is `ArgumentError`; the object itself is an instance of `Argument-Error`, not the class `ArgumentError`.

You get a reprieve from typing `.new`, and your code has a nice high-level look to it, providing enough information to show you what's going on without unnecessary housekeeping details.

RE-RAISING AN EXCEPTION

It's not uncommon to want to re-raise an exception, allowing the next location on the call stack to handle it after your `rescue` block has handled it. You might, for example, want to log something about the exception but still have it treated as an exception by the calling code.

Here's a second version of the begin/end block from the `open_user_file` method a few examples back. This version assumes that you have a `logfile` method that returns a writeable file handle on a log file:

```
begin
  fh = File.open(filename)
```

```
rescue => e
  logfile.puts("User tried to open #{filename}, #{Time.now}")
  logfile.puts("Exception: #{e.message}")
  raise
end
```

The idea here is to intercept the exception, make a note of it in the log file, and then re-raise it by calling `raise`. (Even though there's no argument to `raise`, from inside a `rescue` clause it figures out that you want to re-raise the exception being handled and not the usual generic `RuntimeError`.) The spot in the program that called `open_user_file` in the first place then has to handle the exception—or not, if it's better to allow it to stop program execution.

Another refinement of handling control flow with exceptions is the `ensure` clause, which executes unconditionally no matter what else happens when an exception is raised.

6.4.5 *The ensure clause*

Let's say you want to read a line from a data file and raise an exception if the line doesn't include a particular substring. If it does include the substring, you want to return the line. If it doesn't, you want to raise `ArgumentError`. But whatever happens, you want to close the file handle before the method finishes.

Here's how you might accomplish this, using an `ensure` clause:

```
def line_from_file(filename, substring)
  fh = File.open(filename)
  begin
    line = fh.gets
    raise ArgumentError unless line.include?(substring)
  rescue ArgumentError
    puts "Invalid line!"
    raise
  ensure
    fh.close
  end
  return line
end
```

In this example, the `begin`/`end` block wraps the line that reads from the file, and the rescue clause only handles `ArgumentError`—which means that if something else goes wrong (like the file not existing), it isn't rescued. But if `ArgumentError` is raised based on the test for the inclusion of `substring` in the string `line`, the `rescue` clause is executed.

Moreover, the `ensure` clause is executed whether an exception is raised or not. `ensure` is pegged to the `begin`/`end` structure of which it's a part, and its execution is unconditional. In this example, we want to ensure that the file handle gets closed. The `ensure` clause takes care of this, whatever else may have happened.

NOTE   There's a better way to open a file, involving a code block that wraps the file operations and takes care of closing the file for you. But one thing at a time; you'll see that technique when we look at file and I/O techniques in chapter 12.

One lingering problem with the `line_from_file` method is that `ArgumentError` isn't the best name for the exception we're raising. The best name would be something like `InvalidLineError`, which doesn't exist. Fortunately, you can create your own exception classes and name them whatever you want.

6.4.6   *Creating your own exception classes*

You create a new exception class by inheriting from `Exception` or from a descendant class of `Exception`:

```
class MyNewException < Exception
end
raise MyNewException, "some new kind of error has occurred!"
```

This technique offers two primary benefits. First, by letting you give new names to exception classes, it performs a self-documenting function: when a `MyNewException` gets raised, it's distinct from, say, a `ZeroDivisionError` or a plain-vanilla `RuntimeError`.

Second, this approach lets you pinpoint your rescue operations. Once you've created `MyNewException`, you can rescue it by name:

```
class MyNewException < Exception
end
begin
  puts "About to raise exception..."
  raise MyNewException
rescue MyNewException => e
  puts "Just raised an exception: #{e}"
end
```

The output from this snippet is as follows:

```
About to raise exception...
Just raised an exception: MyNewException
```

Only `MyNewException` errors will be trapped by that `rescue` clause. If another exception is raised first for any reason, it will result in program termination without rescue.

Here's what our `line_from_file` method would look like with a custom exception—along with the code that creates the custom exception class. We'll inherit from `StandardError`, the superclass of `RuntimeError`:

```
class InvalidLineError < StandardError
end
def line_from_file(filename, substring)
  fh = File.open(filename)
  line = fh.gets
  raise InvalidLineError unless line.include?(substring)
  return line
```

```
  rescue InvalidLineError
    puts "Invalid line!"
    raise
  ensure
    fh.close
end
```

This time around, we've fully pinpointed the exception we want to intercept.

Simply by inheriting from StandardError, InvalidLineError provides a meaning-ful exception name and refines the semantics of the rescue operation. Custom exception classes are easy and cheap to produce and can add considerable value. Ruby itself has lots of exception classes—so take the hint, and don't hesitate to create your own any time you feel that none of the built-in exceptions quite expresses what you need. And don't forget that exceptions are classes, classes are constants, and constants can be namespaced, courtesy of nesting:

```
module TextHandler
  class InvalidLineError < StandardError
  end
end
def line_from_file(filename, substring)
  fh = File.open(filename)
  line = fh.gets
  raise TextHandler::InvalidLineError unless line.include?(substring)   <──
```

Nicely namespaced exception name!

Namespacing exceptions this way is polite, in the sense that it lets other people name exceptions as they like without fearing name clashes. It also becomes a necessity once you start creating more than a very small number of exception classes.

With our exploration of exceptions and how they're handled, we've reached the end of this examination of control flow. As you've seen, control can jump around a fair amount—but if you keep in mind the different kinds of jumping (conditionals, loops, iterators, and exceptions), you'll be able to follow any Ruby code and write code that makes productive use of the many flow-related techniques available.

6.5 Summary

In this chapter you've seen

- Conditionals (if/unless and case/when)
- Loops (loop, for, while, and until)
- Iterators and code blocks, including block parameters and variables
- Examples of implementing Ruby methods in Ruby
- Exceptions and exception handling

This chapter has covered several wide-ranging topics, bundled together because they have in common the fact that they involve control flow. Conditionals move control around based on the truth or falsehood of expressions. Loops repeat a segment of code unconditionally, conditionally, or once for each item in a list. Iterators—methods that yield to a code block you provide alongside the call to the method—are among Ruby's most distinctive features. You've learned how to write and call an iterator, techniques you'll encounter frequently later in this book (and beyond).

Exceptions are Ruby's mechanism for handling unrecoverable error conditions. *Unrecoverable* is relative: you can rescue an error condition and continue execution, but you have to stage a deliberate intervention via a `rescue` block and thus divert and gain control of the program where otherwise it would terminate. You can also create your own exception classes through inheritance from the built-in Ruby exception classes.

At this point, we'll delve into Ruby's built-in functionality, starting with some general, pervasive features and techniques, and proceeding to specific classes and modules. Not that you haven't seen and used many built-in features already; but it's time to get more systematic and to go more deeply into how the built-ins work.

Part 2

Built-in classes and modules

In part 2, we come to the heart of the Ruby language: built-in classes and modules.

A great deal of what you'll do as a Rubyist will involve Ruby's built-ins. You've already seen examples involving many of them: strings, arrays, files, and so forth. Ruby provides you with a rich toolset of out-of-the-box built-in data types that you can use and on which you can build.

That's the thing: when you design your own classes and modules, you'll often find that what you need is something similar to an existing Ruby class. If you're writing a DeckOfCards class, for example, one of your first thoughts will probably be that a deck of cards is a lot like an array. Then you'd want to think about whether your cards class should be a subclass of Array—or perhaps each deck object could store an array in an instance variable and put the cards there—and so forth. The point is that Ruby's built-in classes provide you with starting points for your own class and object designs as well as with a set of classes extremely useful in their own right.

We'll start part 2 with a look at built-in essentials (chapter 7). The purpose of this chapter is to provide you with an array (so to speak!) of techniques and tools that you'll find useful across the board in the chapters that follow. To study strings, arrays, and hashes, for example, it's useful to know how Ruby handles the concepts of *true* and *false*—concepts that aren't pegged to any single built-in class but that you need to understand generally.

Following the essentials, we'll turn to specific classes, but grouped into higher-level categories: *scalar* objects first (chapter 8) and then *collections* (chapter 9). Scalars are atomic objects, like strings, numbers, and symbols. Each scalar object represents one value; scalars don't contain other objects. (Strings contain characters, of course; but there's no separate character class in Ruby, so strings are still scalar.) Collection objects contain other objects; the major collection classes in Ruby are arrays and hashes. The collection survey will also include *ranges*, which are hybrid objects that can (but don't always) serve to represent collections of objects. Finally, we'll look at sets, which are implemented in the standard library (rather than the Ruby core) but which merit an exception to the general rule that our focus is on the core itself.

Equal in importance to the specific collection classes are the facilities that all collections in Ruby share: facilities embodied in the `Enumerable` module. `Enumerable` endows collection objects with the knowledge of how to traverse and transform themselves in a great number of ways. Chapter 10 will be devoted to the `Enumerable` module and its ramifications for Ruby programming power.

Part 2 continues in chapter 11 with a look at regular expressions—a string-related topic that, nonetheless, deserves some space of its own—and concludes in chapter 12 with an exploration of file and I/O operations: reading from and writing to files and I/O streams, and related subtopics like error handling and file-status queries. Not surprisingly, Ruby treats all of these things, including regular expressions and I/O streams, as objects.

By the end of part 2, you'll have a rich working knowledge of Ruby's core classes, and your own Ruby horizons will have expanded dramatically.

Built-in essentials

7

This chapter covers

- Literal object constructors
- Syntactic sugar
- "Dangerous" and/or destructive methods
- The `to_*` family of conversion methods
- Boolean states and objects, and `nil`
- Object-comparison techniques
- Runtime inspection of objects' capabilities

The later chapters in this part of the book will cover specific built-in classes: what they are, what you can do with them, and what methods their instances have. This chapter will discuss a selection of topics that cut across a number of built-in classes.

It's more than that, though: it's also a kind of next-generation Ruby literacy guide, a deeper and wider version of chapter 1. Like chapter 1, this chapter has two goals: making it possible to take a certain amount of material for granted in later chapters, where it will arise in various places to varying degrees; and presenting you with information about Ruby that's important and usable in its own right. Throughout this chapter, you'll explore the richness that lies in every Ruby object, as well as some of the syntactic and semantic subsystems that make the language so interesting and versatile.

The chapter moves through a number of topics, so it's probably worth having a look in advance at what you're going to see. Here's a lightly annotated summary:

- *Literal constructors*—Ways to create certain objects with syntax, rather than with a call to `new`
- *Syntactic sugar*—Things Ruby lets you do to make your code look nicer
- *"Dangerous" and/or destructive methods*—Methods that alter their receivers permanently, and other "danger" considerations
- *The `to_*` family of conversion methods*—Methods that produce a conversion from an object to an object of a different class, and the syntactic features that hook into those methods
- *Boolean states and objects, and `nil`*—A close look at `true` and `false` and related concepts in Ruby
- *Object-comparison techniques*—Ruby-wide techniques, both default and customizable, for object-to-object comparison
- *Runtime inspection of objects' capabilities*—An important set of techniques for runtime reflection on the capabilities of an object

You'll find all these topics useful as you read and/or write Ruby code in working through this book and beyond.

You may want to fire up an irb session for this chapter; it makes frequent use of the irb session format for the code examples, and you can often try the examples with small variations to get a feel for how Ruby behaves.

7.1 *Ruby's literal constructors*

Ruby has a lot of built-in classes. Most of them can be instantiated using `new`:

```
str = String.new
arr = Array.new
```

Some can't; for example, you can't create a new instance of the class `Integer`. But for the most part, you can create new instances of the built-in classes.

In addition, a lucky, select few built-in classes enjoy the privilege of having *literal constructors*. That means you can use special notation, instead of a call to `new`, to create a new object of that class.

The classes with literal constructors are shown in table 7.1. When you use one of these literal constructors, you bring a new object into existence. (Although it's not obvious from the table, it's worth noting that there's no `new` constructor for `Symbol` objects. The only way to generate a `Symbol` object is with the literal constructor.)

We'll look in considerable detail at a great deal of functionality in all these classes. Meanwhile, begin getting used to the notation so you can recognize these data types on sight. Literal constructors are never the only way to instantiate an object of a given class, but they're very commonly used.

Table 7.1 Built-in Ruby classes with literal constructors

Class	Literal constructor	Example(s)
String	Quotation marks	`"new string"` `'new string'`
Symbol	Leading colon	`:symbol` `:"symbol with spaces"`
Array	Square brackets	`[1,2,3,4,5]`
Hash	Curly braces	`{"New York" => "NY",` `"Oregon" => "OR"}`
Range	Two or three dots	`0..9` or `0...10`
Regexp	Forward slashes	`/([a-z]+)/`
Proc (lambda)	Dash, arrow, parentheses, braces	`->(x,y) { x * y }`

We'll look next at some of the syntactic sugar that Ruby makes available to you across the spectrum of objects.

Literal constructor characters with more than one meaning

Some of the notation used for literal constructors has more than one meaning in Ruby. Many objects have a method called [] that looks like a literal array constructor but isn't. Code blocks, as you've seen, can be delimited with curly braces—but they're still code blocks, not hash literals. This kind of overloading of notation is a consequence of the finite number of symbols on the keyboard. You can always tell what the notation means by its context, and there are few enough contexts that, with a little practice, it will be easy to differentiate.

7.2 *Recurrent syntactic sugar*

As you know, Ruby sometimes lets you use sugary notation in place of the usual `object.method(args)` method-calling syntax. This lets you do nice-looking things, such as using a plus sign between two numbers, like an operator

```
x = 1 + 2
```

instead of the odd-looking method-style equivalent:

```
x = 1.+(2)
```

As you delve more deeply into Ruby and its built-in methods, be aware that certain methods always get this treatment. The consequence is that you can define how your objects behave in code like this

```
my_object + my_other_object
```

simply by defining the + method. You've seen this process at work, particularly in connection with case equality and defining the === method. But now let's look more extensively at this elegant technique.

7.2.1   *Defining operators by defining methods*

If you define a + method for your class, then objects of your class can use the sugared syntax for addition. Moreover, there's no such thing as defining the meaning of that syntax separately from defining the method. The operator is the method. It just looks nicer as an operator.

Remember, too, that the semantics of methods like + are entirely based on convention. Ruby doesn't know that + means addition. Nothing (other than good judgment) stops you from writing completely nonaddition-like + methods:

```ruby
obj = Object.new
def obj.+(other_obj)
  "Trying to add something to me, eh?"       No addition,
end                                          just output
puts obj + 100
```

The plus sign in the `puts` statement is a call to the + method of `obj`, with the integer 100 as the single (ignored) argument.

Layered on top of the operator-style sugar is the shortcut sugar: x +=1 for x = x + 1. Once again, you automatically reap the sugar harvest if you define the relevant method(s). Here's an example—a bank account class with + and – methods:

```ruby
class Account
  attr_accessor :balance
  def initialize(amount=0)
    self.balance = amount
  end
  def +(x)
    self.balance += x
  end
  def -(x)                           ←❶
    self.balance -= x
  end
  def to_s
    balance.to_s
  end
end
acc = Account.new(20)       ❷
acc -= 5                                 Output: 15
puts acc
```

By defining the – instance method ❶, we gain the -= shortcut, and can subtract from the account using that notation ❷. This is a simple but instructive example of the fact that Ruby encourages you to take advantage of the very same "wiring" that the language itself uses, so as to integrate your programs as smoothly as possible into the underlying technology.

The automatically sugared methods are collected in table 7.2.

Table 7.2   Methods with operator-style syntactic sugar–calling notation

Category	Name	Definition example	Calling example	Sugared notation
Arithmetic method/ operators	+	`def + (x)`	`obj.+(x)`	`obj + x`
	-	`def - (x)`	`obj.-(x)`	`obj - x`
	*	`def * (x)`	`obj.*(x)`	`obj * x`
	/	`def / (x)`	`obj./(x)`	`obj / x`
	% (modulo)	`def % (x)`	`obj.%(x)`	`obj % x`
	** (exponent)	`def ** (x)`	`obj.**(x)`	`obj ** x`
Get/set/append data	[]	`def [] (x)`	`obj.[](x)`	`obj[x]`
	[]=	`def []=(x,y)`	`obj.[]=(x,y)`	`obj[x] = y`
	<<	`def << (x)`	`obj.<<(x)`	`obj << x`
Comparison method/ operators	<=>	`def <=>(x)`	`obj.<=>(x)`	`obj <=> x`
	==	`def == (x)`	`obj.==(x)`	`obj == x`
	>	`def > (x)`	`obj.>(x)`	`obj > x`
	<	`def < (x)`	`obj.<(x)`	`obj < x`
	>=	`def >= (x)`	`obj.>=(x)`	`obj >= x`
	<=	`def <= (x)`	`obj.<=(x)`	`obj <= x`
Case equality operator	===	`def === (x)`	`obj.===(x)`	`obj === x`
Bitwise operators	| (OR)	`def | (x)`	`obj.|(x)`	`obj | x`
	& (AND)	`def & (x)`	`obj.&(x)`	`obj & x`
	^ (XOR)	`def ^ (x)`	`obj.^(x)`	`obj ^ x`

Remembering which methods get the sugar treatment isn't difficult. They fall into several distinct categories, as table 7.2 shows. These categories are for convenience of learning and reference only; Ruby doesn't categorize the methods, and the responsibility for implementing meaningful semantics lies with you. The category names indicate how these method names are used in Ruby's built-in classes and how they're most often used, by convention, when programmers implement them in new classes.

(Don't forget, too, the conditional assignment operator ||=, as well as its rarely spotted cousin &&=, both of which provide the same kind of shortcut as the pseudo-operator methods but are based on operators, namely || and &&, that you can't override.)

The extensive use of this kind of syntactic sugar—where something *looks like* an operator but *is* a method call—tells you a lot about the philosophy behind Ruby as a programming language. The fact that you can define and even redefine elements like the plus sign, minus sign, and square brackets means that Ruby has a great deal of flexibility. But there are limits to what you can redefine in Ruby. You can't redefine any of the literal object constructors: {} is always a hash literal (or a code block, if it appears in that context), "" will always delimit a string, and so forth.

But there's plenty that you can do. You can even define some unary operators via method definitions.

7.2.2   *Customizing unary operators*

The unary operators + and - occur most frequently as signs for numbers, as in -1. But they can be defined; you can specify the behavior of the expressions +obj and -obj for your own objects and classes. You do so by defining the methods +@ and -@.

Let's say that you want + and - to mean uppercase and lowercase for a stringlike object. Here's how you define the appropriate unary operator behavior, using a Banner class as an example:

```
class Banner
  def initialize(text)
    @text = text
  end

  def to_s              <--- 1
    @text
  end

  def +@
    @text.upcase
  end

  def -@
    @text.downcase
  end
end
```

Now create a banner, and manipulate its case using the unary + and - operators:

```
banner = Banner.new("Eat at David's!")
puts banner            <---  Output: Eat at David's!
puts +banner           <--- Output: EAT AT DAVID'S!
puts -banner           <---  Output: eat at david's!
```

The basic string output for the banner text, unchanged, is provided by the to_s conversion method ❶, which you'll see up close in section 7.4.1.

You can also define the ! (logical *not*) operator, by defining the ! method. In fact, defining the ! method gives you both the unary ! and the keyword not. Let's add a definition to Banner:

```
class Banner
  def !
    reverse
  end
end
```

Now examine the banner, "negated." We'll need to use parentheses around the not version to clarify the precedence of expressions (otherwise puts thinks we're trying to print not):

```
puts !banner          ◁─┐  Output: !s'divaD ta taE
puts (not banner)     ◁─┐  Output: !s'divaD ta taE
```

As it so often does, Ruby gives you an object-oriented, method-based way to customize what you might at first think are hardwired syntactic features—even unary operators like !.

Unary negation isn't the only use Ruby makes of the exclamation point.

7.3 Bang (!) methods and "danger"

Ruby methods can end with an exclamation point (!), or bang. The bang has no significance to Ruby internally; bang methods are called and executed just like any other methods. But by convention, the bang labels a method as "dangerous"—specifically, as the dangerous equivalent of a method with the same name but without the bang.

Dangerous can mean whatever the person writing the method wants it to mean. In the case of the built-in classes, it usually means *this method, unlike its nonbang equivalent, permanently modifies its receiver.* It doesn't always, though: exit! is a dangerous alternative to exit, in the sense that it doesn't run any finalizers on the way out of the program. The danger in sub! (a method that substitutes a replacement string for a matched pattern in a string) is partly that it changes its receiver and partly that it returns nil if no change has taken place—unlike sub, which always returns a copy of the original string with the replacement (or no replacement) made.

If "danger" is too melodramatic for you, you can think of the ! in method names as a kind of "Heads up!" And, with very few, very specialized exceptions, every bang method should occur in a pair with a nonbang equivalent. We'll return to questions of best method-naming practice after we've looked at some bang methods in action.

7.3.1 Destructive (receiver-changing) effects as danger

No doubt most of the bang methods you'll come across in the core Ruby language have the bang on them because they're destructive: they change the object on which they're called. Calling upcase on a string gives you a new string consisting of the original string in uppercase; but upcase! turns the original string into its own uppercase equivalent, in place:

```
>> str = "Hello"
=> "Hello"
>> str.upcase
=> "HELLO"
>> str
=> "Hello"                   ◁── ❶
>> str.upcase!
=> "HELLO"
>> str                   ❷
=> "HELLO"           ◁─┘
```

Examining the original string after converting it to uppercase shows that the upper-case version was a copy; the original string is unchanged **❶**. But the bang operation has changed the content of `str` itself **❷**.

Ruby's core classes are full of destructive (receiver-changing) bang methods paired with their nondestructive counterparts: `sort`/`sort!` for arrays, `strip`/`strip!` (strip leading and trailing whitespace) for strings, `reverse`/`reverse!` for strings and arrays, and many more. In each case, if you call the nonbang version of the method on the object, you get a new object. If you call the bang version, you operate in-place on the same object to which you sent the message.

You should always be aware of whether the method you're calling changes its receiver. Neither option is always right or wrong; which is best depends on what you're doing. One consideration, weighing in on the side of modifying objects instead of creating new ones, is efficiency: creating new objects (like a second string that's identical to the first except for one letter) is expensive in terms of memory and processing. This doesn't matter if you're dealing with a small number of objects. But when you get into, say, handling data from large files and using loops and iterators to do so, creating new objects can be a drain on resources.

On the other hand, you need to be cautious about modifying objects in place, because other parts of the program may depend on those objects not to change. For example, let's say you have a database of names. You read the names out of the database into an array. At some point, you need to process the names for printed output—all in capital letters. You may do something like this:

```
names.each do |name|
  capped = name.upcase
  # ...code that does something with capped...
end
```

In this example, `capped` is a new object—an uppercase duplicate of `name`. When you go through the same array later, in a situation where you *do not* want the names in uppercase, such as saving them back to the database, the names will be the way they were originally.

By creating a new string (`capped`) to represent the uppercase version of each name, you avoid the side effect of changing the names permanently. The operation you perform on the names achieves its goals without changing the basic state of the data. Sometimes you'll want to change an object permanently, and sometimes you won't want to. There's nothing wrong with that, as long as you know which you're doing and why.

Furthermore, don't assume a direct correlation between bang methods and destructive methods. They often coincide, but they're not the same thing.

7.3.2 *Destructiveness and "danger" vary independently*

What follows here is some commentary on conventions and best practices. Ruby doesn't care; Ruby is happy to execute methods whose names end in `!` whether they're dangerous, safe, paired with a nonbang method, not paired—whatever. The value of the ! notation as a token of communication between a method author and a user of that method resides entirely in conventions. It's worth gaining a solid understanding of those conventions and why they make sense.

The best advice on when to use bang-terminated method names is…

DON'T USE ! EXCEPT IN M/M! METHOD PAIRS

The ! notation for a method name should only be used when there's a method of the same name without the !, when the relation between those two methods is that they both do substantially the same thing, and when the bang version also has side effects, a different return value, or some other behavior that diverges from its nonbang counterpart.

Don't use the ! just because you think your method is dangerous in some vague, abstract way. All methods do something; that in itself isn't dangerous. The ! is a warning that there may be more going on than the name suggests—and that, in turn, makes sense only if the name is in use for a method that doesn't have the dangerous behavior.

Don't name a method save! just because it writes to a file. Call that method save, and then, if you have another method that writes to a file but (say) doesn't back up the original file (assuming that save does so), go ahead and call that one save!.

If you find yourself writing one method to write to the file, and you put a ! at the end because you're worried the method is too powerful or too unsafe, you should reconsider your method naming. Any experienced Rubyist who sees a save! method documented is going to want to know how it differs from save. The exclamation point doesn't mean anything in isolation; it only makes sense at the end of one of a pair of otherwise identical method names.

DON'T EQUATE ! NOTATION WITH DESTRUCTIVE BEHAVIOR, OR VICE VERSA

Danger in the bang sense usually means object-changing or "destructive" behavior. It's therefore not uncommon to hear people assert that the ! means destructive. From there, it's not much of a leap to start wondering why some destructive methods' names don't end with !.

This line of thinking is problematic from the start. The bang doesn't mean destructive; it means dangerous, possibly unexpected behavior. If you have a method called upcase and you want to write a destructive version of it, you're free to call it destructive_upcase; no rule says you have to add a ! to the original name. It's just a convention, but it's an expressive one.

Destructive methods do not always end with !, nor would that make sense. Many nonbang methods have names that lead you to *expect* the receiver to change. These methods have no nondestructive counterparts. (What would it mean to have a nondestructive version of String#clear, which removes all characters from a string and leaves it equal to ""? If you're not changing the string in place, why wouldn't you just write "" in the first place?) If a method name without a bang already suggests in-place modification or any other kind of "dangerous behavior," then it's not a dangerous method.

You'll almost certainly find that the conventional usage of the ! notation is the most elegant and logical usage. It's best not to slap bangs on names unless you're playing along with those conventions.

Leaving danger behind us, we'll look next at the facilities Ruby provides for converting one object to another.

7.4 Built-in and custom to_* (conversion) methods

Ruby offers a number of built-in methods whose names consist of to_ plus an indicator of a class *to* which the method converts an object: to_s (to string), to_sym (to symbol), to_a (to array), to_i (to integer), and to_f (to float). Not all objects respond to all of these methods. But many objects respond to a lot of them, and the principle is consistent enough to warrant looking at them collectively.

7.4.1 String conversion: to_s

The most commonly used to_ method is probably to_s. Every Ruby object—except instances of BasicObject—responds to to_s, and thus has a way of displaying itself as a string. What to_s does, as the following irb excerpts show, ranges from nothing more than return its own receiver, when the object is already a string

```
>> "I am already a string!".to_s
=> "I am already a string!"
```

to returning a string containing a codelike representation of an object

```
>> ["one", "two", "three", 4, 5, 6].to_s
=> "[\"one\", \"two\", \"three\", 4, 5, 6]"
```

(where the backslash-escaped quotation marks mean there's a literal quotation mark inside the string) to returning an informative, if cryptic, descriptive string about an object:

```
>> Object.new.to_s
=> "#<Object:0x000001030389b0>"
```

The salient point about to_s is that it's used by certain methods and in certain syntactic contexts to provide a canonical string representation of an object. The puts method, for example, calls to_s on its arguments. If you write your own to_s for a class or override it on an object, your to_s will surface when you give your object to puts. You can see this clearly, if a bit nonsensically, using a generic object:

```
>> obj = Object.new
=> #<Object:0x000001011c9ce0>        ← 1
>> puts obj
#<Object:0x000001011c9ce0>           ← 2
=> nil
>> def obj.to_s                      ← 3
>>    "I'm an object!"
>> end
=> :to_s                             ← 4
>> puts obj                          ←
I'm an object!                        5
=> nil
```

The object's default string representation is the usual class and memory-location screen dump ❶. When you call `puts` on the object, that's what you see ❷. But if you define a custom `to_s` method on the object ❸, subsequent calls to `puts` reflect the new definition ❺. (Note that the method definition itself evaluates to a symbol, `:to_s`, representing the name of the method ❹.)

You also get the output of `to_s` when you use an object in string interpolation:

```
>> "My object says: #{obj}"
=> "My object says: I'm an object!"
```

Don't forget, too, that you can call `to_s` explicitly. You don't have to wait for Ruby to go looking for it. But a large percentage of calls to `to_s` are automatic, behind-the-scenes calls on behalf of `puts` or the interpolation mechanism.

> **NOTE** When it comes to generating string representations of their instances, arrays do things a little differently from the norm. If you call `puts` on an array, you get a cyclical representation based on calling `to_s` on each of the elements in the array and outputting one per line. That's a special behavior; it doesn't correspond to what you get when you call `to_s` on an array—namely, a string representation of the array in square brackets.

While we're looking at string representations of objects, let's examine a few related methods. We're drifting a bit from the `to_*` category, perhaps, but these are all methods that generate strings from objects, and a consideration of them is therefore timely.

BORN TO BE OVERRIDDEN: INSPECT

Every Ruby object—once again, with the exception of instances of `BasicObject`—has an `inspect` method. By default—unless a given class overrides `inspect`—the inspect string is a mini-screen-dump of the object's memory location:

```
>> Object.new.inspect
=> "#<Object:0x007fe24a292b68>"
```

Actually, irb uses `inspect` on every value it prints out, so you can see the `inspect` strings of various objects without even explicitly calling `inspect`:

```
>> Object.new
=> #<Object:0x007f91c2a8d1e8>
>> "abc"
=> "abc"
>> [1,2,3]
=> [1, 2, 3]
>> /a regular expression/
=> /a regular expression/
```

If you want a useful inspect string for your classes, you need to define `inspect` explicitly:

```
class Person
  def initialize(name)
    @name = name
  end
```

```
    def inspect
      @name
    end
end

david = Person.new("David")
puts david.inspect               # Output: David
```

(Note that overriding to_s and overriding inspect are two different things. Prior to Ruby 2, inspect piggybacked on to_s, so you could override both by overriding one. That's no longer the case.)

Another, less frequently used, method generates and displays a string representation of an object: display.

USING DISPLAY

You won't see display much. It occurs only once, at last count, in all the Ruby program files in the entire standard library. (inspect occurs 160 times.) It's a specialized output method.

display takes an argument: a writable output stream, in the form of a Ruby I/O object. By default, it uses STDOUT, the standard output stream:

```
>> "Hello".display
Hello=> nil
```

Note that display, unlike puts but like print, doesn't automatically insert a newline character. That's why => nil is run together on one line with the output.

You can redirect the output of display by providing, for example, an open file handle as an argument:

```
>> fh = File.open("/tmp/display.out", "w")
=> #<File:/tmp/display.out>
>> "Hello".display(fh)                          ◁──❶
=> nil
>> fh.close
=> nil
>> puts(File.read("/tmp/display.out"))          ◁──❷
Hello
```

The string "Hello" is "displayed" directly to the file ❶, as we confirm by reading the contents of the file in and printing them out ❷.

Let's leave string territory at this point and look at how conversion techniques play out in the case of the Array class.

7.4.2   *Array conversion with to_a and the * operator*

The to_a (to array) method, if defined, provides an array-like representation of objects. One of to_a's most striking features is that it automatically ties in with the * operator. The * operator (pronounced "star," "unarray," or, among the whimsically inclined, "splat") does a kind of unwrapping of its operand into its components, those components being the elements of its array representation.

You've already seen the star operator used in method parameter lists, where it denotes a parameter that sponges up the optional arguments into an array. In the more general case, the star turns any array, or any object that responds to to_a, into the equivalent of a bare list.

The term *bare list* means several identifiers or literal objects separated by commas. Bare lists are valid syntax only in certain contexts. For example, you can put a bare list inside the literal array constructor brackets:

```
[1,2,3,4,5]
```

It's a subtle distinction, but the notation lying between the brackets isn't an array; it's a list, and the array is constructed from the list, thanks to the brackets.

The star has a kind of bracket-removing or unarraying effect. What starts as an array becomes a list. You can see this if you construct an array from a starred array:

```
>> array = [1,2,3,4,5]
=> [1, 2, 3, 4, 5]
>> [*array]
=> [1, 2, 3, 4, 5]
```

The array in array has been demoted, so to speak, from an array to a bare list, courtesy of the star. Compare this with what happens if you don't use the star:

```
>> [array]
=> [[1, 2, 3, 4, 5]]
```

Here, the list from which the new array gets constructed contains one item: the object array. That object hasn't been mined for its inner elements, as it was in the example with the star.

One implication is that you can use the star in front of a method argument to turn it from an array into a list. You do this in cases where you have objects in an array that you need to send to a method that's expecting a broken-out list of arguments:

```
def combine_names(first_name, last_name)
  first_name + " " + last_name
end
names = ["David", "Black"]                    Output:
puts combine_names(*names)        ◁─┤        David Black
```

If you don't use the unarraying star, you'll send just one argument—an array—to the method, and the method won't be happy.

Let's turn to numbers.

7.4.3 Numerical conversion with to_i and to_f

Unlike some programming languages, such as Perl, Ruby doesn't automatically convert from strings to numbers or numbers to strings. You can't do this

```
>> 1 + "2"          ◁─┤   TypeError: String can't
                          be coerced into Fixnum
```

because Ruby doesn't know how to add a string and an integer together. And you'll get a surprise if you do this:

```
print "Enter a number: "
n = gets.chomp
puts n * 100
```

You'll see the string version of the number printed out 100 times. (This result also tells you that Ruby lets you multiply a string—but it's always treated as a string, even if it consists of digits.) If you want the number, you have to turn it into a number explicitly:

```
n = gets.to_i
```

As you'll see if you experiment with converting strings to integers (which you can do easily in irb with expressions like `"hello".to_i`), the `to_i` conversion value of strings that have no reasonable integer equivalent (including `"Hello"`) is always 0. If your string starts with digits but isn't made up entirely of digits (`"123hello"`), the nondigit parts are ignored and the conversion is performed only on the leading digits.

The `to_f` (to float) conversion gives you, predictably, a floating-point equivalent of any integer. The rules pertaining to nonconforming characters are similar to those governing string-to-integer conversions: `"hello".to_f` is `0.0`, whereas `"1.23hello".to_f` is `1.23`. If you call `to_f` on a float, you get the same float back. Similarly, calling `to_i` on an integer returns that integer.

If the conversion rules for strings seem a little lax to you—if you don't want strings like `"-5xyz"` to succeed in converting themselves to integers or floats—you have a couple of stricter conversion techniques available to you.

STRICTER CONVERSIONS WITH INTEGER AND FLOAT

Ruby provides methods called `Integer` and `Float` (and yes, they look like constants, but they're methods with names that coincide with those of the classes to which they convert). These methods are similar to `to_i` and `to_f`, respectively, but a little stricter: if you feed them anything that doesn't conform to the conversion target type, they raise an exception:

```
>> "123abc".to_i
=> 123
>> Integer("123abc")
ArgumentError: invalid value for Integer(): "123abc"
>> Float("3")
=> 3.0
>> Float("-3")
=> -3.0
>> Float("-3xyz")
ArgumentError: invalid value for Float(): "-3xyz"
```

(Note that converting from an integer to a float is acceptable. It's the letters that cause the problem.)

If you want to be strict about what gets converted and what gets rejected, `Integer` and `Float` can help you out.

> **Conversion vs. typecasting**
>
> When you call methods like `to_s`, `to_i`, and `to_f`, the result is a new object (or the receiver, if you're converting it to its own class). It's not quite the same as typecasting in C and other languages. You're not using the object as a string or an integer; you're asking the object to provide a second object that corresponds to its idea of itself (so to speak) in one of those forms.
>
> The distinction between conversion and typecasting touches on some important aspects of the heart of Ruby. In a sense, all objects are typecasting themselves constantly. Every time you call a method on an object, you're asking the object to behave as a particular type. Correspondingly, an object's "type" is really the aggregate of everything it can do at a particular time.
>
> The closest Ruby gets to traditional typecasting (and it isn't very close) is the role-playing conversion methods, described in section 7.4.4.

Getting back to the `to_*` family of converters: in addition to the straightforward object-conversion methods, Ruby gives you a couple of `to_*` methods that have a little extra intelligence about what their value is expected to do.

7.4.4 Role-playing to_* methods

It's somewhat against the grain in Ruby programming to worry much about what class an object belongs to. All that matters is what the object can do—what methods it can execute.

But in a few cases involving the core classes, strict attention is paid to the class of objects. Don't think of this as a blueprint for "the Ruby way" of thinking about objects. It's more like an expediency that bootstraps you into the world of the core objects in such a way that once you get going, you can devote less thought to your objects' class memberships.

STRING ROLE-PLAYING WITH TO_STR

If you want to print an object, you can define a `to_s` method for it or use whatever `to_s` behavior it's been endowed with by its class. But what if you need an object to *be* a string?

The answer is that you define a `to_str` method for the object. An object's `to_str` representation enters the picture when you call a core method that requires that its argument be a string.

The classic example is string addition. Ruby lets you add two strings together, producing a third string:

```
>> "Hello " + "there."
=> "Hello there."
```

If you try to add a nonstring to a string, you get an error:

```
>> "Hello " + 10
TypeError: no implicit conversion of Float into String
```

This is where to_str comes in. If an object responds to to_str, its to_str representation will be used when the object is used as the argument to String#+.

Here's an example involving a simple Person class. The to_str method is a wrapper around the name method:

```
class Person
  attr_accessor :name
  def to_str
    name
  end
end
```

If you create a Person object and add it to a string, to_str kicks in with the name string:

```
david = Person.new
david.name = "David"                          Output: david is
puts "david is named " + david + "."    ◁──┘  named David.
```

The to_str conversion is also used on arguments to the << (append to string) method. And arrays, like strings, have a role-playing conversion method.

ARRAY ROLE-PLAYING WITH TO_ARY

Objects can masquerade as arrays if they have a to_ary method. If such a method is present, it's called on the object in cases where an array, and only an array, will do—for example, in an array-concatenation operation.

Here's another Person implementation, where the array role is played by an array containing three person attributes:

```
class Person
  attr_accessor :name, :age, :email
  def to_ary
    [name, age, email]
  end
end
```

Concatenating a Person object to an array has the effect of adding the name, age, and email values to the target array:

```
david = Person.new
david.name = "David"
david.age = 55
david.email = "david@wherever"
array = []
array.concat(david)              Output: ["David", 55,
p array                    ◁──┘  "david@wherever"]
```

Like to_str, to_ary provides a way for an object to step into the role of an object of a particular core class. As is usual in Ruby, sensible usage of conventions is left up to you. It's possible to write a to_ary method, for example, that does something other than return an array—but you'll almost certainly get an error message when you try to use it, as Ruby looks to to_ary for an array. So if you're going to use the role-playing to_* methods, be sure to play in Ruby's ballpark.

We'll turn now to the subject of Boolean states and objects in Ruby, a topic we've dipped into already, but one that merits closer inquiry.

7.5   *Boolean states, Boolean objects, and nil*

Every expression in Ruby evaluates to an object, and every object has a Boolean value of either *true* or *false*. Furthermore, `true` and `false` are objects. This idea isn't as convoluted as it sounds. If true and false weren't objects, then a pure Boolean expression like

```
100 > 80
```

would have no object to evaluate *to*. (And > is a method and therefore has to return an object.)

In many cases where you want to get at a truth/falsehood value, such as an if statement or a comparison between two numbers, you don't have to manipulate these special objects directly. In such situations, you can think of truth and falsehood as *states*, rather than objects.

We'll look at `true` and `false` both as states and as special objects, along with the special object `nil`.

7.5.1   *True and false as states*

Every expression in Ruby is either true or false, in a logical or Boolean sense. The best way to get a handle on this is to think in terms of conditional statements. For every expression *e* in Ruby, you can do this

```
if e
```

and Ruby can make sense of it.

For lots of expressions, a conditional test is a stretch; but it can be instructive to try it on a variety of expressions, as the following listing shows.

> **Listing 7.1   Testing the Boolean value of expressions using `if` constructs**

```
if (class MyClass; end)                                    ◁—①
  puts "Empty class definition is true!"
else
  puts "Empty class definition is false!"
end
if (class MyClass; 1; end)                                 ◁—②
  puts "Class definition with the number 1 in it is true!"
else
  puts "Class definition with the number 1 in it is false!"
end
if (def m; return false; end)                              ◁—③
  puts "Method definition is true!"
else
  puts "Method definition is false!"
end
```

```
if "string"
  puts "Strings appear to be true!"                        4
else
  puts "Strings appear to be false!"
end
if 100 > 50                                             ⬅—5
  puts "100 is greater than 50!"
else
  puts "100 is not greater than 50!"
end
```

Here's the output from this listing (minus a warning about using a string literal in a conditional):

```
Empty class definition is false!
Class definition with the number 1 in it is true!
Method definition is true!
Strings appear to be true!
100 is greater than 50!
```

As you can see, empty class definitions ❶ are false; nonempty class definitions evaluate to the same value as the last value they contain ❷ (in this example, the number 1); method definitions are true ❸ (even if a call *to* the method would return false); strings are true ❹ (don't worry about the string literal in condition warning); and 100 is greater than 50 ❺. You can use this simple if technique to explore the Boolean value of any Ruby expression.

The if examples show that every expression in Ruby is either true or false in the sense of either passing or not passing an if test. But these examples don't show what the expressions evaluate to. That's what the if test is testing: it evaluates an expression (such as class MyClass; end) and proceeds on the basis of whether the value produced by that evaluation is true.

To see what values are returned by the expressions whose truth value we've been testing, you can derive those values in irb:

```
>> class MyClass; end                 ⬅—❶
=> nil
>> class MyClass; 1; end               ⬅—❷
=> 1
>> def m; return false; end            ⬅—❸
=> :m
>> "string literal!"                   ⬅—❹
=> "string literal!"
>> 100 > 50                            ⬅—❺
=> true
```

The empty class definition ❶ evaluates to nil, which is a special object (discussed in section 7.5.3). All you need to know for the moment about nil is that it has a Boolean value of false (as you can detect from the behavior of the if clauses that dealt with it in listing 7.1).

The class definition with the number 1 in it ❷ evaluates to the number 1, because every class-definition block evaluates to the last expression contained inside it, or `nil` if the block is empty.

The method definition evaluates to the symbol `:m` ❸, representing the name of the method that's just been defined.

The string `literal` ❹ evaluates to itself; it's a literal object and doesn't have to be calculated or processed into some other form when evaluated. Its value as an expression is itself.

Finally, the comparison expression `100 > 50` ❺ evaluates to true—not just to something that has the Boolean value true, but to the object true. The object `true` does have the Boolean value true. But along with `false`, it has a special role to play in the realm of truth and falsehood and how they're represented in Ruby.

7.5.2 *true and false as objects*

The Boolean objects `true` and `false` are special objects, each being the only instance of a class especially created for it: `TrueClass` and `FalseClass`, respectively. You can ask `true` and `false` to tell you their classes' names, and they will:

```
puts true.class          ←┘  Output: TrueClass
puts false.class         ←┐  Output: FalseClass
```

The terms `true` and `false` are keywords. You can't use them as variable or method names; they're reserved for Ruby's exclusive use.

You can pass the objects `true` and `false` around, assign them to variables, and examine them like any other object. Here's an irb session that puts `true` through its paces in its capacity as a Ruby object:

```
>> a = true
=> true
>> a = 1 unless a
=> nil
>> a
=> true
>> b = a
=> true
```

You'll sometimes see `true` and `false` used as method arguments. For example, if you want a class to show you all of its instance methods but to exclude those defined in ancestral classes, you can provide the argument `false` to your request:

```
>> String.instance_methods(false)
```

The problem with Boolean arguments is that it's very hard to remember what they do. They're rather cryptic. Therefore, it's best to avoid them in your own code, unless there's a case where the true/false distinction is very clear.

Let's summarize the true/false situation in Ruby with a look at Boolean states versus Boolean values.

TRUE/FALSE: STATES VS. VALUES

As you now know, every Ruby expression is true or false in a Boolean sense (as indicated by the `if` test), and there are also objects called `true` and `false`. This double usage of the true/false terminology is sometimes a source of confusion: when you say that something is true, it's not always clear whether you mean it has a Boolean truth value or that it's the object `true`.

Remember that every expression has a Boolean value—including the expression `true` and the expression `false`. It may seem awkward to have to say, "The object `true` is true." But that extra step makes it possible for the model to work consistently.

Building on this point, and on some of the cases you saw in slightly different form in table 7.1, table 7.3 shows a mapping of some sample expressions to both the outcome of their evaluation and their Boolean value.

Note in particular that zero and empty strings (as well as empty arrays and hashes) have a Boolean value of true. The only objects that have a Boolean value of false are `false` and `nil`.

Table 7.3   Mapping sample expressions to their evaluation results and Boolean values

Expression	Object to which expression evaluates	Boolean value of expression
`1`	`1`	True
`0`	`0`	True
`1+1`	`2`	True
`true`	`true`	True
`false`	`false`	False
`nil`	`nil`	False
`"string"`	`"string"`	True
`""`	`""`	True
`puts "string"`	`nil`	False
`100 > 50`	`true`	True
`x = 10`	`10`	True
`def x; end`	`:x`	True
`class C; end`	`nil`	False
`class C; 1; end`	`1`	True

And on the subject of `nil`: it's time for us to look more closely at this unique object.

7.5.3   *The special object nil*

The special object `nil` is, indeed, an object (it's the only instance of a class called `NilClass`). But in practice, it's also a kind of nonobject. The Boolean value of `nil` is false, but that's just the start of its nonobjectness.

nil denotes an absence of anything. You can see this graphically when you inquire into the value of, for example, an instance variable you haven't initialized:

```
puts @x
```

This command prints `nil`. (If you try this with a local variable, you'll get an error; local variables aren't automatically initialized to anything, not even `nil`.) `nil` is also the default value for nonexistent elements of container and collection objects. For example, if you create an array with three elements, and then you try to access the tenth element (at index 9, because array indexing starts at 0), you'll find that it's `nil`:

```
>> ["one","two","three"][9]
=> nil
```

nil is sometimes a difficult object to understand. It's all about absence and nonexistence; but `nil` does exist, and it responds to method calls like other objects:

```
>> nil.to_s
=> ""
>> nil.to_i
=> 0
>> nil.object_id
=> 8
```

The `to_s` conversion of `nil` is an empty string (`""`); the integer representation of `nil` is 0; and `nil`'s object ID is 8. (nil has no special relationship to 8; that just happens to be the number designated as its ID.)

It's not accurate to say that `nil` is empty, because doing so would imply that it has characteristics and dimension, like a number or a collection, which it isn't supposed to. Trying to grasp `nil` can take you into some thorny philosophical territory. You can think of `nil` as an object that exists and that comes equipped with a survival kit of methods but that serves the purpose of representing absence and a state of being undetermined.

Coming full circle, remember that `nil` has a Boolean value of false. `nil` and `false` are the only two objects that do. They're not the only two *expressions* that do; 100 < 50 has a Boolean value of false, because it evaluates to the object `false`. But `nil` and `false` are the only two *objects* in Ruby with a Boolean value of false. All other Ruby objects—numbers, strings, instances of `MyCoolClass`—have a Boolean value of true. Tested directly, they all pass the `if` test.

Boolean values and testing provide a segue into the next topic: comparisons between objects. We'll look at tests involving two objects and ways of determining whether they're equal—and, if they aren't, whether they can be ranked as greater/lesser, and based on what criteria.

7.6   *Comparing two objects*

Ruby objects are created with the capacity to compare themselves to other objects for equality and/or order, using any of several methods. Tests for equality are the most common comparison tests, and we'll start with them. We'll then look at a built-in Ruby module called Comparable, which gives you a quick way to impart knowledge of comparison operations to your classes and objects, and that is used for that purpose by a number of built-in Ruby classes.

7.6.1   *Equality tests*

Inside the Object class, all equality-test methods do the same thing: they tell you whether two objects are exactly the same object. Here they are in action:

```
>> a = Object.new
=> #<Object:0x00000101258af8>
>> b = Object.new
=> #<Object:0x00000101251d70>
>> a == a
=> true
>> a == b
=> false
>> a != b
=> true
>> a.eql?(a)
=> true
>> a.eql?(b)
=> false
>> a.equal?(a)
=> true
>> a.equal?(b)
=> false
```

All three of the positive equality-test methods (==, eql?, and equal?) give the same results in these examples: when you test a against a, the result is true, and when you test a against b, the result is false. (The not-equal or negative equality test method != is the inverse of the == method; in fact, if you define ==, your objects will automatically have the != method.) We have plenty of ways to establish that a is a but not b.

But there isn't much point in having three tests that do the same thing. Further down the road, in classes other than Object, == and/or eql? are typically redefined to do meaningful work for different objects. The equal? method is usually left alone so that you can always use it to check whether two objects are exactly the same object.

Here's an example involving strings. Note that they are == and eql?, but not equal?:

```
>> string1 = "text"
=> "text"
>> string2 = "text"
=> "text"
>> string1 == string2
=> true
>> string1.eql?(string2)
```

```
=> true
>> string1.equal?(string2)
=> false
```

Furthermore, Ruby gives you a suite of tools for object comparisons, and not always just comparison for equality. We'll look next at how equality tests and their redefinitions fit into the overall comparison picture.

7.6.2 *Comparisons and the Comparable module*

The most commonly redefined equality-test method, and the one you'll see used most often, is ==. It's part of the larger family of equality-test methods, and it's also part of a family of comparison methods that includes ==, !=, >, <, >=, and <=.

Not every class of object needs, or should have, all these methods. (It's hard to imagine what it would mean for one Bicycle to be greater than or equal to another. Gears?) But for classes that do need full comparison functionality, Ruby provides a convenient way to get it. If you want objects of class MyClass to have the full suite of comparison methods, all you have to do is the following:

1   Mix a module called Comparable (which comes with Ruby) into MyClass.
2   Define a comparison method with the name <=> as an instance method in MyClass.

The comparison method <=> (usually called the *spaceship operator* or *spaceship method*) is the heart of the matter. Inside this method, you define what you mean by *less than*, *equal to*, and *greater than*. Once you've done that, Ruby has all it needs to provide the corresponding comparison methods.

For example, let's say you're taking bids on a job and using a Ruby script to help you keep track of what bids have come in. You decide it would be handy to be able to compare any two Bid objects, based on an estimate attribute, using simple comparison operators like > and <. *Greater than* means asking for more money, and *less than* means asking for less money.

A simple first version of the Bid class might look like the following listing.

Listing 7.2   Example of a class that mixes in the Comparable module

```
class Bid
  include Comparable
  attr_accessor :estimate
  def <=>(other_bid)                              ◁──❶
    if self.estimate < other_bid.estimate
      -1
    elsif self.estimate > other_bid.estimate
      1
    else
      0
    end
  end
end
```

The spaceship method ❶ consists of a cascading if/elsif/else statement. Depending on which branch is executed, the method returns a negative number (by convention, -1), a positive number (by convention, 1), or 0. Those three return values are predefined, prearranged signals to Ruby. Your <=> method must return one of those three values every time it's called—and they always mean less than, equal to, and greater than, respectively.

You can shorten this method. Bid estimates are either floating-point numbers or integers (the latter, if you don't bother with the cents parts of the figure or if you store the amounts as cents rather than dollars). Numbers already know how to compare themselves to each other, including integers to floats. Bid's <=> method can therefore piggyback on the existing <=> methods of the Integer and Float classes, like this:

```
def <=>(other_bid)
  self.estimate <=> other_bid.estimate
end
```

In this version of the spaceship method, we're punting; we're saying that if you want to know how two bids compare to each other, bump the question to the estimate values for the two bids and use that comparison as the basis for the bid-to-bid comparison.

The payoff for defining the spaceship operator and including Comparable is that you can from then on use the whole set of comparison methods on pairs of your objects. In this example, bid1 wins the contract; it's less than (as determined by <) bid2:

```
>> bid1 = Bid.new
=> #<Bid:0x000001011d5d60>
>> bid2 = Bid.new
=> #<Bid:0x000001011d4320>
>> bid1.estimate = 100
=> 100
>> bid2.estimate = 105
=> 105
>> bid1 < bid2
=> true
```

The < method (along with >, >=, <=, ==, !=, and between?) is defined in terms of <=>, inside the Comparable module. (b.between?(a,c) tells you whether *b* > *a* and *b* < *c*.)

All Ruby numerical classes include Comparable and have a definition for <=>. The same is true of the String class; you can compare strings using the full assortment of Comparable method/operators. Comparable is a handy tool, giving you a lot of functionality in return for, essentially, one method definition.

We'll now turn to the subject of runtime object inspection. In keeping with the spirit of this chapter, we'll look at enough techniques to sustain you through most of the rest of the book. Keep in mind, though, that chapter 15, the last in the book, will come back to the topic of runtime inspection (among others). So you can take this as the first, but not the last, substantial look at the topic.

7.7 *Inspecting object capabilities*

Inspection and *reflection* refer, collectively, to the various ways in which you can get Ruby objects to tell you about themselves during their lifetimes. Much of what you learned earlier about getting objects to show string representations of themselves could be described as inspection. In this section, we'll look at a different kind of runtime reflection: techniques for asking objects about the methods they can execute.

How you do this depends on the object and on exactly what you're looking for. Every object can tell you what methods you can call on it, at least as of the moment you ask it. In addition, class and module objects can give you a breakdown of the methods they provide for the objects that have use of those methods (as instances or via module inclusion).

7.7.1 *Listing an object's methods*

The simplest and most common case is when you want to know what messages an object understands—that is, what methods you can call on it. Ruby gives you a typically simple way to do this. Enter this into irb:

```
>> "I am a String object".methods
```

You'll see a large array of method names. At the least, you'll want to sort them so you can find what you're looking for:

```
>> "I am a String object".methods.sort
```

The `methods` method works with class and module objects, too. But remember, it shows you what the object (the class or module) responds to, not what instances of the class or objects that use the module respond to. For example, asking irb for

```
>> String.methods.sort
```

shows a list of methods that the `Class` object `String` responds to. If you see an item in this list, you know you can send it directly to `String`.

The methods you see when you call `methods` on an object include its singleton methods—those that you've written just for this object—as well as any methods it can call by virtue of the inclusion of one or more modules anywhere in its ancestry. All these methods are presented as equals: the listing of methods flattens the method lookup path and only reports on what methods the object knows about, regardless of where they're defined.

You can verify this in irb. Here's an example where a singleton method is added to a string. If you include the call to `str.methods.sort` at the end, you'll see that `shout` is now among the string's methods:

```
>> str = "A plain old string"
=> "A plain old string"
>> def str.shout
>>   self.upcase + "!!!"
>> end
```

```
=> nil
>> str.shout
=> "A PLAIN OLD STRING!!!"
>> str.methods.sort
```

Conveniently, you can ask just for an object's singleton methods:

```
>> str.singleton_methods
=> [:shout]
```

Similarly, if you mix a module into a class with `include`, instances of that class will report themselves as being able to call the instance methods from that module. Interestingly, you'll get the same result even if you include the module after the instance already exists. Start a new irb session (to clear the memory of the previous example), and try this code. Instead of printing out all the methods, we'll use a couple of less messy techniques to find out whether `str` has the `shout` method:

```
>> str = "Another plain old string."
=> "Another plain old string."
>> module StringExtras
>>   def shout
>>     self.upcase + "!!!"
>>   end
>> end
=> :shout
>> class String                      Makes strings
>>   include StringExtras      ◁──┘  into shouters
>> end
=> String
>> str.methods.include?(:shout)
=> true
```

Including the module affects strings that already exist because when you ask a string to shout, it searches its method lookup path for a `shout` method and finds it in the module. The string really doesn't care when or how the module got inserted into the lookup path.

Any object can tell you what methods it knows. In addition, class and module objects can give you information about the methods they provide.

7.7.2   *Querying class and module objects*

One of the methods you'll find in the list generated by the irb command `String.methods.sort` is `instance_methods`. It tells you all the instance methods that instances of `String` are endowed with:

```
>> String.instance_methods.sort
```

The resulting list is the same as the list of methods, as shown by `methods`, for any given string (unless you've added singleton methods to that string).

You can make a similar request of a module:

```
>> Enumerable.instance_methods.sort
```

In addition to straightforward method and instance-method lists, Ruby provides a certain number of tweaks to help you make more fine-grained queries.

7.7.3 *Filtered and selected method lists*

Sometimes you'll want to see the instance methods defined in a particular class without bothering with the methods every object has. After all, you already know that your object has *those* methods. You can view a class's instance methods without those of the class's ancestors by using the slightly arcane technique, introduced earlier, of providing the argument `false` to the `instance_methods` method:

```
String.instance_methods(false).sort
```

You'll see many fewer methods this way, because you're looking at a list of only those defined in the `String` class, without those defined in any of `String`'s ancestral classes or modules. This approach gives you a restricted picture of the methods available to string objects, but it's useful for looking in a more fine-grained way at how and where the method definitions behind a given object are positioned.

Other method-listing methods include the following (of which you've seen `singleton_methods` already):

- `obj.private_methods`
- `obj.public_methods`
- `obj.protected_methods`
- `obj.singleton_methods`

In addition, classes and modules let you examine their instance methods:

- `MyClass.private_instance_methods`
- `MyClass.protected_instance_methods`
- `MyClass.public_instance_methods`

The last of these, `public_instance_methods`, is a synonym for `instance_methods`.

The mechanisms for examining objects' methods are extensive. As always, be clear in your own mind what the object is (in particular, class/module or "regular" object) that you're querying and what you're asking it to tell you.

We've reached the end of our midbook bootstrap session, survival kit, literacy guide…. Whatever you call it (even "chapter 7"!), it puts us in a good position to look closely at a number of important core classes, which we'll do over the next several chapters.

7.8 *Summary*

In this chapter you've seen

- Ruby's literal constructors
- Syntactic sugar converting methods into operators
- "Destructive" methods and bang methods

- Conversion methods (to_s and friends)
- The inspect and display methods
- Boolean values and Boolean objects
- The special object nil
- Comparing objects and the Comparable module
- Examining an object's methods

This chapter covered several topics that pertain to multiple built-in classes and modules. You've seen Ruby's literal constructors, which provide a concise alternative to calling new on certain built-in classes. You've also seen how Ruby provides syntactic sugar for particular method names, including a large number of methods with names that correspond to arithmetic operators.

We looked at the significance of methods that change their own receivers, which many built-in methods do (many of them bang methods, which end with !). We also examined the to_* methods: built-in methods for performing conversions from one core class to another.

You've also learned a number of important points and techniques concerning Boolean (true/false) values and comparison between objects. You've seen that every object in Ruby has a Boolean value and that Ruby also has special Boolean objects (true and false) that represent those values in their simplest form. A third special object, nil, represents a state of undefinedness or absence. We also discussed techniques for comparing objects using the standard comparison operator (<=>) and the Comparable module.

Finally, we looked at ways to get Ruby objects to tell you what methods they respond to—a kind of reflection technique that can help you see and understand what's going on at a given point in your program. We'll look more deeply at introspection and reflection in chapter 15.

The material in this chapter will put you in a strong position to absorb what you encounter later, in the rest of this book and beyond. When you read statements like "This method has a bang alternative," you'll know what they mean. When you see documentation that tells you a particular method argument defaults to nil, you'll know what that means. And the fact that you've learned about these recurrent topics will help us economize on repetition in the upcoming chapters about built-in Ruby classes and modules and concentrate instead on moving ahead.

Strings, symbols, and other scalar objects

This chapter covers

- String object creation and manipulation
- Methods for transforming strings
- Symbol semantics
- String/symbol comparison
- Integers and floats
- Time and date objects

The term *scalar* means *one-dimensional*. Here, it refers to objects that represent single values, as opposed to collection or container objects that hold multiple values. There are some shades of gray: strings, for example, can be viewed as collections of characters in addition to being single units of text. Scalar is to some extent in the eye of the beholder. Still, as a good first approximation, you can look at the classes discussed in this chapter as classes of one-dimensional, bite-sized objects, in contrast to the collection objects that will be the focus of the next chapter.

The built-in objects we'll look at in this chapter include the following:

- Strings, which are Ruby's standard way of handling textual material of any length

- Symbols, which are (among other things) another way of representing text in Ruby
- Integers
- Floating-point numbers
- `Time`, `Date`, and `DateTime` objects

All of these otherwise rather disparate objects are scalar—they're one-dimensional, noncontainer objects with no further objects lurking inside them the way arrays have. This isn't to say scalars aren't complex and rich in their semantics; as you'll see, they are.

8.1 Working with strings

Ruby provides two built-in classes that, between them, provide all the functionality of text representation and manipulation: the `String` class and the `Symbol` class. Strings and symbols are deeply different from each other, but they're similar enough in their shared capacity to represent text that they merit being discussed in the same chapter. We'll start with strings, which are the standard way to represent bodies of text of arbitrary content and length. You've seen strings in many contexts already; here, we'll get more deeply into some of their semantics and abilities. We'll look first at how you write strings, after which we'll discuss a number of ways in which you can manipulate strings, query them (for example, as to their length), compare them with each other, and transform them (from lowercase to uppercase, and so on). We'll also examine some further details of the process of converting strings with `to_i` and related methods.

8.1.1 String notation

A *string literal* is generally enclosed in quotation marks:

```
"This is a string."
```

Single quotes can also be used:

```
'This is also a string.'
```

But a single-quoted string behaves differently, in some circumstances, than a double-quoted string. The main difference is that string interpolation doesn't work with single-quoted strings. Try these two snippets, and you'll see the difference:

```
puts "Two plus two is #{2 + 2}."
puts 'Two plus two is #{2 + 2}.'
```

As you'll see if you paste these lines into irb, you get two very different results:

```
Two plus two is 4.
Two plus two is #{2 + 2}.
```

Single quotes disable the #{ . . . } interpolation mechanism. If you need that mechanism, you can't use single quotes. Conversely, you can, if necessary, *escape* (and thereby disable) the string interpolation mechanism in a double-quoted string, using backslashes:

```
puts "Escaped interpolation: \"\#{2 + 2}\"."
```

Single- and double-quoted strings also behave differently with respect to the need to escape certain characters. The following statements document and demonstrate the differences. Look closely at which are single-quoted and which are double-quoted, and at how the backslash is used:

```
puts "Backslashes (\\) have to be escaped in double quotes."
puts 'You can just type \ once in a single quoted string.'
puts "But whichever type of quotation mark you use..."
puts "...you have to escape its quotation symbol, such as \"."
puts 'That applies to \' in single-quoted strings too.'
puts 'Backslash-n just looks like \n between single quotes.'
puts "But it means newline\nin a double-quoted string."
puts 'Same with \t, which comes out as \t with single quotes...'
puts "...but inserts a tab character:\tinside double quotes."
puts "You can escape the backslash to get \\n and \\t with double quotes."
```

Here's the output from this barrage of quotations. It doesn't line up line-for-line with the code, but you can see why if you look at the statement that outputs a new-line character:

```
Backslashes (\) have to be escaped in double quotes.
You can just type \ once in a single quoted string.
But whichever type of quotation mark you use...
...you have to escape its quotation symbol, such as ".
That applies to ' in single-quoted strings too.
Backslash-n just looks like \n between single quotes.
But it means newline
in a double-quoted string.
Same with \t, which comes out as \t with single quotes...
...but inserts a tab character:    inside double quotes.
You can escape the backslash to get \n and \t with double quotes.
```

You'll see other cases of string interpolation and character escaping as we proceed. Meanwhile, by far the best way to get a feel for these behaviors firsthand is to experiment with strings in irb.

Ruby gives you several ways to write strings in addition to single and double quotation marks.

OTHER QUOTING MECHANISMS

The alternate quoting mechanisms take the form %*char*{text}, where *char* is one of several special characters and the curly braces stand in for a delimiter of your choosing. Here's an example of one of these mechanisms: %q, which produces a single-quoted string:

```
puts %q{You needn't escape apostrophes when using %q.}
```

As the sample sentence points out, because you're not using the single-quote character as a quote character, you can use it unescaped inside the string.

Also available to you are %Q{}, which generates a double-quoted string, and plain %{} (percent sign and delimiter), which also generates a double-quoted string. Naturally, you don't need to escape the double-quote character inside strings that are represented with either of these notations.

The delimiter for the %-style notations can be just about anything you want, as long as the opening delimiter matches the closing one. *Matching* in this case means either making up a left/right pair of braces (curly, curved, or square) or being two of the same character. Thus all of the following are acceptable:

```
%q-A string-
%Q/Another string/
%[Yet another string]
```

You can't use alphanumeric characters as your delimiters, but if you feel like being obscure, you can use a space. It's hard to see in an example, so the entire following example is surrounded by square brackets that you shouldn't type if you're entering the example in an irb session or Ruby program file:

```
[%q Hello! ]
```

The space-delimited example, aside from being silly (although instructive), brings to mind the question of what happens if you use the delimiter inside the string (because many strings have spaces inside them). If the delimiter is a single character, you have to escape it:

```
[%q Hello\ there! ]
%q-Better escape the \- inside this string!-
```

If you're using left/right matching braces and Ruby sees a left-hand one inside the string, it assumes that the brace is part of the string and looks for a matching right-hand one. If you want to include an unmatched brace of the same type as the ones you're using for delimiters, you have to escape it:

```
%Q[I can put [] in here unescaped.]
%q(I have to escape \( if I use it alone in here.)
%Q(And the same goes for \).)
```

irb doesn't play well with some of this syntax

irb has its own Ruby parser, which has to contend with the fact that as it parses one line, it has no way of knowing what the next line will be. The result is that irb does things a little differently from the Ruby interpreter. In the case of quote mechanisms, you may find that in irb, escaping unmatched square and other brackets produces odd results. Generally, you're better off plugging these examples into the command-line format ruby -e 'puts %q[Example: \[ ]' and similar.

Each of the %*char*-style quoting mechanisms generates either a single- or double-quoted string. That distinction pervades stringdom; every string is one or the other, no matter which notation you use—including the next one we'll look at, the "here" document syntax.

"HERE" DOCUMENTS

A *"here" document*, or *here-doc*, is a string, usually a multiline string, that often takes the form of a template or a set of data lines. It's said to be "here" because it's physically present in the program file, not read in from a separate text file.

Here-docs come into being through the << operator, as shown in this irb excerpt:

```
>> text = <<EOM
This is the first line of text.
This is the second line.
Now we're done.
EOM
=> "This is the first line of text.\nThis is the second line.\n
Now we're done.\n"
```

The expression <<EOM means *the text that follows, up to but not including the next occurrence of "EOM."* The delimiter can be any string; EOM (end of message) is a common choice. It has to be flush-left, and it has to be the only thing on the line where it occurs. You can switch off the flush-left requirement by putting a hyphen before the << operator:

```
>> text = <<-EOM
The EOM doesn't have to be flush left!
        EOM
=> "The EOM doesn't have to be flush left!\n"
```

The EOM that stops the reading of this here-doc (only a one-line document this time) is in the middle of the line.

By default, here-docs are read in as double-quoted strings. Thus they can include string interpolation and use of escape characters like \n and \t. If you want a single-quoted here-doc, put the closing delimiter in single quotes when you start the document. To make the difference clearer, this example includes a puts of the here-doc:

```
>> text = <<-'EOM'
Single-quoted!
Note the literal \n.
And the literal #{2+2}.
EOM
=> "Single-quoted!\nNote the literal \\n.\nAnd the literal \#{2+2}.\n"
>> puts text
Single-quoted!
Note the literal \n.
And the literal #{2+2}.
```

The <<EOM (or equivalent) doesn't have to be the last thing on its line. Wherever it occurs, it serves as a placeholder for the upcoming here-doc. Here's one that gets converted to an integer and multiplied by 10:

```
a = <<EOM.to_i * 10
5
EOM                          Output: 50
puts a
```

You can even use a here-doc in a literal object constructor. Here's an example where a string gets put into an array, creating the string as a here-doc:

```
array = [1,2,3, <<EOM, 4]
This is the here-doc!
It becomes array[3].
EOM
p array
```

The output is

```
[1, 2, 3, "This is the here-doc!\nIt becomes array[3].\n", 4]
```

And you can use the <<EOM notation as a method argument; the argument becomes the here-doc that follows the line on which the method call occurs. This can be useful if you want to avoid cramming too much text into your argument list:

```
do_something_with_args(a, b, <<EOM)
http://some_very_long_url_or_other_text_best_put_on_its_own_line
EOM
```

In addition to creating strings, you need to know what you can do with them. You can do a lot, and we'll look at much of it in detail, starting with the basics of string manipulation.

8.1.2   Basic string manipulation

Basic in this context means manipulating the object at the lowest levels: retrieving and setting substrings, and combining strings with each other. From Ruby's perspective, these techniques aren't any more basic than those that come later in our survey of strings; but conceptually, they're closer to the string metal, so to speak.

GETTING AND SETTING SUBSTRINGS

To retrieve the *n*th character in a string, you use the [] operator/method, giving it the index, on a zero-origin basis, for the character you want. Negative numbers index from the end of the string:

```
>> string = "Ruby is a cool language."
=> "Ruby is a cool language."
>> string[5]
=> "i"
>> string[-12]
=> "o"
```

If you provide a second integer argument, *m*, you'll get a substring of *m* characters, starting at the index you've specified:

```
>> string[5,10]
=> "is a cool "
```

You can also provide a single *range* object as the argument. We'll look at ranges in more depth later; for now, you can think of *n..m* as all of the values between *n* and *m*, inclusive (or exclusive of *m*, if you use three dots instead of two). The range can use negative numbers, which count from the end of the string backward, but the second index always has to be closer to the end of the string than the first index; the index logic only goes from left to right:

```
>> string[7..14]
=> " a cool "
>> string[-12..-3]
=> "ol languag"
>> string[-12..20]
=> "ol langua"
>> string[15..-1]
=> "language."
```

You can also grab substrings based on an explicit substring search. If the substring is found, it's returned; if not, the return value is `nil`:

```
>> string["cool lang"]
=> "cool lang"
>> string["very cool lang"]
=> nil
```

It's also possible to search for a pattern match using the `[]` technique with a regular expression—`[]` is a method, and what's inside it are the arguments, so it can do whatever it's programmed to do:

```
>> string[/c[ol ]+/]
=> "cool l"
```

We'll look at regular expressions separately in chapter 11, at which point you'll get a sense of the possibilities of this way of looking for substrings.

The `[]` method is also available under the name `slice`. Furthermore, a receiver-changing version of `slice`, namely `slice!`, removes the character(s) from the string permanently:

```
>> string.slice!("cool ")
=> "cool "
>> string
=> "Ruby is a language."
```

To set part of a string to a new value, you use the `[]=` method. It takes the same kinds of indexing arguments as `[]` but changes the values to what you specify. Putting the preceding little string through its paces, here are some substring-setting examples, with an examination of the changed string after each one:

```
>> string = "Ruby is a cool language."
=> "Ruby is a cool language."
>> string["cool"] = "great"
=> "great"
>> string
=> "Ruby is a great language."
>> string[-1] = "!"
=> "!"
>> string
```

```
=> "Ruby is a great language!"
>> string[-9..-1] = "thing to learn!"
=> "thing to learn!"
>> string
=> "Ruby is a great thing to learn!"
```

Integers, ranges, strings, and regular expressions can thus all work as index or substring specifiers. If you try to set part of the string that doesn't exist—that is, a too-high or too-low numerical index, or a string or regular expression that doesn't match the string—you get a fatal error.

In addition to changing individual strings, you can also combine strings with each other.

COMBINING STRINGS

There are several techniques for combining strings. These techniques differ as to whether the second string is permanently added to the first or whether a new, third string is created out of the first two—in other words, whether the operation changes the receiver.

To create a new string consisting of two or more strings, you can use the + method/operator to run the original strings together. Here's what irb has to say about adding strings:

```
>> "a" + "b"
=> "ab"
>> "a" + "b" + "c"
=> "abc"
```

The string you get back from + is always a new string. You can test this by assigning a string to a variable, using it in a + operation, and checking to see what its value is after the operation:

```
>> str = "Hi "
=> "Hi "
>> str + "there."        ❶
=> "Hi there."
>> str                   ❷
=> "Hi "
```

The expression `str + "there."` (which is syntactic sugar for the method call `str.+("there")`) evaluates to the new string `"Hi there."` ❶ but leaves `str` unchanged ❷.

To add (append) a second string permanently to an existing string, use the `<<` method, which also has a syntactic sugar, pseudo-operator form:

```
>> str = "Hi "
=> "Hi "
>> str << "there."
=> "Hi there."
>> str                   ❶
=> "Hi there."
```

In this example, the original string `str` has had the new string appended to it, as you can see from the evaluation of `str` at the end ❶.

String interpolation is (among other things) another way to combine strings. You've seen it in action already, but let's take the opportunity to look at a couple of details of how it works.

STRING COMBINATION VIA INTERPOLATION

At its simplest, string interpolation involves dropping one existing string into another:

```
>> str = "Hi "
=> "Hi "
>> "#{str} there."
=> "Hi there."
```

The result is a new string: "Hi there." However, it's good to keep in mind that the interpolation can involve any Ruby expression:

```
>> "The sum is #{2 + 2}."
=> "The sum is 4."
```

The code inside the curly braces can be anything. (They do have to be curly braces; it's not like %q{}, where you can choose your own delimiter.) It's unusual to make the code terribly complex, because that detracts from the structure and readability of the program—but Ruby is happy with any interpolated code and will obligingly place a string representation of the value of the code in your string:

```
>> "My name is #{class Person
              attr_accessor :name
          end
          d = Person.new
          d.name = "David"
          d.name
          }."
=> "My name is David."
```

You really, *really* don't want to do this, but it's important to understand that you can interpolate any code you want. Ruby patiently waits for it all to run and then snags the final value of the whole thing (d.name, in this case, because that's the last expression inside the interpolation block) and interpolates it.

There's a much nicer way to accomplish something similar. Ruby interpolates by calling to_s on the object to which the interpolation code evaluates. You can take advantage of this to streamline string construction, by defining your own to_s methods appropriately:

```
>> class Person
>>   attr_accessor :name
>>   def to_s
>>     name
>>   end
>> end
=> :to_s
>> david = Person.new
=> #<Person:0x00000101a73cb0>
>> david.name = "David"
```

```
=> "David"
>> "Hello, #{david}!"
=> "Hello, David!"
```

Here the object `david` serves as the interpolated code, and produces the result of its `to_s` operation, which is defined as a wrapper around the `name` getter method. Using the `to_s` hook is a useful way to control your objects' behavior in interpolated strings. Remember, though, that you can also say (in the preceding example) `david.name`. So if you have a broader use for a class's `to_s` than a very specific interpolation scenario, you can usually accommodate it.

After you've created and possibly altered a string, you can ask it for a considerable amount of information about itself. We'll look now at how to query strings.

8.1.3   Querying strings

String queries come in a couple of flavors. Some give you a Boolean (true or false) response, and some give you a kind of status report on the current state of the string. We'll organize our exploration of string query methods along these lines.

BOOLEAN STRING QUERIES

You can ask a string whether it includes a given substring, using `include?`. Given the string used earlier (`"Ruby is a cool language."`), inclusion queries might look like this:

```
>> string.include?("Ruby")
=> true
>> string.include?("English")
=> false
```

You can test for a given start or end to a string with `start_with?` and `end_with?`:

```
>> string.start_with?("Ruby")
=> true
>> string.end_with?("!!!")
=> false
```

And you can test for the absence of content—that is, for the presence of any characters at all—with the `empty?` method:

```
>> string.empty?
=> false
>> "".empty?
=> true
```

Keep in mind that whitespace counts as characters; the string `" "` isn't empty.

CONTENT QUERIES

The `size` and `length` methods (they're synonyms for the same method) do what their names suggest they do:

```
>> string.size
=> 24
```

If you want to know how many times a given letter or set of letters occurs in a string, use count. To count occurrences of one letter, provide that one letter as the argument. Still using the string "Ruby is a cool language.", there are three occurrences of "a":

```
>> string.count("a")
=> 3
```

To count how many of a range of letters there are, you can use a hyphen-separated range:

```
>> string.count("g-m")
=> 5
```

Character specifications are case-sensitive:

```
>> string.count("A-Z")
=> 1
```

You can also provide a written-out set of characters you want to count:

```
>> string.count("aey. ")          ◁──┐   Three letters plus period
=> 10                                │   and space characters
```

To negate the search—that is, to count the number of characters that don't match the ones you specify—put a ^ (caret) at the beginning of your specification:

```
>> string.count("^aey. ")
=> 14
>> string.count("^g-m")
=> 19
```

(If you're familiar with regular expressions, you'll recognize the caret technique as a close cousin of regular expression character class negation.) You can combine the specification syntaxes and even provide more than one argument:

```
>> string.count("ag-m")
=> 8                                     Count "a" and "g-m"
>> string.count("ag-m", "^l")    ◁──┘   except for "l"
=> 6
```

Another way to query strings as to their content is with the index method. index is sort of the inverse of using [] with a numerical index: instead of looking up a substring at a particular index, it returns the index at which a given substring occurs. The first occurrence from the left is returned. If you want the first occurrence from the right, use rindex:

```
>> string.index("cool")
=> 10
>> string.index("l")
=> 13
>> string.rindex("l")
=> 15
```

Although strings are made up of characters, Ruby has no separate character class. One-character strings can tell you their ordinal code, courtesy of the ord method:

```
>> "a".ord
=> 97
```

If you take the ord of a longer string, you get the code for the first character:

```
>> "abc".ord
=> 97
```

The reverse operation is available as the chr method on integers:

```
>> 97.chr
=> "a"
```

Asking a number that doesn't correspond to any character for its chr equivalent causes a fatal error.

In addition to providing information about themselves, strings can compare themselves with other strings, to test for equality and order.

8.1.4 *String comparison and ordering*

The String class mixes in the Comparable module and defines a <=> method. Strings are therefore good to go when it comes to comparisons based on character code (ASCII or otherwise) order:

```
>> "a" <=> "b"
=> -1
>> "b" > "a"
=> true
>> "a" > "A"
=> true
>> "." > ","
=> true
```

Remember that the spaceship method/operator returns -1 if the right object is greater, 1 if the left object is greater, and 0 if the two objects are equal. In the first case in the previous sequence, it returns -1 because the string "b" is greater than the string "a". But "a" is greater than "A", because the order is done by character value and the character values for "a" and "A" are 97 and 65, respectively, in Ruby's default encoding of UTF-8. Similarly, the string "." is greater than "," because the value for a period is 46 and that for a comma is 44. (See section 8.1.7 for more on encoding.)

Like Ruby objects in general, strings have several methods for testing equality.

COMPARING TWO STRINGS FOR EQUALITY

The most common string comparison method is ==, which tests for equality of string content:

```
>> "string" == "string"
=> true
>> "string" == "house"
=> false
```

The two literal "string" objects are different objects, but they have the same content. Therefore, they pass the == test. The string "house" has different content and is therefore not considered equal, based on ==, with "string".

Another equality-test method, String#eql?, tests two strings for identical content. In practice, it usually returns the same result as ==. (There are subtle differences in the implementations of these two methods, but you can use either. You'll find that == is more common.) A third method, String#equal?, behaves like equal? usually does: it tests whether two strings are the same object—or for that matter, whether a string and any other object are the same object:

```
>> "a" == "a"
=> true
>> "a".equal?("a")
=> false
>> "a".equal?(100)
=> false
```

The first test succeeds because the two strings have the same contents. The second test fails because the first string isn't the same object as the second string. (And of course no string is the same object as the integer 100, so that test fails too.) This is a good reminder of the fact that strings that appear identical to the eye may, to Ruby, have different object identities.

The next two sections will present string *transformations* and *conversions*, in that order. The difference between the two is that a transformation involves applying some kind of algorithm or procedure to the content of a string, whereas a conversion means deriving a second, unrelated object—usually not even a string—from the string.

8.1.5 *String transformation*

String transformations in Ruby fall informally into three categories: case, formatting, and content transformations. We'll look at each in turn.

CASE TRANSFORMATIONS
Strings let you raise, lower, and swap their case. All of the case-changing methods have receiver-modifying bang equivalents:

```
>> string = "David A. Black"
=> "David A. Black"
>> string.upcase
=> "DAVID A. BLACK"
>> string.downcase
=> "david a. black"
>> string.swapcase
=> "dAVID a. bLACK"
```

There's also a nice refinement that lets you capitalize the string:

```
>> string = "david"
=> "david"
>> string.capitalize
=> "David"
```

Like the other case transformers, `capitalize` has an in-place equivalent, `capitalize!`.

You can perform a number of transformations on the format of a string, most of which are designed to help you make your strings look nicer.

FORMATTING TRANSFORMATIONS

Strictly speaking, format transformations are a subset of content transformations; if the sequence of characters represented by the string didn't change, it wouldn't be much of a transformation. We'll group under the formatting heading some transformations whose main purpose is to enhance the presentation of strings.

The `rjust` and `ljust` methods expand the size of your string to the length you provide in the first argument, padding with blank spaces as necessary:

```
>> string = "David A. Black"
=> "David A. Black"
>> string.rjust(25)
=> "           David A. Black"
>> string.ljust(25)
=> "David A. Black           "
```

If you supply a second argument, it's used as padding. This second argument can be more than one character long:

```
>> string.rjust(25,'.')
=> "...........David A. Black"
>> string.rjust(25,'><')
=> "><><><><><>David A. Black"
```

The padding pattern is repeated as many times as it will fit, truncating the last placement if necessary.

And to round things out in the justification realm, there's a `center` method, which behaves like `rjust` and `ljust` but puts the characters of the string in the center:

```
>> "The middle".center(20, "*")
=> "*****The middle*****"
```

Odd-numbered padding spots are rendered right-heavy:

```
>> "The middle".center(21, "*")
=> "*****The middle******"
```

Finally, you can prettify your strings by stripping whitespace from either or both sides, using the `strip`, `lstrip`, and `rstrip` methods:

```
>> string = "   David A. Black   "
=> "   David A. Black   "
>> string.strip
=> "David A. Black"
>> string.lstrip
=> "David A. Black   "
>> string.rstrip
=> "   David A. Black"
```

All three of the string-stripping methods have `!` versions that change the string permanently in place.

CONTENT TRANSFORMATIONS

We'll look at some, though not all, of the ways you can transform a string by changing its contents.

The `chop` and `chomp` methods are both in the business of removing characters from the ends of strings—but they go about it differently. The main difference is that `chop` removes a character unconditionally, whereas `chomp` removes a target substring if it finds that substring at the end of the string. By default, `chomp`'s target substring is the newline character, `\n`. You can override the target by providing `chomp` with an argument:

```
>> "David A. Black".chop
=> "David A. Blac"
>> "David A. Black\n".chomp
=> "David A. Black"
>> "David A. Black".chomp('ck')
=> "David A. Bla"
```

By far the most common use of either `chop` or `chomp` is the use of `chomp` to remove newlines from the ends of strings, usually strings that come to the program in the form of lines of a file or keyboard input.

Both `chop` and `chomp` have bang equivalents that change the string in place.

On the more radical end of character removal stands the `clear` method, which empties a string of all its characters, leaving the empty string:

```
>> string = "David A. Black"
=> "David A. Black"
>> string.clear
=> ""
>> string
=> ""
```

`String#clear` is a great example of a method that changes its receiver but doesn't end with the `!` character. The name `clear` makes it clear, so to speak, that something is happening to the string. There would be no point in having a `clear` method that didn't change the string in place; it would just be a long-winded way to say `""` (the empty string).

If you want to swap out all your characters without necessarily leaving your string bereft of content, you can use `replace`, which takes a string argument and replaces the current content of the string with the content of that argument:

```
>> string = "(to be named later)"
=> "(to be named later)"
>> string.replace("David A. Black")
=> "David A. Black"
```

As with `clear`, the `replace` method permanently changes the string—as suggested, once again, by the name.

You can target certain characters for removal from a string with `delete`. The arguments to `delete` follow the same rules as the arguments to `count` (see section 8.1.3):

```
>> "David A. Black".delete("abc")
=> "Dvid A. Blk"
>> "David A. Black".delete("^abc")
=> "aac"
>> "David A. Black".delete("a-e","^c")
=> "Dvi A. Blck"
```

Another specialized string transformation is `crypt`, which performs a Data Encryption Standard (DES) encryption on the string, similar to the Unix `crypt(3)` library function. The single argument to `crypt` is a two-character salt string:

```
>> "David A. Black".crypt("34")
=> "3470EY.7YRmio"
```

Make sure you read up on the robustness of any encryption techniques you use, including `crypt`.

The last transformation technique we'll look at is string incrementation. You can get the next-highest string with the `succ` method (also available under the name `next`). The ordering of strings is engineered to make sense, even at the expense of strict character-code order: `"a"` comes after `"`"` (the backtick character) as it does in ASCII, but after `"z"` comes `"aa"`, not `"{"`. Incrementation continues, odometer-style, throughout the alphabet:

```
>> "a".succ
=> "b"
>> "abc".succ
=> "abd"
>> "azz".succ
=> "baa"
```

The ability to increment strings comes in handy in cases where you need batch-generated unique strings, perhaps to use as filenames.

As you've already seen, strings (like other objects) can convert themselves with methods in the `to_*` family. We'll look next at some further details of string conversion.

8.1.6   *String conversions*

The `to_i` method you saw in the last chapter is one of the conversion methods available to strings. This method offers an additional feature: if you give it a positive integer argument in the range 2–36, the string you're converting is interpreted as representing a number in the base corresponding to the argument.

For example, if you want to interpret 100 as a base 17 number, you can do so like this:

```
>> "100".to_i(17)
=> 289
```

The output is the decimal equivalent of 100, base 17.

Base 8 and base 16 are considered special cases and have dedicated methods so you don't have to go the `to_i` route. These methods are `oct` and `hex`, respectively:

```
>> "100".oct
=> 64
>> "100".hex
=> 256
```

Other conversion methods available to strings include `to_f` (to float), `to_s` (to string; it returns its receiver), and `to_sym` or `intern`, which converts the string to a `Symbol` object. None of these hold any particular surprises:

```
>> "1.2345".to_f
=> 1.2345
>> "Hello".to_s
=> "Hello"
>> "abcde".to_sym
=> :abcde
>> "1.2345and some words".to_f
=> 1.2345
>> "just some words".to_i
=> 0
```

Every string consists of a sequence of bytes. The bytes map to characters. Exactly *how* they map to characters—how many bytes make up a character, and what those characters are—is a matter of *encoding*, which we'll now take a brief look at.

8.1.7 *String encoding: A brief introduction*

The subject of character encoding is interesting but vast. Encodings are many, and there's far from a global consensus on a single best one. Ruby 1.9 added a great deal of encoding intelligence and functionality to strings. The big change in Ruby 2 was the use of UTF-8, rather than US-ASCII, as the default encoding for Ruby scripts. Encoding in Ruby continues to be an area of ongoing discussion and development. We won't explore it deeply here, but we'll put it on our radar and look at some important encoding-related techniques.

SETTING THE ENCODING OF THE SOURCE FILE

To start with, your source code uses a certain encoding. By default, Ruby source files use UTF-8 encoding. You can determine this by asking Ruby to display the value `__ENCODING__`. Put this line in a file, and run it:

```
puts __ENCODING__        ⟵── Output: UTF-8
```

You need to put the line in a file because you may get different results if you run the command directly from the command line. The reason for the difference is that a file-less Ruby run takes its encoding from the current locale setting. You can verify this by observing the effect of running the same command with the `LANG` environment variable set to a different value:

```
LANG=en_US.iso885915 ruby -e 'puts __ENCODING__'        ⟵── Output: US-ASCII
```

To change the encoding of a source file, you need to use a *magic comment* at the top of the file. The magic comment takes the form

```
# encoding: encoding
```

where *encoding* is an identifier for an encoding. For example, to encode a source file in US-ASCII, you put this line at the top of the file:

```
# encoding: ASCII
```

This line (which can use the word *coding* rather than the word *encoding*, if you prefer) is sometimes referred to as a "magic comment."

In addition to your source file, you can also query and set the encoding of individual strings.

ENCODING OF INDIVIDUAL STRINGS

Strings will tell you their encoding:

```
>> str = "Test string"
=> "Test string"
>> str.encoding
=> #<Encoding:UTF-8>
```

You can encode a string with a different encoding, as long as the conversion from the original encoding to the new one—the *transcoding*—is permitted (which depends on the capability of the string with the new encoding):

```
>> str.encode("US-ASCII")
=> "Test string"
```

If you need to, you can force an encoding with the force_encoding method, which bypasses the table of "permitted" encodings and encodes the bytes of the string with the encoding you specify, unconditionally.

The bang version of encode changes the encoding of the string permanently:

```
>> str.encode!("US-ASCII")
=> "Test string"
>> str.encoding
=> #<Encoding:US-ASCII>
```

The encoding of a string is also affected by the presence of certain characters in a string and/or by the amending of the string with certain characters. You can represent arbitrary characters in a string using either the \x escape sequence, for a two-digit hexadecimal number representing a byte, or the \u escape sequence, which is followed by a UTF-8 code, and inserts the corresponding character.

The effect on the string's encoding depends on the character. Given an encoding of US-ASCII, adding an escaped character in the range 0–127 (0x00-0x7F in hexadecimal) leaves the encoding unchanged. If the character is in the range 128–255 (0xA0-0xFF), the encoding switches to UTF-8. If you add a UTF-8 character in the range 0x0000–0x007F, the ASCII string's encoding is unaffected. UTF-8 codes higher than 0x007F cause the string's encoding to switch to UTF-8. Here's an example:

```
>> str = "Test string"
=> "Test string"
>> str.encode!("US-ASCII")
>> str << ". Euro symbol: \u20AC"          <--●
=> "Test string. Euro symbol: €"
>> str.encoding
=> #<Encoding:UTF-8>
```

The \u escape sequence ● lets you insert any UTF-8 character, whether you can type it directly or not.

There's a great deal more to the topic of character and string encoding, but you've seen enough at this point to know the kinds of operations that are available. How deeply you end up exploring encoding will depend on your needs as a Ruby developer. Again, be aware that encoding has tended to be the focus of particularly intense discussion and development in Ruby (and elsewhere).

At this point, we'll wrap up our survey of string methods and turn to a class with some strong affinities with the `String` class but also some interesting differences: the `Symbol` class.

8.2 Symbols and their uses

Symbols are instances of the built-in Ruby class `Symbol`. They have a literal constructor: the leading colon. You can always recognize a symbol literal (and distinguish it from a string, a variable name, a method name, or anything else) by this token:

```
:a
:book
:"Here's how to make a symbol with spaces in it."
```

You can also create a symbol programmatically by calling the `to_sym` method (also known by the synonym `intern`) on a string, as you saw in the last section:

```
>> "a".to_sym
=> :a
>> "Converting string to symbol with intern....".intern
=> :"Converting string to symbol with intern...."
```

Note the telltale leading colons on the evaluation results returned by irb.

You can easily convert a symbol to a string:

```
>> :a.to_s
=> "a"
```

That's just the beginning, though. Symbols differ from strings in important ways. Let's look at symbols on their own terms and then come back to a comparative look at symbols and strings.

8.2.1 Chief characteristics of symbols

Symbols are a hard nut to crack for many people learning Ruby. They're not quite like anything else, and they don't correspond exactly to data types most people have come across previously. In some respects they're rather stringlike, but at the same time, they have a lot in common with integers. It's definitely worth a close look at their chief characteristics: immutability and uniqueness.

IMMUTABILITY

Symbols are immutable. There's no such thing as appending characters to a symbol; once the symbol exists, that's it. You'll never see :abc << :d or anything of that kind.

That's not to say that there's no symbol :abcd. There is, but it's a completely different symbol from :abc. You can't change :abc itself. Like an integer, a symbol can't be changed. When you want to refer to 5, you don't change the object 4 by adding 1 to it. You can add 1 to 4 by calling 4.+(1) (or 4 + 1), but you can't cause the object 4 to be the object 5. Similarly, although you can use a symbol as a hint to Ruby for the generation of another symbol, you can't alter a given symbol.

UNIQUENESS

Symbols are unique. Whenever you see :abc, you're seeing a representation of the same object. Again, symbols are more like integers than strings in this respect. When you see the notation "abc" in two places, you're looking at representations of two different string objects; the literal string constructor "" creates a new string. But :abc is always the same Symbol object, just as 100 is always the same object.

You can see the difference between strings and symbols in the matter of uniqueness by querying objects as to their object_id, which is unique for every separate object:

```
>> "abc".object_id
=> 2707250
>> "abc".object_id
=> 2704780
>> :abc.object_id
=> 160488
>> :abc.object_id
=> 160488
```

The "abc" notation creates a new string each time, as you can see from the fact that each such string has a different object ID. But the :abc notation always represents the same object; :abc identifies itself with the same ID number no matter how many times you ask it.

Because symbols are unique, there's no point having a constructor for them; Ruby has no Symbol#new method. You can't create a symbol any more than you can create a new integer. In both cases, you can only refer to them.

The word *symbol* has broad connotations; it sounds like it might refer to any identifier or token. It's important to get a handle on the relation between symbol objects and symbols in a more generic sense.

8.2.2 Symbols and identifiers

This code includes one Symbol object (:x) and one local variable identifier (s):

```
s = :x
```

But it's not unusual to refer to the s as a symbol. And it *is* a symbol, in the sense that it represents something other than itself. In fact, one of the potential causes of confusion surrounding the `Symbol` class and symbol objects is the fact that symbol objects *don't* represent anything other than themselves. In a sense, a variable name is more "symbolic" than a symbol.

And a connection exists between symbol objects and symbolic identifiers. Internally, Ruby uses symbols to keep track of all the names it's created for variables, methods, and constants. You can see a list of them, using the `Symbol.all_symbols` class method. Be warned; there are a lot of them! Here's the tip of the iceberg:

```
>> Symbol.all_symbols
=> [:inspect, :intern, :object_id, :const_missing, :method_missing,
:method_added, :singleton_method_added, :method_removed,
:singleton_method_removed,
```

And on it goes, listing more than 3,000 symbols.

When you assign a value to a variable or constant, or create a class or write a method, the identifier you choose goes into Ruby's internal symbol table. You can check for evidence of this with some array-probing techniques:

```
>> Symbol.all_symbols.size
=> 3118
>> abc = 1
=> 1
>> Symbol.all_symbols.size
=> 3119
>> Symbol.all_symbols.grep(/abc/)     ◁———  Use grep rather than include?
=> [:abc]                                    (see following note)
```

You can see from the measurement of the size of the array returned by `all_symbols` that it grows by 1 when you make an assignment to abc. In addition, the symbol `:abc` is now present in the array, as demonstrated by the `grep` operation.

Tests for symbol inclusion are always true

`grep` is a regular expression–based way of looking for matching elements in an array. Why not just say this?

```
>> Symbol.all_symbols.include?(:abc)
```

Because it will always be true! The very act of writing `:abc` in the `include?` test puts the symbol `:abc` into the symbol table, so the test passes even if there was no previous assignment to the identifier abc.

The symbol table is just that: a symbol table. It's not an object table. If you use an identifier for more than one purpose—say, as a local variable and also as a method name—the corresponding symbol will still only appear once in the symbol table:

```
>> def abc; end          ◁———  Reuses "abc" identifier
=> :abc                                        ◁——  Method definitions return
>> Symbol.all_symbols.size                            their names as symbols
=> 3119                  ◁——  Same size; :abc is in
                               table only once
```

Ruby keeps track of what symbols it's supposed to know about so it can look them up quickly. The inclusion of a symbol in the symbol table doesn't tell you anything about what the symbol is for.

Coming full circle, you can also see that when you assign a symbol to a variable, that symbol gets added to the table:

```
>> abc = :my_symbol
=> :my_symbol
>> Symbol.all_symbols.size
=> 3020
>> Symbol.all_symbols.grep(/my_symbol/)
=> [:my_symbol]
```

Not only symbols matching variable and method names are put in the table; any symbol Ruby sees anywhere in the program is added. The fact that :my_symbol gets stored in the symbol table by virtue of your having used it means that the next time you use it, Ruby will be able to look it up quickly. And unlike a symbol that corresponds to an identifier to which you've assigned a more complex object, like a string or array, a symbol that you're using purely as a symbol, like :my_symbol, doesn't require any further lookup. It's just itself: the symbol :my_symbol.

Ruby is letting you, the programmer, use the same symbol-storage mechanism that Ruby uses to track identifiers. Only you're not tracking identifiers; you're using symbols for your own purposes. But you still get the benefits of Ruby exposing the whole symbol mechanism for programmer-side use.

What do you do with symbols?

8.2.3   *Symbols in practice*

Symbols have a number of uses, but most appearances fall into one of two categories: method arguments and hash keys.

SYMBOLS AS METHOD ARGUMENTS

A number of core Ruby methods take symbols as arguments. Many such methods can also take strings. You've already seen a couple of examples from the attr_* method family:

```
attr_accessor :name
attr_reader :age
```

The send method, which sends a message to an object without the dot, can take a symbol:

```
"abc".send(:upcase)
```

You don't normally need send if you know the whole method name in advance. But the lesson here is that send can take a symbol, which remains true even if the symbol is stored in a variable, rather than written out, and/or determined dynamically at runtime.

At the same time, most methods that take symbols can also take strings. You can replace :upcase with "upcase" in the previous send example, and it will work. The difference is that by supplying :upcase, you're saving Ruby the trouble of translating the string upcase to a symbol internally on its way to locating the method.

It's possible to go overboard. You'll occasionally see code like this:

```
some_object.send(method_name.to_sym)
```

An extra step is taken (the to_sym conversion) on the way to passing an argument to send. There's no point in doing this unless the method being called can only handle symbols. If it can handle strings and you've got a string, pass the string. Let the method handle the conversion if one is needed.

Consider allowing symbols or strings as method arguments

When you're writing a method that will take an argument that could conceivably be a string or a symbol, it's often nice to allow both. It's not necessary in cases where you're dealing with user-generated, arbitrary strings, or where text read in from a file is involved; those won't be in symbol form anyway. But if you have a method that expects, say, a method name, or perhaps a value from a finite table of tags or labels, it's polite to allow either strings or symbols. That means avoiding doing anything to the object that requires it to be one or the other and that will cause an error if it's the wrong one. You can normalize the argument with a call to to_sym (or to_s, if you want to normalize to strings) so that whatever gets passed in fits into the operations you need to perform.

Next up: symbols as hash keys. We won't look in depth at hashes until chapter 9, but the use of symbols as hash keys is extremely widespread and worth putting on our radar now.

SYMBOLS AS HASH KEYS

A *hash* is a keyed data structure: you insert values into it by assigning the value to a key, and you retrieve a value by providing a reference to a key. Ruby puts no constraints on hash keys. You can use an array, a class, another hash, a string, or any object you like as a hash key. But in most cases you're likely to use strings or symbols.

Here's the creation of a hash with symbols as keys, followed by the retrieval of one of the values:

```
>> d_hash = { :name => "David", :age => 55 }
=> {:name=>"David", :age=>55}
>> d_hash[:age]
=> 55
```

And here's a similar hash with string keys:

```
>> d_hash = { "name" => "David", "age" => 55 }
=> {"name"=>"David", "age"=>55}
>> d_hash["name"]
=> "David"
```

There's nothing terrible about using strings as hash keys, especially if you already have a collection of strings on hand and need to incorporate them into a hash. But symbols have a few advantages in the hash-key department.

First, Ruby can process symbols faster, so if you're doing a lot of hash lookups, you'll save a little time. You won't notice a difference if you're only processing small amounts of data, but if you need to tweak for efficiency, symbol hash keys are probably a good idea.

Second, symbols look good as hash keys. Looking good is, of course, not a technical characteristic, and opinion about what looks good varies widely. But symbols do have a kind of frozen, label-like look that lends itself well to cases where your hash keys are meant to be static identifiers (like `:name` and `:age`), whereas strings have a malleability that's a good fit for the representation of arbitrary values (like someone's name). Perhaps this is a case of projecting the technical basis of the two objects—strings being mutable, symbols not—onto the aesthetic plane. Be that as it may, Ruby programmers tend to use symbols more than strings as hash keys.

The third reason to use symbols rather than strings as hash keys, when possible, is that Ruby allows a special form of symbol representation in the hash-key position, with the colon after the symbol instead of before it and the hash separator arrow removed. In other words,

```
hash = { :name => "David", :age => 55 }
```

can also be written as

```
hash = { name: "David", age: 55 }
```

As it so often does, Ruby goes out of its way to let you write things in an uncluttered, simple way. Of course, if you prefer the version with the standard symbol notation and the hash arrows, you can still use that form.

So far, and by design, we've looked at symbols mainly by the light of how they differ from strings. But you'll have noticed that strings enter the discussion regularly, no matter how much we try to separate the two. It's worth having centered the spotlight on symbols, but now let's widen it and look at some specific points of comparison between symbols and strings.

8.2.4   *Strings and symbols in comparison*

Symbols have become increasingly stringlike in successive versions of Ruby. That's not to say that they've shed their salient features; they're still immutable and unique. But they present a considerably more stringlike interface than they used to.

By way of a rough demonstration of the changes, here are two lists of methods. The first comes from Ruby 1.8.6:

```
>> Symbol.instance_methods(false).sort
=> ["===", "id2name", "inspect", "to_i", "to_int", "to_s", "to_sym"]
```

The second is from Ruby 2:

```
>> Symbol.instance_methods(false).sort
=> [:<=>, :==, :===, :=~, :[], :capitalize, :casecmp, :downcase, :empty?,
:encoding, :id2name, :inspect, :intern, :length, :match, :next, :size,
:slice, :succ, :swapcase, :to_proc, :to_s, :to_sym, :upcase]
```

Somewhere along the line, symbols have learned to do lots of new things, mostly from the string domain. But note that there are no bang versions of the various case-changing and incrementation methods. For strings, `upcase!` means *upcase yourself in place*. Symbols, on the other hand, are immutable; the symbol `:a` can show you the symbol `:A`, but it can't be the symbol `:A`.

In general, the semantics of the stringlike symbol methods are the same as the string equivalents, including incrementation:

```
>> sym = :david
=> :david
>> sym.upcase
=> :DAVID
>> sym.succ
=> :davie
>> sym[2]
=> "v"                    <--●
>> sym.casecmp(:david)
=> 0
```

Note that indexing into a symbol returns a substring ❶, not a symbol. From the programmer's perspective, symbols acknowledge the fact that they're representations of text by giving you a number of ways to manipulate their content. But it isn't really content; `:david` doesn't contain "david" any more than `100` contains "100." It's a matter of the interface and of a characteristically Ruby-like confluence of object theory and programming practicality.

Underneath, symbols are more like integers than strings. (The symbol table is basically an integer-based hash.) They share with integers not only immutability and uniqueness, but also immediacy: a variable to which a symbol is bound provides the actual symbol value, not a reference to it. If you're puzzled over exactly how symbols work, or over why both strings and symbols exist when they seem to be duplicating each other's efforts in representing text, think of symbols as integer-like entities dressed up in characters. It sounds odd, but it explains a lot.

The integer-like qualities of symbols also provide a nice transition to the topic of numerical objects.

8.3 Numerical objects

In Ruby, numbers are objects. You can send messages to them, just as you can to any object:

```
n = 99.6
m = n.round
puts m                    <--●
x = 12
if x.zero?
  puts "x is zero"
else
  puts "x is not zero"    <--❷
end
puts "The ASCII character equivalent of 97 is #{97.chr}"    <--❸
```

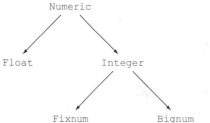

Figure 8.1 Numerical class hierarchy

As you'll see if you run this code, floating-point numbers know how to round themselves ❶ (up or down). Numbers in general know ❷ whether they're zero. And integers can convert themselves to the character that corresponds to their ASCII value ❸.

Numbers are objects; therefore, they have classes—a whole family tree of them.

8.3.1 *Numerical classes*

Several classes make up the numerical landscape. Figure 8.1 shows a slightly simplified view (mixed-in modules aren't shown) of those classes, illustrating the inheritance relations among them.

The top class in the hierarchy of numerical classes is Numeric; all the others descend from it. The first branch in the tree is between floating-point and integral numbers: the Float and Integer classes. Integers are broken into two classes: Fixnum and Bignum. Bignums, as you may surmise, are large integers. When you use or calculate an integer that's big enough to be a Bignum rather than a Fixnum, Ruby handles the conversion automatically for you; you don't have to worry about it.

8.3.2 *Performing arithmetic operations*

For the most part, numbers in Ruby behave as the rules of arithmetic and the usual conventions of arithmetic notation lead you to expect. The examples in table 8.1 should be reassuring in their boringness.

Note that when you divide integers, the result is always an integer. If you want floating-point division, you have to feed Ruby floating-point numbers (even if all you're doing is adding .0 to the end of an integer).

Table 8.1 Common arithmetic expressions and their evaluative results

Expression	Result	Comments
1 + 1	2	Addition
10/5	2	Integer division
16/5	3	Integer division (no automatic floating-point conversion)
10/3.3	3.3333333333	Floating-point division
1.2 + 3.4	4.6	Floating-point addition

Table 8.1   Common arithmetic expressions and their evaluative results *(continued)*

Expression	Result	Comments
-12 - -7	–5	Subtraction
10 % 3	1	Modulo (remainder)

Ruby also lets you manipulate numbers in nondecimal bases. Hexadecimal integers are indicated by a leading 0x. Here are some irb evaluations of hexadecimal integer expressions:

```
>> 0x12
=> 18
>> 0x12 + 12        ⬷——❶
=> 30
```

The second 12 in the last expression ❶ is a decimal 12; the 0x prefix applies only to the numbers it appears on.

Integers beginning with 0 are interpreted as *octal* (base 8):

```
>> 012
=> 10
>> 012 + 12
=> 22
>> 012 + 0x12
=> 28
```

As you saw in section 8.1.6, you can also use the to_i method of strings to convert numbers in any base to decimal. To perform such a conversion, you need to supply the base you want to convert *from* as an argument to to_i. The string is then interpreted as an integer in that base, and the whole expression returns the decimal equivalent. You can use any base from 2 to 36, inclusive. Here are some examples:

```
>> "10".to_i(17)
=> 17
>> "12345".to_i(13)
=> 33519
>> "ruby".to_i(35)
=> 1194794
```

Keep in mind that most of the arithmetic operators you see in Ruby are *methods*. They don't look that way because of the operator-like syntactic sugar that Ruby gives them. But they are methods, and they can be called as methods:

```
>> 1.+(1)
=> 2
>> 12./(3)
=> 4
>> -12.-(-7)
=> -5
```

In practice, no one writes arithmetic operations that way; you'll always see the syntactic sugar equivalents (1 + 1 and so forth). But seeing examples of the method-call form is a good reminder of the fact that they're methods—and also of the fact that if you define, say, a method called + in a class of your own, you can use the operator's syntactic sugar. (And if you see arithmetic operators behaving weirdly, it may be that someone has redefined their underlying methods.)

We'll turn now to the next and last category of scalar objects we'll discuss in this chapter: time and date objects.

8.4   *Times and dates*

Ruby gives you lots of ways to manipulate times and dates. In fact, the extent and variety of the classes that represent times and/or dates, and the class and instance methods available through those classes, can be bewildering. So can the different ways in which instances of the various classes represent themselves. Want to know what the day we call April 24, 1705, would have been called in England prior to the calendar reform of 1752? Load the date package, and then ask

```
>> require 'date'
=> true
>> Date.parse("April 24 1705").england.strftime("%B %d %Y")
=> "April 13 1705"
```

On the less exotic side, you can perform a number of useful and convenient manipulations on time and date objects.

Times and dates are manipulated through three classes: Time, Date, and DateTime. (For convenience, the instances of all of these classes can be referred to collectively as *date/time objects.*) To reap their full benefits, you have to pull one or both of the date and time libraries into your program or irb session:

```
require 'date'
require 'time'
```

Here, the first line provides the Date and DateTime classes, and the second line enhances the Time class. (Actually, even if you don't require 'date' you'll be able to see the Date class. But it can't do anything yet.) At some point in the future, all the available date- and time-related functionality may be unified into one library and made available to programs by default. But for the moment, you have to do the require operations if you want the full functionality.

In what follows, we'll examine a large handful of date/time operations—not all of them, but most of the common ones and enough to give you a grounding for further development. Specifically, we'll look at how to instantiate date/time objects, how to query them, and how to convert them from one form or format to another.

8.4.1   *Instantiating date/time objects*

How you instantiate a date/time object depends on exactly which object is involved. We'll look at the Date, Time, and DateTime classes, in that order.

CREATING DATE OBJECTS

You can get today's date with the `Date.today` constructor:

```
>> Date.today
=> #<Date: 2013-11-02 ((2456599j,0s,0n),+0s,2299161j)>
```

You can get a simpler string by running to_s on the date, or by putsing it:

```
>> puts Date.today
2013-11-02
```

You can also create date objects with `Date.new` (also available as `Date.civil`). Send along a year, month, and day:

```
>> puts Date.new(1959,2,1)
1959-02-01
```

If not provided, the month and day (or just day) default to 1. If you provide no arguments, the year defaults to –4712—probably not the most useful value.

Finally, you can create a new date with the `parse` constructor, which expects a string representing a date:

```
>> puts Date.parse("2003/6/9")          Assumes year/
2003-06-09                              month/day order
```

By default, Ruby expands the century for you if you provide a one- or two-digit number. If the number is 69 or greater, then the offset added is 1900; if it's between 0 and 68, the offset is 2000. (This distinction has to do with the beginning of the Unix "epoch" at the start of 1970.)

```
>> puts Date.parse("03/6/9")
2003-06-09
>> puts Date.parse("33/6/9")
2033-06-09
>> puts Date.parse("77/6/9")
1977-06-09
```

`Date.parse` makes an effort to make sense of whatever you throw at it, and it's pretty good at its job:

```
>> puts Date.parse("November 2 2013")
2013-11-02
>> puts Date.parse("Nov 2 2013")
2013-11-02
>> puts Date.parse("2 Nov 2013")
2013-11-02
>> puts Date.parse("2013/11/2")
2013-11-02
```

You can create Julian and commercial (Monday-based rather than Sunday-based day-of-week counting) `Date` objects with the methods `jd` and `commercial`, respectively. You can also scan a string against a format specification, generating a `Date` object, with `strptime`. These constructor techniques are more specialized than the others, and we won't go into them in detail here; but if your needs are similarly specialized, the Date class can address them.

The Time class, like the Date class, has multiple constructors.

CREATING TIME OBJECTS

You can create a time object using any of several constructors: new (a.k.a. now), at, local (a.k.a. mktime), and parse. This plethora of constructors, excessive though it may seem at first, does provide a variety of functionalities, all of them useful. Here are some examples, irb-style:

```
>> Time.new                           ❶
=> 2013-11-02 12:16:21 +0000
>> Time.at(100000000)                 ❷
=> 1973-03-03 09:46:40 +0000
>> Time.mktime(2007,10,3,14,3,6)      ❸
=> 2007-10-03 14:03:06 +0100
>> require 'time'                     ❹
=> true
>> Time.parse("March 22, 1985, 10:35 PM")   ❺
=> 1985-03-22 22:35:00 +0000
```

Time.new (or Time.now) creates a time object representing the current time ❶. Time.at(seconds) gives you a time object for the number of seconds since the epoch (midnight on January 1, 1970, GMT) represented by the seconds argument ❷. Time.mktime (or Time.local) expects year, month, day, hour, minute, and second arguments. You don't have to provide all of them; as you drop arguments off from the right, Time.mktime fills in with reasonable defaults (1 for month and day; 0 for hour, minute, and second) ❸.

To use Time.parse, you have to load the time library ❹. Once you do, Time.parse makes as much sense as it can of the arguments you give it, much like Date.parse ❺.

CREATING DATE/TIME OBJECTS

DateTime is a subclass of Date, but its constructors are a little different thanks to some overrides. The most common constructors are new (also available as civil), now, and parse:

```
>> puts DateTime.new(2009, 1, 2, 3, 4, 5)
2009-01-02T03:04:05+00:00
=> nil
>> puts DateTime.now
2013-11-03T04:44:52-08:00
=> nil
>> puts DateTime.parse("October 23, 1973, 10:34 AM")
1973-10-23T10:34:00+00:00
```

DateTime also features the specialized jd (Julian date), commercial, and strptime constructors mentioned earlier in connection with the Date class.

Let's turn now to the various ways in which you can query date/time objects.

8.4.2 Date/time query methods

In general, the time and date objects have the query methods you'd expect them to have. Time objects can be queried as to their year, month, day, hour, minute, and second, as can date/time objects. Date objects can be queried as to their year, month, and day:

```
>> dt = DateTime.now
=> #<DateTime: 2014-02-21T06:33:38-05:00
((2456710j,41618s,552942000n),-18000s,2299161j)>
>> dt.year
=> 2014
>> dt.hour
=> 6
>> dt.minute
=> 33
>> dt.second
=> 38
>> t = Time.now
=> 2014-02-21 06:33:50 -0500
>> t.month
=> 2
>> t.sec
=> 50
>> d = Date.today
=> #<Date: 2014-02-21 ((2456710j,0s,0n),+0s,2299161j)>
>> d.day
=> 21
```

Note that date/time objects have a `second` method, as well as `sec`. Time objects have only `sec`.

Some convenient day-of-week methods work equally for all three classes. Through them, you can determine whether the given date/time is or isn't a particular day of the week:

```
>> d.monday?
=> false
>> dt.friday?
=> true
```

Other available queries include Boolean ones for leap year (`leap?`) and daylight saving time (`dst?`, for time objects only).

As you've seen, the string representations of date/time objects differ considerably, depending on exactly what you've asked for and which of the three classes you're dealing with. In practice, the default string representations aren't used much. Instead, the objects are typically formatted using methods designed for that purpose.

8.4.3 Date/time formatting methods

All date/time objects have the `strftime` method, which allows you to format their fields in a flexible way using format strings, in the style of the Unix `strftime(3)` system library:

```
>> t = Time.now
=> 2014-02-21 06:37:59 -0500
>> t.strftime("%m-%d-%y")
=> "02-21-14"
```

In the example, the format specifiers used are %m (two-digit month), %d (two-digit day), and %Y (four-digit year). The hyphens between the fields are reproduced in the output as literal hyphens.

Some useful format specifiers for strftime are shown in table 8.2.

Table 8.2 Common time and date format specifiers

Specifier	Description
%Y	Year (four digits)
%y	Year (last two digits)
%b, %B	Short month, full month
%m	Month (number)
%d	Day of month (left-padded with zeros)
%e	Day of month (left-padded with blanks)
%a, %A	Short day name, full day name
%H, %I	Hour (24-hour clock), hour (12-hour clock)
%M	Minute
%S	Second
%c	Equivalent to "%a %b %d %H:%M:%S %Y"
%x	Equivalent to "%m/%d/%y"

WARNING The %c and %x specifiers, which involve convenience combinations of other specifiers, may differ from one locale to another; for instance, some systems put the day before the month in the %x format. This is good, because it means a particular country's style isn't hard-coded into these formats. But you do need to be aware of it, so you don't count on specific behavior that you may not always get. When in doubt, you can use a format string made up of smaller specifiers.

Here are some more examples of the format specifiers in action:

```
>> t.strftime("Today is %x")
=> "Today is 11/03/13"
>> t.strftime("Otherwise known as %d-%b-%y")
=> "Otherwise known as 03-Nov-13"
>> t.strftime("Or even day %e of %B, %Y.")
=> "Or even day  3 of November, 2013."
>> t.strftime("The time is %H:%m.")
=> "The time is 04:11."
```

In addition to the facilities provided by strftime, the Date and DateTime classes give you a handful of precooked output formats for specialized cases like RFC 2822 (email) compliance and the HTTP format specified in RFC 2616:

```
>> Date.today.rfc2822
=> "Sun, 3 Nov 2013 00:00:00 +0000"
>> DateTime.now.httpdate
=> "Sun, 03 Nov 2013 12:49:48 GMT"
```

One way or another, you can get your times and dates to look the way you want them to. Date/time objects also allow for conversions of various kinds, from one class of object to another.

8.4.4 *Date/time conversion methods*

All of the date/time classes allow for conversion to each other; that is, Time has to_date and to_datetime methods, Date has to_time and to_datetime, and Date-Time has to_time and to_date. In all cases where the target class has more information than the source class, the missing fields are set to 0—essentially, midnight, because all three classes have date information but only two have time information.

You can also move around the calendar with certain time-arithmetic methods and operators.

DATE/TIME ARITHMETIC

Time objects let you add and subtract seconds from them, returning a new time object:

```
>> t = Time.now
=> 2013-11-03 04:50:49 -0800
>> t - 20
=> 2013-11-03 04:50:29 -0800
>> t + 20
=> 2013-11-03 04:51:09 -0800
```

Date and date/time objects interpret + and - as day-wise operations, and they allow for month-wise conversions with << and >>:

```
>> dt = DateTime.now
=> #<DateTime: 2013-11-03T04:51:05-08:00 ... >
>> puts dt + 100
2014-02-11T04:51:05-08:00
>> puts dt >> 3
2014-02-03T04:51:05-08:00
>> puts dt << 10
2013-01-03T04:51:05-08:00
```

You can also move ahead one using the next (a.k.a. succ) method. A whole family of next_unit and prev_unit methods lets you move back and forth by day(s), month(s), or year(s):

```
>> d = Date.today
=> #<Date: 2013-11-03 ((2456600j,0s,0n),+0s,2299161j)>
>> puts d.next
2013-11-04
```

```
>> puts d.next_year
2014-11-03
>> puts d.next_month(3)
2014-02-03
>> puts d.prev_day(10)
2013-10-24
```

Furthermore, date and date/time objects allow you to iterate over a range of them, using the `upto` and `downto` methods, each of which takes a time, date, or date/time object. Here's an `upto` example:

```
>> d = Date.today
=> #<Date: 2013-11-03 ((2456600j,0s,0n),+0s,2299161j)>
>> next_week = d + 7
=> #<Date: 2013-11-10 ((2456607j,0s,0n),+0s,2299161j)>
>> d.upto(next_week) {|date| puts "#{date} is a #{date.strftime("%A")}" }
2013-11-03 is a Sunday
2013-11-04 is a Monday
2013-11-05 is a Tuesday
2013-11-06 is a Wednesday
2013-11-07 is a Thursday
2013-11-08 is a Friday
2013-11-09 is a Saturday
2013-11-10 is a Sunday
```

The date/time classes offer much more than what you've seen here. But the features we've covered are the most common and, in all likelihood, most useful. Don't forget that you can always use the command-line tool `ri` to get information about methods! If you try `ri Date`, for example, you'll get information about the class as well as a list of available class and instance methods—any of which you can run `ri` on separately.

We've reached the end of our survey of scalar objects in Ruby. Next, in chapter 9, we'll look at collections and container objects.

8.5 Summary

In this chapter you've seen

- String creation and manipulation
- The workings of symbols
- Numerical objects, including floats and integers
- Date, time, and date/time objects and how to query and manipulate them

In short, we've covered the basics of the most common and important scalar objects in Ruby. Some of these topics involved consolidating points made earlier in the book; others were new in this chapter. At each point, we've examined a selection of important, common methods. We've also looked at how some of the scalar-object classes relate to each other. Strings and symbols both represent text, and although they're different kinds of objects, conversions from one to the other are easy and common. Numbers and strings interact, too. Conversions aren't automatic, as they are (for example) in Perl; but Ruby supplies conversion methods to go from string to numerical object and back, as well as ways to convert strings to integers in as many bases as 10 digits and the 26 letters of the English alphabet can accommodate.

Time and date objects have a foot in both the string and numerical camps. You can perform calculations on them, such as adding *n* months to a given date, and you can also put them through their paces as strings, using techniques like the `Time#strftime` method in conjunction with output format specifiers.

The world of scalar objects in Ruby is rich and dynamic. Most of what you do with both Ruby and Rails will spring from what you've learned here about scalar objects: direct manipulation of these objects, manipulation of objects that share some of their traits (for example, CGI parameters whose contents are strings), or collections of multiple objects in these categories. Scalar objects aren't everything, but they lie at the root of virtually everything else. The tour we've taken of important scalar classes and methods in this chapter will stand you in good stead as we proceed next to look at collections and containers—the two- (and sometimes more) dimensional citizens of Ruby's object world.

Collection and
container objects

This chapter covers

- Sequentially ordered collections with arrays
- Keyed collections with hashes
- Inclusion and membership tests with ranges
- Unique, unordered collections with sets
- Named arguments using hash syntax

In programming, you generally deal not only with individual objects but with *collections* of objects. You search through collections to find an object that matches certain criteria (like a magazine object containing a particular article); you sort collections for further processing or visual presentation; you filter collections to include or exclude particular items; and so forth. All of these operations, and similar ones, depend on objects being accessible in collections.

Ruby represents collections of objects by putting them inside *container* objects. In Ruby, two built-in classes dominate the container-object landscape: *arrays* and *hashes*. We'll start this chapter by looking at the Array and Hash classes: first in comparison with each other, to establish an overall understanding, and then separately.

We'll look at two other classes: Range and Set. Ranges are a bit of a hybrid: they work partly as Boolean filters (in the sense that you can perform a true/false test as to whether a given value lies inside a given range), but also, in some contexts, as collections. Sets are collections through and through. The only reason the Set class requires special introduction is that it isn't a core Ruby class; it's a standard library class, and although we're not looking at many of those in depth in this book, sets fall nicely into place beside arrays and hashes and merit our attention.

While reading this chapter, keep in mind that it represents a first pass through a kind of mega-topic that we'll visit in the next chapter, too. Ruby implements collections principally through the technique of defining classes that mix in the Enumerable module. That module gives you a package deal on methods that sort, sift, filter, count, and transform collections. In this chapter, we'll look primarily at what you can do with the major collection classes *other* than take advantage of their Enumerable nature. Chapter 10 will deal directly with Enumerable and how it's used. We'll look at enough of enumerability here to bootstrap this chapter, and then we'll come back to it in the next.

Finally, this chapter includes a throwback to chapter 2. In that chapter we looked in depth at method parameter and argument lists, and at how arguments bind to parameters. Once we've looked more closely at hashes, we'll fill in a gap in chapter 2 by looking at Ruby's *named arguments*, which use hash syntax.

Also, keep in mind that collections are, themselves, objects. You send them messages, assign them to variables, and so forth, in normal object fashion. They just have an extra dimension, beyond the scalar.

9.1 Arrays and hashes in comparison

An *array* is an ordered collection of objects—*ordered* in the sense that you can select objects from the collection based on a consistent, consecutive numerical index. You'll have noticed that we've already used arrays in some of the examples earlier in the book. It's hard *not* to use arrays in Ruby. An array's job is to store other objects. Any object can be stored in an array, including other arrays, hashes, file handles, classes, true and false...any object at all. The contents of an array always remain in the same order unless you explicitly move objects around (or add or remove them).

Hashes in recent versions of Ruby are also ordered collections—and that's a big change from previous versions, where hashes are unordered (in the sense that they have no idea of what their first, last, or *n*th element is). Hashes store objects in pairs, each pair consisting of a *key* and a *value*. You retrieve a value by means of the key. Hashes remember the order in which their keys were inserted; that's the order in which the hash replays itself for you if you iterate through the pairs in it or print a string representation of it to the screen.

Any Ruby object can serve as a hash key and/or value, but keys are unique per hash: you can have only one key/value pair for any given key. Hashes (or similar data storage types) are sometimes called *dictionaries* or *associative arrays* in other languages. They offer a tremendously—sometimes surprisingly—powerful way of storing and retrieving data.

Arrays and hashes are closely connected. An array is, in a sense, a hash, where the keys happen to be consecutive integers. Hashes are, in a sense, arrays, where the indexes are allowed to be anything, not just integers. If you do use consecutive integers as hash keys, arrays and hashes start behaving similarly when you do lookups:

```
array = ["ruby", "diamond", "emerald"]
hash = { 0 => "ruby", 1 => "diamond", 2 => "emerald" }
puts array[0]    # ruby
puts hash[0]     # ruby
```

Even if you don't use integers, hashes exhibit a kind of "meta-index" property, based on the fact that they have a certain number of key/value pairs and that those pairs can be counted off consecutively. You can see this property in action by stepping through a hash with the with_index method, which yields a counter value to the block along with the key and value:

```
hash = { "red" => "ruby", "white" => "diamond", "green" => "emerald" }
hash.each.with_index {|(key,value),i|
  puts "Pair #{i} is: #{key}/#{value}"
}
```

The output from this code snippet is

```
Pair 0 is: red/ruby
Pair 1 is: white/diamond
Pair 2 is: green/emerald
```

The *index* is an integer counter, maintained as the pairs go by. The pairs are the actual content of the hash.

> **TIP** The parentheses in the block parameters (key,value) serve to split apart an array. Each key/value pair comes at the block as an array of two elements. If the parameters were key,value,i, then the parameter key would end up bound to the entire [key,value] array; value would be bound to the index; and i would be nil. That's obviously not what you want. The parenthetical grouping of (key,value) is a signal that you want the array to be distributed across those two parameters, element by element.

Conversions of various kinds between arrays and hashes are common. Some such conversions are automatic: if you perform certain operations of selection or extraction of pairs from a hash, you'll get back an array. Other conversions require explicit instructions, such as turning a flat array ([1,2,3,4]) into a hash ({1 => 2, 3 => 4}). You'll see a good amount of back and forth between these two collection classes, both here in this chapter and in lots of Ruby code.

In the next two sections, we'll look at arrays and hashes in depth. Let's start with arrays.

9.2   *Collection handling with arrays*

Arrays are the bread-and-butter way to handle collections of objects. We'll put arrays through their paces in this section: we'll look at the varied techniques available for creating arrays; how to insert, retrieve, and remove array elements; combining arrays with each other; transforming arrays (for example, flattening a nested array into a one-dimensional array); and querying arrays as to their properties and state.

9.2.1 Creating a new array

You can create an array in one of four ways:

- With the `Array.new` method
- With the literal array constructor (square brackets)
- With a top-level method called `Array`
- With the special `%w{...}` and `%i{...}` notations

You'll see all of these techniques in heavy rotation in Ruby code, so they're all worth knowing. We'll look at each in turn.

ARRAY.NEW

The `new` method on the array class works in the usual way:

```
a = Array.new
```

You can then add objects to the array using techniques we'll look at later.

`Array.new` lets you specify the size of the array and, if you wish, initialize its contents. Here's an irb exchange that illustrates both possibilities:

```
>> Array.new(3)                    ◀━❶
=> [nil, nil, nil]
>> Array.new(3,"abc")              ◀━❷
=> ["abc", "abc", "abc"]
```

If you give one argument to `Array.new` ❶, you get an array of the size you asked for, with all elements set to `nil`. If you give two arguments ❷, you get an array of the size you asked for, with each element initialized to contain the second argument.

You can even supply a code block to `Array.new`. In that case, the elements of the array are initialized by repeated calls to the block:

```
>> n = 0
=> 0                                    ❶
>> Array.new(3) { n += 1; n * 10 }   ◀━┘   ❷
=> [10, 20, 30]                             ◀━┘
```

In this example, the new array has a size of 3. Each of the three elements is set to the return value of the code block. The code inside the block ❶, executed three times, produces the values 10, 20, and 30—and those are the initial values in the array ❷.

> **WARNING** When you initialize multiple elements of an array using a second argument to `Array.new`—as in `Array.new(3, "abc")`—all the elements of the array are initialized to the same object. If you do `a = Array.new(3,"abc");` `a[0] << "def"; puts a[1]`, you'll find that the second element of the array is now `"abcdef"`, even though you appended `"def"` to the first element. That's because the first and second positions in the array contain the same string

object, not two different strings that happen to both consist of `"abc"`. To create an array that inserts a different `"abc"` string into each slot, you should use `Array.new(3) { "abc" }`. The code block runs three times, each time generating a new string (same characters, different string object).

Preinitializing arrays isn't always necessary, because your arrays grow as you add elements to them. But if and when you need this functionality—and/or if you see it in use and want to understand it—it's there.

THE LITERAL ARRAY CONSTRUCTOR: [ ]

The second way to create an array is by using the *literal array constructor* `[]` (square brackets):

```
a = []
```

When you create an array with the literal constructor, you can put objects into the array at the same time:

```
a = [1,2,"three",4, []]
```

Notice that the last element in this array is another array. That's perfectly legitimate; you can nest arrays to as many levels as you wish.

Square brackets can mean a lot of different things in Ruby: array construction, array indexing (as well as string and hash indexing), character classes in regular expressions, delimiters in `%q[]`-style string notation, even the calling of an anonymous function. You can make an initial division of the various uses of square brackets by distinguishing cases where they're a semantic construct from cases where they're the name of a method. It's worth practicing on a few examples like this to get a feel for the way the square brackets play out in different contexts:

```
[1,2,3][1]
```
          ◁─── **Index 1 on array [1,2,3]**

Now back to array creation.

THE ARRAY METHOD

The third way to create an array is with a *method* (even though it looks like a class name!) called `Array`. As you know from having seen the `Integer` and `Float` methods, it's legal to define methods whose names begin with capital letters. Those names look exactly like constants, and in core Ruby itself, capitalized methods tend to have the same names as classes to which they're related.

Some more built-in methods that start with uppercase letters

In addition to the `Array` method and the two uppercase-style conversion methods you've already seen (`Integer` and `Float`, the "fussy" versions of `to_i` and `to_f`), Ruby provides a few other top-level methods whose names look like class names: `Complex`, `Rational`, and `String`. In each case, the method returns an object of the class that its name looks like.

(continued)

The String method is a wrapper around to_s, meaning String(obj) is equivalent to obj.to_s. Complex and Rational correspond to the to_c and to_r methods available for numerics and strings—except Complex and Rational, like Integer and Float, are fussy: they don't take kindly to non-numeric strings. "abc".to_c gives you (0+0i), but Complex("abc") raises ArgumentError, and Rational and to_r behave similarly.

We're not covering rational and complex numbers here, but now you know how to generate them, in case they're of interest to you!

The Array method creates an array from its single argument. If the argument object has a to_ary method defined, then Array calls that method on the object to generate an array. (Remember that to_ary is the quasi-typecasting array conversion method.) If there's no to_ary method, it tries to call to_a. If to_a isn't defined either, Array wraps the object in an array and returns that:

```
>> string = "A string"
=> "A string"
>> string.respond_to?(:to_ary)
=> false
>> string.respond_to?(:to_a)
=> false
>> Array(string)                <--- ❶
=> ["A string"]
>> def string.to_a              <--- ❷
>>   split(//)
>> end
=> nil
>> Array(string)
=> ["A", " ", "s", "t", "r", "i", "n", "g"]
```

In this example, the first attempt to run Array on the string ❶ results in a one-element array, where the one element is the string. That's because strings have neither a to_ary nor a to_a method. But after to_a is defined for the string ❷, the result of calling Array is different: it now runs the to_a method and uses that as its return value. (The to_a method splits the string into individual characters.)

Among the various array constructors, the literal [] is the most common, followed by Array.new and the Array method, in that order. But each has its place. The literal constructor is the most succinct; when you learn what it means, it clearly announces "array" when you see it. The Array method is constrained by the need for there to be a to_ary or to_a method available.

THE %W AND %W ARRAY CONSTRUCTORS

As a special dispensation to help you create arrays of strings, Ruby provides a %w operator, much in the same family as the %q-style operators you've seen already, that automatically generates an array of strings from the space-separated strings you put inside it. You can see how it works by using it in irb and looking at the result:

```
>> %w{ David A. Black }
=> ["David", "A.", "Black"]
```

If any string in the list contains a whitespace character, you need to escape that character with a backslash:

```
>> %w{ David\ A.\ Black is a Rubyist. }
=> ["David A. Black", "is", "a", "Rubyist."]
```

The strings in the list are parsed as single-quoted strings. But if you need double-quoted strings, you can use %W instead of %w:

```
>> %W{ David is #{2014 - 1959} years old. }
=> ["David", "is", "55", "years", "old."]
```

THE %I AND %I ARRAY CONSTRUCTORS

Just as you can create arrays of strings using %w and %W, you can also create arrays of symbols using %i and %I. The i/I distinction, like the w/W distinction, pertains to single- versus double-quoted string interpretation:

```
>> %i{ a b c }
=> [:a, :b, :c]
>> d = "David"
=> "David"
>> %I{"#{d}"}
=> [:"\"David\""]
```

Let's proceed now to the matter of handling array elements.

The `try_convert` family of methods

Each of several built-in classes in Ruby has a class method called `try_convert`, which always takes one argument. `try_convert` looks for a conversion method on the argument object. If the method exists, it gets called; if not, `try_convert` returns `nil`. If the conversion method returns an object of a class other than the class to which conversion is being attempted, it's a fatal error (`TypeError`).

The classes implementing `try_convert` (and the names of the required conversion methods) are Array (to_ary), Hash (to_hash), IO (to_io), Regexp (to_regexp), and String (to_str). Here's an example of an object putting Array.try_convert through its paces. (The other `try_convert` methods work similarly.)

```
>> obj = Object.new
=> #<Object:0x000001028033a8>
>> Array.try_convert(obj)
=> nil
>> def obj.to_ary
>>   [1,2,3]
>> end
```

```
(continued)
=> :to_ary
>> Array.try_convert(obj)
=> [1, 2, 3]
>> def obj.to_ary
>>   "Not an array!"
>> end
=> :to_ary
>> Array.try_convert(obj)
TypeError: can't convert Object to Array (Object#to_ary gives String
```

9.2.2 *Inserting, retrieving, and removing array elements*

An array is a numerically ordered collection. Any object you add to the array goes at the beginning, at the end, or somewhere in the middle. The most general technique for inserting one or more items into an array is the setter method `[]=` (square brackets and equal sign). This looks odd as a method name in the middle of a paragraph like this, but thanks to its syntactic sugar equivalent, `[]=` works smoothly in practice.

To use `[]=`, you need to know that each item (or element) in an array occupies a numbered position. The first element is at position *zero* (not position *one*). The second element is at position one, and so forth.

To insert an element with the `[]=` method—using the syntactic sugar that allows you to avoid the usual method-calling dot—do this:

```
a = []
a[0] = "first"
```

The second line is syntactic sugar for `a.[]=(0,"first")`. In this example, you end up with a one-element array whose first (and only) element is the string `"first"`.

When you have objects in an array, you can retrieve those objects by using the `[]` method, which is the getter equivalent of the `[]=` setter method:

```
a = [1,2,3,4,5]
p a[2]
```

In this case, the second line is syntactic sugar for `a.[](2)`. You're asking for the third element (based on the zero-origin indexing), which is the integer 3.

You can also perform these get and set methods on more than one element at a time.

SETTING OR GETTING MORE THAN ONE ARRAY ELEMENT AT A TIME

If you give either `Array#[]` or `Array#[]=` (the get or set method) a second argument, it's treated as a length—a number of elements to set or retrieve. In the case of retrieval, the results are returned inside a new array.

Here's some irb dialogue, illustrating the multi-element operations of the `[]` and `[]=` methods:

```
>> a = ["red","orange","yellow","purple","gray","indigo","violet"]
=> ["red", "orange", "yellow", "purple", "gray", "indigo", "violet"]     ❶
>> a[3,2]
=> ["purple", "gray"]
>> a[3,2] = "green", "blue"          Syntactic sugar for
❷ => ["green", "blue"]               a.[]=(3,2,["green", "blue"])
>> a
=> ["red", "orange", "yellow", "green", "blue", "indigo", "violet"]     ◁—❸
```

After initializing the array a, we grab two elements ❶, starting at index 3 (the fourth element) of a. The two elements are returned in an array. Next, we set the fourth and fifth elements, using the [3,2] notation ❷, to new values; these new values are then present in the whole array ❸ when we ask irb to display it at the end.

There's a synonym for the [] method: slice. Like [], slice takes two arguments: a starting index and an optional length. In addition, a method called slice! removes the sliced items permanently from the array.

Another technique for extracting multiple array elements is the values_at method. values_at takes one or more arguments representing indexes and returns an array consisting of the values stored at those indexes in the receiver array:

```
array = ["the", "dog", "ate", "the", "cat"]
articles = array.values_at(0,3)          Output:
p articles                               ["the", "the"]
```

You can perform set and get operations on elements anywhere in an array. But operations specifically affecting the beginnings and ends of arrays crop up most often. Accordingly, a number of methods exist for the special purpose of adding items to or removing them from the beginning or end of an array, as you'll now see.

SPECIAL METHODS FOR MANIPULATING THE BEGINNINGS AND ENDS OF ARRAYS

To add an object to the beginning of an array, you can use unshift. After this operation

```
a = [1,2,3,4]
a.unshift(0)
```

the array a now looks like this: [0,1,2,3,4].

To add an object to the end of an array, you use push. Doing this

```
a = [1,2,3,4]
a.push(5)
```

results in the array a having a fifth element: [1,2,3,4,5].

You can also use a method called << (two less-than signs), which places an object on the end of the array. Like many methods whose names resemble operators, << offers the syntactic sugar of usage as an infix operator. The following code adds 5 as the fifth element of a, just like the push operation in the last example:

```
a = [1,2,3,4]
a << 5
```

The methods << and push differ in that push can take more than one argument. The code

```
a = [1,2,3,4,5]
a.push(6,7,8)
```

adds three elements to a, resulting in [1,2,3,4,5,6,7,8].

Corresponding to unshift and push but with opposite effect are shift and pop. shift removes one object from the beginning of the array (thereby "shifting" the remaining objects to the left by one position), and pop removes an object from the end of the array. shift and pop both return the array element they have removed, as this example shows:

```
a = [1,2,3,4,5]
print "The original array: "
p a
popped = a.pop
print "The popped item: "
puts popped
print "The new state of the array: "
p a
shifted = a.shift
print "The shifted item: "
puts shifted
print "The new state of the array: "
p a
```

The output is

```
The original array: [1, 2, 3, 4, 5]
The popped item: 5
The new state of the array: [1, 2, 3, 4]
The shifted item: 1
The new state of the array: [2, 3, 4]
```

As you can see from the running commentary in the output, the return value of pop and shift is the item that was removed from the array. The array is permanently changed by these operations; the elements are removed, not just referred to or captured.

shift and pop can remove more than one element at a time. Just provide an integer argument, and that number of elements will be removed. The removed items will be returned as an array (even if the number you provide is 1):

```
>> a = %w{ one two three four five }
=> ["one", "two", "three", "four", "five"]
>> a.pop(2)
=> ["four", "five"]
>> a
=> ["one", "two", "three"]
>> a.shift(2)
=> ["one", "two"]
>> a
=> ["three"]
```

We'll turn next from manipulating one array to looking at ways to combine two or more arrays.

9.2.3 Combining arrays with other arrays

Several methods allow you to combine multiple arrays in various ways—something that, it turns out, is common and useful when you begin manipulating lots of data in lists. Remember that in every case, even though you're dealing with two (or more) arrays, one array is always the receiver of the message. The other arrays involved in the operation are arguments to the method.

To add the contents of one array to another array, you can use concat:

```
>> [1,2,3].concat([4,5,6])
=> [1, 2, 3, 4, 5, 6]
```

Note that concat differs in an important way from push. Try replacing concat with push in the example and see what happens.

concat permanently changes the contents of its receiver. If you want to combine two arrays into a third, new array, you can do so with the + method:

```
>> a = [1,2,3]
=> [1, 2, 3]
>> b = a + [4,5,6]
=> [1, 2, 3, 4, 5, 6]
>> a
=> [1, 2, 3]                    ❶
```

The receiver of the + message—in this case, the array a—remains unchanged by the operation (as irb tells you ❶).

Another useful array-combining method, at least given a fairly liberal interpretation of the concept of "combining," is replace. As the name implies, replace replaces the contents of one array with the contents of another:

```
>> a = [1,2,3]
=> [1, 2, 3]
>> a.replace([4,5,6])      ◁━❶
=> [4, 5, 6]
>> a
=> [4, 5, 6]
```

The original contents of a are gone, replaced ❶ by the contents of the argument array [4,5,6]. Remember that a replace operation is different from reassignment. If you do this

```
a = [1,2,3]
a = [4,5,6]
```

the second assignment causes the variable a to refer to a completely different array object than the first. That's not the same as replacing the elements of the *same* array object. This starts to matter, in particular, when you have another variable that refers to the original array, as in this code:

```
>> a = [1,2,3]
=> [1, 2, 3]
>> b = a                          ◄——❶
=> [1, 2, 3]
>> a.replace([4,5,6])
=> [4, 5, 6]
>> b                              ◄——❷
=> [4, 5, 6]
>> a = [7,8,9]              ◄——❸
=> [7, 8, 9]
>> b
=> [4, 5, 6]            ◄——❹
```

Once you've performed the assignment of a to b ❶, replacing the contents of a means you've replaced the contents of b ❷, because the two variables refer to the same array. But when you reassign to a ❸, you break the binding between a and the array; a and b now refer to different array objects: b to the same old array ❹, a to a new one.

In addition to combining multiple arrays, you can also transform individual arrays to different forms. We'll look next at techniques along these lines.

9.2.4 *Array transformations*

A useful array transformation is flatten, which does an un-nesting of inner arrays. You can specify how many levels of flattening you want, with the default being the full un-nesting.

Here's a triple-nested array being flattened by various levels:

```
>> array = [1,2,[3,4,[5],[6,[7,8]]]]
=> [1, 2, [3, 4, [5], [6, [7, 8]]]]
>> array.flatten                              ◄——   Flattens completely
=> [1, 2, 3, 4, 5, 6, 7, 8]
>> array.flatten(1)                      ◄——   Flattens by
=> [1, 2, 3, 4, [5], [6, [7, 8]]]             one level
>> array.flatten(2)                  ◄——   Flattens by
=> [1, 2, 3, 4, 5, 6, [7, 8]]                 two levels
```

There's also an in-place flatten! method, which makes the change permanently in the array.

Another array-transformation method is reverse, which does exactly what it says:

```
>>[1,2,3,4].reverse
=>   [4, 3, 2, 1]
```

Like its string counterpart, Array#reverse also has a bang (!) version, which permanently reverses the array that calls it.

Another important array-transformation method is join. The return value of join isn't an array but a string, consisting of the string representation of all the elements of the array strung together:

```
>> ["abc", "def", 123].join
=> "abcdef123"
```

join takes an optional argument; if given, the argument is placed between each pair of elements:

```
>> ["abc", "def", 123].join(", ")
=> "abc, def, 123"
```

Joining with commas (or comma-space, as in the last example) is a fairly common operation.

In a great example of Ruby's design style, there's another way to join an array: the * method. It looks like you're multiplying the array by a string, but you're actually performing a join operation:

```
>> a = %w{ one two three }
=> ["one", "two", "three"]
>> a * "-"
=> "one-two-three"
```

You can also transform an array with uniq. uniq gives you a new array, consisting of the elements of the original array with all duplicate elements removed:

```
>> [1,2,3,1,4,3,5,1].uniq
=> [1, 2, 3, 4, 5]
```

Duplicate status is determined by testing pairs of elements with the == method. Any two elements for which the == test returns true are considered duplicates of each other. uniq also has a bang version, uniq!, which removes duplicates permanently from the original array.

Sometimes you have an array that includes one or more occurrences of nil, and you want to get rid of them. You might, for example, have an array of the ZIP codes of all the members of an organization. But maybe some of them don't have ZIP codes. If you want to do a histogram on the ZIP codes, you'd want to get rid of the nil ones first.

You can do this with the compact method. This method returns a new array identical to the original array, except that all occurrences of nil have been removed:

```
>> zip_codes = ["06511", "08902", "08902", nil, "10027",
"08902", nil, "06511"]
=> ["06511", "08902", "08902", nil, "10027", "08902", nil, "06511"]
>> zip_codes.compact
=> ["06511", "08902", "08902", "10027", "08902", "06511"]
```

Once again, there's a bang version (compact!) available.

In addition to transforming arrays in various ways, you can query arrays on various criteria.

9.2.5   *Array querying*

Several methods allow you to gather information about an array from the array. Table 9.1 summarizes some of them. Other query methods arise from Array's inclusion of the Enumerable module and will therefore come into view in the next chapter.

Table 9.1 Summary of common array query methods

Method name/Sample call	Meaning
`a.size` (synonym: `length`)	Number of elements in the array
`a.empty?`	True if a is an empty array; false if it has any elements
`a.include?(item)`	True if the array includes items; false otherwise
`a.count(item)`	Number of occurrences of `item` in array
`a.first(n=1)`	First *n* elements of array
`a.last(n=1)`	Last *n* elements of array
`a.sample(n=1)`	*n* random elements from array

In the cases of `first`, `last`, and `sample`, if you don't pass in an argument, you get just one element back. If you do pass in an argument *n*, you get an array of *n* elements back—even if *n* is 1.

Next up: hashes. They've crossed our path here and there along the way, and now we'll look at them in detail.

9.3 Hashes

Like an array, a hash is a collection of objects. A hash consists of key/value pairs, where any key and any value can be any Ruby object. Hashes let you perform lookup operations based on keys. In addition to simple key-based value retrieval, you can also perform more complex filtering and selection operations.

A typical use of a hash is to store complete strings along with their abbreviations. Here's a hash containing a selection of names and two-letter state abbreviations, along with some code that exercises it. The `=>` operator connects a key on the left with the value corresponding to it on the right:

```
state_hash = { "Connecticut" => "CT",
               "Delaware"    => "DE",
               "New Jersey"  => "NJ",
               "Virginia"    => "VA" }
print "Enter the name of a state: "
state = gets.chomp
abbr = state_hash[state]
puts "The abbreviation is #{abbr}."
```

When you run this snippet (assuming you enter one of the states defined in the hash), you see the abbreviation.

Hashes remember the insertion order of their keys. Insertion order isn't always terribly important; one of the merits of a hash is that it provides quick lookup in better-than-linear time. And in many cases, items get added to hashes in no particular order; ordering, if any, comes later, when you want to turn, say, a hash of names and birthdays that you've created over time into a chronologically or alphabetically sorted array. Still, however useful it may or may not be for them to do so, hashes remember their key-insertion order and observe that order when you iterate over them or examine them.

Like arrays, hashes can be created in several different ways.

9.3.1   *Creating a new hash*

There are four ways to create a hash:

- With the literal constructor (curly braces)
- With the Hash.new method
- With the Hash.[] method (a square-bracket class method of Hash)
- With the top-level method whose name is Hash

These hash-creation techniques are listed here, as closely as possible, in descending order of commonness. In other words, we'll start with the most common technique and proceed from there.

CREATING A LITERAL HASH

When you type out a literal hash inside curly braces, you separate keys from values with the => operator (unless you're using the special { key: value } syntax for symbol keys). After each complete key/value pair you put a comma (except for the last pair, where it's optional).

The literal hash constructor is convenient when you have values you wish to hash that aren't going to change; you'll type them into the program file once and refer to them from the program. State abbreviations are a good example.

You can use the literal hash constructor to create an empty hash:

```
h = {}
```

You'd presumably want to add items to the empty hash at some point; techniques for doing so will be forthcoming in section 9.3.2.

The second way to create a hash is with the traditional new constructor.

THE HASH.NEW CONSTRUCTOR

Hash.new creates an empty hash. But if you provide an argument to Hash.new, it's treated as the default value for nonexistent hash keys. We'll return to the matter of default values, and some bells and whistles on Hash.new, once we've looked at key/value insertion and retrieval.

THE HASH.[ ] CLASS METHOD

The third way to create a hash involves another class method of the Hash class: the method [] (square brackets). This method takes a comma-separated list of items and, assuming there's an even number of arguments, treats them as alternating keys and values, which it uses to construct a hash. Thanks to Ruby's syntactic sugar, you can put the arguments to [] directly inside the brackets and dispense them with the method-calling dot:

```
>> Hash["Connecticut", "CT", "Delaware", "DE" ]
=> {"Connecticut"=>"CT", "Delaware"=>"DE"}
```

If you provide an odd number of arguments, a fatal error is raised, because an odd number of arguments can't be mapped to a series of key/value pairs. However, you can pass in an array of arrays, where each subarray consists of two elements. Hash. [] will use the inner arrays as key/value pairs:

```
>> Hash[ [[1,2], [3,4], [5,6]] ]
=> {1=>2, 3=>4, 5=>6}
```

You can also pass in anything that has a method called to_hash. The new hash will be the result of calling that method.

Another hash-creation technique involves the top-level Hash method.

THE HASH METHOD

The Hash method has slightly idiosyncratic behavior. If called with an empty array ([]) or nil, it returns an empty hash. Otherwise, it calls to_hash on its single argument. If the argument doesn't have a to_hash method, a fatal error (TypeError) is raised.

You've now seen a number of ways to create hashes. Remember that they're in approximate descending order by commonness. You'll see a lot more literal hash constructors and calls to Hash.new than you will the rest of the techniques presented. Still, it's good to know what's available and how the various techniques work.

Now let's turn to the matter of manipulating a hash's contents. We'll follow much the same path as we did with arrays, looking at insertion and retrieval operations, combining hashes with other hashes, hash transformations, and querying hashes. Along the way, we'll also take a separate look at setting default values for nonexistent hash keys.

9.3.2 *Inserting, retrieving, and removing hash pairs*

As you'll see, hashes have a lot in common with arrays when it comes to the get- and set-style operations—though there are some important differences and some techniques that are specific to each.

ADDING A KEY/VALUE PAIR TO A HASH

To add a key/value pair to a hash, you use essentially the same technique as for adding an item to an array: the [] = method plus syntactic sugar.

To add a state to state_hash, do this

```
state_hash["New York"] = "NY"
```

which is the sugared version of this:

```
state_hash.[]=("New York", "NY")
```

You can also use the synonymous method store for this operation. store takes two arguments (a key and a value):

```
state_hash.store("New York", "NY")
```

When you're adding to a hash, keep in mind the important principle that keys are unique. You can have only one entry with a given key. Hash values don't have to be unique; you can assign the same value to two or more keys. But you can't have duplicate keys.

If you add a key/value pair to a hash that already has an entry for the key you're adding, the old entry is overwritten. Here's an example:

```
h = Hash.new
h["a"] = 1
h["a"] = 2
puts h["a"]          ◁─┘  Output: 2
```

This code assigns two values to the "a" key of the hash h. The second assignment clobbers the first, as the puts statement shows by outputting 2.

If you reassign to a given hash key, that key still maintains its place in the insertion order of the hash. The change in the value paired with the key isn't considered a new insertion into the hash.

RETRIEVING VALUES FROM A HASH

The workhorse technique for retrieving hash values is the [] method. For example, to retrieve "CT" from state_hash and assign it to a variable, do this:

```
conn_abbrev = state_hash["Connecticut"]
```

Using a hash key is much like indexing an array—except that the index (the key) can be anything, whereas in an array it's always an integer.

Hashes also have a fetch method, which gives you an alternative way of retrieving values by key:

```
conn_abbrev = state_hash.fetch("Connecticut")
```

fetch differs from [] in the way it behaves when you ask it to look up a nonexistent key: fetch raises an exception, whereas [] gives you either nil or a default you've specified (as discussed in the next section). If you provide a second argument to hash, that argument will be returned, instead of an exception being raised if the key isn't found. For example, this code

```
state_hash.fetch("Nebraska", "Unknown state")
```

evaluates to the string "Unknown state".

You can also retrieve values for multiple keys in one operation, with values_at:

```
two_states = state_hash.values_at("New Jersey","Delaware")
```

This code returns an array consisting of ["NJ","DE"] and assigns it to the variable two_states.

Now that you have a sense of the mechanics of getting information into and out of a hash, let's circle back and look at the matter of supplying a default value (or default code block) when you create a hash.

9.3.3 *Specifying default hash values and behavior*

By default, when you ask a hash for the value corresponding to a nonexistent key, you get `nil`:

```
>> h = Hash.new
=> {}
>> h["no such key!"]
=> nil
```

But you can specify a different default value by supplying an argument to `Hash.new`:

```
>> h = Hash.new(0)
=> {}
>> h["no such key!"]
=> 0
```

Here we get back the hash's default value, 0, when we use a nonexistent key. (You can also set the default on an already existing hash with the `default` method.)

It's important to remember that whatever you specify as the default value is what you get when you specify a *nonexistent* key—and that the key remains nonexistent until you assign a value to it. In other words, saying `h["blah"]` doesn't mean that h now has a `"blah"` key. If you want that key in the hash, you have to put it there. You can verify the fact that the hash h has no keys by examining it after performing the nonexistent key lookup in the last example:

```
>> h
=> {}
```

If you want references to nonexistent keys to cause the keys to come into existence, you can arrange this by supplying a code block to `Hash.new`. The code block will be executed every time a nonexistent key is referenced. Two objects will be yielded to the block: the hash and the (nonexistent) key.

This technique gives you a foot in the door when it comes to setting keys automatically when they're first used. It's not the most elegant or streamlined technique in Ruby, but it does work. You write a block that grabs the hash and the key, and you do a set operation.

For example, if you want every nonexistent key to be added to the hash with a value of 0, create your hash like this:

```
h = Hash.new {|hash,key| hash[key] = 0 }
```

When the hash h is asked to retrieve the value for a key it doesn't have, the block is executed with `hash` set to the hash itself and `key` set to the nonexistent key. And thanks to the code in the block, the key is added to the hash after all, with the value 0.

Given this assignment of a new hash to h, you can trigger the block like this:

```
>> h["new key!"]          ⬅—❶
=> 0
>> h                      ⬅—❷
=> {"new key!"=>0}
```

When you try to look up the key "new key!" ❶, it's not there; but thanks to the block, it gets added, with the value 0. Next, when you ask irb to show you the whole hash ❷, it contains the automatically added pair.

This technique has lots of uses. It lets you make assumptions about what's in a hash, even if nothing is there to start with. It also shows you another facet of Ruby's extensive repertoire of dynamic programming techniques and the flexibility of hashes.

We'll turn now to ways you can combine hashes with each other, as we did with strings and arrays.

9.3.4   *Combining hashes with other hashes*

The process of combining two hashes into one comes in two flavors: the destructive flavor, where the first hash has the key/value pairs from the second hash added to it directly; and the nondestructive flavor, where a new, third hash is created that combines the elements of the original two.

The destructive operation is performed with the update method. Entries in the first hash are overwritten permanently if the second hash has a corresponding key:

```
h1 = {"Smith" => "John",
      "Jones" => "Jane" }
h2 = {"Smith" => "Jim" }
h1.update(h2)
puts h1["Smith"]          ←┘   Output: Jim
```

In this example, h1's "Smith" entry has been changed (updated) to the value it has in h2. You're asking for a refresh of your hash to reflect the contents of the second hash. That's the destructive version of combining hashes.

To perform nondestructive combining of two hashes, use the merge method, which gives you a third hash and leaves the original unchanged:

```
h1 = {"Smith" => "John",
      "Jones" => "Jane" }
h2 = {"Smith" => "Jim" }
h3 = h1.merge(h2)
p h1["Smith"]            ←┘   Output: John
```

Here h1's "Smith"/"John" pair isn't overwritten by h2's "Smith"/"Jim" pair. Instead, a new hash is created, with pairs from both of the other two. That hash will look like this, if examined:

```
{"Smith"=>"Jim", "Jones"=>"Jane"}
```

Note that h3 has a decision to make: which of the two Smith entries should it contain? The answer is that when the two hashes being merged share a key, the second hash (h2, in this example) wins. h3's value for the key "Smith" will be "Jim".

Incidentally, merge!—the bang version of merge—is a synonym for update. You can use either name when you want to perform that operation.

In addition to being combined with other hashes, hashes can also be transformed in a number of ways, as you'll see next.

9.3.5 *Hash transformations*

You can perform several transformations on hashes. *Transformation*, in this context, means that the method is called on a hash, and the result of the operation (the method's return value) is a hash. In chapter 10, you'll see other filtering and selecting methods on hashes that return their result sets in arrays. Here we're looking at hash-to-hash operations.

SELECTING AND REJECTING ELEMENTS FROM A HASH

To derive a subhash from an existing hash, use the `select` method. Key/value pairs will be passed in succession to the code block you provide. Any pair for which the block returns a true value will be included in the result hash:

```
>> h = Hash[1,2,3,4,5,6]
=> {1=>2, 3=>4, 5=>6}
>> h.select {|k,v| k > 1 }
=> {3=>4, 5=>6}
```

Rejecting elements from a hash works in the opposite way—those key/value pairs for which the block returns true are excluded from the result hash:

```
>> h.reject {|k,v| k > 1 }
=> {1=>2}
```

`select` and `reject` have in-place equivalents (versions that change the original hash permanently, rather than returning a new hash): `select!` and `reject!`. These two methods return `nil` if the hash doesn't change. To do an in-place operation that returns your original hash (even if it's unchanged), you can use `keep_if` and `delete_if`.

INVERTING A HASH

`Hash#invert` flips the keys and the values. Values become keys, and keys become values:

```
>> h = { 1 => "one", 2 => "two" }
=> {1=>"one", 2=>"two"}
>> h.invert
=> {"two"=>2, "one"=>1}
```

Be careful when you invert hashes. Because hash keys are unique, but values aren't, when you turn duplicate values into keys, one of the pairs is discarded:

```
>> h = { 1 => "one", 2 => "more than 1", 3 => "more than 1" }
=> {1=>"one", 2=>"more than 1", 3=>"more than 1"}
>> h.invert
=> {"one"=>1, "more than 1"=>3}
```

Only one of the two `"more than 1"` values can survive as a key when the inversion is performed; the other is discarded. You should invert a hash only when you're certain the values as well as the keys are unique.

CLEARING A HASH

`Hash#clear` empties the hash:

```
>> {1 => "one", 2 => "two" }.clear
=> {}
```

This is an in-place operation: the empty hash is the same hash (the same object) as the one to which you send the `clear` message.

REPLACING THE CONTENTS OF A HASH

Like strings and arrays, hashes have a `replace` method:

```
>> { 1 => "one", 2 => "two" }.replace({ 10 => "ten", 20 => "twenty"})
=> {10 => "ten", 20 => "twenty"}
```

This is also an in-place operation, as the name `replace` implies.

We'll turn next to hash query methods.

9.3.6   *Hash querying*

Like arrays (and many other Ruby objects), hashes provide a number of methods with which you can query the state of the object. Table 9.2 shows some common hash query methods.

Table 9.2   Common hash query methods and their meanings

Method name/Sample call	Meaning
h.has_key?(1)	True if h has the key 1
h.include?(1)	Synonym for has_key?
h.key?(1)	Synonym for has_key?
h.member?(1)	Synonym for has_key?
h.has_value?("three")	True if any value in h is "three"
h.value?("three")	Synonym for has_value?
h.empty?	True if h has no key/value pairs
h.size	Number of key/value pairs in h

None of the methods in table 9.2 should offer any surprises at this point; they're similar in spirit, and in some cases in letter, to those you've seen for arrays. With the exception of `size`, they all return either true or false. The only surprise may be how many of them are synonyms. Four methods test for the presence of a particular key: has_key?, include?, key?, and member?. A case could be made that this is two or even three synonyms too many. has_key? seems to be the most popular of the four and is the most to-the-point with respect to what the method tests for.

The has_value? method has one synonym: value?. As with its key counterpart, has_value? seems to be more popular.

The other methods—empty? and size—tell you whether the hash is empty and what its size is. (size can also be called as length.) The size of a hash is the number of key/value pairs it contains.

Hashes get special dispensation in method argument lists, as you'll see next.

9.3.7 *Hashes as final method arguments*

If you call a method in such a way that the *last* argument in the argument list is a hash, Ruby allows you to write the hash without curly braces. This perhaps trivial-sounding special rule can, in practice, make argument lists look much nicer than they otherwise would.

Here's an example. The first argument to `add_to_city_database` is the name of the city; the second argument is a hash of data about the city, written without curly braces (and using the special `key: value` symbol notation):

```
add_to_city_database("New York City",
  state: "New York",
  population: 7000000,
  nickname: "Big Apple")
```

The method `add_to_city_database` has to do more work to gain access to the data being passed to it than it would if it were binding parameters to arguments in left-to-right order through a list:

```
def add_to_city_database(name, info)
  c = City.new
  c.name = name
  c.state = info[:state]
  c.population = info[:population]
  # etc.
```

Hashes as first arguments

In addition to learning about the special syntax available to you for using hashes as final method arguments without curly braces, it's worth noting a pitfall of using a hash as the first argument to a method. The rule in this case is that you must not only put curly braces around the hash but also put the entire argument list in parentheses. If you don't, Ruby will think your hash is a code block. In other words, when you do this

```
my_method { "NY" => "New York" }, 100, "another argument"
```

Ruby interprets the expression in braces as a block. If you want to send a hash along as an argument in this position, you have to use parentheses around the entire argument list to make it clear that the curly braces are hash-related and not block-related.

Of course, the exact process involved in unwrapping the hash will vary from one case to another. (Perhaps `City` objects store their information as a hash; that would make the method's job a little easier.) But one way or another, the method has to handle the hash.

Keep in mind that although you get to leave the curly braces off the hash literal when it's the last thing in an argument list, you can have as many hashes as you wish as method arguments, in any position. Just remember that it's only when a hash is in the final argument position that you're allowed to dispense with the braces.

Until Ruby 2 came along, hash arguments of this kind were the closest one could get to named or keyword arguments. That's all changed, though. Ruby now has real named arguments. Their syntax is very hashlike, which is why we're looking at them here rather than in chapter 2.

9.3.8   *A detour back to argument syntax: Named (keyword) arguments*

Using named arguments saves you the trouble of "unwrapping" hashes in your methods. Here's a barebones example that shows the most basic version of named arguments:

```
>> def m(a:, b:)
>>    p a,b
>> end
=> :m
>> m(a: 1, b: 2)
1
2
=> [1, 2]
```

On the method end, there are two parameters ending with colons. On the calling end, there's something that looks a lot like a hash. Ruby matches everything up so that the values for a and b bind as expected. There's no need to probe into a hash.

In the preceding example, a and b indicate required keyword arguments. You can't call the method without them:

```
>> m
ArgumentError: missing keywords: a, b
>> m(a: 1)
ArgumentError: missing keyword: b
```

You can make keyword arguments optional by supplying default values for your named parameters—which makes the parameter list look even more hashlike:

```
>> def m(a: 1, b: 2)
>>    p a,b
>> end
=> :m
>> m                    <──❶
1
2
=> [1, 2]
>> m(a:10)              <──❷
10
2
=> [10, 2]
```

When you call m with no arguments ❶, the defaults for a and b kick in. If you provide an a but no b ❷, you get the a you've provided and the default b.

What if you go in the other direction and call a method using keyword arguments that the method doesn't declare? If the method's parameter list includes a double-starred name, the variable of that name will sponge up all unknown keyword arguments into a hash, as follows:

```
>> def m(a: 1, b: 2, **c)
>>    p a,b,c
>> end
```

```
=> :m
>> m(x: 1, y: 2)
1
2
{:x=>1, :y=>2}
=> [1, 2, {:x=>1, :y=>2}]
```

If there's no keyword sponge parameter, a method call like m(x:1, y:2) is just passing along a hash, which may or may not fail, depending on what arguments the method is expecting.

And of course, you can combine keyword and nonkeyword arguments:

```
>> def m(x, y, *z, a: 1, b:, **c, &block)
>>    p x,y,z,a,b,c
>> end
=> :m
>> m(1,2,3,4,5,b:10,p:20,q:30)
1
2
[3, 4, 5]
1
10
{:p=>20, :q=>30}
=> [1, 2, [3, 4, 5], 1, 10, {:p=>20, :q=>30}]
```

Here the method m

- Takes two required positional arguments (x and y, bound to 1 and 2)
- Has a "sponge" parameter (z) that takes care of extra arguments following the positional ones (3, 4, 5)
- Has one optional and one required keyword argument (a and b, respectively, bound to 1 and 10)
- Has a keyword "sponge" (c) to absorb unknown named arguments (the p and q hash)
- Has a variable for binding to the code block, if any (block)

You'll rarely see method signatures of this complexity, so if you can keep track of the elements in this one, you're probably all set!

We'll look next at ranges—which aren't exactly collection objects, arguably, but which turn out to have a lot in common with collection objects.

9.4   Ranges

A *range* is an object with a start point and an end point. The semantics of range operations involve two major concepts:

- *Inclusion*—Does a given value fall inside the range?
- *Enumeration*—The range is treated as a traversable collection of individual items.

The logic of inclusion applies to all ranges; you can always test for inclusion. The logic of enumeration kicks in only with certain ranges—namely, those that include a finite number of discrete, identifiable values. You can't iterate over a range that lies between two floating-point numbers, because the range encompasses an infinite number of values. But you can iterate over a range between two integers.

We'll save further analysis of range iteration and enumeration logic for the next chapter, where we'll look at enumeration and the `Enumerable` module in depth. In this section, we'll look primarily at the other semantic concept: inclusion logic. We'll start with some range-creation techniques.

9.4.1 Creating a range

You can create range objects with `Range.new`. If you do so in irb, you're rewarded with a view of the syntax for literal range construction:

```
>> r = Range.new(1,100)
=> 1..100
```

The literal syntax can, of course, also be used directly to create a range:

```
>> r = 1..100
=> 1..100
```

When you see a range with two dots between the start-point and end-point values, as in the previous example, you're seeing an *inclusive* range. A range with three dots in the middle is an *exclusive* range:

```
>> r = 1...100
=> 1...100
```

The difference lies in whether the end point is considered to lie inside the range. Coming full circle, you can also specify inclusive or exclusive behavior when you create a range with `Range.new`: the default is an inclusive range, but you can force an exclusive range by passing a third argument of `true` to the constructor:

```
>> Range.new(1,100)
=> 1..100
>> Range.new(1,100,true)
=> 1...100
```

Unfortunately, there's no way to remember which behavior is the default and which is triggered by the `true` argument, except to memorize it.

Also notoriously hard to remember is which number of dots goes with which type of range.

REMEMBERING .. VS. ...

If you follow Ruby discussion forums, you'll periodically see messages and posts from people who find it difficult to remember which is which: two versus three dots, inclusive versus exclusive range.

One way to remember is to think of a range as always reaching to the point represented by whatever follows the second dot. In an inclusive range, the point after the second dot is the end value of the range. In this example, the value `100` is included in the range:

```
1..100
```

But in this exclusive range, the value `100` lies beyond the effective end of the range:

```
1...100
```

In other words, you can think of `100` as having been "pushed" to the right in such a way that it now sits outside the range.

We'll turn now to range-inclusion logic—a section that closely corresponds to the "query" sections from the discussions of strings, arrays, and hashes, because most of what you do with ranges involves querying them on criteria of inclusion.

9.4.2 *Range-inclusion logic*

Ranges have `begin` and `end` methods, which report back their starting and ending points:

```
>> r = 1..10
=> 1..10
>> r.begin
=> 1
>> r.end
=> 10
```

A range also knows whether it's an exclusive (three-dot) range:

```
>> r.exclude_end?
=> false
```

With the goal posts in place, you can start to test for inclusion.

Two methods are available for testing inclusion of a value in a range: `cover?` and `include?` (which is also aliased as `member?`).

TESTING RANGE INCLUSION WITH COVER?

The `cover?` method performs a simple test: if the argument to the method is greater than the range's start point and less than its end point (or equal to it, for an inclusive range), then the range is said to *cover* the object. The tests are performed using Boolean comparison tests, with a false result in cases where the comparison makes no sense.

All of the following comparisons make sense; one of them fails because the item isn't in the range:

```
>> r = "a".."z"
=> "a".."z"
>> r.cover?("a")        <──┤ true: "a" >= "a"
=> true                      and "a" <= "z"
>> r.cover?("abc")      <──┤ true: "abc" >= "a"
=> true                      and "abc" <= "z"
>> r.cover?("A")        <──┐ false: "A" < "a"
=> false
```

But this next test fails because the item being tested for inclusion isn't comparable with the range's start and end points:

```
>> r.cover?([])
=> false
```

It's meaningless to ask whether an array is greater than the string "a". If you try such a comparison on its own, you'll get a fatal error. Fortunately, ranges take a more conservative approach and tell you that the item isn't covered by the range.

Whereas cover? performs start- and end-point comparisons, the other inclusion test, include? (or member?), takes a more collection-based approach.

TESTING RANGE INCLUSION WITH INCLUDE?

The include? test treats the range as a kind of crypto-array—that is, a collection of values. The "a".."z" range, for example, is considered to include (as measured by include?) only the 26 values that lie inclusively between "a" and "z".

Therefore, include? produces results that differ from those of cover?:

```
>> r.include?("a")
=> true
>> r.include?("abc")
=> false
```

In cases where the range can't be interpreted as a finite collection, such as a range of floats, the include? method falls back on numerical order and comparison:

```
>> r = 1.0..2.0
=> 1.0..2.0
>> r.include?(1.5)
=> true
```

Are there backward ranges?

The anticlimactic answer to the question of backward ranges is this: yes and no. You can create a backward range, but it won't do what you probably want it to:

```
>> r = 100...1
=> 100...1
>> r.include?(50)
=> false
```

The range happily performs its usual inclusion test for you. The test calculates whether the candidate for inclusion is greater than the start point of the range and less than the end point. Because 50 is neither greater than 100 nor less than 1, the test fails. And it fails silently; this is a logic error, not a fatal syntax or runtime error.

Backward ranges do show up in one particular set of use cases: as index arguments to strings and arrays. They typically take the form of a positive start point and a negative end point, with the negative end point counting in from the right:

```
>> "This is a sample string"[10..-5]
=> "sample st"
>> ['a','b','c','d'][0..-2]
=> ["a", "b", "c"]
```

> **(continued)**
>
> You can even use an exclusive backward range:
>
> ```
> >> ['a','b','c','d'][0...-2]
> => ["a", "b"]
> ```
>
> In these cases, what doesn't work (at least, in the way you might have expected) in a range on its own does work when applied to a string or an array.

You'll see more about ranges as quasi-collections in the next chapter, as promised. In this chapter, we've got one more basic collection class to examine: the Set class.

9.5 Sets

Set is the one class under discussion in this chapter that isn't, strictly speaking, a Ruby core class. It's a standard library class, which means that to use it, you have to do this:

```
require 'set'
```

The general rule in this book is that we're looking at the core language rather than the standard library, but the Set class makes a worthy exception because it fits in so nicely with the other container and collection classes we've looked at.

A *set* is a unique collection of objects. The objects can be anything—strings, integers, arrays, other sets—but no object can occur more than once in the set. Uniqueness is also enforced at the commonsense content level: if the set contains the string "New York", you can't add the string "New York" to it, even though the two strings may technically be different objects. The same is true of arrays with equivalent content.

> **NOTE** Internally, sets use a hash to enforce the uniqueness of their contents. When an element is added to a set, the internal hash for that set gets a new key. Therefore, any two objects that would count as duplicates if used as hash keys can't occur together in a set.

Let's look now at how to create sets.

9.5.1 Set creation

To create a set, you use the Set.new constructor. You can create an empty set, or you can pass in a collection object (defined as an object that responds to each or each_entry). In the latter case, all the elements of the collection are placed individually in the set:

```
>> new_england = ["Connecticut", "Maine", "Massachusetts",
                   "New Hampshire", "Rhode Island", "Vermont"]
=> ["Connecticut", "Maine", "Massachusetts",
    "New Hampshire","Rhode Island", "Vermont"]
>> state_set = Set.new(new_england)
=> #<Set: {"Connecticut", "Maine", "Massachusetts",
           "New Hampshire", "Rhode Island", "Vermont"}>
```

Here, we've created an array, new_england, and used it as the constructor argument for the creation of the state_set set. Note that there's no literal set constructor (no equivalent to [] for arrays or {} for hashes). There can't be: sets are part of the standard library, not the core, and the core syntax of the language is already in place before the set library gets loaded.

You can also provide a code block to the constructor, in which case every item in the collection object you supply is passed through the block (yielded to it) with the resulting value being inserted into the set. For example, here's a way to initialize a set to a list of uppercased strings:

```
>> names = ["David", "Yukihiro", "Chad", "Amy"]
=> ["David", "Yukihiro", "Chad", "Amy"]
>> name_set = Set.new(names) {|name| name.upcase }
=> #<Set: {"AMY", "YUKIHIRO", "CHAD", "DAVID"}>
```

Rather than using the array of names as its initial values, the set constructor yields each name to the block and inserts what it gets back (an uppercase version of the string) into the set.

Now that we've got a set, we can manipulate it.

9.5.2 *Manipulating set elements*

Like arrays, sets have two modes of adding elements: either inserting a new element into the set or drawing on another collection object as a source for multiple new elements. In the array world, this is the difference between << and concat. For sets, the distinction is reflected in a variety of methods, which we'll look at here.

ADDING/REMOVING ONE OBJECT TO/FROM A SET

To add a single object to a set, you can use the << operator/method:

```
>> tri_state = Set.new(["New Jersey", "New York"])          Whoops,
=> #<Set: {"New Jersey", "New York"}>                       only two!
>> tri_state << "Connecticut"
=> #<Set: {"New Jersey", "New York", "Connecticut"}>    Adds third
```

Here, as with arrays, strings, and other objects, << connotes appending to a collection or mutable object. If you try to add an object that's already in the set (or an object that's content-equal to one that's in the set), nothing happens:

```
>> tri_state << "Connecticut"
=> #<Set: {"New Jersey", "New York", "Connecticut"}>    Second time
```

To remove an object, use delete:

```
>> tri_state << "Pennsylvania"
=> #<Set: {"New Jersey", "New York", "Connecticut", "Pennsylvania"}>
>> tri_state.delete("Connecticut")
=> #<Set: {"New Jersey", "New York", "Pennsylvania"}>
```

Deleting an object that isn't in the set doesn't raise an error. As with adding a duplicate object, nothing happens.

The << method is also available as add. There's also a method called add?, which differs from add in that it returns nil (rather than returning the set itself) if the set is unchanged after the operation:

```
>> tri_state.add?("Pennsylvania")
=> nil
```

You can test the return value of add? to determine whether to take a different conditional branch if the element you've attempted to add was already there.

SET INTERSECTION, UNION, AND DIFFERENCE

Sets have a concept of their own intersection, union, and difference with other sets— and, indeed, with other enumerable objects. The Set class comes with the necessary methods to perform these operations.

These methods have English names and symbolic aliases. The names are

- intersection, aliased as &
- union, aliased as + and |
- difference, aliased as -

Each of these methods returns a new set consisting of the original set, plus or minus the appropriate elements from the object provided as the method argument. The original set is unaffected.

Let's shift our tri-state grouping back to the East and look at some set operations:

```
>> tri_state = Set.new(["Connecticut", "New Jersey", "New York"])
=> #<Set: {"Connecticut", "New Jersey", "New York"}>
# Subtraction (difference/-)
>> state_set - tri_state
=> #<Set: {"Maine", "Massachusetts", "New Hampshire", "Rhode Island",
"Vermont"}>
# Addition (union/+/|)
>> state_set + tri_state
=> #<Set: {"Connecticut", "Maine", "Massachusetts", "New Hampshire",
"Rhode Island", "Vermont", "New Jersey", "New York"}>
# Intersection (&)
>> state_set & tri_state
=> #<Set: {"Connecticut"}>
>> state_set | tri_state
=> #<Set: {"Connecticut", "Maine", "Massachusetts", "New Hampshire",
"Rhode Island", "Vermont", "New Jersey", "New York"}>
```

There's also an exclusive-or operator, ^, which you can use to take the exclusive union between a set and an enumerable—that is, a set consisting of all elements that occur in either the set or the enumerable but not both:

```
>> state_set ^ tri_state
=> #<Set: {"New Jersey", "New York", "Maine", "Massachusetts",
  "New Hampshire", "Rhode Island", "Vermont"}>
```

You can extend an existing set using a technique very similar in effect to the Set.new technique: the merge method, which can take as its argument any object that responds to each or each_entry. That includes arrays, hashes, and ranges—and, of course, other sets.

MERGING A COLLECTION INTO ANOTHER SET

What happens when you merge another object into a set depends on what that object's idea of iterating over itself consists of. Here's an array example, including a check on object_id to confirm that the original set has been altered in place:

```
>> tri_state = Set.new(["Connecticut", "New Jersey"])
=> #<Set: {"Connecticut", "New Jersey"}>
>> tri_state.object_id
=> 2703420
>> tri_state.merge(["New York"])
=> #<Set: {"Connecticut", "New Jersey", "New York"}>
>> tri_state.object_id
=> 2703420
```

Merging a hash into a set results in the addition of two-element, key/value arrays to the set—because that's how hashes break themselves down when you iterate through them. Here's a slightly non-real-world example that demonstrates the technology:

```
>> s = Set.new([1,2,3])
=> #<Set: {1, 2, 3}>
>> s.merge({ "New Jersey" => "NJ", "Maine" => "ME" })
=> #<Set: {1, 2, 3, ["New Jersey", "NJ"], ["Maine", "ME"]}>
```

If you provide a hash argument to Set.new, the behavior is the same: you get a new set with two-element arrays based on the hash.

You might want to merge just the keys of a hash, rather than the entire hash, into a set. After all, set membership is based on hash key uniqueness, under the hood. You can do that with the keys method:

```
>> state_set = Set.new(["New York", "New Jersey"])
=> #<Set: {"New York", "New Jersey"}>
>> state_hash = { "Maine" => "ME", "Vermont" => "VT" }
=> {"Maine"=>"ME", "Vermont"=>"VT"}
>> state_set.merge(state_hash.keys)
=> #<Set: {"New York", "New Jersey", "Maine", "Vermont"}>
```

Try out some permutations of set merging, and you'll see that it's quite open-ended (just like set creation), as long as the argument is an object with an each or each _entry method.

Sets wouldn't be sets without subsets and supersets, and Ruby's set objects are sub- and super-aware.

9.5.3   *Subsets and supersets*

You can test for subset/superset relationships between sets (and the arguments have to be sets, not arrays, hashes, or any other kind of enumerable or collection) using the unsurprisingly named subset and superset methods:

```
>> small_states = Set.new(["Connecticut", "Delaware", "Rhode Island"])
=> #<Set: {"Connecticut", "Delaware", "Rhode Island"}>
>> tiny_states = Set.new(["Delaware", "Rhode Island"])
=> #<Set: {"Delaware", "Rhode Island"}>
>> tiny_states.subset?(small_states)
=> true
>> small_states.superset?(tiny_states)
=> true
```

The proper_subset and proper_superset methods are also available to you. A *proper subset* is a subset that's smaller than the parent set by at least one element. If the two sets are equal, they're subsets of each other but not proper subsets. Similarly, a *proper superset* of a set is a second set that contains all the elements of the first set plus at least one element not present in the first set. The "proper" concept is a way of filtering out the case where a set is a superset or subset of itself—because all sets are both.

We'll pick up the set thread in the next chapter, where we'll take another pass through collection objects in the interest of getting more deeply into the Enumerable module and the collection-based services it provides.

9.6   *Summary*

In this chapter you've seen

- How to create, manipulate, and transform collection objects, including
  - Arrays
  - Hashes
  - Ranges
  - Sets
- Named arguments

We've looked closely at Ruby's major core container classes, Array and Hash. We've also looked at ranges, which principally operate as inclusion test criteria but know how to behave as collections when their makeup permits them to (a point that will make more sense after you've seen more about the Enumerable module). After ranges, we looked at sets, which are defined in the standard library and add another important tool to Ruby's collection toolset. The source code for the Set class is written in Ruby; that gave us an opportunity to look at some real production Ruby code.

We also took a detour into named arguments, which prevent you from having to use hash keys as pseudo-keywords and "unpacking" argument hashes in your methods.

The concept of the *collection* in Ruby is closely associated with the Enumerable module and its principle of dependence on an each method. In the next chapter, we'll go more deeply into Enumerable—which means looking at the many searching, filtering, sorting, and transforming operations available on objects whose classes mix in that module.

Collections central: Enumerable and Enumerator

This chapter covers

- Mixing `Enumerable` into your classes
- The use of `Enumerable` methods in collection objects
- Strings as quasi-enumerable objects
- Sorting enumerables with the `Comparable` module
- Enumerators

All collection objects aren't created equal—but an awful lot of them have many characteristics in common. In Ruby, common characteristics among many objects tend to reside in modules. Collections are no exception: collection objects in Ruby typically include the `Enumerable` module.

Classes that use `Enumerable` enter into a kind of contract: the class has to define an instance method called `each`, and in return, `Enumerable` endows the objects of the class with all sorts of collection-related behaviors. The methods behind these behaviors are defined in terms of `each`. In some respects, you might say the whole concept of a "collection" in Ruby is pegged to the `Enumerable` module and the methods it defines on top of `each`.

You've already seen a bit of each in action. Here, you'll see a lot more. Keep in mind, though, that although every major collection class partakes of the Enumerable module, each of them has its own methods too. The methods of an array aren't identical to those of a set; those of a range aren't identical to those of a hash. And sometimes collection classes share method names but the methods don't do exactly the same thing. They *can't* always do the same thing; the whole point is to have multiple collection classes but to extract as much common behavior as possible into a common module.

You can mix Enumerable into your own classes:

```
class C
  include Enumerable
end
```

By itself, that doesn't do much. To tap into the benefits of Enumerable, you must define an each instance method in your class:

```
class C
  include Enumerable
  def each
    # relevant code here
  end
end
```

At this point, objects of class C will have the ability to call any instance method defined in Enumerable.

In addition to the Enumerable module, in this chapter we'll look at a closely related class called Enumerator. *Enumerators* are objects that encapsulate knowledge of how to iterate through a particular collection. By packaging iteration intelligence in an object that's separate from the collection itself, enumerators add a further and powerful dimension to Ruby's already considerable collection-manipulation facilities.

Let's start by looking more closely at each and its role as the engine for enumerable behavior.

10.1 Gaining enumerability through each

Any class that aspires to be enumerable must have an each method whose job is to yield items to a supplied code block, one at a time.

Exactly what each does will vary from one class to another. In the case of an array, each yields the first element, then the second, and so forth. In the case of a hash, it yields key/value pairs in the form of two-element arrays. In the case of a file handle, it yields one line of the file at a time. Ranges iterate by first deciding whether iterating is possible (which it isn't, for example, if the start point is a float) and then pretending to be an array. And if you define an each in a class of your own, it can mean whatever you want it to mean—as long as it yields something. So each has different semantics for different classes. But however each is implemented, the methods in the Enumerable module depend on being able to call it.

You can get a good sense of how Enumerable works by writing a small, proof-of-concept class that uses it. The following listing shows such a class: Rainbow. This class has an each method that yields one color at a time. Because the class mixes in Enumerable, its instances are automatically endowed with the instance methods defined in that module.

> **Listing 10.1   An Enumerable class and its deployment of the each method**

```
class Rainbow
  include Enumerable
  def each
    yield "red"
    yield "orange"
    yield "yellow"
    yield "green"
    yield "blue"
    yield "indigo"
    yield "violet"
  end
end
```

Every instance of Rainbow will know how to iterate through the colors. In the simplest case, we can use the each method:

```
r = Rainbow.new
r.each do |color|
  puts "Next color: #{color}"
end
```

The output of this simple iteration is as follows:

```
Next color: red
Next color: orange
Next color: yellow
Next color: green
Next color: blue
Next color: indigo
Next color: violet
```

But that's just the beginning. Because Rainbow mixed in the Enumerable module, rainbows are automatically endowed with a whole slew of methods built on top of the each method.

Here's an example: find, which returns the first element in an enumerable object for which the code block provided returns true. Let's say we want to find the first color that begins with the letter y. We can do it with find, like this:

```
r = Rainbow.new
y_color = r.find {|color| color.start_with?('y') }
puts "First color starting with 'y' is #{y_color}."
```

> **Output: First color starting with 'y' is yellow.**

find works by calling each. each yields items, and find uses the code block we've given it to test those items one at a time for a match. When each gets around to yielding yellow, find runs it through the block and it passes the test. The variable y_color therefore receives the value yellow. Notice that there's no need to define find. It's part of Enumerable, which we've mixed in. It knows what to do and how to use each to do it.

Defining each, together with mixing in Enumerable, buys you a great deal of functionality for your objects. Much of the searching and querying functionality you see in Ruby arrays, hashes, and other collection objects comes directly from Enumerable. If you want to know which methods Enumerable provides, ask it:

```
>> Enumerable.instance_methods(false).sort
=> [:all?, :any?, :chunk, :collect, :collect_concat, :count, :cycle, :detect,
:drop, :drop_while, :each_cons, :each_entry, :each_slice, :each_with_index,
:each_with_object, :entries, :find, :find_all, :find_index, :first,
:flat_map, :grep, :group_by, :include?, :inject, :lazy, :map, :max, :max_by,
:member?, :min, :min_by, :minmax, :minmax_by, :none?, :one?, :partition,
:reduce, :reject, :reverse_each, :select, :slice_before, :sort, :sort_by,
:take, :take_while, :to_a, :to_h, :zip]
```

Thanks to the false argument, the list includes only the methods defined in the Enumerable module itself. Each of these methods is built on top of each.

In the sections that follow, you'll see examples of many of these methods. Some of the others will crop up in later chapters. The examples throughout the rest of this chapter will draw on all four of the major collection classes—Array, Hash, Range, and Set—more or less arbitrarily. Chapter 9 introduced you to these classes individually. Armed with a sense of what makes each of them tick, you're in a good position to study what they have in common.

Some of the methods in Ruby's enumerable classes are actually overwritten in those classes. For example, you'll find implementations of map, select, sort, and other Enumerable instance methods in the source-code file array.c; the Array class doesn't simply provide an each method and mix in Enumerable (though it does do that, and it gains behaviors that way). These overwrites are done either because a given class requires special behavior in the face of a given Enumerable method, or for the sake of efficiency. We're not going to scrutinize all the overwrites. The main point here is to explore the ways in which all of the collection classes share behaviors and interface.

In what follows, we'll look at several categories of methods from Enumerable. We'll start with some Boolean methods.

10.2 *Enumerable Boolean queries*

A number of Enumerable methods return true or false depending on whether one or more element matches certain criteria. Given an array states, containing the names of all the states in the United States of America, here's how you might perform some of these Boolean queries:

```
# Does the array include Louisiana?
>> states.include?("Louisiana")
=> true
# Do all states include a space?
>> states.all? {|state| state =~ / / }
=> false
```

```
# Does any state include a space?
>> states.any? {|state| state =~ / / }
=> true
# Is there one, and only one, state with "West" in its name?
>> states.one? {|state| state =~ /West/ }
=> true
# Are there no states with "East" in their names?
>> states.none? {|state| state =~ /East/ }
=> true
```

If states were, instead, a hash with state names as keys and abbreviations as values, you could run similar tests, although you'd need to adjust for the fact that Hash#each yields both a key and a value each time through. The Hash#include? method checks for key inclusion, as you saw in chapter 9, but the other methods in the previous example handle key/value pairs:

```
# Does the hash include Louisiana?
>> states.include?("Louisiana")                     include? consults
=> true                                          ⤺  hash's keys
# Do all states include a space?
>> states.all? {|state, abbr| state =~ / / }        Hash yields key/value
=> false                                         ⤺  pairs to block
# Is there one, and only one, state with "West" in its name?
>> states.one? {|state, abbr| state =~ /West/ }
=> true
```

In all of these cases, you could grab an array via states.keys and perform the tests on that array directly:

```
# Do all states include a space?
>> states.keys.all? {|state, abbr| state =~ / / }
=> false
```

Generating the entire keys array in advance, rather than walking through the hash that's already there, is slightly wasteful of memory. Still, the new array contains the key objects that already exist, so it only "wastes" the memory devoted to wrapping the keys in an array. The memory taken up by the keys themselves doesn't increase.

Hashes iterate with two-element arrays

When you iterate through a hash with each or any other built-in iterator, the hash is yielded to your code block one key/value pair at a time—and the pairs are two-element arrays. You can, if you wish, provide just one block parameter and capture the whole little array:

```
hash.each {|pair| ... }
```

In such a case, you'll find the key at pair[0] and the value at pair[1]. Normally, it makes more sense to grab the key and value in separate block parameters. But all that's happening is that the two are wrapped up in a two-element array, and that array is yielded. If you want to operate on the data in that form, you may.

What about sets and ranges? Set iteration works much like array iteration for Boolean query (and most other) purposes: if `states` were a set, you could run exactly the same queries as the ones in the example with the same results. With ranges, enumerability gets a little trickier.

It's more meaningful to view some ranges as enumerable—as collections of items that you can step through—than others. The `include?` method works for any range. But the other Boolean `Enumerable` methods force the enumerability issue: if the range can be expressed as a list of discrete elements, then those methods work; but if it can't, as with a range of floats, then calling any of the methods triggers a fatal error:

```
>> r = Range.new(1, 10)
=> 1..10
>> r.one? {|n| n == 5 }
=> true
>> r.none? {|n| n % 2 == 0 }
=> false
>> r = Range.new(1.0, 10.0)
=> 1.0..10.0
>> r.one? {|n| n == 5 }
TypeError: can't iterate from Float
>> r = Range.new(1, 10.3)
=> 1..10.3
>> r.any? {|n| n > 5 }
=> true
```

① **②** **③** **④**

Given a range spanning two integers, you can run tests like one? and none? **①** because the range can easily slip into behaving like a collection: in effect, the range `1..10` adopts the API of the corresponding array, `[1,2,3,4,5,6,7,8,9,10]`.

But a range between two floats **②** can't behave like a finite collection of discrete values. It's meaningless to produce "each" float inside a range. The range has the each method, but the method is written in such a way as to refuse to iterate over floats **③**. (The fact that the error is `TypeError` rather than `NoMethodError` indicates that the each method exists but can't function on this range.)

You can use a float as a range's end point and still get enumeration, as long as the start point is an integer **④**. When you call each (or one of the methods built on top of each), the range behaves like a collection of integers starting at the start point and ending at the end point rounded down to the nearest integer. That integer is considered to be included in the range, whether the range is inclusive or exclusive (because, after all, the official end point is a float that's higher than the integer below it).

In addition to answering various true/false questions about their contents, enumerable objects excel at performing search and select operations. We'll turn to those now.

10.3 *Enumerable searching and selecting*

It's common to want to filter a collection of objects based on one or more selection criteria. For example, if you have a database of people registering for a conference, and you want to send payment reminders to the people who haven't paid, you can filter a complete list based on payment status. Or you might need to narrow a list of numbers to only the even ones. And so forth; the use cases for selecting elements from enumerable objects are unlimited.

The Enumerable module provides several facilities for filtering collections and for searching collections to find one or more elements that match one or more criteria. We'll look at several filtering and searching methods here. All of them are iterators: they all expect you to provide a code block. The code block is the selection filter. You define your selection criteria (your tests for inclusion or exclusion) inside the block. The return value of the entire method may, depending on which method you're using and on what it finds, be one object, an array (possibly empty) of objects matching your criteria, or nil, indicating that the criteria weren't met.

We'll start with a one-object search using find and then work our way through several techniques for deriving a multiple-object result set from an enumerable query.

10.3.1   *Getting the first match with find*

find (also available as the synonymous detect) locates the first element in an array for which the code block, when called with that element as an argument, returns true. For example, to find the first number greater than 5 in an array of integers, you can use find like this:

```
>> [1,2,3,4,5,6,7,8,9,10].find {|n| n > 5 }
=> 6
```

find iterates through the array, yielding each element in turn to the block. If the block returns anything with the Boolean value of true, the element yielded "wins," and find stops iterating. If find fails to find an element that passes the code-block test, it returns nil. (Try changing n > 5 to n > 100 in the example, and you'll see.) It's interesting to ponder the case where your array has nil as one of its elements, and your code block looks for an element equal to nil:

```
[1,2,3,nil,4,5,6].find {|n| n.nil? }
```

In these circumstances, find always returns nil—whether the search succeeds or fails! That means the test is useless; you can't tell whether it succeeded. You can work around this situation with other techniques, such as the include? method, with which you can find out whether an array has nil as an element. You can also provide a "nothing found" function—a Proc object—as an argument to find, in which case that function will be called if the find operation fails. We haven't looked at Proc objects in depth yet, although you've seen some examples of them in connection with the handling of code blocks. For future reference, here's an example of how to supply find with a failure-handling function:

```
>> failure = lambda { 11 }                              ←── ❶
=> #<Proc:0x434810@(irb):6 (lambda)>
>> over_ten = [1,2,3,4,5,6].find(failure) {|n| n > 10 }
=> 11
```

In this example, the anonymous function (the `Proc` object) returns 11 **❶**, so even if there's no number greater than 10 in the array, you get one anyway. (You'll see lambdas and `Proc` objects up close in chapter 14.)

Although `find` always returns one object, `find_all`, also known as `select`, always returns an array, as does its negative equivalent `reject`.

The dominance of the array

Arrays serve generically as the containers for most of the results that come back from enumerable selecting and filtering operations, whether or not the object being selected from or filtered is an array. There are some exceptions to this quasi-rule, but it holds true widely.

The plainest way to see it is by creating an enumerable class of your own and watching what you get back from your select queries. Look again at the `Rainbow` class in listing 10.1. Now look at what you get back when you perform some queries:

```
>> r = Rainbow.new
=> #<Rainbow:0x45b708>
>> r.select {|color| color.size == 6 }
=> ["orange", "yellow", "indigo", "violet"]
>> r.map {|color| color[0,3] }
=> ["red", "ora", "yel", "gre", "blu", "ind", "vio"]
>> r.drop_while {|color| color.size < 5 }
=> ["orange", "yellow", "green", "blue", "indigo", "violet"]
```

In every case, the result set comes back in an array.

The array is the most generic container and therefore the logical candidate for the role of universal result format. A few exceptions arise. A hash returns a hash from a `select` or `reject` operation. Sets return arrays from `map`, but you can call `map!` on a set to change the elements of the set in place. For the most part, though, enumerable selection and filtering operations come back to you inside arrays.

10.3.2 Getting all matches with find_all (a.k.a. select) and reject

`find_all` (the same method as `select`) returns a new collection containing all the elements of the original collection that match the criteria in the code block, not just the first such element (as with `find`). If no matching elements are found, `find_all` returns an empty collection object.

In the general case—for example, when you use `Enumerable` in your own classes—the "collection" returned by `select` will be an array. Ruby makes special arrangements for hashes and sets, though: if you `select` on a hash or set, you get back a hash or set. This is enhanced behavior that isn't strictly part of `Enumerable`.

We'll stick to array examples here:

```
>> a = [1,2,3,4,5,6,7,8,9,10]
=> [1, 2, 3, 4, 5, 6, 7, 8, 9, 10]
>> a.find_all {|item| item > 5 }          ❶
=> [6, 7, 8, 9, 10]
```

```
>> a.select {|item| item > 100 }
=> []                                    ◁──②
```

The first `find_all` operation returns an array of all the elements that pass the test in the block: all elements that are greater than 5 ❶. The second operation also returns an array, this time of all the elements in the original array that are greater than 10. There aren't any, so an empty array is returned ❷.

(Arrays, hashes, and sets have a bang version, `select!`, that reduces the collection permanently to only those elements that passed the selection test. There's no `find_all!` synonym; you have to use `select!`.)

Just as you can select items, so you can reject items, meaning that you find out which elements of an array do not return a true value when yielded to the block. Using the a array from the previous example, you can do this to get the array minus any and all elements that are greater than 5:

```
>> a.reject {|item| item > 5 }
=> [1, 2, 3, 4, 5]
```

(Once again there's a bang, in-place version, `reject!`, specifically for arrays, hashes, and sets.)

If you've ever used the command-line utility `grep`, the next method will ring a bell. If you haven't, you'll get the hang of it anyway.

10.3.3 *Selecting on threequal matches with grep*

The `Enumerable#grep` method lets you select from an enumerable object based on the case equality operator, `===`. The most common application of `grep` is the one that corresponds most closely to the common operation of the command-line utility of the same name, pattern matching for strings:

```
>> colors = %w{ red orange yellow green blue indigo violet }
=> ["red", "orange", "yellow", "green", "blue", "indigo", "violet"]
>> colors.grep(/o/)
=> ["orange", "yellow", "indigo", "violet"]
```

But the generality of `===` lets you do some fancy things with grep:

```
>> miscellany = [75, "hello", 10...20, "goodbye"]
=> [75, "hello", 10...20, "goodbye"]
>> miscellany.grep(String)               ❶
=> ["hello", "goodbye"]
>> miscellany.grep(50..100)              ❷
=> [75]
```

`String === object` is true for the two strings in the array, so an array of those two strings is what you get back from grepping for `String` ❶. Ranges implement `===` as an inclusion test. The range `50..100` includes 75; hence the result from grepping `miscellany` for that range ❷.

In general, the statement `enumerable.grep(expression)` is functionally equivalent to this:

```
enumerable.select {|element| expression === element }
```

In other words, it selects for a truth value based on calling `===`. In addition, `grep` can take a block, in which case it yields each element of its result set to the block before returning the results:

```
>> colors = %w{ red orange yellow green blue indigo violet }
=> ["red", "orange", "yellow", "green", "blue", "indigo", "violet"]
>> colors.grep(/o/) {|color| color.capitalize }
=> ["Orange", "Yellow", "Indigo", "Violet"]
```

The full `grep` syntax

```
enumerable.grep(expression) {|item| ... }
```

thus operates in effect like this:

```
enumerable.select {|item| expression === item}.map {|item| ... }
```

Again, you'll mostly see (and probably mostly use) `grep` as a pattern-based string selector. But keep in mind that grepping is pegged to case equality (`===`) and can be used accordingly in a variety of situations.

Whether carried out as `select` or `grep` or some other operation, selection scenarios often call for grouping of results into clusters or categories. The `Enumerable` #group_by and #partition methods make convenient provisions for exactly this kind of grouping.

10.3.4 *Organizing selection results with group_by and partition*

A `group_by` operation on an enumerable object takes a block and returns a hash. The block is executed for each object. For each unique block return value, the result hash gets a key; the value for that key is an array of all the elements of the enumerable for which the block returned that value.

An example should make the operation clear:

```
>> colors = %w{ red orange yellow green blue indigo violet }
=> ["red", "orange", "yellow", "green", "blue", "indigo", "violet"]
>> colors.group_by {|color| color.size }
=> {3=>["red"], 6=>["orange", "yellow", "indigo", "violet"],
    5=>["green"], 4=>["blue"]}
```

The block `{|color| color.size }` returns an integer for each color. The hash returned by the entire `group_by` operation is keyed to the various sizes (3, 4, 5, 6), and the values are arrays containing all the strings from the original array that are of the size represented by the respective keys.

The `partition` method is similar to `group_by`, but it splits the elements of the enumerable into two arrays based on whether the code block returns true for the element.

There's no hash, just an array of two arrays. The two arrays are always returned in true/false order.

Consider a `Person` class, where every person has an age. The class also defines an instance method `teenager?`, which is true if the person's age is between 13 and 19, inclusive:

```
class Person
  attr_accessor :age
  def initialize(options)
    self.age = options[:age]
  end
  def teenager?
    (13..19) === age
  end
end
```

Now let's generate an array of people:

```
people = 10.step(25,3).map {|i| Person.new(:age => i) }
```

This code does an iteration from 10 to 25 in steps of 3 (10, 13, 16, 19, 22, 25), passing each of the values to the block in turn. Each time through, a new `Person` is created with the age corresponding to the increment. Thanks to `map`, the person objects are all accumulated into an array, which is assigned to `people`. (The chaining of the iterator `map` to the iterator `step` is made possible by the fact that `step` returns an enumerator. You'll learn more about enumerators presently.)

We've got our six people; now let's partition them into teens and non-teens:

```
teens =  people.partition {|person| person.teenager? }
```

The `teens` array has the following content:

```
[[#<Person:0x000001019d1a50 @age=13>, #<Person:0x000001019d19d8 @age=16>,
#<Person:0x000001019d1988 @age=19>], [#<Person:0x000001019d1ac8 @age=10>,
#<Person:0x000001019d1910 @age=22>, #<Person:0x000001019d1898 @age=25>]]
```

Note that this is an array containing two subarrays. The first contains those people for whom `person.teenager?` returned true; the second is the non-teens.

We can now use the information, for example, to find out how many teens and non-teens we have:

```
puts "#{teens[0].size} teens; #{teens[1].size} non-teens"
```

The output from this statement reflects the fact that half of our people are teens and half aren't:

```
3 teens; 3 non-teens
```

Let's look now at some "element-wise" operations—methods that involve relatively fine-grained manipulation of specific collection elements.

10.4 *Element-wise enumerable operations*

Collections are born to be traversed, but they also contain special-status individual objects: the first or last in the collection, and the greatest (largest) or least (smallest). Enumerable objects come with several tools for element handling along these lines.

10.4.1 *The first method*

Enumerable#first, as the name suggests, returns the first item encountered when iterating over the enumerable:

```
>> [1,2,3,4].first
=> 1
>> (1..10).first
=> 1
>> {1 => 2, "one" => "two"}.first
=> [1, 2]
```

The object returned by first is the same as the first object you get when you iterate through the parent object. In other words, it's the first thing yielded by each. In keeping with the fact that hashes yield key/value pairs in two-element arrays, taking the first element of a hash gives you a two-element array containing the first pair that was inserted into the hash (or the first key inserted and its new value, if you've changed that value at any point):

```
>> hash = { 3 => "three", 1 => "one", 2 => "two" }
=> {3=>"three", 1=>"one", 2=>"two"}          first means first
>> hash.first                            ◁─┘ inserted
=> [3, "three"]
>> hash[3] = "trois"
=> "trois"                           New value doesn't
>> hash.first                    ◁─┘ change insertion order
=> [3, "trois"]
```

Perhaps the most noteworthy point about Enumerable#first is that there's no Enumerable#last. That's because finding the end of the iteration isn't as straightforward as finding the beginning. Consider a case where the iteration goes on forever. Here's a little Die class (die as in the singular of dice). It iterates by rolling the die forever and yielding the result each time:

```
class Die
  include Enumerable
  def each
    loop do
      yield rand(6) + 1
    end
  end
end
```

The loop uses the method Kernel#rand. Called with no argument, this method generates a random floating-point number n such that $0 <= n < 1$. With an argument i, it returns a random integer n such that $0 <= n < i$. Thus rand(6) produces an integer in the range (0..5). Adding one to that number gives a number between 1 and 6, which corresponds to what you get when you roll a die.

But the main point is that Die#each goes on forever. If you're using the Die class, you have to make provisions to break out of the loop. Here's a little game where you win as soon as the die turns up 6:

```
puts "Welcome to 'You Win If You Roll a 6'!"
d = Die.new
d.each do |roll|
  puts "You rolled a #{roll}."
  if roll == 6
    puts "You win!"
    break
  end
end
```

A typical run might look like this:

```
Welcome to 'You Win If You Roll a 6'
You rolled a 3.
You rolled a 2.
You rolled a 2.
You rolled a 1.
You rolled a 6.
You win!
```

The triviality of the game aside, the point is that it would be meaningless to call `last` on your die object, because there's no last roll of the die. Unlike taking the first element, taking the last element of an enumerable has no generalizable meaning.

For the same reason—the unreachability of the end of the enumeration—an enumerable class with an infinitely yielding each method can't do much with methods like `select` and `map`, which don't return their results until the underlying iteration is complete. Occasions for infinite iteration are, in any event, few; but observing the behavior and impact of an endless each can be instructive for what it reveals about the more common, finite case.

Keep in mind, though, that some enumerable classes do have a `last` method: notably, `Array` and `Range`. Moreover, all enumerables have a `take` method, a kind of generalization of `first`, and a companion method called `drop`.

10.4.2 *The take and drop methods*

Enumerables know how to "take" a certain number of elements from the beginning of themselves and conversely how to "drop" a certain number of elements. The `take` and `drop` operations basically do the same thing—they divide the collection at a specific point—but they differ in what they return:

```
>> states = %w{ NJ NY CT MA VT FL }
=> ["NJ", "NY", "CT", "MA", "VT", "FL"]          Grabs first two
>> states.take(2)                             ◄── elements
=> ["NJ", "NY"]
>> states.drop(2)                                    Grabs collection except
=> ["CT", "MA", "VT", "FL"]                   ◄──    first two elements
```

When you take elements, you get those elements. When you drop elements, you get the original collection minus the elements you've dropped. You can constrain the `take` and `drop` operations by providing a block and using the variant forms `take_while` and `drop_while`, which determine the size of the "take" not by an integer argument but by the truth value of the block:

```
>> states.take_while {|s| /N/.match(s) }
=> ["NJ", "NY"]
>> states.drop_while {|s| /N/.match(s) }
=> ["CT", "MA", "VT", "FL"]
```

The `take` and `drop` operations are a kind of hybrid of `first` and `select`. They're anchored to the beginning of the iteration and terminate once they've satisfied the quantity requirement or encountered a block failure.

You can also determine the minimum and maximum values in an enumerable collection.

10.4.3 *The min and max methods*

The `min` and `max` methods do what they sound like they'll do:

```
>> [1,3,5,4,2].max
=> 5
>> %w{ Ruby C APL Perl Smalltalk }.min
=> "APL"
```

Minimum and maximum are determined by the `<=>` (spaceship comparison operator) logic, which for the array of strings puts `"APL"` first in ascending order. If you want to perform a minimum or maximum test based on nondefault criteria, you can provide a code block:

```
>> %w{ Ruby C APL Perl Smalltalk }.min {|a,b| a.size <=> b.size }
=> "C"
```

A more streamlined block-based approach, though, is to use `min_by` or `max_by`, which perform the comparison implicitly:

```
>> %w{ Ruby C APL Perl Smalltalk }.min_by {|lang| lang.size }  ◁─┤  No need to compare
=> "C"                                                               two parameters
                                                                     explicitly in code block
```

There's also a `minmax` method (and the corresponding `minmax_by` method), which gives you a pair of values, one for the minimum and one for the maximum:

```
>> %w{ Ruby C APL Perl Smalltalk }.minmax
=> ["APL", "Smalltalk"]
>> %w{ Ruby C APL Perl Smalltalk }.minmax_by {|lang| lang.size }
=> ["C", "Smalltalk"]
```

Keep in mind that the `min`/`max` family of enumerable methods is always available, even when using it isn't a good idea. You wouldn't want to do this, for example:

```
die = Die.new
puts die.max
```

The infinite loop with which Die#each is implemented won't allow a maximum value ever to be determined. Your program will hang.

In the case of hashes, min and max use the keys to determine ordering. If you want to use values, the *_by members of the min/max family can help you:

```
>> state_hash = {"New York" => "NY", "Maine" => "ME",
"Alaska" => "AK", "Alabama" => "AL" }
=> {"New York"=>"NY", "Maine"=>"ME", "Alaska"=>"AK", "Alabama"=>"AL"}
>> state_hash.min                                        ⟵┐ Minimum pair, by key
=> ["Alabama", "AL"]
>> state_hash.min_by {|name, abbr| name }    ⟵┐ Same as min
=> ["Alabama", "AL"]
>> state_hash.min_by {|name, abbr| abbr }  ⟵┐ Minimum pair, by value
=> ["Alaska", "AK"]
```

And of course you can, if you wish, perform calculations inside the block that involve both the key and the value.

At this point, we've looked at examples of each methods and how they link up to a number of methods that are built on top of them. It's time now to look at some methods that are similar to each but a little more specialized. The most important of these is map. In fact, map is important enough that we'll look at it separately in its own section. First, let's discuss some other each relatives.

10.5 Relatives of each

Enumerable makes several methods available to you that are similar to each, in that they go through the whole collection and yield elements from it, not stopping until they've gone all the way through (and in one case, not even then!). Each member of this family of methods has its own particular semantics and niche. The methods include reverse_each, each_with_index, each_slice, each_cons, cycle, and inject. We'll look at them in that order.

10.5.1 reverse_each

The reverse_each method does what it sounds like it will do: it iterates backwards through an enumerable. For example, the code

```
[1,2,3].reverse_each {|e| puts e * 10 }
```

produces this output:

```
30
20
10
```

You have to be careful with reverse_each: don't use it on an infinite iterator, since the concept of going in reverse depends on the concept of knowing what the last element is—which is a meaningless concept in the case of an infinite iterator. Try calling reverse_each on an instance of the Die class shown earlier—but be ready to hit Ctrl-c to get out of the infinite loop.

10.5.2 *The each_with_index method (and each.with_index)*

Enumerable#each_with_index differs from each in that it yields an extra item each time through the collection: namely, an integer representing the ordinal position of the item. This index can be useful for labeling objects, among other purposes:

```
>> names = ["George Washington", "John Adams", "Thomas Jefferson",
"James Madison"]
=> ["George Washington", "John Adams", "Thomas Jefferson",
"James Madison"]
>> names.each_with_index do |pres, i|
?>   puts "#{i+1}. #{pres}"                    ◁――┐  Adds 1 to avoid
>> end                                             │  0th list entry
1. George Washington
2. John Adams
3. Thomas Jefferson
4. James Madison
```

An anomaly is involved in each_with_index: every enumerable object has it, but not every enumerable object has knowledge of what an index is. You can see this by asking enumerables to perform an each_index (as opposed to each_with_index) operation. The results vary from one enumerable to another:

```
>> %w{a b c }.each_index {|i| puts i }
0
1
2
=> ["a", "b", "c"]
```

Arrays, then, have a fundamental sense of an index. Hashes don't—although they do have a sense of with index:

```
>> letters = {"a" => "ay", "b" => "bee", "c" => "see" }
=> {"a"=>"ay", "b"=>"bee", "c"=>"see"}
>> letters.each_with_index {|(key,value),i| puts i }
0
1
2
=> {"a"=>"ay", "b"=>"bee", "c"=>"see"}
>> letters.each_index {|(key,value),i| puts i }
NoMethodError: undefined method `each_index' for {"a"=>"ay",
"b"=>"bee", "c"=>"see"}:Hash
```

We could posit that a hash's keys are its indexes and that the ordinal numbers generated by the each_with_index iteration are extra or meta-indexes. It's an interesting theoretical question; but in practice it doesn't end up mattering much, because it's extremely unusual to need to perform an each_with_index operation on a hash.

  Enumerable#each_with_index works, but it's somewhat deprecated. Instead, consider using the #with_index method of the enumerator you get back from calling each. You've already seen this technique in chapter 9:

```
>> array = %w{ red yellow blue }
=> ["red", "yellow", "blue"]
```

```
>> array.each.with_index do |color, i|
?>   puts "Color number #{i} is #{color}."
>> end
```

It's as simple as changing an underscore to a period ... though there's a little more to it under the hood, as you'll see when you learn more about enumerators a little later. (See section 10.11.2 for more on each_index.) Using each_index also buys you some functionality: you can provide an argument that will be used as the first index value, thus avoiding the need to add one to the index in a case like the previous list of presidents:

```
>> names.each.with_index(1) do |pres, i|
?>   puts "#{i} #{pres}"
>> end
```

Another subfamily of each relatives is the pair of methods each_slice and each_cons.

10.5.3 *The each_slice and each_cons methods*

The each_slice and each_cons methods are specializations of each that walk through a collection a certain number of elements at a time, yielding an array of that many elements to the block on each iteration. The difference between them is that each_slice handles each element only once, whereas each_cons takes a new grouping at each element and thus produces overlapping yielded arrays.

Here's an illustration of the difference:

```
>> array = [1,2,3,4,5,6,7,8,9,10]
=> [1, 2, 3, 4, 5, 6, 7, 8, 9, 10]
>> array.each_slice(3) {|slice| p slice }
[1, 2, 3]
[4, 5, 6]
[7, 8, 9]
[10]
=> nil
>> array.each_cons(3) {|cons| p cons }
[1, 2, 3]
[2, 3, 4]
[3, 4, 5]
[4, 5, 6]
[5, 6, 7]
[6, 7, 8]
[7, 8, 9]
[8, 9, 10]
=> nil
```

The each_slice operation yields the collection progressively in slices of size n (or less than n, if fewer than n elements remain). By contrast, each_cons moves through the collection one element at a time and at each point yields an array of n elements, stopping when the last element in the collection has been yielded once.

Yet another generic way to iterate through an enumerable is with the cycle method.

10.5.4 *The cycle method*

Enumerable#cycle yields all the elements in the object again and again in a loop. If you provide an integer argument, the loop will be run that many times. If you don't, it will be run infinitely.

You can use cycle to decide dynamically how many times you want to iterate through a collection—essentially, how many each-like runs you want to perform consecutively. Here's an example involving a deck of playing cards:

```ruby
class PlayingCard
  SUITS = %w{ clubs diamonds hearts spades }          ❶
  RANKS = %w{ 2 3 4 5 6 7 8 9 10 J Q K A }
  class Deck                                           ❷
    attr_reader :cards
    def initialize(n=1)                                ❸
      @cards = []
      SUITS.cycle(n) do |s|                            ❹
        RANKS.cycle(1) do |r|                          ❺
          @cards << "#{r} of #{s}"                     
        end                                            ❻
      end
    end
  end
end
```

The class PlayingCard defines constants representing suits and ranks ❶, whereas the PlayingCard::Deck class models the deck. The cards are stored in an array in the deck's @cards instance variable, available also as a reader attribute ❷. Thanks to cycle, it's easy to arrange for the possibility of combining two or more decks. Deck.new takes an argument, defaulting to 1 ❸. If you override the default, the process by which the @cards array is populated is augmented.

For example, this command produces a double deck of cards containing two of each card for a total of 104:

```ruby
deck = PlayingCard::Deck.new(2)
```

That's because the method cycles through the suits twice, cycling through the ranks once per suit iteration ❹. The ranks cycle is always done only once ❺; cycle(1) is, in effect, another way of saying each. For each permutation, a new card, represented by a descriptive string, is inserted into the deck ❻.

Last on the each-family method tour is inject, also known as reduce.

10.5.5 *Enumerable reduction with inject*

The inject method (a.k.a. reduce and similar to "fold" methods in functional languages) works by initializing an accumulator object and then iterating through a collection (an enumerable object), performing a calculation on each iteration and resetting the accumulator, for purposes of the next iteration, to the result of that calculation.

The classic example of injecting is the summing up of numbers in an array. Here's how to do it:

```
>> [1,2,3,4].inject(0) {|acc,n| acc + n }
=> 10
```

And here's how it works:

1. The accumulator is initialized to 0, courtesy of the 0 argument to `inject`.

2. The first time through the iteration—the code block—acc is 0, and n is set to 1 (the first item in the array). The result of the calculation inside the block is 0 + 1, or 1.

3. The second time through, acc is set to 1 (the block's result from the previous time through), and n is set to 2 (the second element in the array). The block therefore evaluates to 3.

4. The third time through, acc and n are 3 (previous block result) and 3 (next value in the array). The block evaluates to 6.

5. The fourth time through, acc and n are 6 and 4. The block evaluates to 10. Because this is the last time through, the value from the block serves as the return value of the entire call to `inject`. Thus the entire call evaluates to 10, as shown by irb.

If you don't supply an argument to `inject`, it uses the first element in the enumerable object as the initial value for acc. In this example, that would produce the same result, because the first iteration added 0 to 1 and set acc to 1 anyway.

Here's a souped-up example, with some commentary printed out on each iteration so that you can see what's happening:

```
>> [1,2,3,4].inject do |acc,n|
     puts "adding #{acc} and #{n}...#{acc+n}"
     acc + n
   end
adding 1 and 2...3
adding 3 and 3...6
adding 6 and 4...10
=> 10
```

The `puts` statement is a pure side effect (and, on its own, evaluates to nil), so you still have to end the block with acc + n to make sure the block evaluates to the correct value.

We've saved perhaps the most important relative of each for last: `Enumerable#map`.

10.6   *The map method*

The `map` method (also callable as `collect`) is one of the most powerful and important enumerable or collection operations available in Ruby. You've met it before (in chapter 6), but there's more to see, especially now that we're inside the overall topic of enumerability.

Whatever enumerable it starts with, map always returns an array. The returned array is always the same size as the original enumerable. Its elements consist of the accumulated result of calling the code block on each element in the original object in turn.

For example, here's how you map an array of names to their uppercase equivalents:

```
>> names = %w{ David Yukihiro Chad Amy }
=> ["David", "Yukihiro", "Chad", "Amy"]
>> names.map {|name| name.upcase }
=> ["DAVID", "YUKIHIRO", "CHAD", "AMY"]
```

The new array is the same size as the original array, and each of its elements corresponds to the element in the same position in the original array. But each element has been run through the block.

Using a symbol argument as a block

You can use a symbol such as :upcase with a & in front of it in method-argument position, and the result will be the same as if you used a code block that called the method with the same name as the symbol on each element. Thus you could rewrite the block in the last example, which calls upcase on each element, like this:

```
names.map(&:upcase)
```

You'll see an in-depth explanation of this idiom when you read about callable objects in chapter 14.

It may be obvious, but it's important to note that what matters about map is its return value.

10.6.1 *The return value of map*

The return value of map, and the usefulness of that return value, is what distinguishes map from each. The return value of each doesn't matter. You'll almost never see this:

```
result = array.each {|x| # code here... }
```

Why? Because each returns its receiver. You might as well do this:

```
result = array
array.each {|x| ... }
```

On the other hand, map returns a new object: a mapping of the original object to a new object. So you'll often see—and do—things like this:

```
result = array.map {|x| # code here... }
```

The difference between map and each is a good reminder that each exists purely for the side effects from the execution of the block. The value returned by the block each time through is discarded. That's why each returns its receiver; it doesn't have anything else to return, because it hasn't saved anything. map, on the other hand, maintains an accumulator array of the results from the block.

This doesn't mean that map is better or more useful than each. It means they're different in some important ways. But the semantics of map do mean that you have to be careful about the side effects that make each useful.

BE CAREFUL WITH BLOCK EVALUATION

Have a look at this code, and see if you can predict what the array `result` will contain when the code is executed:

```
array = [1,2,3,4,5]
result = array.map {|n| puts n * 100 }
```

The answer is that `result` will be this:

```
[nil, nil, nil, nil, nil]
```

Why? Because the return value of `puts` is always `nil`. That's all `map` cares about. Yes, the five values represented by n * 100 will be printed to the screen, but that's because the code in the block gets executed. The result of the operation—the mapping itself—is all `nil`s because every call to this particular block will return `nil`.

There's an in-place version of map for arrays and sets: `map!` (a.k.a. `collect!`).

10.6.2 *In-place mapping with map!*

Consider again the `names` array:

```
names = %w{ David Yukihiro Chad Amy }
```

To change the `names` array in place, run it through `map!`, the destructive version of `map`:

```
names.map!(&:upcase)   ⊲── See tip, above!
```

The `map!` method of `Array` is defined in `Array`, not in `Enumerable`. Because map operations generally return arrays, whatever the class of their receiver may be, doing an in-place mapping doesn't make sense unless the object is already an array. It would be difficult, for example, to imagine what an in-place mapping of a range would consist of. But the `Set#map!` method does an in-place mapping of a set back to itself—which makes sense, given that a set is in many respects similar to an array.

We're going to look next at a class that isn't enumerable: `String`. Strings are a bit like ranges in that they do and don't behave like collections. In the case of ranges, their collection-like properties are enough that the class warrants the mixing in of `Enumerable`. In the case of strings, `Enumerable` isn't in play; but the semantics of strings, when you treat them as iterable sequences of characters or bytes, is similar enough to enumerable semantics that we'll address it here.

10.7 *Strings as quasi-enumerables*

You can iterate through the raw bytes or the characters of a string using convenient iterator methods that treat the string as a collection of bytes, characters, code points, or lines. Each of these four ways of iterating through a string has an each–style method associated with it. To iterate through bytes, use `each_byte`:

```
str = "abcde"
str.each_byte {|b| p b }
```

The output of this code is

```
97
98
99
100
101
```

If you want each character, rather than its byte code, use each_char:

```
str = "abcde"
str.each_char {|c| p c }
```

This time, the output is

```
"a"
"b"
"c"
"d"
"e"
```

Iterating by code point provides character codes (integers) at the rate of exactly one per character:

```
>> str = "100\u20ac"
=> "100€"
>> str.each_codepoint {|cp| p cp }
49
48
48
8364
```

Compare this last example with what happens if you iterate over the same string byte by byte:

```
>> str.each_byte {|b| p b }
49
48
48
226
130
172
```

Due to the encoding, the number of bytes is greater than the number of code points (or the number of characters, which is equal to the number of code points).

Finally, if you want to go line by line, use each_line:

```
str = "This string\nhas three\nlines"
str.each_line {|l| puts "Next line: #{l}" }
```

The output of this example is

```
Next line: This string
Next line: has three
Next line: lines
```

The string is split at the end of each line—or, more strictly speaking, at every occurrence of the current value of the global variable $/. If you change this variable, you're changing the delimiter for what Ruby considers the next line in a string:

```
str = "David!Alan!Black"
$/ = "!"
str.each_line {|l| puts "Next line: #{l}" }
```

Now Ruby's concept of a "line" will be based on the ! character:

```
Next line: David!
Next line: Alan!
Next line: Black
```

Even though Ruby strings aren't enumerable in the technical sense (`String` doesn't include `Enumerable`), the language thus provides you with the necessary tools to traverse them as character, byte, code point, and/or line collections when you need to.

The four each-style methods described here operate by creating an enumerator. You'll learn more about enumerators in section 10.9. The important lesson for the moment is that you've got another set of options if you simply want an array of all bytes, characters, code points, or lines: drop the `each_` and pluralize the method name. For example, here's how you'd get an array of all the bytes in a string:

```
string = "Hello"
p string.bytes
```

The output is

```
[72, 101, 108, 108, 111]
```

You can do likewise with the methods `chars`, `codepoints`, and `lines`.

We've searched, transformed, filtered, and queried a variety of collection objects using an even bigger variety of methods. The one thing we haven't done is *sort* collections. We'll do that next.

10.8 *Sorting enumerables*

If you have a class, and you want to be able to arrange multiple instances of it in order, you need to do the following:

1. Define a comparison method for the class (`<=>`).
2. Place the multiple instances in a container, probably an array.
3. Sort the container.

The key point is that although the ability to sort is granted by `Enumerable`, your class doesn't have to mix in `Enumerable`. Rather, you put your objects into a container object that does mix in `Enumerable`. That container object, as an enumerable, has two sorting methods, `sort` and `sort_by`, which you can use to sort the collection.

In the vast majority of cases, the container into which you place objects you want sorted will be an array. Sometimes it will be a hash, in which case the result will be an array (an array of two-element key/value pair arrays, sorted by a key or some other criterion).

Normally, you don't have to create an array of items explicitly before you sort them. More often, you sort a collection that your program has already generated automatically. For instance, you may perform a `select` operation on a collection of objects and sort the ones you've selected. The manual stuffing of lists of objects into square brackets to create array examples in this section is therefore a bit contrived. But the goal is to focus directly on techniques for sorting, and that's what we'll do.

Here's a simple sorting example involving an array of integers:

```
>> [3,2,5,4,1].sort
=> [1, 2, 3, 4, 5]
```

Doing this is easy when you have numbers or even strings (where a sort gives you alphabetical order). The array you put them in has a sorting mechanism, and the integers or strings have some knowledge of what it means to be in order.

But what if you want to sort, say, an array of `Painting` objects?

```
>> [pa1, pa2, pa3, pa4, pa5].sort
```

For paintings to have enough knowledge to participate in a sort operation, you have to define the spaceship operator (see section 7.6.2): `Painting#<=>`. Each painting will then know what it means to be greater or less than another painting, and that will enable the array to sort its contents. Remember, it's the array you're sorting, not each painting; but to sort the array, its elements have to have a sense of how they compare to each other. (You don't have to mix in the `Comparable` module; you just need the spaceship method. We'll come back to `Comparable` shortly.)

Let's say you want paintings to sort in increasing order of price, and let's assume paintings have a `price` attribute. Somewhere in your `Painting` class you would do this:

```
def <=>(other_painting)
  self.price <=> other_painting.price
end
```

Now any array of paintings you sort will come out in price-sorted order:

```
price_sorted = [pa1, pa2, pa3, pa4, pa5].sort
```

Ruby applies the `<=>` test to these elements, two at a time, building up enough information to perform the complete sort.

A more fleshed-out account of the steps involved might go like this:

1 Teach your objects how to compare themselves with each other, using `<=>`.

2 Put those objects inside an enumerable object (probably an array).

3 Ask that object to sort itself. It does this by asking the objects to compare themselves to each other with `<=>`.

If you keep this division of labor in mind, you'll understand how sorting operates and how it relates to `Enumerable`. But what about `Comparable`?

10.8.1 *Where the Comparable module fits into enumerable sorting (or doesn't)*

When we first encountered the spaceship operator, it was in the context of including `Comparable` and letting that module build its various methods (`>`, `<`, and so on) on top of `<=>`. But in prepping objects to be sortable inside enumerable containers, all we've done is define `<=>`; we haven't mixed in `Comparable`.

The whole picture fits together if you think of it as several separate, layered techniques:

- If you define `<=>` for a class, then instances of that class can be put inside an array or other enumerable for sorting.
- If you don't define `<=>`, you can still sort objects if you put them inside an array and provide a code block telling the array how it should rank any two of the objects. (This is discussed next in section 10.8.2.)
- If you define `<=>` and also include `Comparable` in your class, then you get sort-ability inside an array *and* you can perform all the comparison operations between any two of your objects (`>`, `<`, and so on), as per the discussion of `Comparable` in chapter 9.

In other words, the `<=>` method is useful both for classes whose instances you wish to sort and for classes whose instances you wish to compare with each other in a more fine-grained way using the full complement of comparison operators.

Back we go to enumerable sorting—and, in particular, to the variant of sorting where you provide a code block instead of a `<=>` method to specify how objects should be compared and ordered.

10.8.2 *Defining sort-order logic with a block*

In cases where no `<=>` method is defined for these objects, you can supply a block on-the-fly to indicate how you want your objects sorted. If there's a `<=>` method, you can override it for the current sort operation by providing a block.

Let's say, for example, that you've defined `Painting#<=>` in such a way that it sorts by price, as earlier. But now you want to sort by year. You can force a year-based sort by using a block:

```
year_sort = [pa1, pa2, pa3, pa4, pa5].sort do |a,b|
  a.year <=> b.year
end
```

The block takes two arguments, a and b. This enables Ruby to use the block as many times as needed to compare one painting with another. The code inside the block does a `<=>` comparison between the respective years of the two paintings. For this call to `sort`, the code in the block is used instead of the code in the `<=>` method of the `Painting` class.

You can use this code-block form of `sort` to handle cases where your objects don't have a `<=>` method and therefore don't know how to compare themselves to each other. It can also come in handy when the objects being sorted are of different classes and by default don't know how to compare themselves to each other. Integers and strings, for example, can't be compared directly: an expression like `"2" <=> 4` causes a fatal error. But if you do a conversion first, you can pull it off:

```
>> ["2",1,5,"3",4,"6"].sort {|a,b| a.to_i <=> b.to_i }
=> [1, "2", "3", 4, 5, "6"]
```

The elements in the sorted output array are the same as those in the input array: a mixture of strings and integers. But they're ordered as they would be if they were all integers. Inside the code block, both strings and integers are normalized to integer form with `to_i`. As far as the sort engine is concerned, it's performing a sort based on a series of integer comparisons. It then applies the order it comes up with to the original array.

`sort` with a block can thus help you where the existing comparison methods won't get the job done. And there's an even more concise way to sort a collection with a code block: the `sort_by` method.

10.8.3 *Concise sorting with sort_by*

Like `sort`, `sort_by` is an instance method of `Enumerable`. The main difference is that `sort_by` always takes a block, and it only requires that you show it how to treat one item in the collection. `sort_by` figures out that you want to do the same thing to both items every time it compares a pair of objects.

The previous array-sorting example can be written like this, using `sort_by`:

```
>> ["2",1,5,"3",4,"6"].sort_by {|a| a.to_i }          ⟵  Or sort_by(&:to_i)
=> [1, "2", "3", 4, 5, "6"]
```

All we have to do in the block is show (once) what action needs to be performed to prep each object for the sort operation. We don't have to call `to_i` on two objects; nor do we need to use the `<=>` method explicitly.

In addition to the `Enumerable` module, and still in the realm of enumerability, Ruby provides a class called `Enumerator`. Enumerators add a whole dimension of collection manipulation power to Ruby. We'll look at them in depth now.

10.9 *Enumerators and the next dimension of enumerability*

Enumerators are closely related to iterators, but they aren't the same thing. An iterator is a method that yields one or more values to a code block. An enumerator is an *object*, not a method.

At heart, an enumerator is a simple enumerable object. It has an `each` method, and it employs the `Enumerable` module to define all the usual methods—`select`, `inject`, `map`, and friends—directly on top of its `each`.

The twist in the plot, though, is how the enumerator's `each` method is engineered.

An enumerator isn't a container object. It has no "natural" basis for an `each` operation, the way an array does (start at element 0; yield it; go to element 1; yield it; and so on). The `each` iteration logic of every enumerator has to be explicitly specified. After you've told it how to do each, the enumerator takes over from there and figures out how to do map, find, take, drop, and all the rest.

An enumerator is like a brain in a science-fiction movie, sitting on a table with no connection to a body but still able to think. It just needs an "each" algorithm, so that it can set into motion the things it already knows how to do. And this it can learn in one of two ways: either you call Enumerator.new with a code block, so that the code block contains the each logic you want the enumerator to follow; or you create an enumerator based on an existing enumerable object (an array, a hash, and so forth) in such a way that the enumerator's each method draws its elements, for iteration, from a specific method of that enumerable object.

We'll start by looking at the code block approach to creating enumerators. But most of the rest of the discussion of enumerators will focus on the second approach, where you "hook up" an enumerator to an iterator on another object. (If you find the block-based technique difficult to follow, no harm will come if you skim section 10.9.1 for now and focus on section 10.9.2.) Which techniques you use and how you combine them will ultimately depend on your exact needs in a given situation.

10.9.1 Creating enumerators with a code block

Here's a simple example of the instantiation of an enumerator with a code block:

```
e = Enumerator.new do |y|
  y << 1
  y << 2
  y << 3
end
```

Now, first things first: what is y?

y is a *yielder*, an instance of Enumerator::Yielder, automatically passed to your block. Yielders encapsulate the yielding scenario that you want your enumerator to follow. In this example, what we're saying is *when you (the enumerator) get an* each *call, please take that to mean that you should yield 1, then 2, then 3*. The << method (in infix operator position, as usual) serves to instruct the yielder as to what it should yield. (You can also write y.yield(1) and so forth, although the similarity of the yield method to the yield keyword might be more confusing than it's worth.) Upon being asked to iterate, the enumerator consults the yielder and makes the next move—the next yield—based on the instructions that the yielder has stored.

What happens when you use e, the enumerator? Here's an irb session where it's put through its paces (given that the code in the example has already been executed):

```
>> e.to_a                       ⟵  Array representation of yielded elements
=> [1, 2, 3]
>> e.map {|x| x * 10 }          ⟵  Mapping, based on each
=> [10, 20, 30]
>> e.select {|x| x > 1 }        ⟵  Selection, based on each
=> [2, 3]
>> e.take(2)                    ⟵  Takes first two elements yielded
  => [1, 2]
```

The enumerator e is an enumerating machine. It doesn't contain objects; it has code associated with it—the original code block—that tells it what to do when it's addressed in terms that it recognizes as coming from the `Enumerable` module.

The enumerator iterates once for every time that << (or the `yield` method) is called on the yielder. If you put calls to << inside a loop or other iterator inside the code block, you can introduce just about any iteration logic you want. Here's a rewrite of the previous example, using an iterator inside the block:

```
e = Enumerator.new do |y|
  (1..3).each {|i| y << i }
end
```

The behavior of e will be the same, given this definition, as it is in the previous examples. We've arranged for << to be called three times; that means e.each will do three iterations. Again, the behavior of the enumerator can be traced ultimately to the calls to << inside the code block with which it was initialized.

Note in particular that you don't yield from the block; that is, you *don't* do this:

```
e = Enumerator.new do          ⟵  Wrong!
  yield 1
  yield 2                      This is what
  yield 3                      you don't do!
end
```

Rather, you populate your yielder (y, in the first examples) with specifications for how you want the iteration to proceed at such time as you call an iterative method on the enumerator.

Every time you call an iterator method on the enumerator, the code block gets executed once. Any variables you initialize in the block are initialized once at the start of each such method call. You can trace the execution sequence by adding some verbosity and calling multiple methods:

```
e = Enumerator.new do |y|
  puts "Starting up the block!"
  (1..3).each {|i| y << i }
  puts "Exiting the block!"
end
p e.to_a
p e.select {|x| x > 2 }
```

The output from this code is

```
Starting up the block!     ⟵  Call to to_a
Exiting the block!
[1, 2, 3]
Starting up the block!     ⟵  Call to select
Exiting the block!
[3]
```

You can see that the block is executed once for each iterator called on e.

It's also possible to involve other objects in the code block for an enumerator. Here's a somewhat abstract example in which the enumerator performs a calculation involving the elements of an array while removing those elements from the array permanently:

```
a = [1,2,3,4,5]
e = Enumerator.new do |y|
  total = 0
  until a.empty?
    total += a.pop
    y << total
  end
end
```

Now let's look at the fate of poor a, in irb:

```
>> e.take(2)
=> [5, 9]
>> a
=> [1, 2, 3]
>> e.to_a
=> [3, 5, 6]
>> a
=> []
```

The take operation produces a result array of two elements (the value of total for two successive iterations) and leaves a with three elements. Calling to_a on e, at this point, causes the original code block to be executed again, because the to_a call isn't part of the same iteration as the call to take. Therefore, total starts again at 0, and the until loop is executed with the result that three values are yielded and a is left empty.

It's not fair to ambush a separate object by removing its elements as a side effect of calling an enumerator. But the example shows you the mechanism—and it also provides a reasonable segue into the other half of the topic of creating enumerators: creating enumerators whose each methods are tied to specific methods on existing enumerable objects.

10.9.2 *Attaching enumerators to other objects*

The other way to endow an enumerator with each logic is to hook the enumerator up to another object—specifically, to an iterator (often each, but potentially any method that yields one or more values) on another object. This gives the enumerator a basis for its own iteration: when it needs to yield something, it gets the necessary value by triggering the next yield from the object to which it is attached, via the designated method. The enumerator thus acts as part proxy, part parasite, defining its own each in terms of another object's iteration.

You create an enumerator with this approach by calling enum_for (a.k.a. to_enum) on the object from which you want the enumerator to draw its iterations. You provide as the first argument the name of the method onto which the enumerator will attach its each method. This argument defaults to :each, although it's common to attach the enumerator to a different method, as in this example:

```
names = %w{ David Black Yukihiro Matsumoto }
e = names.enum_for(:select)
```

Specifying :select as the argument means that we want to bind this enumerator to the select method of the names array. That means the enumerator's each will serve as a kind of front end to array's select:

```
e.each {|n| n.include?('a') }
```
◁—| **Output: ["David", "Black", "Matsumoto"]**

You can also provide further arguments to enum_for. Any such arguments are passed through to the method to which the enumerator is being attached. For example, here's how to create an enumerator for inject so that when inject is called on to feed values to the enumerator's each, it's called with a starting value of "Names: ":

```
>> e = names.enum_for(:inject, "Names: ")
=> #<Enumerator: ["David", "Black", "Yukihiro", "Matsumoto"]:inject("Names: ")>
>> e.each {|string, name| string << "#{name}..." }
=> "Names: David...Black...Yukihiro...Matsumoto..."
```

But be careful! That starting string "Names: " has had some names added to it, but it's still alive inside the enumerator. That means if you run the same inject operation again, it adds to the same string (the line in the output in the following code is broken across two lines to make it fit):

```
>> e.each {|string, name| string << "#{name}..." }
=> "Names: David...Black...Yukihiro...Matsumoto...
David...Black...Yukihiro...Matsumoto..."
```

When you create the enumerator, the arguments you give it for the purpose of supplying its proxied method with arguments are the arguments—the objects—it will use permanently. So watch for side effects. (In this particular case, you can avoid the side effect by adding strings—string + "#{name}..."—instead of appending to the string with <<, because the addition operation creates a new string object. Still, the cautionary tale is generally useful.)

> **NOTE** You can call Enumerator.new(obj, method_name, arg1, arg2...) as an equivalent to obj.enum_for(method_name, arg1, arg2...). But using this form of Enumerator.new is discouraged. Use enum_for for the method-attachment scenario and Enumerator.new for the block-based scenario described in section 10.9.1.

Now you know how to create enumerators of both kinds: the kind whose knowledge of how to iterate is conveyed to it in a code block, and the kind that gets that knowledge from another object. Enumerators are also created implicitly when you make block-less calls to certain iterator methods.

10.9.3 *Implicit creation of enumerators by blockless iterator calls*

By definition, an iterator is a method that yields one or more values to a block. But what if there's no block?

The answer is that most built-in iterators return an enumerator when they're called without a block. Here's an example from the `String` class: the `each_byte` method (see section 10.7). First, here's a classic iterator usage of the method, without an enumerator but with a block:

```
>> str = "Hello"
=> "Hello"
>> str.each_byte {|b| puts b }
72
101
108
108
111
=> "Hello"
```

`each_byte` iterates over the bytes in the string and returns its receiver (the string). But if you call `each_byte` with no block, you get an enumerator:

```
>> str.each_byte
=> #<Enumerator: "Hello":each_byte>
```

The enumerator you get is equivalent to what you would get if you did this:

```
>> str.enum_for(:each_byte)
```

You'll find that lots of methods from `Enumerable` return enumerators when you call them without a block (including `each`, `map`, `select`, `inject`, and others). The main use case for these automatically returned enumerators is *chaining*: calling another method immediately on the enumerator. We'll look at chaining as part of the coverage of enumerator semantics in the next section.

10.10 *Enumerator semantics and uses*

Now that you know how enumerators are wired and how to create them, we're going to look at how they're used—and why they're used.

Perhaps the hardest thing about enumerators, because it's the most difficult to interpret visually, is how things play out when you call the each method. We'll start by looking at that; then, we'll examine the practicalities of enumerators, particularly the ways in which an enumerator can protect an object from change and how you can use an enumerator to do fine-grained, controlled iterations. We'll then look at how enumerators fit into method chains in general and we'll see a couple of important specific cases.

10.10.1 *How to use an enumerator's each method*

An enumerator's each method is hooked up to a method on another object, possibly a method other than each. If you use it directly, it behaves like that other method, including with respect to its return value.

This can produce some odd-looking results where calls to each return filtered, sorted, or mapped collections:

```
>> array = %w{ cat dog rabbit }
=> ["cat", "dog", "rabbit"]
>> e = array.map
=> #<Enumerator: ["cat", "dog", "rabbit"]:map>    ┐ Returns
>> e.each {|animal| animal.capitalize }         ◁─┘ mapping
=> ["Cat", "Dog", "Rabbit"]
```

There's nothing mysterious here. The enumerator isn't the same object as the array; it has its own ideas about what each means. Still, the overall effect of connecting an enumerator to the map method of an array is that you get an each operation with an array mapping as its return value. The usual each iteration of an array, as you've seen, exists principally for its side effects and returns its receiver (the array). But an enumerator's each serves as a kind of conduit to the method from which it pulls its values and behaves the same way in the matter of return value.

Another characteristic of enumerators that you should be aware of is the fact that they perform a kind of *un-overriding* of methods in Enumerable.

THE UN-OVERRIDING PHENOMENON

If a class defines each and includes Enumerable, its instances automatically get map, select, inject, and all the rest of Enumerable's methods. All those methods are defined in terms of each.

But sometimes a given class has already overridden Enumerable's version of a method with its own. A good example is Hash#select. The standard, out-of-the-box select method from Enumerable always returns an array, whatever the class of the object using it might be. A select operation on a hash, on the other hand, returns a hash:

```
>> h = { "cat" => "feline", "dog" => "canine", "cow" => "bovine" }
=> {"cat"=>"feline", "dog"=>"canine", "cow"=>"bovine"}
>> h.select {|key,value| key =~ /c/ }
=> {"cat"=>"feline", "cow"=>"bovine"}
```

So far, so good (and nothing new). And if we hook up an enumerator to the select method, it gives us an each method that works like that method:

```
>> e = h.enum_for(:select)
=> #<Enumerator: {"cat"=>"feline", "dog"=>"canine", "cow"=>"bovine"}:select>
>> e.each {|key,value| key =~ /c/ }
=> {"cat"=>"feline", "cow"=>"bovine"}
```

But what about an enumerator hooked up not to the hash's select method but to the hash's each method? We can get one by using to_enum and letting the target method default to each:

```
>> e = h.to_enum
=> #<Enumerator: {"cat"=>"feline", "dog"=>"canine", "cow"=>"bovine"}:each>
```

Hash#each, called with a block, returns the hash. The same is true of the enumerator's each—because it's just a front end to the hash's each. The blocks in these examples are empty because we're only concerned with the return values:

```
>> h.each { }
=> {"cat"=>"feline", "dog"=>"canine", "cow"=>"bovine"}
>> e.each { }
=> {"cat"=>"feline", "dog"=>"canine", "cow"=>"bovine"}
```

So far, it looks like the enumerator's each is a stand-in for the hash's each. But what happens if we use this each to perform a select operation?

```
>> e.select {|key,value| key =~ /c/ }
=> [["cat", "feline"], ["cow", "bovine"]]
```

The answer, as you can see, is that we get back an array, not a hash.

Why? If e.each is pegged to h.each, how does the return value of e.select get unpegged from the return value of h.select?

The key is that the call to select in the last example is a call to the select method of the *enumerator*, not the hash. And the select method of the enumerator is built directly on the enumerator's each method. In fact, the enumerator's select method is Enumerable#select, which always returns an array. The fact that Hash#select doesn't return an array is of no interest to the enumerator.

In this sense, the enumerator is adding enumerability to the hash, even though the hash is already enumerable. It's also un-overriding Enumerable#select; the select provided by the enumerator is Enumerable#select, even if the hash's select wasn't. (Technically it's not an un-override, but it does produce the sensation that the enumerator is occluding the select logic of the original hash.)

The lesson is that it's important to remember that an enumerator is a different object from the collection from which it siphons its iterated objects. Although this difference between objects can give rise to some possibly odd results, like select being rerouted through the Enumerable module, it's definitely beneficial in at least one important way: accessing a collection through an enumerator, rather than through the collection itself, protects the collection object from change.

10.10.2 *Protecting objects with enumerators*

Consider a method that expects, say, an array as its argument. (Yes, it's a bit un-Ruby-like to focus on the object's class, but you'll see that that isn't the main point here.)

```
def give_me_an_array(array)
```

If you pass an array object to this method, the method can alter that object:

```
array << "new element"
```

If you want to protect the original array from change, you can duplicate it and pass along the duplicate—or you can pass along an enumerator instead:

```
give_me_an_array(array.to_enum)
```

The enumerator will happily allow for iterations through the array, but it won't absorb changes. (It will respond with a fatal error if you try calling << on it.) In other words, an enumerator can serve as a kind of gateway to a collection object such that it allows iteration and examination of elements but disallows destructive operations.

The deck of cards code from section 10.5.4 provides a nice opportunity for some object protection. In that code, the Deck class has a reader attribute cards. When a deck is created, its @cards instance variable is initialized to an array containing all the cards. There's a vulnerability here: What if someone gets hold of the @cards array through the cards reader attribute and alters it?

```
deck = PlayingCard::Deck.new
deck.cards << "JOKER!!"
```

Ideally, we'd like to be able to read from the cards array but not alter it. (We could freeze it with the freeze method, which prevents further changes to objects, but we'll need to change the deck inside the Deck class when it's dealt from.) Enumerators provide a solution. Instead of a reader attribute, let's make the cards method return an enumerator:

```
class PlayingCard
  SUITS = %w{ clubs diamonds hearts spades }
  RANKS = %w{ 2 3 4 5 6 7 8 9 10 J Q K A }
  class Deck
    def cards
      @cards.to_enum
    end
    def initialize(n=1)
      @cards = []
      SUITS.cycle(n) do |s|
        RANKS.cycle(1) do |r|
          @cards << "#{r} of #{s}"
        end
      end
    end
  end
end
```

It's still possible to pry into the @cards array and mess it up if you're determined. But the enumerator provides a significant amount of protection:

```
deck = PlayingCard::Deck.new
deck.cards << "Joker!!"                ◄─── NoMethodError: undefined method '<<'
                                            for #<Enumerator:0x000001020643b8>
```

Of course, if you want the calling code to be able to address the cards as an array, returning an enumerator may be counterproductive. (And at least one other technique protects objects under circumstances like this: return @cards.dup.) But if it's a good fit, the protective qualities of an enumerator can be convenient.

Because enumerators are objects, they have state. Furthermore, they use their state to track their own progress so you can stop and start their iterations. We'll look now at the techniques for controlling enumerators in this way.

10.10.3 Fine-grained iteration with enumerators

Enumerators maintain state: they keep track of where they are in their enumeration. Several methods make direct use of this information. Consider this example:

```
names = %w{ David Yukihiro }
e = names.to_enum
puts e.next
puts e.next
e.rewind
puts e.next
```

The output from these commands is

```
David
Yukihiro
David
```

The enumerator allows you to move in slow motion, so to speak, through the enumeration of the array, stopping and restarting at will. In this respect, it's like one of those editing tables where a film editor cranks the film manually. Unlike a projector, which you switch on and let it do its thing, the editing table allows you to influence the progress of the film as it proceeds.

This point also sheds light on the difference between an enumerator and an iterator. An enumerator is an object, and can therefore maintain state. It remembers where it is in the enumeration. An iterator is a method. When you call it, the call is atomic; the entire call happens, and then it's over. Thanks to code blocks, there is of course a certain useful complexity to Ruby method calls: the method can call back to the block, and decisions can be made that affect the outcome. But it's still a method. An iterator doesn't have state. An enumerator is an enumerable object.

Interestingly, you can use an enumerator on a non-enumerable object. All you need is for your object to have a method that yields something so the enumerator can adopt that method as the basis for its own each method. As a result, the non-enumerable object becomes, in effect, enumerable.

10.10.4 Adding enumerability with an enumerator

An enumerator can add enumerability to objects that don't have it. It's a matter of wiring: if you hook up an enumerator's each method to any iterator, then you can use the enumerator to perform enumerable operations on the object that owns the iterator, whether that object considers itself enumerable or not.

When you hook up an enumerator to the String#bytes method, you're effectively adding enumerability to an object (a string) that doesn't have it, in the sense that String doesn't mix in Enumerable. You can achieve much the same effect with classes of your own. Consider the following class, which doesn't mix in Enumerable but does have one iterator method:

```
module Music
  class Scale
    NOTES = %w{ c c# d d# e f f# g a a# b }
```

```
    def play
      NOTES.each {|note| yield note }
    end
  end
end
```

Given this class, it's possible to iterate through the notes of a scale

```
scale = Music::Scale.new
scale.play {|note| puts "Next note is #{note}" }
```

with the result

```
Next note is c
Next note is c#
Next note is d
```

and so forth. But the scale isn't technically an enumerable. The standard methods from Enumerable won't work because the class Music::Scale doesn't mix in Enumerable and doesn't define each:

```
scale.map {|note| note.upcase }
```

The result is

```
NoMethodError: unknown method `map' for #<Music::Scale:0x3b0aec>
```

Now, in practice, if you wanted scales to be fully enumerable, you'd almost certainly mix in Enumerable and change the name of play to each. But you can also make a scale enumerable by hooking it up to an enumerator.

Here's how to create an enumerator for the scale object, tied in to the play method:

```
enum = scale.enum_for(:play)          ⊲—— Or scale.to_enum(:play)
```

The enumerator, enum, has an each method; that method performs the same iteration that the scale's play method performs. Furthermore, unlike the scale, the enumerator *is* an enumerable object; it has map, select, inject, and all the other standard methods from Enumerable. If you use the enumerator, you get enumerable operations on a fundamentally non-enumerable object:

```
p enum.map {|note| note.upcase }
p enum.select {|note| note.include?('f') }
```

The first line's output is

```
["C", "C#", "D", "D#", "E", "F", "F#", "G", "A", "A#", "B"]
```

and the second line's output is

```
["f", "f#"]
```

An enumerator, then, attaches itself to a particular method on a particular object and uses that method as the foundation method—the each—for the entire enumerable toolset.

Attaching an enumerator to a non-enumerable object like the scale object is a good exercise because it illustrates the difference between the original object and the enumerator so sharply. But in the vast majority of cases, the objects for which enumerators are created are themselves enumerables: arrays, hashes, and so forth. Most of the examples in what follows will involve enumerable objects (the exception being strings). In addition to taking us into the realm of the most common practices, this will allow us to look more broadly at the possible advantages of using enumerators.

Throughout, keep in mind the lesson of the `Music::Scale` object and its enumerator: an enumerator is an enumerable object whose `each` method operates as a kind of siphon, pulling values from an iterator defined on a different object.

We'll conclude our examination of enumerators with a look at techniques that involve chaining enumerators and method calls.

10.11 Enumerator method chaining

Method chaining is a common technique in Ruby programming. It's common in part because it's so easy. Want to print out a comma-separated list of uppercased names beginning with A through N? Just string a few methods together:

```
puts names.select {|n| n[0] < 'M' }.map(&:upcase).join(", ")
```

> Output (given previous list of names): **DAVID, BLACK**

The left-to-right, conveyor-belt style of processing data is powerful and, for the most part, straightforward. But it comes at a price: the creation of intermediate objects. Method chaining usually creates a new object for every link in the chain. In the previous code, assuming that `names` is an array of strings, Ruby ends up creating two more arrays (one as the output of `select`, one from `map`) and a string (from `join`).

Enumerators don't solve all the problems of method chaining. But they do mitigate the problem of creating intermediate objects in some cases. And enumerator-based chaining has some semantics unto itself that it's good to get a handle on.

10.11.1 Economizing on intermediate objects

Remember that many methods from the `Enumerable` module return an enumerator if you call them without a block. In most such cases, there's no reason to chain the enumerator directly to another method. `names.each.inject`, for example, might as well be `names.inject`. Similarly, `names.map.select` doesn't buy you anything over `names.select`. The `map` enumerator doesn't have any knowledge of what function to map to; therefore, it can't do much other than pass the original array of values down the chain.

But consider `names.each_slice(2)`. The enumerator generated by this expression does carry some useful information; it knows that it's expected to produce two-element-long slices of the `names` array. If you place it inside a method chain, it has an effect:

```
>> names = %w{ David Black Yukihiro Matsumoto }
=> ["David", "Black", "Yukihiro", "Matsumoto"]
>> names.each_slice(2).map do |first, last|
     "First name: #{first}, last name: #{last}\n"
   end
=> ["First name: David, last name: Black\n",
    "First name: Yukihiro, last name: Matsumoto\n"]
```

The code block attached to the map operation gets handed items from the names array two at a time, because of the each_slice(2) enumerator. The enumerator can proceed in "lazy" fashion: rather than create an entire array of two-element slices in memory, it can create the slices as they're needed by the map operation.

Enumerator literacy

One consequence of the way enumerators work, and of their being returned automatically from blockless iterator calls, is that it takes a little practice to read enumerator code correctly. Consider this snippet, which returns an array of integers:

```
string = "An arbitrary string"
string.each_byte.map {|b| b + 1 }
```

Probably not useful business logic...but the point is that it looks much like string.each_byte is returning an array. The presence of map as the next operation, although not conclusive evidence of an array, certainly evokes the presence of a collection on the left.

Let's put it another way. Judging by its appearance, you might expect that if you peel off the whole map call, you'll be left with a collection.

In fact, string.each_byte returns an enumerator. The key is that an enumerator *is* a collection. It's an enumerable object as much as an array or a hash is. It just may take a little getting used to.

Enumerable methods that take arguments and return enumerators, like each_slice, are candidates for this kind of compression or optimizationEven if an enumerable method doesn't return an enumerator, you can create one for it, incorporating the argument so that it's remembered by the enumerator. You've seen an example of this technique already, approached from a slightly different angle, in section 10.9.2:

```
e = names.enum_for(:inject, "Names: ")
```

The enumerator remembers not only that it's attached to the inject method of names but also that it represents a call to inject with an argument of "Names".

In addition to the general practice of including enumerators in method chains, the specialized method with_index—one of the few that the Enumerator class implements separately from those in Enumerable—adds considerable value to enumerations.

10.11.2 Indexing enumerables with with_index

In the days when Rubyists used the `each_with_index` method, a number of us lobbied for a corresponding `map_with_index` method. We never got it—but we ended up with something even better. Enumerators have a `with_index` method that adds numerical indexing, as a second block parameter, to any enumeration. Here's how you would use `with_index` to do the letter/number mapping:

```
('a'..'z').map.with_index {|letter,i| [letter, i] }
```
⟵ **Output: [["a", 0], ["b", 1], etc.]**

Note that it's `map.with_index` (two methods, chained), not `map_with_index` (a composite method name). And `with_index` can be chained to any enumerator. Remember the musical scale from section 10.10.4? Let's say we enumerator-ize the `play` method:

```
def play
  NOTES.to_enum
end
```

The original example of walking through the notes will now work without the creation of an intermediate enumerator.

```
scale.play {|note| puts "Next note: #{note}" }
```

And now this will work too:

```
scale.play.with_index(1) {|note,i| puts "Note #{i}: #{note}" }
```
⟵ **Provide 1 as the first value for the index**

The output will be a numbered list of notes:

```
Note 1: c
Note 2: c#
Note 3: d
# etc.
```

Thus the `with_index` method generalizes what would otherwise be a restricted functionality.

We'll look at one more enumerator chaining example, which nicely pulls together several enumerator and iteration techniques and also introduces a couple of new methods you may find handy.

10.11.3 Exclusive-or operations on strings with enumerators

Running an exclusive-or (or *XOR*) operation on a string means XOR-ing each of its bytes with some value. XOR-ing a byte is a bitwise operation: each byte is represented by an integer, and the result of the XOR operation is an exclusive-or-ing of that integer with another number.

If your string is `"a"`, for example, it contains one byte with the value 97. The binary representation of 97 is 1100001. Let's say we want to XOR it with the character #, which has an ASCII value of 35, or 100011 in binary. Looking at it purely numerically, and not in terms of strings, we're doing 97 ^ 35, or 1100001 ^ 100011 in binary terms.

An XOR produces a result that, in binary representation (that is, in terms of its bits) contains a 1 where either of the source numbers, *but not both*, contained a 1, and a 0 where both of the source numbers contains the same value, whether 0 or 1. In the case of our two numbers, the XOR operation produces 1000010 or 66.

A distinguishing property of bitwise XOR operations is that if you perform the same operation twice, you get back the original value. In other words, (a ^ b) ^ b == a. Thus if we xor 66 with 35, we get 97. This behavior makes xor-ing strings a useful obfuscation technique, especially if you xor a long string byte for byte against a second string. Say your string is "This is a string." If you xor it character for character against, say, #%.3u, repeating the xor string as necessary to reach the length of the original string, you get the rather daunting result wMG@UJV\x0ERUPQ\\Z\eD\v. If you xor that monstrosity against #%.3u again, you get back "This is a string."

Now let's write a method that will do this. We'll add it to the String class—not necessarily the best way to go about changing the functionality of core Ruby objects (as you'll see in chapter 13), but expedient for purposes of illustration. The following listing shows the instance method String#^.

Listing 10.2 An exclusive-or method for strings

```
class String
  def ^(key)                                              ←① 1
    kenum = key.each_byte.cycle                           ←② 2
      each_byte.map {|byte| byte ^ kenum.next }.pack("C*")  ←
  end                                                       ③ 3
end
```

The method takes one argument: the string that will be used as the basis of the xor operation (the *key*) ①. We have to deal with cases where the key is shorter than the original string by looping through the key as many times as necessary to provide enough characters for the whole operation. That's where enumerators come in.

The variable kenum is bound to an enumerator based on chaining two methods off the key string: each_byte, which itself returns an enumerator traversing the string byte by byte, and cycle, which iterates over and over again through a collection, resuming at the beginning when it reaches the end ②. The enumerator kenum embodies both of these operations: each iteration through it provides another byte from the string; and when it's finished providing all the bytes, it goes back to the beginning of the string and iterates over the bytes again. That's exactly the behavior we want, to make sure we've got enough bytes to match whatever string we're xor-ing, even if it's a string that's longer than the key. In effect, we've made the key string infinitely long.

Now comes the actual xor operation ③. Here, we use each_byte to iterate over the bytes of the string that's being xor'ed. The enumerator returned by each_byte gets chained to map. Inside the map block, each byte of the original string is xor'ed with the "next" byte from the enumerator that's cycling infinitely through the bytes of the key string. The whole map operation, then, produces an array of xor'ed bytes. All that remains is to put those bytes back into a result string.

Enter the pack method. This method turns an array into a string, interpreting each element of the array in a manner specified by the argument. In this case, the argument is `"C*"`, which means *treat each element of the array as an unsigned integer representing a single character* (that's the "C"), *and process all of them* (that's the "*"). Packing the array into a string of characters is thus the equivalent of transforming each array element into a character and then doing a join on the whole array.

Now we can xor strings. Here's what the process looks like:

```
>> str = "Nice little string."
=> "Nice little string."
>> key = "secret!"
=> "secret!"
>> x = str ^ key
   => "=\f\x00\x17E\x18H\a\x11\x0F\x17E\aU\x01\f\r\x15K"
>> orig = x ^ key
=> "Nice little string."
```

As you can see, XOR-ing twice with the same key gets you back to the original string. And it's all thanks to a two-line method that uses three enumerators!

Forcing an encoding

The `String#^` as implemented in the previous snippet is vulnerable to encoding issues: if you xor, say, a UTF-8 string against an ASCII string twice, you'll get back a string encoded in ASCII-8BIT. To guard against this, add a call to `force_encoding`:

```
each_byte.map {|byte| byte ^ kenum.next }.pack("C*").
                      force_encoding(self.encoding)
```

This will ensure that the byte sequence generated by the mapping gets encoded in the original string's encoding.

Enumerators add a completely new tool to the already rich Ruby toolkit for collection management and iteration. They're conceptually and technically different from iterators, but if you try them out on their own terms, you're sure to find uses for them alongside the other collection-related techniques you've seen.

We'll conclude our look at enumerators with a variant called a lazy enumerator.

10.12 *Lazy enumerators*

Lazy enumerators make it easy to enumerate selectively over infinitely large collections. To illustrate what this means, let's start with a case where an operation tries to enumerate over an infinitely large collection and gets stuck. What if you want to know the first 10 multiples of 3? To use an infinite collection we'll create a range that goes from 1 to the special value `Float::INFINITY`. Using such a range, a first approach to the task at hand might be

```
(1..Float::INFINITY).select {|n| n % 3 == 0 }.first(10)
```

But this line of code runs forever. The `select` operation never finishes, so the chained-on `first` command never gets executed.

You can get a finite result from an infinite collection by using a lazy enumerator. Calling the `lazy` method directly on a range object will produce a lazy enumerator over that range:

```
>> (1..Float::INFINITY).lazy
=> #<Enumerator::Lazy: 1..Infinity>
```

You can then wire this lazy enumerator up to `select`, creating a cascade of lazy enumerators:

```
>>(1..Float::INFINITY).lazy.select {|n| n % 3 == 0 }
=> #<Enumerator::Lazy: #<Enumerator::Lazy: 1..Infinity>:select>
```

Since we're now lazily enumerating, it's possible to grab result sets from our operations without waiting for the completion of infinite tasks. Specifically, we can now ask for the first 10 results from the select test on the infinite list, and the infinite list is happy to enumerate only as much as is necessary to produce those 10 results:

```
>> (1..Float::INFINITY).lazy.select {|n| n % 3 == 0 }.first(10)
=> [3, 6, 9, 12, 15, 18, 21, 24, 27, 30]
```

As a variation on the same theme, you can create the lazy `select` enumerator and then use `take` on it. This allows you to choose how many multiples of 3 you want to see without hard-coding the number. Note that you have to call `force` on the result of `take`; otherwise you'll end up with yet another lazy enumerator, rather than an actual result set:

```
>> my_enum = (1..Float::INFINITY).lazy.select {|n| n % 3 == 0 }
=> #<Enumerator::Lazy: #<Enumerator::Lazy: 1..Infinity>:select>
>> my_enum.take(5).force
=> [3, 6, 9, 12, 15]
>> my_enum.take(10).force
=> [3, 6, 9, 12, 15, 18, 21, 24, 27, 30]
```

Lazy enumerators are a somewhat specialized tool, and you probably won't need them too often. But they're very handy if you have an infinite collection and want to deal only with a finite result set from operations on that collection.

10.12.1 FizzBuzz with a lazy enumerator

The `FizzBuzz` problem, in its classic form, involves printing out the integers from 1 to 100 ... except you apply the following rules:

- If the number is divisible by 15, print `"FizzBuzz"`.
- Else if the number is divisible by 3, print `"Fizz"`.
- Else if the number is divisible by 5, print `"Buzz"`.
- Else print the number.

You can use a lazy enumerator to write a version of `FizzBuzz` that can handle any range of numbers. Here's what it might look like:

```
def fb_calc(i)
  case 0
  when i % 15
    "FizzBuzz"
  when i % 3
    "Fizz"
  when i % 5
    "Buzz"
  else
    i.to_s
  end
end

def fb(n)
  (1..Float::INFINITY).lazy.map {|i| fb_calc(i) }.first(n)
end
```

Now you can examine, say, the `FizzBuzz` output for the first 15 positive integers like this:

```
p fb(15)
```

The output will be

```
["1", "2", "Fizz", "4", "Buzz", "Fizz", "7", "8", "Fizz", "Buzz", "11",
    "Fizz", "13", "14", "FizzBuzz"]
```

Without creating a lazy enumerator on the range, the map operation would go on forever. Instead, the lazy enumeration ensures that the whole process will stop once we've got what we want.

10.13 Summary

In this chapter you've seen

- The `Enumerable` module and its instance methods
- Using `Enumerable` in your own classes
- Enumerator basics
- Creating enumerators
- Iterating over strings
- Lazy enumerators

This chapter focused on the `Enumerable` module and the `Enumerator` class, two entities with close ties. First, we explored the instance methods of `Enumerable`, which are defined in terms of an `each` method and which are available to your objects as long as those objects respond to `each` and your class mixes in `Enumerable`. Second, we looked at enumerators, objects that encapsulate the iteration process of another object, binding themselves—specifically, their `each` methods—to a designated method on another object and using that parasitic `each`-binding to deliver the full range of enumerable functionality.

Enumerators can be tricky. They build entirely on `Enumerable`; and in cases where an enumerator gets hooked up to an object that has overridden some of `Enumerable`'s methods, it's important to remember that the enumerator will have its own ideas of what those methods are. It's not a general-purpose proxy to another object; it siphons off values from one method on the other object.

One way or another—be it through the use of enumerators or the use of the more classic Ruby style of iteration and collection management—you'll almost certainly use the enumeration-related facilities of the language virtually every time you write a Ruby program. It's worth getting to know `Enumerable` intimately; it's as powerful a unit of functionality as there is anywhere in Ruby.

We'll turn next to the subject of regular expressions and pattern matching. As you'll see, there's some payoff to looking at both strings and collection objects prior to studying regular expressions: a number of pattern-matching methods performed on strings return their results to you in collection form and therefore lend themselves to iteration. Looking at regular expressions will help you develop a full-featured toolkit for processing strings and bodies of text.

11

Regular expressions and regexp-based string operations

This chapter covers

- Regular expression syntax
- Pattern-matching operations
- The `MatchData` class
- Built-in methods based on pattern matching

In this chapter, we'll explore Ruby's facilities for pattern matching and text processing, centering around the use of regular expressions. A *regular expression* in Ruby serves the same purposes it does in other languages: it specifies a pattern of characters, a pattern that may or may not correctly predict (that is, match) a given string. Pattern-match operations are used for conditional branching (match/no match), pinpointing substrings (parts of a string that match parts of the pattern), and various text-filtering techniques.

Regular expressions in Ruby are objects. You send messages *to* a regular expression. Regular expressions add something to the Ruby landscape but, as objects, they also fit nicely into the landscape.

We'll start with an overview of regular expressions. From there, we'll move on to the details of how to write them and, of course, how to use them. In the latter category, we'll look at using regular expressions both in simple match operations and in methods where they play a role in a larger process, such as filtering a collection or repeatedly scanning a string.

11.1 *What are regular expressions?*

Regular expressions appear in many programming languages, with minor differences among the incarnations. Their purpose is to specify character patterns that subsequently are determined to match (or not match) strings. Pattern matching, in turn, serves as the basis for operations like parsing log files, testing keyboard input for validity, and isolating substrings—operations, in other words, of frequent and considerable use to anyone who has to process strings and text.

Regular expressions have a weird reputation. Using them is a powerful, concentrated technique; they burn through a large subset of text-processing problems like acid through a padlock. They're also, in the view of many people (including people who understand them well), difficult to use, difficult to read, opaque, unmaintainable, and ultimately counterproductive.

You have to judge for yourself. The one thing you should *not* do is shy away from learning at least the basics of how regular expressions work and how to use the Ruby methods that utilize them. Even if you decide you aren't a "regular expression person," you need a reading knowledge of them. And you'll by no means be alone if you end up using them in your own programs more than you anticipated.

A number of Ruby built-in methods take regular expressions as arguments and perform selection or modification on one or more string objects. Regular expressions are used, for example, to *scan* a string for multiple occurrences of a pattern, to *substitute* a replacement string for a substring, and to *split* a string into multiple substrings based on a matching separator.

If you're familiar with regular expressions from Perl, sed, vi, Emacs, or any other source, you may want to skim or skip the expository material here and pick up in section 11.5, where we talk about Ruby methods that use regular expressions. But note that Ruby regular expressions aren't identical to those in any other language. You'll almost certainly be able to read them, but you may need to study the differences (such as whether parentheses are special by default or special when escaped) if you get into writing them.

Let's turn now to writing some regular expressions.

11.2 *Writing regular expressions*

Regular expressions are written with familiar characters—of course—but you have to learn to read and write them as things unto themselves. They're not strings, and their meaning isn't always as obvious as that of strings. They're representations of *patterns*.

11.2.1 *Seeing patterns*

A regular expression (regexp or regex) specifies a pattern. For every such pattern, every string in the world either matches the pattern or doesn't match it. The Ruby methods that use regular expressions use them either to determine whether a given string matches a given pattern or to make that determination and also take some action based on the answer.

Patterns of the kind specified by regular expressions are most easily understood, initially, in plain language. Here are several examples of patterns expressed this way:

- The letter a, followed by a digit
- Any uppercase letter, followed by at least one lowercase letter
- Three digits, followed by a hyphen, followed by four digits

A pattern can also include components and constraints related to positioning inside the string:

- The beginning of a line, followed by one or more whitespace characters
- The character . (period) at the end of a string
- An uppercase letter at the beginning of a word

Pattern components like "the beginning of a line," which match a condition rather than a character in a string, are nonetheless expressed with characters or sequences of characters in the regexp.

Regular expressions provide a language for expressing patterns. Learning to write them consists principally of learning how various things are expressed inside a regexp. The most commonly applied rules of regexp construction are fairly easy to learn. You just have to remember that a regexp, although it contains characters, isn't a string. It's a special notation for expressing a pattern that may or may not correctly describe some or all of any given string.

11.2.2 *Simple matching with literal regular expressions*

Regular expressions are instances of the `Regexp` class, which is one of the Ruby classes that has a literal constructor for easy instantiation. The regexp literal constructor is a pair of forward slashes:

```
//
```

As odd as this may look, it really is a regexp, if a skeletal one. You can verify that it gives you an instance of the `Regexp` class in irb:

```
>> //.class
=> Regexp
```

The specifics of the regexp go between the slashes. We'll start to construct a few simple regular expressions as we look at the basics of the matching process.

Any pattern-matching operation has two main players: a regexp and a string. The regexp expresses predictions about the string. Either the string fulfills those predictions (matches the pattern) or it doesn't.

The simplest way to find out whether there's a match between a pattern and a string is with the `match` method. You can do this either direction—regexp objects and string objects both respond to match, and both of these examples succeed and print "Match!":

```
puts "Match!" if /abc/.match("The alphabet starts with abc.")
puts "Match!" if "The alphabet starts with abc.".match(/abc/)
```

The string version of match (the second line of the two) differs from the regexp version in that it converts a string argument *to* a regexp. (We'll return to that a little later.) In the example, the argument is already a regexp (/abc/), so no conversion is necessary.

In addition to the match method, Ruby also features a pattern-matching operator, =~ (equal sign and tilde), which goes between a string and a regexp:

```
puts "Match!" if /abc/ =~ "The alphabet starts with abc."
puts "Match!" if "The alphabet starts with abc." =~ /abc/
```

As you might guess, this pattern-matching "operator" is an instance method of both the String and Regexp classes. It's one of the many Ruby methods that provide the syntactic sugar of an infix-operator usage style.

The match method and the =~ operator are equally useful when you're after a simple yes/no answer to the question of whether there's a match between a string and a pattern. If there's no match, you get back nil. That's handy for conditionals; all four of the previous examples test the results of their match operations with an if test. Where match and =~ differ from each other chiefly is in what they return when there *is* a match: =~ returns the numerical index of the character in the string where the match started, whereas match returns an instance of the class MatchData:

```
>> "The alphabet starts with abc" =~ /abc/
=> 25
>> /abc/.match("The alphabet starts with abc.")
=> #<MatchData "abc">
```

The first example finds a match in position 25 of the string. In the second example, the creation of a MatchData object means that a match was found.

We'll examine MatchData objects a little further on. For the moment, we'll be concerned mainly with getting a yes/no answer to an attempted match, so any of the techniques shown thus far will work. For the sake of consistency, and because we'll be more concerned with MatchData objects than numerical indexes of substrings, most of the examples in this chapter will stick to the Regexp#match method.

Now, let's look in more detail at the composition of a regexp.

11.3 *Building a pattern in a regular expression*

When you write a regexp, you put the definition of your pattern between the forward slashes. Remember that what you're putting there isn't a string but a set of predictions and constraints that you want to look for in a string.

The possible components of a regexp include the following:

- *Literal characters*, meaning "match this character"
- The *dot wildcard character (.)*, meaning "match any character" (except \n, the newline character)
- *Character classes*, meaning "match one of these characters"

We'll discuss each of these in turn. We'll then use that knowledge to look more deeply at match operations.

11.3.1 *Literal characters in patterns*

Any literal character you put in a regexp matches *itself* in the string. Thus the regexp

```
/a/
```

matches any string containing the letter a.

Some characters have special meanings to the regexp parser (as you'll see in detail shortly). When you want to match one of these special characters as itself, you have to escape it with a backslash (\). For example, to match the character ? (question mark), you have to write this:

```
/\?/
```

The backslash means "don't treat the next character as special; treat it as itself."

The special characters include those listed between the parentheses here: (^ $? . / \ [ ] { } ( ) + *). Among them, as you can see, is the dot, which is a special character in regular expressions.

11.3.2 *The dot wildcard character (.)*

Sometimes you'll want to match *any character* at some point in your pattern. You do this with the special dot wildcard character (.). A dot matches any character with the exception of a newline. (There's a way to make it match newlines too, which you'll see a little later.)

The pattern in this regexp matches both "dejected" and "rejected":

```
/.ejected/
```

It also matches "%ejected" and "8ejected":

```
puts "Match!" if /.ejected/.match("%ejected")
```

The wildcard dot is handy, but sometimes it gives you more matches than you want. You can impose constraints on matches while still allowing for multiple possible strings, using character classes.

11.3.3 *Character classes*

A *character class* is an explicit list of characters placed inside the regexp in square brackets:

```
/[dr]ejected/
```

This means "match either *d* or *r*, followed by *ejected*." This new pattern matches either "dejected" or "rejected" but not "&ejected." A character class is a kind of partial or constrained wildcard: it allows for multiple possible characters, but only a limited number of them.

Inside a character class, you can also insert a *range* of characters. A common case is this, for lowercase letters:

```
/[a-z]/
```

To match a hexadecimal digit, you might use several ranges inside a character class:

```
/[A-Fa-f0-9]/
```

This matches any character *a* through *f* (upper- or lowercase) or any digit.

Character classes are longer than what they match

Even a short character class like [a] takes up more than one space in a regexp. But remember, each character class matches *one character* in the string. When you look at a character class like /[dr]/, it may look like it's going to match the substring dr. But it isn't: it's going to match either d or r.

Sometimes you need to match any character *except* those on a special list. You may, for example, be looking for the first character in a string that is *not* a valid hexadecimal digit.

You perform this kind of negative search by negating a character class. To do so, you put a caret (^) at the beginning of the class. For example, here's a character class that matches any character except a valid hexadecimal digit:

```
/[^A-Fa-f0-9]/
```

And here's how you might find the index of the first occurrence of a non-hex character in a string:

```
>> string = "ABC3934 is a hex number."
=> "ABC3934 is a hex number."
>> string =~ /[^A-Fa-f0-9]/
=> 7
```

A character class, positive or negative, can contain any characters. Some character classes are so common that they have special abbreviations.

SPECIAL ESCAPE SEQUENCES FOR COMMON CHARACTER CLASSES
To match any digit, you can do this:

```
/[0-9]/
```

You can also accomplish the same thing more concisely with the special escape sequence \d:

```
/\d/
```

Notice that there are no square brackets here; it's just \d. Two other useful escape sequences for predefined character classes are these:

- \w matches any digit, alphabetical character, or underscore (_).
- \s matches any whitespace character (space, tab, newline).

Each of these predefined character classes also has a negated form. You can match any character that isn't a digit by doing this:

```
/\D/
```

Similarly, \W matches any character other than an alphanumeric character or underscore, and \S matches any non-whitespace character.

A successful call to `match` returns a `MatchData` object. Let's look at `MatchData` objects and their capabilities up close.

11.4 Matching, substring captures, and MatchData

So far, we've looked at basic match operations:

```
regex.match(string)
string.match(regex)
```

These are essentially true/false tests: either there's a match or there isn't. Now we'll examine what happens on successful and unsuccessful matches and what a match operation can do for you beyond the yes/no answer.

11.4.1 Capturing submatches with parentheses

One of the most important techniques of regexp construction is the use of parentheses to specify *captures*.

The idea is this. When you test for a match between a string—say, a line from a file—and a pattern, it's usually because you want to do something with the string or, more commonly, with part of the string. The capture notation allows you to isolate and save substrings of the string that match particular subpatterns.

For example, let's say we have a string containing information about a person:

```
Peel,Emma,Mrs.,talented amateur
```

From this string, we need to harvest the person's last name and title. We know the fields are comma separated, and we know what order they come in: last name, first name, title, occupation.

To construct a pattern that matches such a string, we might think in English along the following lines:

First some alphabetical characters,
then a comma,
then some alphabetical characters,
then a comma,
then either 'Mr.' or 'Mrs.'

We're keeping it simple: no hyphenated names, no doctors or professors, no leaving off the final period on Mr. and Mrs. (which would be done in British usage). The regexp, then, might look like this:

```
/[A-Za-z]+,[A-Za-z]+,Mrs?\./
```

(The question mark after the *s* means *match zero or one s*. Expressing it that way lets us match either "Mr." and "Mrs." concisely.) The pattern matches the string, as irb attests:

```
>> /[A-Za-z]+,[A-Za-z]+,Mrs?\./.match("Peel,Emma,Mrs.,talented amateur")
=> #<MatchData "Peel,Emma,Mrs.">
```

We got a `MatchData` object rather than `nil`; there was a match.

But now what? How do we isolate the substrings we're interested in (`"Peel"` and `"Mrs."`)?

This is where parenthetical groupings come in. We want two such groupings: one around the subpattern that matches the last name, and one around the subpattern that matches the title:

```
/([A-Za-z]+),[A-Za-z]+,(Mrs?\.)/
```

Now, when we perform the match

```
/([A-Za-z]+),[A-Za-z]+,(Mrs?\.)/.match("Peel,Emma,Mrs.,talented amateur")
```

two things happen:

- We get a `MatchData` object that gives us access to the submatches (discussed in a moment).
- Ruby automatically populates a series of variables for us, which also give us access to those submatches.

The variables that Ruby populates are global variables, and their names are based on numbers: $1, $2, and so forth. $1 contains the substring matched by the subpattern inside the *first* set of parentheses from the left in the regexp. Examining $1 after the previous match (for example, with `puts $1`) displays `Peel`. $2 contains the substring matched by the *second* subpattern; and so forth. In general, the rule is this: after a successful match operation, the variable $*n* (where *n* is a number) contains the substring matched by the subpattern inside the *n*th set of parentheses from the left in the regexp.

> **NOTE** If you've used Perl, you may have seen the variable $0, which represents not a specific captured subpattern but the entire substring that has been successfully matched. Ruby uses $0 for something else: it contains the name of the Ruby program file from which the current program or script was initially started up. Instead of $0 for pattern matches, Ruby provides a method; you call `string` on the `MatchData` object returned by the match. You'll see an example of the `string` method in section 11.4.2.

We can combine these techniques with string interpolation to generate a salutation for a letter, based on performing the match and grabbing the $1 and $2 variables:

```
line_from_file = "Peel,Emma,Mrs.,talented amateur"
/([A-Za-z]+),[A-Za-z]+,(Mrs?\.)/.match(line_from_file)
puts "Dear #{$2} #{$1},"
```

Output: Dear Mrs. Peel,

The $n-style variables are handy for grabbing submatches. But you can accomplish the same thing in a more structured, programmatic way by querying the `MatchData` object returned by your match operation.

11.4.2 *Match success and failure*

Every match operation either succeeds or fails. Let's start with the simpler case: failure. When you try to match a string to a pattern and the string doesn't match, the result is always `nil`:

```
>> /a/.match("b")
=> nil
```

Unlike `nil`, the `MatchData` object returned by a successful match has a Boolean value of true, which makes it handy for simple match/no-match tests. Beyond this, it also stores information about the match, which you can pry out with the appropriate methods: where the match began (at what character in the string), how much of the string it covered, what was captured in the parenthetical groups, and so forth.

To use the `MatchData` object, you must first save it. Consider an example where you want to pluck a phone number from a string and save the various parts of it (area code, exchange, number) in groupings. The following listing shows how you might do this. It's also written as a clinic on how to use some of `MatchData`'s more common methods.

Listing 11.1   Matching a phone number and querying the resulting `MatchData` object

```
string = "My phone number is (123) 555-1234."
phone_re = /\((\d{3})\)\s+(\d{3})-(\d{4})/
m = phone_re.match(string)
unless m
  puts "There was no match—sorry."                    Terminates
  exit                                                 program
end
print "The whole string we started with: "
puts m.string                                          ❶
print "The entire part of the string that matched: "
puts m[0]                                              ❷
puts "The three captures: "
3.times do |index|                                     ❸
  puts "Capture ##{index + 1}: #{m.captures[index]}"
end
puts "Here's another way to get at the first capture:"
print "Capture #1: "
puts m[1]                                              ❹
```

In this code, we've used the string method of MatchData ❶, which returns the entire string on which the match operation was performed. To get the part of the string that matched our pattern, we address the MatchData object with square brackets, with an index of 0 ❷. We also use the nifty times method ❸ to iterate exactly three times through a code block and print out the submatches (the parenthetical captures) in succession. Inside that code block, a method called captures fishes out the substrings that matched the parenthesized parts of the pattern. Finally, we take another look at the first capture, this time through a different technique ❹: indexing the MatchData object directly with square brackets and positive integers, each integer corresponding to a capture.

Here's the output of the listing:

```
The whole string we started with: My phone number is (123) 555-1234.
The entire part of the string that matched: (123) 555-1234
The three captures:
Capture #1: 123
Capture #2: 555
Capture #3: 1234
Here's another way to get at the first capture:
Capture #1: 123
```

This gives you a taste of the kinds of match data you can extract from a MatchData object. You can see that there are two ways of retrieving captures. Let's zoom in on those techniques.

11.4.3 *Two ways of getting the captures*

One way to get the parenthetical captures from a MatchData object is by directly indexing the object, array-style:

```
m[1]
m[2]
#etc.
```

The first line will show the first capture (the first set of parentheses from the left), the second line will show the second capture, and so on.

As listing 11.1 shows, an index of 0 gives you the entire string that was matched. From 1 onward, an index of n gives you the nth capture, based on counting opening parentheses from the left. (And n, where $n > 0$, always corresponds to the number in the global $n variable.)

The other technique for getting the parenthetical captures from a MatchData object is the captures method, which returns all the captured substrings in a single array. Because this is a regular array, the first item in it—essentially, the same as the global variable $1—is item 0, not item 1. In other words, the following equivalencies apply:

```
m[1] == m.captures[0]
m[2] == m.captures[1]
```

and so forth.

A word about this recurrent "counting parentheses from the left" thing. Some regular expressions can be confusing as to their capture parentheses if you don't know the rule. Take this one, for example:

```
/((a)((b)c))/.match("abc")
```

What will be in the various captures? Well, just count opening parentheses from the left. For each opening parenthesis, find its counterpart on the right. Everything inside that pair will be capture number *n*, for whatever *n* you've gotten up to.

That means the first capture will be "abc", because that's the part of the string that matches the pattern between the outermost parentheses. The next parentheses surround "a"; that will be the second capture. Next comes "bc", followed by "b". And that's the last of the opening parentheses.

The string representation of the `MatchData` object you get from this match will obligingly show you the captures:

```
>> /((a)((b)c))/.match("abc")
=> #<MatchData "abc" 1:"abc" 2:"a" 3:"bc" 4:"b">
```

Sure enough, they correspond rigorously to what was matched between the pairs of parentheses counted off from the left.

NAMED CAPTURES

Capturing subexpressions indexed by number is certainly handy, but there's another, sometimes more reader-friendly way, that you can label subexpressions: named captures.

Here's an example. This regular expression will match a name of the form "David A. Black" or, equally, "David Black" (with no middle initial):

```
>> re = /(?<first>\w+)\s+((?<middle>\w\.)\s+)?(?<last>\w+)/
```

What are the words `first`, `middle`, and `last` doing there? They're providing named captures: parenthetical captures that you can recover from the `MatchData` object using words instead of numbers.

If you perform a match using this regular expression, you'll see evidence of the named captures in the screen output representing the `MatchData` object:

```
>> m = re.match("David A. Black")
=> #<MatchData "David A. Black" first:"David" middle:"A." last:"Black">
```

Now you can query the object for its named captures:

```
>> m[:first]
=> "David"
```

Named captures can bulk up your regular expressions, but with the payback that the semantics of retrieving captures from the match become word-based rather than number-based, and therefore potentially clearer and more self-documenting. You also don't have to count pairs of parentheses to derive a reference to your captured substrings.

`MatchData` objects provide information beyond the parenthetical captures, information you can take and use if you need it.

11.4.4 *Other MatchData information*

The code in the following listing, which is designed to be grafted onto listing 11.1, gives some quick examples of several further `MatchData` methods.

Listing 11.2 Supplemental code for phone number–matching operations

```
print "The part of the string before the part that matched was: "
puts m.pre_match
print "The part of the string after the part that matched was: "
puts m.post_match
print "The second capture began at character "
puts m.begin(2)
print "The third capture ended at character "
puts m.end(3)
```

The output from this supplemental code is as follows:

```
The string up to the part that matched was: My phone number is
The string after the part that matched was: .
The second capture began at character 25
The third capture ended at character 33
```

The `pre_match` and `post_match` methods you see in this listing depend on the fact that when you successfully match a string, the string can then be thought of as being made up of three parts: the part before the part that matched the pattern; the part that matched the pattern; and the part after the part that matched the pattern. Any or all of these can be an empty string. In this listing, they're not: the `pre_match` and `post_match` strings both contain characters (albeit only one character in the case of `post_match`).

You can also see the `begin` and `end` methods in this listing. These methods tell you where the various parenthetical captures, if any, begin and end. To get the information for capture *n*, you provide *n* as the argument to `begin` and/or `end`.

The `MatchData` object is a kind of clearinghouse for information about what happened when the pattern met the string. With that knowledge in place, let's continue looking at techniques you can use to build and use regular expressions. We'll start with a fistful of important regexp components: quantifiers, anchors, and modifiers. Learning about these components will help you both with the writing of your own regular expressions and with your regexp literacy. If matching `/abc/` makes sense to you now, matching `/^x?[yz]{2}.*\z/i` will make sense to you shortly.

> #### The global `MatchData` object `$~`
> Whenever you perform a successful match operation, using either `match` or `=~`, Ruby sets the global variable `$~` to a `MatchData` object representing the match. On an unsuccessful match, `$~` gets set to `nil`. Thus you can always get at a `MatchData` object, for analytical purposes, even if you use `=~`.

11.5   *Fine-tuning regular expressions with quantifiers, anchors, and modifiers*

Quantifiers let you specify how many times in a row you want something to match. *Anchors* let you stipulate that the match occur at a certain structural point in a string (beginning of string, end of line, at a word boundary, and so on). *Modifiers* are like switches you can flip to change the behavior of the regexp engine; for example, by making it case-insensitive or altering how it handles whitespace.

We'll look at quantifiers, anchors, and modifiers here, in that order.

11.5.1   *Constraining matches with quantifiers*

Regexp syntax gives you ways to specify not only what you want but also how many: exactly one of a particular character, 5–10 repetitions of a subpattern, and so forth.

All the quantifiers operate either on a single character (which may be represented by a character class) or on a parenthetical group. When you specify that you want to match, say, three consecutive occurrences of a particular subpattern, that subpattern can thus be just one character, or it can be a longer subpattern placed inside parentheses.

ZERO OR ONE

You've already seen a zero-or-one quantifier example. Let's review it and go a little more deeply into it.

You want to match either "Mr" or "Mrs"—and, just to make it more interesting, you want to accommodate both the American versions, which end with periods, and the British versions, which don't. You might describe the pattern as follows:

```
the character M, followed by the character r, followed by
zero or one of the character s, followed by
zero or one of the character '.'
```

Regexp notation has a special character to represent the zero-or-one situation: the question mark (?). The pattern just described would be expressed in regexp notation as follows:

```
/Mrs?\.?/
```

The question mark after the *s* means that a string with an *s* in that position will match the pattern, and so will a string without an *s*. The same principle applies to the literal period (note the backslash, indicating that this is an actual period, not a special wildcard dot) followed by a question mark. The whole pattern, then, will match "Mr," "Mrs," "Mr.," or "Mrs." (It will also match "ABCMr." and "Mrs!," but you'll see how to delimit a match more precisely when we look at anchors in section 11.5.3.)

The question mark is often used with character classes to indicate zero or one of any of a number of characters. If you're looking for either one or two digits in a row, for example, you might express that part of your pattern like this:

```
\d\d?
```

This sequence will match "1," "55," "03," and so forth.

Along with the zero-or-one, there's a zero-or-more quantifier.

ZERO OR MORE

A fairly common case is one in which a string you want to match contains whitespace, but you're not sure how much. Let's say you're trying to match closing `</poem>` tags in an XML document. Such a tag may or may not contain whitespace. All of these are equivalent:

```
</poem>
< /poem>
</    poem>
</poem
>
```

In order to match the tag, you have to allow for unpredictable amounts of whitespace in your pattern—including none.

This is a case for the *zero-or-more* quantifier—the asterisk or star (*):

```
/<\s*\/\s*poem\s*>/
```

Each time it appears, the sequence `\s*` means the string being matched is allowed to contain zero or more whitespace characters at this point in the match. (Note the necessity of escaping the forward slash in the pattern with a backslash. Otherwise, it would be interpreted as the slash signaling the end of the regexp.)

Regular expressions, it should be noted, can't do everything. In particular, it's a commonplace and correct observation that you can't parse arbitrary XML with regular expressions, for reasons having to do with the nesting of elements and the ways in which character data is represented. Still, if you're scanning a document because you want to get a rough count of how many poems are in it, and you match and count poem tags, the likelihood that you'll get the information you're looking for is high.

Next among the quantifiers is one or more.

ONE OR MORE

The one-or-more quantifier is the plus sign (+) placed after the character or parenthetical grouping you wish to match one or more of. The match succeeds if the string contains at least one occurrence of the specified subpattern at the appropriate point. For example, the pattern

```
/\d+/
```

matches any sequence of one or more consecutive digits:

```
/\d+/.match("There's a digit here somewh3re...")      ←—— Succeeds
/\d+/.match("No digits here. Move along.")            ←—— Fails
/\d+/.match("Digits-R-Us 2345")                       ←—— Succeeds
```

Of course, if you throw in parentheses, you can find out what got matched:

```
/(\d+)/.match("Digits-R-Us 2345")
puts $1
```

The output here is 2345.

Here's a question, though. The job of the pattern \d+ is to match one or more digits. That means as soon as the regexp engine (the part of the interpreter that's doing all this pattern matching) sees that the string has the digit 2 in it, it has enough information to conclude that yes, there's a match. Yet it clearly keeps going; it doesn't stop matching the string until it gets all the way to the 5. You can deduce this from the value of $1: the fact that $1 is 2345 means that the subexpression \d+, which is what's in the first set of parentheses, is considered to have matched that substring of four digits.

But why match four digits when all you need to prove you're right is one digit? The answer, as it so often is in life as well as regexp analysis, is greed.

11.5.2   *Greedy (and non-greedy) quantifiers*

The * (zero-or-more) and + (one-or-more) quantifiers are *greedy*. This means they match as many characters as possible, consistent with allowing the rest of the pattern to match.

Look at what .* matches in this snippet:

```
string = "abc!def!ghi!"
match = /.+!/.match(string)
puts match[0]
```

Output:
abc!def!ghi!

We've asked for one or more characters (using the wildcard dot) followed by an exclamation point. You might expect to get back the substring "abc!", which fits that description.

Instead, we get "abc!def!ghi!". The + quantifier greedily eats up as much of the string as it can and only stops at the *last* exclamation point, not the first.

We can make + as well as * into non-greedy quantifiers by putting a question mark after them. Watch what happens when we do that with the last example:

```
string = "abc!def!ghi!"
match = /.+?!/.match(string)
puts match[0]
```

Output: **abc!**

This version says, "Give me one or more wildcard characters, but only as many as you see up to the *first* exclamation point, which should also be included." Sure enough, this time we get "abc!".

If we add the question mark to the quantifier in the digits example, it will stop after it sees the 2:

```
/(\d+?)/.match("Digits-R-Us 2345")
puts $1
```

In this case, the output is 2.

What does it mean to say that greedy quantifiers give you as many characters as they can, "consistent with allowing the rest of the pattern to match"?

Consider this match:

```
/\d+5/.match("Digits-R-Us 2345")
```

If the one-or-more quantifier's greediness were absolute, the \d+ would match all four digits—and then the 5 in the pattern wouldn't match anything, so the whole match would fail. But greediness always subordinates itself to ensuring a successful match. What happens, in this case, is that after the match fails, the regexp engine backtracks: it unmatches the 5 and tries the pattern again. This time, it succeeds: it has satisfied both the \d+ requirement (with 234) and the requirement that 5 follow the digits that \d+ matched.

Once again, you can get an informative X-ray of the proceedings by capturing parts of the matched string and examining what you've captured. Let's let irb and the MatchData object show us the relevant captures:

```
>> /(\d+)(5)/.match("Digits-R-Us 2345")
=> #<MatchData "2345" 1:"234" 2:"5">
```

The first capture is "234" and the second is "5". The one-or-more quantifier, although greedy, has settled for getting only three digits, instead of four, in the interest of allowing the regexp engine to find a way to make the whole pattern match the string.

In addition to using the zero-/one-or-more-style modifiers, you can also require an exact number or number range of repetitions of a given subpattern.

SPECIFIC NUMBERS OF REPETITIONS

To specify exactly how many repetitions of a part of your pattern you want matched, put the number in curly braces ({}) right after the relevant subexpression, as this example shows:

```
/\d{3}-\d{4}/
```

This example matches exactly three digits, a hyphen, and then four digits: 555-1212 and other phone number–like sequences.

You can also specify a range inside the braces:

```
/\d{1,10}/
```

This example matches any string containing 1–10 consecutive digits. A single number followed by a comma is interpreted as a minimum (*n* or more repetitions). You can therefore match "three or more digits" like this:

```
/\d{3,}/
```

Ruby's regexp engine is smart enough to let you know if your range is impossible; you'll get a fatal error if you try to match, say, {10,2} (at least 10 but no more than 2) occurrences of a subpattern.

You can specify that a repetition count not only for single characters or character classes but also for any regexp *atom*—the more technical term for "part of your pattern." Atoms include parenthetical subpatterns and character classes as well as individual characters. Thus you can do this, to match five consecutive uppercase letters:

```
/([A-Z]){5}/.match("David BLACK")
```

But there's an important potential pitfall to be aware of in cases like this.

THE LIMITATION ON PARENTHESES

If you run that last line of code and look at what the `MatchData` object tells you about the first capture, you may expect to see `"BLACK"`. But you don't:

```
>> /([A-Z]){5}/.match("David BLACK")
=> #<MatchData "BLACK" 1:"K">
```

It's just `"K"`. Why isn't `"BLACK"` captured in its entirety?

The reason is that the parentheses don't "know" that they're being repeated five times. They just know that they're the first parentheses from the left (in this particular case) and that what they've captured should be stashed in the first capture slot (`$1`, or `captures[1]` of the `MatchData` object). The expression inside the parentheses, `[A-Z]`, can only match one character. If it matches one character five times in a row, it's still only matched one at a time—and it will only "remember" the last one.

In other words, matching one character five times isn't the same as matching five characters one time.

If you want to capture all five characters, you need to move the parentheses so they enclose the entire five-part match:

```
>> /([A-Z]{5})/.match("David BLACK")
=> #<MatchData "BLACK" 1:"BLACK">
```

Be careful and literal-minded when it comes to figuring out what will be captured.

We'll look next at ways in which you can specify conditions under which you want matches to occur, rather than the content you expect the string to have.

11.5.3 *Regular expression anchors and assertions*

Assertions and anchors are different types of creatures from characters. When you match a character (even based on a character class or wildcard), you're said to be *consuming* a character in the string you're matching. An assertion or an anchor, on the other hand, doesn't consume any characters. Instead, it expresses a *constraint*: a condition that must be met before the matching of characters is allowed to proceed.

The most common anchors are *beginning of line* (`^`) and *end of line* (`$`). You might use the beginning-of-line anchor for a task like removing all the comment lines from a Ruby program file. You'd accomplish this by going through all the lines in the file and printing out only those that did *not* start with a hash mark (`#`) or with whitespace followed by a hash mark. To determine which lines are comment lines, you can use this regexp:

```
/^\s*#/
```

The `^` (caret) in this pattern *anchors* the match at the beginning of a line. If the rest of the pattern matches, but *not* at the beginning of the line, that doesn't count—as you can see with a couple of tests:

```
>> comment_regexp = /^\s*#/
=> /^\s*#/
>> comment_regexp.match("  # Pure comment!")
```

```
=> #<MatchData "  #">
>> comment_regexp.match("  x = 1  # Code plus comment!")
=> nil
```

Only the line that starts with some whitespace and the hash character is a match for the comment pattern. The other line doesn't match the pattern and therefore wouldn't be deleted if you used this regexp to filter comments out of a file.

Table 11.1 shows a number of anchors, including start and end of line and start and end of string.

Table 11.1 Regular expression anchors

Notation	Description	Example	Sample matching string
^	Beginning of line	/^\s*#/	" # A Ruby comment line with leading spaces"
$	End of line	/\.$/	"one\ntwo\nthree.\nfour"
\A	Beginning of string	/\AFour score/	"Four score"
\z	End of string	/from the earth.\z/	"from the earth."
\Z	End of string (except for final newline)	/from the earth.\Z/	"from the earth\n"
\b	Word boundary	/\b\w+\b/	"!!!word***" (matches "word")

Note that \z matches the absolute end of the string, whereas \Z matches the end of the string except for an optional trailing newline. \Z is useful in cases where you're not sure whether your string has a newline character at the end—perhaps the last line read out of a text file—and you don't want to have to worry about it.

Hand-in-hand with anchors go *assertions*, which, similarly, tell the regexp processor that you want a match to count only under certain conditions.

LOOKAHEAD ASSERTIONS

Let's say you want to match a sequence of numbers only if it ends with a period. But you don't want the period itself to count as part of the match.

One way to do this is with a *lookahead assertion*—or, to be complete, a zero-width, positive lookahead assertion. Here, followed by further explanation, is how you do it:

```
str = "123 456. 789"
m = /\d+(?=\.)/.match(str)
```

At this point, m[0] (representing the entire stretch of the string that the pattern matched) contains 456—the one sequence of numbers that's followed by a period.

Here's a little more commentary on some of the terminology:

- *Zero-width* means it doesn't consume any characters in the string. The presence of the period is noted, but you can still match the period if your pattern continues.

- *Positive* means you want to stipulate that the period be present. There are also *negative* lookaheads; they use `(?!...)` rather than `(?=...)`.
- *Lookahead assertion* means you want to know that you're specifying what *would* be next, without matching it.

When you use a lookahead assertion, the parentheses in which you place the lookahead part of the match don't count; `$1` won't be set by the match operation in the example. And the dot after the 6 won't be consumed by the match. (Keep this last point in mind if you're ever puzzled by lookahead behavior; the puzzlement often comes from forgetting that looking ahead isn't the same as moving ahead.)

LOOKBEHIND ASSERTIONS

The lookahead assertions have lookbehind equivalents. Here's a regexp that matches the string `BLACK` only when it's preceded by "David ":

```
re = /(?<=David )BLACK/
```

Conversely, here's one that matches it only when it isn't preceded by "David ":

```
re = /(?<!David )BLACK/
```

Once again, keep in mind that these are zero-width assertions. They represent constraints on the string (*"David " has to be before it, or this "BLACK" doesn't count as a match*), but they don't match or consume any characters.

Non-capturing parentheses

If you want to match something—not just assert that it's next, but actually match it—using parentheses, but you don't want it to count as one of the numbered parenthetical captures resulting from the match, use the `(?:...)` construct. Anything inside a `(?:)` grouping will be matched based on the grouping, but not saved to a capture. Note that the `MatchData` object resulting from the following match only has two captures; the `def` grouping doesn't count, because of the `?:` notation:

```
>> str = "abc def ghi"
=> "abc def ghi"
>> m = /(abc) (?:def) (ghi)/.match(str)
=> #<MatchData "abc def ghi" 1:"abc" 2:"ghi">
```

Unlike a zero-width assertion, a `(?:)` group does consume characters. It just doesn't save them as a capture.

There's also such a thing as a *conditional match*.

CONDITIONAL MATCHES

While it probably won't be among your everyday regular expression practices, it's interesting to note the existence of conditional matches in Ruby 2.0's regular expression engine (project name Onigmo). A conditional match tests for a particular capture (by number or name), and matches one of two subexpressions based on whether or not the capture was found.

Here's a simple example. The conditional expression `(?(1)b|c)` matches b if capture number 1 is matched; otherwise it matches c:

```
>> re = /(a)?(?(1)b|c)/
=> /(a)?(?(1)b|c)/
>> re.match("ab")                    ❶
=> #<MatchData "ab" 1:"a">         ←┘
>> re.match("b")                     ❷
=> nil                            ←┘
>> re.match("c")                     ❸
=> #<MatchData "c" 1:nil>          ←┘
```

The regular expression `re` matches the string `"ab"` ❶, with `"a"` as the first parenthetical capture and the conditional subexpression matching `"a"`. However, `re` doesn't match the string `"b"` ❷. Because there's no first parenthetical capture, the conditional subexpression tries to match `"c"`, and fails ❸. That's also why `re` *does* match the string `"c"`: the condition `(?(1)...)` isn't met, so the expression tries to match the "else" part of itself, which is the subexpression `/c/`.

You can also write conditional regular expressions using named captures. The preceding example would look like this:

```
/(?<first>a)?(?(<first>)b|c)/
```

and the results of the various matches would be the same.

Anchors, assertions, and conditional matches add richness and granularity to the pattern language with which you express the matches you're looking for. Also in the language-enrichment category are regexp modifiers.

11.5.4 *Modifiers*

A regexp *modifier* is a letter placed after the final, closing forward slash of the regex literal:

```
/abc/i
```

The `i` modifier shown here causes match operations involving this regexp to be case-insensitive. The other most common modifier is `m`. The `m` (multiline) modifier has the effect that the wildcard dot character, which normally matches *any character except newline*, will match *any character, including newline*. This is useful when you want to capture everything that lies between, say, an opening parenthesis and a closing one, and you don't know (or care) whether they're on the same line.

Here's an example; note the embedded newline characters (`\n`) in the string:

```
str = "This (including\nwhat's in parens\n) takes up three lines."
m = /\(.*?\)/m.match(str)
```

The non-greedy wildcard subpattern `.*?` matches:

```
(including\nwhat's in parens\n)
```

Without the `m` modifier, the dot in the subpattern wouldn't match the newline characters. The match operation would hit the first newline and, not finding a `)` character by that point, would fail.

Another often-used regexp modifier is x. The x modifier changes the way the regexp parser treats whitespace. Instead of including it literally in the pattern, it ignores it unless it's escaped with a backslash. The point of the x modifier is to let you add comments to your regular expressions:

```
/
 \((\d{3})\)   # 3 digits inside literal parens (area code)
   \s          # One space character
 (\d{3})       # 3 digits (exchange)
   -           # Hyphen
 (\d{4})       # 4 digits (second part of number
/x
```

The previous regexp is exactly the same as this one but with expanded syntax and comments:

```
/\((\d{3})\)\s(\d{3})-(\d{4})/
```

Be careful with the x modifier. When you first discover it, it's tempting to bust all your patterns wide open:

```
/ (?<=  David\ )    BLACK  /x
```

(Note the backslash-escaped literal space character, the only such character that will be considered part of the pattern.) But remember that a lot of programmers have trained themselves to understand regular expressions without a lot of ostensibly user-friendly extra whitespace thrown in. It's not easy to un-x a regexp as you read it, if you're used to the standard syntax.

For the most part, the x modifier is best saved for cases where you want to break the regexp out onto multiple lines for the sake of adding comments, as in the telephone number example. Don't assume that whitespace automatically makes regular expressions more readable.

We'll look next at techniques for converting back and forth between two different but closely connected classes: String and Regexp.

11.6 *Converting strings and regular expressions to each other*

The fact that regular expressions aren't strings is easy to absorb at a glance in the case of regular expressions like this:

```
/[a-c]{3}/
```

With its special character-class and repetition syntax, this pattern doesn't look much like any of the strings it matches ("aaa", "aab", "aac", and so forth).

It gets a little harder *not* to see a direct link between a regexp and a string when faced with a regexp like this:

```
/abc/
```

This regexp isn't the string `"abc"`. Moreover, it matches not only `"abc"` but any string with the substring `"abc"` somewhere inside it (like "Now I know my abcs."). There's no unique relationship between a string and a similar-looking regexp.

Still, although the visual resemblance between some strings and some regular expressions doesn't mean they're the same thing, regular expressions and strings do interact in important ways. Let's look at some flow in the string-to-regexp direction and then some going the opposite way.

11.6.1 *String-to-regexp idioms*

To begin with, you can perform string (or string-style) interpolation inside a regexp. You do so with the familiar #{ . . . } interpolation technique:

```
>> str = "def"
=> "def"
>> /abc#{str}/
=> /abcdef/
```

The value of `str` is dropped into the regexp and made part of it, just as it would be if you were using the same technique to interpolate it into a string.

The interpolation technique becomes more complicated when the string you're interpolating contains regexp special characters. For example, consider a string containing a period (.). As you know, the period or dot has a special meaning in regular expressions: it matches any single character except newline. In a string, it's just a dot. When it comes to interpolating strings into regular expressions, this has the potential to cause confusion:

```
>> str = "a.c"
=> "a.c"
>> re = /#{str}/
=> /a.c/
>> re.match("a.c")
=> #<MatchData "a.c">
>> re.match("abc")
=> #<MatchData "abc">
```

Both matches succeed; they return `MatchData` objects rather than `nil`. The dot in the pattern matches a dot in the string `"a.c"`. But it also matches the b in `"abc"`. The dot, which started life as just a dot inside `str`, takes on special meaning when it becomes part of the regexp.

But you can *escape* the special characters inside a string before you drop the string into a regexp. You don't have to do this manually: the `Regexp` class provides a `Regexp.escape` class method that does it for you. You can see what this method does by running it on a couple of strings in isolation:

```
>> Regexp.escape("a.c")
=> "a\\.c"
>> Regexp.escape("^abc")
=> "\\^abc"
```

(irb doubles the backslashes because it's outputting double-quoted strings. If you wish, you can `puts` the expressions, and you'll see them in their real form with single backslashes.)

As a result of this kind of escaping, you can constrain your regular expressions to match exactly the strings you interpolate into them:

```
>> str = "a.c"
=> "a.c"
>> re = /#{Regexp.escape(str)}/
=> /a\.c/
>> re.match("a.c")
=> #<MatchData "a.c">
>> re.match("abc")
=> nil
```

This time, the attempt to use the dot as a wildcard match character fails; `"abc"` isn't a match for the escaped, interpolated string.

It's also possible to instantiate a regexp from a string by passing the string to `Regexp.new`:

```
>> Regexp.new('(.*)\s+Black')
=> /(.*)\s+Black/
```

The usual character-escaping and/or regexp-escaping logic applies:

```
>> Regexp.new('Mr\. David Black')
=> /Mr\. David Black/
>> Regexp.new(Regexp.escape("Mr. David Black"))
=> /Mr\.\ David\ Black/
```

Notice that the literal space characters have been escaped with backslashes—not strictly necessary unless you're using the x modifier, but not detrimental either.

You can also pass a literal regexp to `Regexp.new`, in which case you get back a new, identical regexp. Because you can always just use the literal regexp in the first place, `Regexp.new` is more commonly used to convert strings to regexps.

The use of single-quoted strings makes it unnecessary to double up on the backslashes. If you use double quotes (which you may have to, depending on what sorts of interpolation you need to do), remember that you need to write `Mr\\.` so the backslash is part of the string passed to the regexp constructor. Otherwise, it will only have the effect of placing a literal dot in the string—which was going to happen anyway—and that dot will make it into the regexp without a slash and will therefore be interpreted as a wildcard dot.

Now let's look at some conversion techniques in the other direction: regexp to string. This is something you'll do mostly for debugging and analysis purposes.

11.6.2   *Going from a regular expression to a string*

Like all Ruby objects, regular expressions can represent themselves in string form. The way they do this may look odd at first:

```
>> puts /abc/
(?-mix:abc)
```

This is an alternate regexp notation—one that rarely sees the light of day except when generated by the `to_s` instance method of regexp objects. What looks like *mix* is a list of modifiers (`m`, `i`, and `x`) with a minus sign in front indicating that the modifiers are all switched off.

You can play with `puts`ing regular expressions in irb, and you'll see more about how this notation works. We won't pursue it here, in part because there's another way to get a string representation of a regexp that looks more like what you probably typed—by calling `inspect` or `p` (which in turn calls `inspect`):

```
>> /abc/.inspect
=> "/abc/"
```

Going from regular expressions to strings is useful primarily when you're studying and/or troubleshooting regular expressions. It's a good way to make sure your regular expressions are what you think they are.

At this point, we'll bring regular expressions full circle by examining the roles they play in some important methods of other classes. We've gotten this far using the `match` method almost exclusively; but `match` is just the beginning.

11.7 Common methods that use regular expressions

The payoff for gaining facility with regular expressions in Ruby is the ability to use the methods that take regular expressions as arguments and do something with them.

To begin with, you can always use a `match` operation as a test in, say, a `find` or `find_all` operation on a collection. For example, to find all strings longer than 10 characters and containing at least 1 digit, from an array of strings called `array`, you can do this:

```
array.find_all {|e| e.size > 10 and /\d/.match(e) }
```

But a number of methods, mostly pertaining to strings, are based more directly on the use of regular expressions. We'll look at several of them in this section.

11.7.1 String#scan

The `scan` method goes from left to right through a string, testing repeatedly for a match with the pattern you specify. The results are returned in an array.

For example, if you want to harvest all the digits in a string, you can do this:

```
>> "testing 1 2 3 testing 4 5 6".scan(/\d/)
=> ["1", "2", "3", "4", "5", "6"]
```

Note that `scan` jumps over things that don't match its pattern and looks for a match later in the string. This behavior is different from that of `match`, which stops for good when it finishes matching the pattern completely once.

If you use parenthetical groupings in the regexp you give to `scan`, the operation returns an array of arrays. Each inner array contains the results of one scan through the string:

```
>> str = "Leopold Auer was the teacher of Jascha Heifetz."
=> "Leopold Auer was the teacher of Jascha Heifetz."
>> violinists = str.scan(/([A-Z]\w+)\s+([A-Z]\w+)/)
=> [["Leopold", "Auer"], ["Jascha", "Heifetz"]]
```

This example nets you an array of arrays, where each inner array contains the first name and the last name of a person. Having each complete name stored in its own array makes it easy to iterate over the whole list of names, which we've conveniently stashed in the variable `violinists`:

```
violinists.each do |fname,lname|
  puts "#{lname}'s first name was #{fname}."
end
```

The output from this snippet is as follows:

```
Auer's first name was Leopold.
Heifetz's first name was Jascha.
```

The regexp used for names in this example is, of course, overly simple: it neglects hyphens, middle names, and so forth. But it's a good illustration of how to use captures with `scan`.

String#scan can also take a code block—and that technique can, at times, save you a step. `scan` yields its results to the block, and the details of the yielding depend on whether you're using parenthetical captures. Here's a scan-block-based rewrite of the previous code:

```
str.scan(/([A-Z]\w+)\s+([A-Z]\w+)/) do |fname, lname|
  puts "#{lname}'s first name was #{fname}."
end
```

Each time through the string, the block receives the captures in an array. If you're not doing any capturing, the block receives the matched substrings successively. Scanning for clumps of \w characters (\w is the character class consisting of letters, numbers, and underscore) might look like this

```
"one two three".scan(/\w+/) {|n| puts "Next number: #{n}" }
```

which would produce this output:

```
Next number: one
Next number: two
Next number: three
```

Note that if you provide a block, `scan` doesn't store the results up an array and return them; it sends each result to the block and then discards it. That way, you can scan through long strings, doing something with the results along the way, and avoid taking up memory with the substrings you've already seen and used.

Another common regexp-based string operation is `split`.

Even more string scanning with the `StringScanner` class

The standard library includes an extension called `strscan`, which provides the `StringScanner` class. `StringScanner` objects extend the available toolkit for scanning and examining strings. A `StringScanner` object maintains a pointer into the string, allowing for back-and-forth movement through the string using position and pointer semantics.

Here are some examples of the methods in `StringScanner`:

```
>> require 'strscan'                                        ⟵ Loads scanner library
=> true
>> ss = StringScanner.new("Testing string scanning")       ⟵ Creates scanner
=> #<StringScanner 0/23 @ "Testi...">
>> ss.scan_until(/ing/)                                     ⟵ Scans string until
=> "Testing"                                                    regexp matches
>> ss.pos                                                   ⟵ Examines new
=> 7                                                            pointer position
>> ss.peek(7)                                               ⟵ Looks at next 7 bytes (but
=> " string"                                                    doesn't advance pointer)
>> ss.unscan
=> #<StringScanner 0/23 @ "Testi...">                      ⟵ Undoes previous scan
>> ss.pos
=> 0
>> ss.skip(/Test/)                                          ⟵ Moves pointer past regexp
=> 4
>> ss.rest                                                  ⟵ Examines part of string
=> "ing string scanning"                                        to right of pointer
```

Using the notion of a pointer into the string, `StringScanner` lets you traverse across the string as well as examine what's already been matched and what remains. `String-Scanner` is a useful complement to the built-in string scanning facilities.

11.7.2 *String#split*

In keeping with its name, `split` splits a string into multiple substrings, returning those substrings as an array. `split` can take either a regexp or a plain string as the separator for the split operation. It's commonly used to get an array consisting of all the characters in a string. To do this, you use an empty regexp:

```
>> "Ruby".split(//)
=> ["R", "u", "b", "y"]
```

`split` is often used in the course of converting flat, text-based configuration files to Ruby data structures. Typically, this involves going through a file line by line and converting each line. A single-line conversion might look like this:

```
line = "first_name=david;last_name=black;country=usa"
record = line.split(/=|;/)
```

This leaves `record` containing an array:

```
["first_name", "david", "last_name", "black", "country", "usa"]
```

With a little more work, you can populate a hash with entries of this kind:

```
data = []
record = Hash[*line.split(/=|;/)]          ◁──    Use * to turn array into
data.push(record)                                 bare list to feed to Hash[ ]
```

If you do this for every line in a file, you'll have an array of hashes representing all the records. That array of hashes, in turn, can be used as the pivot point to a further operation—perhaps embedding the information in a report or feeding it to a library routine that can save it to a database table as a sequence of column/value pairs.

You can provide a second argument to `split`; this argument limits the number of items returned. In this example

```
>> "a,b,c,d,e".split(/,/,3)
=> ["a", "b", "c,d,e"]
```

`split` stops splitting once it has three elements to return and puts everything that's left (commas and all) in the third string.

In addition to breaking a string into parts by scanning and splitting, you can also change parts of a string with substitution operations, as you'll see next.

11.7.3   *sub/sub! and gsub/gsub!*

`sub` and `gsub` (along with their bang, in-place equivalents) are the most common tools for changing the contents of strings in Ruby. The difference between them is that `gsub` (*global sub*stitution) makes changes throughout a string, whereas `sub` makes at most one substitution.

SINGLE SUBSTITUTIONS WITH SUB

`sub` takes two arguments: a regexp (or string) and a replacement string. Whatever part of the string matches the regexp, if any, is removed from the string and replaced with the replacement string:

```
>> "typigraphical error".sub(/i/,"o")
=> "typographical error"
```

You can use a code block *instead of* the replacement-string argument. The block is called (yielded to) if there's a match. The call passes in the string being replaced as an argument:

```
>> "capitalize the first vowel".sub(/[aeiou]/) {|s| s.upcase }
=> "cApitalize the first vowel"
```

If you've done any parenthetical grouping, the global $n variables are set and available for use inside the block.

GLOBAL SUBSTITUTIONS WITH GSUB

`gsub` is like `sub`, except it keeps substituting as long as the pattern matches anywhere in the string. For example, here's how you can replace the first letter of every word in a string with the corresponding capital letter:

```
>> "capitalize every word".gsub(/\b\w/) {|s| s.upcase }
=> "Capitalize Every Word"
```

As with `sub`, `gsub` gives you access to the $n parenthetical capture variables in the code block.

USING THE CAPTURES IN A REPLACEMENT STRING

You can access the parenthetical captures by using a special notation consisting of backslash-escaped numbers. For example, you can correct an occurrence of a lower-case letter followed by an uppercase letter (assuming you're dealing with a situation where this is a mistake) like this:

```
>> "aDvid".sub(/([a-z])([A-Z])/, '\2\1')
=> "David"
```

Note the use of single quotation marks for the replacement string. With double quotes, you'd have to double the backslashes to escape the backslash character.

To double every word in a string, you can do something similar, but using `gsub`:

```
>> "double every word".gsub(/\b(\w+)/, '\1 \1')
=> "double double every every word word"
```

> ### A global capture variable pitfall
>
> Beware: You can use the global capture variables ($1, etc.) in your substitution string, but they may not do what you think they will. Specifically, you'll be vulnerable to left-over values for those variables. Consider this example:
>
> ```
> >> /(abc)/.match("abc")
> => #<MatchData "abc" 1:"abc">
> >> "aDvid".sub(/([a-z])([A-Z])/, "#{$2}#{$1}")
> => "abcvid"
> ```
>
> Here, $1 from the previous match ("abc") ended up infiltrating the substitution string in the second match. In general, sticking to the \1-style references to your captures is safer than using the global capture variables in `sub` and `gsub` substitution strings.

We'll conclude our look at regexp-based tools with two techniques having in common their dependence on the case equality operator (`===`): case statements (which aren't method calls but which do incorporate calls to the threequal operator) and `Enumerable#grep`.

11.7.4 Case equality and grep

As you know, all Ruby objects understand the `===` message. If it hasn't been overridden in a given class or for a given object, it's a synonym for `==`. If it has been overridden, it's whatever the new version makes it be.

Case equality for regular expressions is a match test: for any given *regexp* and *string*, *regexp* `===` *string* is true if *string* matches *regexp*. You can use `===` explicitly as a match test:

```
puts "Match!" if re.match(string)
puts "Match!" if string =~ re
puts "Match!" if re === string
```

And, of course, you have to use whichever test will give you what you need: `nil` or `MatchData` object for `match`; `nil` or integer offset for `=~`; `true` or `false` for `===`.

In case statements, `===` is used implicitly. To test for various pattern matches in a case statement, proceed along the following lines:

```
print "Continue? (y/n) "
answer = gets
case answer
when /^y/i
  puts "Great!"
when /^n/i
  puts "Bye!"
  exit
else
  puts "Huh?"
end
```

Each when clause is a call to `===`: `/^y/i === answer`, and so forth.

The other technique you've seen that uses the `===` method/operator, also implicitly, is `Enumerable#grep`. You can refer back to section 10.3.3. Here, we'll put the spotlight on a couple of aspects of how it handles strings and regular expressions.

`grep` does a filtering operation from an enumerable object based on the case equality operator (`===`), returning all the elements in the enumerable that return a true value when threequaled against grep's argument. Thus if the argument to `grep` is a regexp, the selection is based on pattern matches, as per the behavior of `Regexp#===`:

```
>> ["USA", "UK", "France", "Germany"].grep(/[a-z]/)
=> ["France", "Germany"]
```

You can accomplish the same thing with `select`, but it's a bit wordier:

```
["USA", "UK", "France", "Germany"].select {|c| /[a-z]/ === c }
```

`grep` uses the generalized threequal technique to make specialized `select` operations, including but not limited to those involving strings, concise and convenient.

You can also supply a code block to `grep`, in which case you get a combined select/map operation: the results of the filtering operation are yielded one at a time to the block, and the return value of the whole grep call is the cumulative result of those yields. For example, to select countries and then collect them in uppercase, you can do this:

```
>> ["USA", "UK", "France", "Germany"].grep(/[a-z]/) {|c| c.upcase }
=> ["FRANCE", "GERMANY"]
```

Keep in mind that `grep` selects based on the case equality operator (`===`), so it won't select anything other than strings when you give it a regexp as an argument—and there's no automatic conversion between numbers and strings. Thus if you try this

```
[1,2,3].grep(/1/)
```

you get back an empty array; the array has no string element that matches the regexp /1/, no element for which it's true that /1/ === element.

This brings us to the end of our survey of regular expressions and some of the methods that use them. There's more to learn; pattern matching is a sprawling subject. But this chapter has introduced you to much of what you're likely to need and see as you proceed with your study and use of Ruby.

11.8 Summary

In this chapter you've seen

- The underlying principles behind regular expression pattern matching
- The match and =~ techniques
- Character classes
- Parenthetical captures
- Quantifiers
- Anchors
- MatchData objects
- String/regexp interpolation and conversion
- Ruby methods that use regexps: scan, split, grep, sub, gsub

This chapter has introduced you to the fundamentals of regular expressions in Ruby, including character classes, parenthetical captures, and anchors. You've seen that regular expressions are objects—specifically, objects of the Regexp class—and that they respond to messages (such as "match"). We looked at the MatchData class, instances of which hold information about the results of a match operation. You've also learned how to interpolate strings into regular expressions (escaped or unescaped, depending on whether you want the special characters in the string to be treated as special in the regexp), how to instantiate a regexp from a string, and how to generate a string representation of a regexp.

Methods like String#scan, String#split, Enumerable#grep, and the "sub" family of String methods use regular expressions and pattern matching as a way of determining how their actions should be applied. Gaining knowledge about regular expressions gives you access not only to relatively simple matching methods but also to a suite of string-handling tools that otherwise wouldn't be usable.

As we continue our investigation of Ruby's built-in facilities, we'll move in chapter 12 to the subject of I/O operations in general and file handling in particular.

File and I/O operations

12

> **This chapter covers**
> - Keyboard input and screen output
> - The `IO` and `File` classes
> - Standard library file facilities, including `FileUtils` and `Pathname`
> - The `StringIO` and `open-uri` library features

As you'll see once you dive in, Ruby keeps even file and I/O operations object-oriented. Input and output streams, like the standard input stream or, for that matter, any file handle, are objects. Some I/O-related commands are more procedural: `puts`, for example, or the `system` method that lets you execute a system command. But `puts` is only procedural when it's operating on the standard output stream. When you `puts` a line to a file, you explicitly send the message "puts" to a `File` object.

The memory space of a Ruby program is a kind of idealized space, where objects come into existence and talk to each other. Given the fact that I/O and system command execution involve stepping outside this idealized space, Ruby does a lot to keep objects in the mix.

You'll see more discussion of standard library (as opposed to core) packages in this chapter than anywhere else in the book. That's because the file-handling facilities in the standard library—highlighted by the `FileUtils`, `Pathname`, and `StringIO` packages—are so powerful and so versatile that they've achieved a kind of quasi-core status. The odds are that if you do any kind of file-intensive Ruby programming, you'll get to the point where you load those packages almost without thinking about it.

12.1 How Ruby's I/O system is put together

The `IO` class handles all input and output streams either by itself or via its descendant classes, particularly `File`. To a large extent, `IO`'s API consists of wrappers around system library calls, with some enhancements and modifications. The more familiar you are with the C standard library, the more at home you'll feel with methods like `seek`, `getc`, and `eof?`. Likewise, if you've used another high-level language that also has a fairly close-fitting wrapper API around those library methods, you'll recognize their equivalents in Ruby. But even if you're not a systems or C programmer, you'll get the hang of it quickly.

12.1.1 The IO class

`IO` objects represent readable and/or writable connections to disk files, keyboards, screens, and other devices. You treat an `IO` object like any other object: you send it messages, and it executes methods and returns the results.

When a Ruby program starts up, it's aware of the standard input, output, and error streams. All three are encapsulated in instances of `IO`. You can use them to get a sense of how a simple `IO` object works:

```
>> STDERR.class                    ❶
=> IO
>> STDERR.puts("Problem!")         ❷
Problem!
=> nil
>> STDERR.write("Problem!\n")
Problem!                           ❸
=> 9
```

The constants `STDERR`, `STDIN`, and `STDOUT` (all of which will be covered in detail in section 12.1.3) are automatically set when the program starts. `STDERR` is an `IO` object ❶. If an `IO` object is open for writing (which `STDERR` is, because the whole point is to output status and error messages to it), you can call `puts` on it, and whatever you `puts` will be written to that `IO` object's output stream ❷. In the case of `STDERR`—at least, in the default startup situation—that's a fancy way of saying that it will be written to the screen.

In addition to `puts`, `IO` objects have the `print` method and a `write` method. If you `write` to an `IO` object, there's no automatic newline output (`write` is like `print` rather than `puts` in that respect), and the return value is the number of bytes written ❸.

`IO` is a Ruby class, and as a class it's entitled to mix in modules. And so it does. In particular, `IO` objects are enumerable.

12.1.2 *IO objects as enumerables*

An enumerable, as you know, must have an each method so that it can iterate. IO objects iterate based on the global input record separator, which, as you saw in connection with strings and their each_line method in section 10.7, is stored in the global variable $/.

In the following examples, Ruby's output is indicated by **bold** type; regular type indicates keyboard input. The code performs an iteration on STDIN, the standard input stream. (We'll look more closely at STDIN and friends in the next section.) At first, STDIN treats the newline character as the signal that one iteration has finished; it thus prints each line as you enter it:

```
>> STDIN.each {|line| p line }
This is line 1
```
"This is line 1\n"
```
This is line 2
```
"This is line 2\n"
```
All separated by $/, which is a newline character
```
"All separated by $/, which is a newline character\n"

But if you change the value of $/, STDIN's idea of what constitutes an iteration also changes. Terminate the first iteration with Ctrl-d (or Ctrl-c, if necessary!), and try this example:

```
>> $/ = "NEXT"
```
=> "NEXT"
```
>> STDIN.each {|line| p line}
First line
NEXT
```
"First line\nNEXT"
```
Next line
where "line" really means
until we see... NEXT
```
"\nNext line\nwhere \"line\" really means\nuntil we see... NEXT"

Here, Ruby accepts keyboard input until it hits the string "NEXT", at which point it considers the entry of the record to be complete.

So $/ determines an IO object's sense of "each." And because IO objects are enumerable, you can perform the usual enumerable operations on them. (You can assume that $/ has been returned to its original value in these examples.) The ^D notation indicates that the typist entered Ctrl-d at that point:

```
>> STDIN.select {|line| line =~ /\A[A-Z]/ }
We're only interested in
lines that begin with
Uppercase letters
^D
```
=> ["We're only interested in\n", "Uppercase letters\n"]
```
>> STDIN.map {|line| line.reverse }
senil esehT
terces a niatnoc
.egassem
^D
```
=> ["\nThese lines", "\ncontain a secret", "\nmessage."]

We'll come back to the enumerable behaviors of IO objects in the context of file handling in section 12.2. Meanwhile, the three basic IO objects—STDIN, STDOUT, and STDERR—are worth a closer look.

12.1.3 *STDIN, STDOUT, STDERR*

If you've written programs and/or shell scripts that use any kind of I/O piping, then you're probably familiar with the concept of the *standard* input, output, and error streams. They're basically defaults: unless told otherwise, Ruby assumes that all input will come from the keyboard, and all normal output will go to the terminal. *Assuming*, in this context, means that the unadorned, procedural I/O methods, like puts and gets, operate on STDOUT and STDIN, respectively.

Error messages and STDERR are a little more involved. Nothing goes to STDERR unless someone tells it to. So if you want to use STDERR for output, you have to name it explicitly:

```
if broken?
  STDERR.puts "There's a problem!"
end
```

In addition to the three constants, Ruby also gives you three global variables: $stdin, $stdout, and $stderr.

THE STANDARD I/O GLOBAL VARIABLES

The main difference between STDIN and $stdin (and the other pairs likewise) is that you're not supposed to reassign to the constant but you can reassign to the variable. The variables give you a way to modify default standard I/O stream behaviors without losing the original streams.

For example, perhaps you want all output going to a file, including standard out and standard error. You can achieve this with some assignments to the global variables. Save this code in outputs.rb:

```
record = File.open("/tmp/record", "w")
old_stdout = $stdout
$stdout = record
$stderr = $stdout
puts "This is a record"
z = 10/0
```

The first step is to open the file to which you want to write. (If you don't have a /tmp directory on your system, you can change the filename so that it points to a different path, as long as you have write permission to it.) Next, save the current $stdout to a variable, in case you want to switch back to it later.

Now comes the little dance of the I/O handles. First, $stdout is redefined as the output handle record. Next, $stderr is set equivalent to $stdout. At this point, any plain-old puts statement results in output being written to the file /tmp/record, because plain puts statements output to $stdout—and that's where $stdout is now pointing. $stderr output (like the error message resulting from a division by zero) also goes to the file, because $stderr, too, has been reassigned that file handle.

The result is that when you run the program, you see nothing on your screen; but /tmp/record looks like this:

```
This is a record
outputs.rb:6:in `/': divided by 0 (ZeroDivisionError)
    from outputs.rb:6:in `<main>'
```

Of course, you can also send standard output to one file and standard error to another. The global variables let you manipulate the streams any way you need to.

We'll move on to files soon, but while we're talking about I/O in general and the standard streams in particular, let's look more closely at the keyboard.

12.1.4 *A little more about keyboard input*

Keyboard input is accomplished, for the most part, with gets and getc. As you've seen, gets returns a single line of input. getc returns one character.

One difference between these two methods is that in the case of getc, you need to name your input stream explicitly:

```
line = gets
char = STDIN.getc
```

In both cases, input is buffered: you have to press Enter before anything happens. It's possible to make getc behave in an unbuffered manner so that it takes its input as soon as the character is struck, but there's no portable way to do this across Ruby platforms. (On UNIX-ish platforms, you can set the terminal to "raw" mode with the stty command. You need to use the system method, described in chapter 14, to do this from inside Ruby.)

If for some reason you've got $stdin set to something other than the keyboard, you can still read keyboard input by using STDIN explicitly as the receiver of gets:

```
line = STDIN.gets
```

Assuming you've followed the advice in the previous section and done all your standard I/O stream juggling through the use of the global variables rather than the constants, STDIN will still be the keyboard input stream, even if $stdin isn't.

At this point, we're going to turn to Ruby's facilities for reading, writing, and manipulating files.

12.2 *Basic file operations*

The built-in class File provides the facilities for manipulating files in Ruby. File is a subclass of IO, so File objects share certain properties with IO objects, although the File class adds and changes certain behaviors.

We'll look first at basic file operations, including opening, reading, writing, and closing files in various modes. Then, we'll look at a more "Rubyish" way to handle file reading and writing: with code blocks. After that, we'll go more deeply into the enumerability of files, and then end the section with an overview of some of the common exceptions and error messages you may get in the course of manipulating files.

12.2.1 *The basics of reading from files*

Reading from a file can be performed one byte at a time, a specified number of bytes at a time, or one line at a time (where *line* is defined by the $/ delimiter). You can also change the position of the next read operation in the file by moving forward or backward a certain number of bytes or by advancing the File object's internal pointer to a specific byte offset in the file.

All of these operations are performed courtesy of File objects. So, the first step is to create a File object. The simplest way to do this is with File.new. Pass a filename to this constructor, and, assuming the file exists, you'll get back a file handle opened for reading. The following examples involve a file called ticket2.rb that contains the code in listing 3.2 and that's stored in a directory called code:

```
>> f = File.new("code/ticket2.rb")
=> #<File:code/ticket2.rb>
```

(If the file doesn't exist, an exception will be raised.) At this point, you can use the file instance to read from the file. A number of methods are at your disposal. The absolute simplest is the read method; it reads in the entire file as a single string:

```
>> f.read
=> "class Ticket\n  def initialize(venue, date)\n
        @venue = venue\n    @date = date\n  end\n\n etc.
```

Although using read is tempting in many situations and appropriate in some, it can be inefficient and a bit sledgehammer-like when you need more granularity in your data reading and processing.

We'll look here at a large selection of Ruby's file-reading methods, handling them in groups: first line-based read methods and then byte-based read methods.

> **Close your file handles**
>
> When you're finished reading from and/or writing to a file, you need to close it. File objects have a close method (for example, f.close) for this purpose. You'll learn about a way to open files so that Ruby handles the file closing for you, by scoping the whole file operation to a code block. But if you're doing it the old-fashioned way, as in the examples involving File.new in this part of the chapter, you should close your files explicitly. (They'll get closed when you exit irb too, but it's good practice to close the ones you've opened.)

12.2.2 *Line-based file reading*

The easiest way to read the next line from a file is with gets:

```
>> f.gets
=> "class Ticket\n"
>> f.gets
=> "  def initialize(venue, date)\n"
>> f.gets
=> "    @venue = venue\n"
```

The `readline` method does much of what `gets` does: it reads one line from the file. The difference lies in how the two methods behave when you try to read beyond the end of a file: `gets` returns `nil`, and `readline` raises a fatal error. You can see the difference if you do a read on a File object to get to the end of the file and then try the two methods on the object:

```
>> f.read
=> "  def initialize(venue, date)\n     @venue = venue\n
   @date = date\n  end\n\n
   etc.
>> f.gets
=> nil
>> f.readline
EOFError: end of file reached
```

If you want to get the entire file at once as an array of lines, use `readlines` (a close relative of read). Note also the `rewind` operation, which moves the File object's internal position pointer back to the beginning of the file:

```
>> f.rewind
=> 0
>> f.readlines
=> ["class Ticket\n", "  def initialize(venue, date)\n",
   "    @venue = venue\n", "    @date = date\n" etc.
```

Keep in mind that File objects are enumerable. That means you can iterate through the lines one at a time rather than reading the whole file into memory. The `each` method of File objects (also known by the synonym `each_line`) serves this purpose:

```
>> f.each {|line| puts "Next line: #{line}" }
Next line: class Ticket
Next line:   def initialize(venue, date)
Next line:     @venue = venue
etc.
```

> **NOTE** In the previous example and several that follow, a rewind of the File object is assumed. If you're following along in irb, you'll want to type `f.rewind` to get back to the beginning of the file.

The enumerability of File objects merits a discussion of its own, and we'll look at it shortly. Meanwhile, let's look at byte-wise simple read operations.

12.2.3 *Byte- and character-based file reading*

If an entire line is too much, how about one character? The `getc` method reads and returns one character from the file:

```
>> f.getc
=> "c"
```

You can also "un-get" a character—that is, put a specific character back onto the file-input stream so it's the first character read on the next read:

```
>> f.getc
=> "c"
```

```
>> f.ungetc("X")
=> nil
>> f.gets
=> "Xlass Ticket\n"
```

Every character is represented by one or more bytes. How bytes map to characters depends on the encoding. Whatever the encoding, you can move byte-wise as well as character-wise through a file, using getbyte. Depending on the encoding, the number of bytes and the number of characters in your file may or may not be equal, and getc and getbyte, at a given position in the file, may or may not return the same thing.

Just as readline differs from gets in that readline raises a fatal error if you use it at the end of a file, the methods readchar and readbyte differ from getc and getbyte, respectively, in the same way. Assuming you've already read to the end of the File object f, you get the following results:

```
>> f.getc
=> nil
>> f.readchar
EOFError: end of file reached
>> f.getbyte
=> nil
>> f.readbyte
EOFError: end of file reached
```

During all these operations, the File object (like any IO object) has a sense of where it is in the input stream. As you've seen, you can easily rewind this internal pointer to the beginning of the file. You can also manipulate the pointer in some more fine-grained ways.

12.2.4 *Seeking and querying file position*

The File object has a sense of where in the file it has left off reading. You can both read and change this internal pointer explicitly, using the File object's pos (position) attribute and/or the seek method.

With pos, you can tell where in the file the pointer is currently pointing:

```
>> f.rewind
=> 0
>> f.pos
=> 0
>> f.gets
=> "class Ticket\n"
>> f.pos
=> 13
```

Here, the position is 0 after a rewind and 13 after a reading of one 13-byte line. You can assign to the position value, which moves the pointer to a specific location in the file:

```
>> f.pos = 10
=> 10
>> f.gets
=> "et\n"
```

The string returned is what the `File` object considers a "line" as of byte 10: everything from that position onward until the next occurrence of newline (or, strictly speaking, of $/).

The `seek` method lets you move around in a file by moving the position pointer to a new location. The location can be a specific offset into the file, or it can be relative to either the current pointer position or the end of the file. You specify what you want using special constants from the `IO` class:

```
f.seek(20, IO::SEEK_SET)
f.seek(15, IO::SEEK_CUR)
f.seek(-10, IO::SEEK_END)
```

In this example, the first line seeks to byte 20. The second line advances the pointer 15 bytes from its current position, and the last line seeks to 10 bytes before the end of the file. Using `IO::SEEK_SET` is optional; a plain `f.seek(20)` does the same thing (as does `f.pos = 20`).

We've looked at several ways to read from files, starting with the all-at-once read method, progressing through the line-by-line approach, and winding up with the most fine-grained reads based on character and position. All of these file-reading techniques involve `File` objects—that is, instances of the `File` class. That class itself also offers some reading techniques.

12.2.5 *Reading files with File class methods*

A little later, you'll see more of the facilities available as class methods of `File`. For now, we'll look at two methods that handle file reading at the class level: `File.read` and `File.readlines`.

These two methods do the same thing their same-named instance-method counterparts do; but instead of creating an instance, you use the `File` class, the method name, and the name of the file:

```
full_text = File.read("myfile.txt")
lines_of_text = File.readlines("myfile.txt")
```

In the first case, you get a string containing the entire contents of the file. In the second case, you get an array of lines.

These two class methods exist purely for convenience. They take care of opening and closing the file handle for you; you don't have to do any system-level housekeeping. Most of the time, you'll want to do something more complex and/or more efficient than reading the entire contents of a file into a string or an array at one time. Given that even the `read` and `readlines` instance methods are relatively coarse-grained tools, if you decide to read a file in all at once, you may as well go all the way and use the class-method versions.

You now have a good toolkit for reading files and dealing with the results. At this point, we'll turn to the other side of the equation: writing to files.

> ### Low-level I/O methods
>
> In addition to the various I/O and `File` methods we'll look at closely here, the `IO` class gives you a toolkit of system-level methods with which you can do low-level I/O operations. These include `sysseek`, `sysread`, and `syswrite`. These methods correspond to the system calls on which some of the higher-level methods are built.
>
> The `sys-` methods perform raw, unbuffered data operations and shouldn't be mixed with higher-level methods. Here's an example of what not to do:
>
> ```
> File.open("output.txt", "w") do |f|
>   f.print("Hello")
>   f.syswrite(" there!")
> end
> puts File.read("output.txt")
> ```
>
> If you run this little program, here's what you'll see:
>
> ```
> syswrite.rb:3: warning: syswrite for buffered IO
>  there!Hello
> ```
>
> In addition to a warning, you get the second string (the one written with `syswrite`) stuck in the file before the first string. That's because `syswrite` and `print` don't operate according to the same rules and don't play nicely together. It's best to stick with the higher-level methods unless you have a particular reason to use the others.

12.2.6 Writing to files

Writing to a file involves using `puts`, `print`, or `write` on a `File` object that's opened in write or append mode. Write mode is indicated by `w` as the second argument to `new`. In this mode, the file is created (assuming you have permission to create it); if it existed already, the old version is overwritten. In append mode (indicated by `a`), whatever you write to the file is appended to what's already there. If the file doesn't exist yet, opening it in append mode creates it.

This example performs some simple write and append operations, pausing along the way to use the mighty `File.read` to check the contents of the file:

```
>> f = File.new("data.out", "w")
=> #<File:data.out>
>> f.puts "David A. Black, Rubyist"
=> nil
>> f.close
=> nil
>> puts File.read("data.out")
David A. Black, Rubyist
=> nil
>> f = File.new("data.out", "a")
=> #<File:data.out>
>> f.puts "Yukihiro Matsumoto, Ruby creator"
=> nil
>> f.close
=> nil
```

```
>> puts File.read("data.out")
David A. Black, Rubyist
Yukihiro Matsumoto, Ruby creator
```

The return value of a call to puts on a File object is the same as the return value of any call to puts: nil. The same is true of print. If you use the lower-level write method, which is an instance method of the IO class (and therefore available to File objects, because File inherits from IO), the return value is the number of bytes written to the file.

Ruby lets you economize on explicit closing of File objects—and enables you to keep your code nicely encapsulated—by providing a way to perform file operations inside a code block. We'll look at this elegant and common technique next.

12.2.7 *Using blocks to scope file operations*

Using File.new to create a File object has the disadvantage that you end up having to close the file yourself. Ruby provides an alternate way to open files that puts the housekeeping task of closing the file in the hands of Ruby: File.open with a code block.

If you call File.open with a code block, the block receives the File object as its single argument. You use that File object inside the block. When the block ends, the File object is automatically closed.

Here's an example in which a file is opened and read in line by line for processing. First, create a file called records.txt containing one record per line:

```
Pablo Casals|Catalan|cello|1876-1973
Jascha Heifetz|Russian-American|violin|1901-1988
Emanuel Feuermann|Austrian-American|cello|1902-1942
```

Now write the code that will read this file, line by line, and report on what it finds. It uses the block-based version of File.open:

```
File.open("records.txt") do |f|
  while record = f.gets
    name, nationality, instrument, dates = record.chomp.split('|')
    puts "#{name} (#{dates}), who was #{nationality},
    played #{instrument}. "
  end
end
```

The program consists entirely of a call to File.open along with its code block. (If you call File.open without a block, it acts like File.new.) The block parameter, f, receives the File object. Inside the block, the file is read one line at a time using f. The while test succeeds as long as lines are coming in from the file. When the program hits the end of the input file, gets returns nil, and the while condition fails.

Inside the while loop, the current line is chomped so as to remove the final newline character, if any, and split on the pipe character. The resulting values are stored in the four local variables on the left, and those variables are then interpolated into a pretty-looking report for output:

```
Pablo Casals (1876-1973), who was Catalan, played cello.
Jascha Heifetz (1901-1988), who was Russian-American, played violin.
Emanuel Feuermann (1902-1942), who was Austrian-American, played cello.
```

The use of a code block to scope a `File.open` operation is common. It sometimes leads to misunderstandings, though. In particular, remember that the block that provides you with the `File` object doesn't do anything else. There's no implicit loop. If you want to read what's in the file, you still have to do something like a `while` loop using the `File` object. It's just nice that you get to do it inside a code block and that you don't have to worry about closing the `File` object afterward.

And don't forget that `File` objects are enumerable.

12.2.8 *File enumerability*

Thanks to the fact that `Enumerable` is among the ancestors of `File`, you can replace the `while` idiom in the previous example with `each`:

```
File.open("records.txt") do |f|
  f.each do |record|
    name, nationality, instrument, dates = record.chomp.split('|')
    puts "#{name} (#{dates}), who was #{nationality},
    played #{instrument}. "
  end
end
```

Ruby gracefully stops iterating when it hits the end of the file.

As enumerables, `File` objects can perform many of the same functions that arrays, hashes, and other collections do. Understanding how file enumeration works requires a slightly different mental model: whereas an array exists already and walks through its elements in the course of iteration, `File` objects have to manage line-by-line reading behind the scenes when you iterate through them. But the similarity of the idioms—the common use of the methods from `Enumerable`—means you don't have to think in much detail about the file-reading process when you iterate through a file.

Most important, don't forget that you can iterate through files and address them as enumerables. It's tempting to read a whole file into an array and then process the array. But why not just iterate on the file and avoid wasting the space required to hold the file's contents in memory?

You could, for example, read in an entire file of plain-text records and then perform an inject operation on the resulting array to get the average of a particular field:

```
# Sample record in members.txt:
# David Black male 55
count = 0
total_ages = File.readlines("members.txt").inject(0) do |total,line|
  count += 1
  fields = line.split
  age = fields[3].to_i
  total + age
end
puts "Average age of group: #{total_ages / count}."
```

But you can also perform the inject operation directly on the `File` object:

```
count = 0
total_ages = File.open("members.txt") do |f|
  f.inject(0) do |total,line|
    count += 1
    fields = line.split
    age = fields[3].to_i
    total + age
  end
end
puts "Average age of group: #{total_ages / count}."
```

With this approach, no intermediate array is created. The `File` object does its own work.

One way or another, you'll definitely run into cases where something goes wrong with your file operations. Ruby will leave you in no doubt that there's a problem, but it's helpful to see in advance what some of the possible problems are and how they're reported.

12.2.9 *File I/O exceptions and errors*

When something goes wrong with file operations, Ruby raises an exception. Most of the errors you'll get in the course of working with files can be found in the `Errno` namespace: `Errno::EACCES` (permission denied), `Errno::ENOENT` (no such entity—a file or directory), `Errno:EISDIR` (is a directory—an error you get when you try to open a directory as if it were a file), and others. You'll always get a message along with the exception:

```
>> File.open("no_file_with_this_name")
Errno::ENOENT: No such file or directory - no_file_with_this_name
>> f = File.open("/tmp")
=> #<File:/tmp>
>> f.gets
Errno::EISDIR: Is a directory - /tmp
>> File.open("/var/root")
Errno::EACCES: Permission denied - /var/root
```

The `Errno` family of errors includes not only file-related errors but also other system errors. The underlying system typically maps errors to integers (for example, on Linux, the "not a directory" error is represented by the C macro `ENOTDIR`, which is defined as the number 20). Ruby's `Errno` class wraps these error-to-number mappings in a bundle of exception classes.

Each `Errno` exception class contains knowledge of the integer to which its corresponding system error maps. You can get these numbers via the `Errno` constant of each `Errno` class—and if that sounds obscure, an example will make it clearer:

```
>> Errno::ENOTDIR::Errno
=> 20
```

You'll rarely, if ever, have to concern yourself with the mapping of Ruby's `Errno` exception classes to the integers to which your operating system maps errors. But you should be aware that any `Errno` exception is basically a system error percolating up through Ruby.

These aren't Ruby-specific errors, like syntax errors or missing method errors; they involve things going wrong at the system level. In these situations, Ruby is just the messenger.

Let's go back to what you can do when things go right. We'll look next at some ways in which you can ask IO and File objects for information about themselves and their state.

12.3 *Querying IO and File objects*

IO and File objects can be queried on numerous criteria. The IO class includes some query methods; the File class adds more.

One class and one module closely related to File also get into the act: File::Stat and FileTest. File::Stat returns objects whose attributes correspond to the fields of the stat structure defined by the C library call stat(2). Some of these fields are system-specific and not meaningful on all platforms. The FileTest module offers numerous methods for getting status information about files.

The File class also has some query methods. In some cases, you can get the same information about a file several ways:

```
>> File.size("code/ticket2.rb")
=> 219
>> FileTest.size("code/ticket2.rb")
=> 219
>> File::Stat.new("code/ticket2.rb").size
=> 219
```

In what follows, we'll look at a large selection of query methods. In some cases, they're available in more than one way.

12.3.1 *Getting information from the File class and the FileTest module*

File and FileTest offer numerous query methods that can give you lots of information about a file. These are the main categories of query: *What is it? What can it do? How big is it?*

The methods available as class methods of File and FileTest are almost identical; they're mostly aliases of each other. The examples will only use FileTest, but you can use File too.

Here are some questions you might want to ask about a given file, along with the techniques for asking them. All of these methods return either true or false except size, which returns an integer. Keep in mind that these file-testing methods are happy to take directories, links, sockets, and other filelike entities as their arguments. They're not restricted to regular files:

- *Does a file exist?*

    ```
    FileTest.exist?("/usr/local/src/ruby/README")
    ```

- *Is the file a directory? A regular file? A symbolic link?*

    ```
    FileTest.directory?("/home/users/dblack/info")
    FileTest.file?("/home/users/dblack/info")
    FileTest.symlink?("/home/users/dblack/info")
    ```

This family of query methods also includes `blockdev?`, `pipe?`, `chardev?`, and `socket?`.

■   *Is a file readable? Writable? Executable?*

```
FileTest.readable?("/tmp")
FileTest.writable?("/tmp")
FileTest.executable?("/home/users/dblack/setup")
```

This family of query methods includes `world_readable?` and `world_writable?`, which test for more permissive permissions. It also includes variants of the basic three methods with `_real` appended. These test the permissions of the script's actual runtime ID as opposed to its effective user ID.

■   *What is the size of this file? Is the file empty (zero bytes)?*

```
FileTest.size("/home/users/dblack/setup")
FileTest.zero?("/tmp/tempfile")
```

Getting file information with Kernel#test

Among the top-level methods at your disposal (that is, private methods of the `Kernel` module, which you can call anywhere without a receiver, like `puts`) is a method called `test`. You use `test` by passing it two arguments: the first represents the test, and the second is a file or directory. The choice of test is indicated by a character. You can represent the value using the `?c` notation, where `c` is the character, or as a one-character string.

Here's an example that finds out whether `/tmp` exists:

```
test ?e, "/tmp"
```

Other common test characters include `?d` (the test is true if the second argument is a directory), `?f` (true if the second argument is a regular file), and `?z` (true if the second argument is a zero-length file). For every test available through `Kernel#test`, there's usually a way to get the result by calling a method of one of the classes discussed in this section. But the `Kernel#test` notation is shorter and can be handy for that reason.

In addition to the query and Boolean methods available through `FileTest` (and `File`), you can also consult objects of the `File::Stat` class for file information.

12.3.2   *Deriving file information with File::Stat*

`File::Stat` objects have attributes corresponding to the stat structure in the standard C library. You can create a `File::Stat` object in either of two ways: with the `new` method or with the `stat` method on an existing `File` object:

```
>> File::Stat.new("code/ticket2.rb")
=> #<File::Stat dev=0x1000002, ino=11531534, mode=0100644,
nlink=1, uid=501, gid=20, rdev=0x0, size=219, blksize=4096,
blocks=8, atime=2014-03-23 08:31:49 -0400,
mtime=2014-02-25 06:24:43 -0500, ctime=2014-02-25 06:24:43 -0500>

>> File.open("code/ticket2.rb") {|f| f.stat }
```

Same output

The screen output from the `File::Stat.new` method shows you the attributes of the object, including its times of creation (`ctime`), last modification (`mtime`), and last access (`atime`).

> **TIP** The code block given to `File.open` in this example, `{ |f| f.stat }`, evaluates to the last expression inside it. Because the last (indeed, only) expression is `f.stat`, the value of the block is a `File::Stat` object. In general, when you use `File.open` with a code block, the call to `File.open` returns the last value from the block. Called without a block, `File.open` (like `File.new`) returns the newly created `File` object.

Much of the information available from `File::Stat` is built off of UNIX-like metrics, such as inode number, access mode (permissions), and user and group ID. The relevance of this information depends on your operating system. We won't go into the details here because it's not cross-platform; but whatever information your system maintains about files is available if you need it.

Manipulating and querying files often involves doing likewise to directories. Ruby provides facilities for directory operations in the `Dir` class. You'll also see such operations in some of the standard library tools we'll discuss a little later. First, let's look at `Dir`.

12.4 Directory manipulation with the Dir class

Like `File`, the `Dir` class provides useful class and instance methods. To create a `Dir` instance, you pass a directory path to `new`:

```
>> d = Dir.new("/usr/local/src/ruby/lib/minitest")    ◁─┐  Adjust path as needed
=> #<Dir:/usr/local/src/ruby/lib/minitest>              │  for your system
```

The most common and useful `Dir`-related technique is iteration through the entries (files, links, other directories) in a directory.

12.4.1 Reading a directory's entries

You can get hold of the entries in one of two ways: using the `entries` method or using the `glob` technique. The main difference is that *globbing* the directory doesn't return hidden entries, which on many operating systems (including all UNIX-like systems) means entries whose names start with a period. Globbing also allows for wildcard matching and for recursive matching in subdirectories.

THE ENTRIES METHOD
Both the `Dir` class itself and instances of the `Dir` class can give you a directory's entries. Given the instance of `Dir` created earlier, you can do this:

```
>> d.entries
=> [".", "..", ".document", "autorun.rb", "benchmark.rb", "hell.rb",
"mock.rb", "parallel_each.rb", "pride.rb", "README.txt", "spec.rb",
"unit.rb"]
```

Or you can use the class-method approach:

```
>> Dir.entries("/usr/local/src/ruby/lib/minitest")
=> [".", "..", ".document", "autorun.rb", "benchmark.rb", "hell.rb",
"mock.rb", "parallel_each.rb", "pride.rb", "README.txt", "spec.rb",
"unit.rb"]
```

Note that the single- and double-dot entries (current directory and parent directory, respectively) are present, as is the hidden .document entry. If you want to iterate through the entries, only processing files, you need to make sure you filter out the names starting with dots.

Let's say we want to add up the sizes of all non-hidden regular files in a directory. Here's a first iteration (we'll develop a shorter one later):

```
d = Dir.new("/usr/local/src/ruby/lib/minitest")
entries = d.entries
entries.delete_if {|entry| entry =~ /^\./ }
entries.map! {|entry| File.join(d.path, entry) }
entries.delete_if {|entry| !File.file?(entry) }
print "Total bytes: "
puts entries.inject(0) {|total, entry| total + File.size(entry) }
```

First, we create a Dir object for the target directory and grab its entries. Next comes a sequence of manipulations on the array of entries. Using the delete_if array method, we remove all that begin with a dot. Then, we do an in-place mapping of the entry array so that each entry includes the full path to the file. This is accomplished with two useful methods: the instance method Dir#path, which returns the original directory path underlying this particular Dir instance (/usr/local/src/ruby/lib/minitest); and File.join, which joins the path to the filename with the correct separator (usually /, but it's somewhat system-dependent).

Now that the entries have been massaged to represent full pathnames, we do another delete_if operation to delete all the entries that aren't regular files, as measured by the File.file? test method. The entries array now contains full pathnames of all the regular files in the original directory. The last step is to add up their sizes, a task for which inject is perfectly suited.

Among other ways to shorten this code, you can use directory globbing instead of the entries method.

DIRECTORY GLOBBING
Globbing in Ruby takes its semantics largely from shell globbing, the syntax that lets you do things like this in the shell:

```
$ ls *.rb
$ rm *.?xt
$ for f in [A-Z]*    # etc.
```

The details differ from one shell to another, of course; but the point is that this whole family of name-expansion techniques is where Ruby gets its globbing syntax. An asterisk represents a wildcard match on any number of characters; a question mark represents one wildcard character. Regexp-style character classes are available for matching.

To glob a directory, you can use the `Dir.glob` method or `Dir.[]` (square brackets). The square-bracket version of the method allows you to use index-style syntax, as you would with the square-bracket method on an array or hash. You get back an array containing the result set:

```
>> Dir["/usr/local/src/ruby/include/ruby/r*.h"]
=> ["/usr/local/src/ruby/include/ruby/re.h", "/usr/local/src/ruby/include/
   ruby/regex.h", "/usr/local/src/ruby/include/ruby/ruby.h"]
```

The `glob` method is largely equivalent to the `[]` method but a little more versatile: you can give it not only a glob pattern but also one or more flag arguments that control its behavior. For example, if you want to do a case-insensitive glob, you can pass the `File::FNM_CASEFOLD` flag:

```
Dir.glob("info*")        # []
Dir.glob("info", File::FNM_CASEFOLD   # ["Info", "INFORMATION"]
```

Another useful flag is `FNM_DOTMATCH`, which includes hidden dot files in the results.

If you want to use two flags, you combine them with the bitwise OR operator, which consists of a single pipe character. In this example, progressively more files are found as the more permissive flags are added:

```
>> Dir.glob("*info*")
=> []
>> Dir.glob("*info*", File::FNM_DOTMATCH)
=> [".information"]
>> Dir.glob("*info*", File::FNM_DOTMATCH | File::FNM_CASEFOLD)
=> [".information", ".INFO", "Info"]
```

The flags are, literally, numbers. The value of `File::FNM_DOTMATCH`, for example, is 4. The specific numbers don't matter (they derive ultimately from the flags in the system library function `fnmatch`). What does matter is the fact that they're exponents of two accounts for the use of the OR operation to combine them.

> **NOTE** As you can see from the first two lines of the previous example, a `glob` operation on a directory can find nothing and still not complain. It gives you an empty array. Not finding anything isn't considered a failure when you're globbing.

Globbing with square brackets is the same as globbing without providing any flags. In other words, doing this

```
Dir["*info*"]
```

is like doing this

```
Dir.glob("*info*", 0)
```

which, because the default is that none of the flags is in effect, is like doing this

```
Dir.glob("*info*")
```

The square-bracket method of `Dir` gives you a kind of shorthand for the most common case. If you need more granularity, use `Dir.glob`.

By default, globbing doesn't include filenames that start with dots. Also, as you can see, globbing returns full pathnames, not just filenames. Together, these facts let us trim down the file-size totaling example:

```
dir = "/usr/local/src/ruby/lib/minitest"
entries = Dir["#{dir}/*"].select {|entry| File.file?(entry) }
print "Total bytes: "
puts entries.inject(0) {|total, entry| total + File.size(entry) }
```

With their exclusion of dot files and their inclusion of full paths, glob results often correspond more closely than `Dir.entries` results to the ways that many of us deal with files and directories on a day-to-day basis.

There's more to directory management than just seeing what's there. We'll look next at some techniques that let you go more deeply into the process.

12.4.2 *Directory manipulation and querying*

The `Dir` class includes several query methods for getting information about a directory or about the current directory, as well as methods for creating and removing directories. These methods are, like so many, best illustrated by example.

Here, we'll create a new directory (`mkdir`), navigate to it (`chdir`), add and examine a file, and delete the directory (`rmdir`):

```
newdir = "/tmp/newdir"                          ◄──❶
newfile = "newfile"
Dir.mkdir(newdir)
Dir.chdir(newdir) do                            ◄──❷
  File.open(newfile, "w") do |f|
    f.puts "Sample file in new directory"       ◄──❸
  end
  puts "Current directory: #{Dir.pwd}"          ◄──❹
  puts "Directory listing: "
  p Dir.entries(".")
  File.unlink(newfile)                          ◄──❺
end
Dir.rmdir(newdir)                               ◄──❻
print "Does #{newdir} still exist? "
if File.exist?(newdir)                          ◄──❼
  puts "Yes"
else
  puts "No"
end
```

After initializing a couple of convenience variables ❶, we create the new directory with `mkdir`. With `Dir.chdir`, we change to that directory; also, using a block with `chdir` means that after the block exits, we're back in the previous directory ❷. (Using `chdir` without a block changes the current directory until it's explicitly changed back.)

As a kind of token directory-populating step, we create a single file with a single line in it ❸. We then examine the current directory name using `Dir.pwd` and look at a listing of the entries in the directory ❹. Next, we unlink (delete) the recently created file ❺, at which point the chdir block is finished.

Back in whatever directory we started in, we remove the sample directory using Dir.rmdir (also callable as unlink or delete) ❻. Finally, we test for the existence of newdir, fully expecting an answer of No (because rmdir would have raised a fatal error if it hadn't found the directory and successfully removed it) ❼.

As promised in the introduction to this chapter, we'll now look at some standard library facilities for manipulating and handling files.

12.5   *File tools from the standard library*

File handling is an area where the standard library's offerings are particularly rich. Accordingly, we'll delve into those offerings more deeply here than anywhere else in the book. This isn't to say that the rest of the standard library isn't worth getting to know, but that the extensions available for file manipulation are so central to how most people do file manipulation in Ruby that you can't get a firm grounding in the process without them.

We'll look at the versatile FileUtils package first and then at the more specialized but useful Pathname class. Next you'll meet StringIO, a class whose objects are, essentially, strings with an I/O interface; you can rewind them, seek through them, getc from them, and so forth. Finally, we'll explore open-uri, a package that lets you "open" URIs and read them into strings as easily as if they were local files.

12.5.1   *The FileUtils module*

The FileUtils module provides some practical and convenient methods that make it easy to manipulate files from Ruby in a concise manner in ways that correspond to familiar system commands. The methods' names will be particularly familiar to users of UNIX and UNIX-like operating systems. They can be easily learned by those who don't know them already.

Many of the methods in FileUtils are named in honor of system commands with particular command-line options. For example, FileUtils.rm_rf emulates the rm -rf command (force unconditional recursive removal of a file or directory). You can create a symbolic link from *filename* to *linkname* with FileUtils.ln_s(filename, linkname), much in the manner of the ln -s command.

As you can see, some of the methods in FileUtils are operating-system specific. If your system doesn't support symbolic links, then ln_s won't work. But the majority of the module's methods are portable. We'll look here at examples of some of the most useful ones.

COPYING, MOVING, AND DELETING FILES

FileUtils provides several concise, high-level methods for these operations. The cp method emulates the traditional UNIX method of the same name. You can cp one file to another or several files to a directory:

```
>> require 'fileutils'
=> true
>> FileUtils.cp("baker.rb", "baker.rb.bak")
=> nil
>> FileUtils.mkdir("backup")                        <--①
=> ["backup"]
>> FileUtils.cp(["ensure.rb", "super.rb"], "backup")
=> ["ensure.rb", "super.rb"]
>> Dir["backup/*"]                                  <--②
=> ["backup/ensure.rb", "backup/super.rb"]
```

This example also illustrates the mkdir method ① as well as the use of Dir#[] ② to verify the presence of the copied files in the new backup directory.

Just as you can copy files, you can also move them, individually or severally:

```
>> FileUtils.mv("baker.rb.bak", "backup")
=> 0
>> Dir["backup/*"]
=> ["backup/baker.rb.bak", "backup/ensure.rb", "backup/super.rb"]
```

And you can remove files and directories easily:

```
>> File.exist?("backup/super.rb")
=> true
>> FileUtils.rm("./backup/super.rb")
=> ["./backup/super.rb"]
>> File.exist?("backup/super.rb")
=> false
```

The rm_rf method recursively and unconditionally removes a directory:

```
>> FileUtils.rm_rf("backup")
=> ["backup"]
>> File.exist?("backup")
=> false
```

FileUtils gives you a useful toolkit for quick and easy file maintenance. But it goes further: it lets you try commands without executing them.

THE DRYRUN AND NOWRITE MODULES

If you want to see what would happen if you were to run a particular FileUtils command, you can send the command to FileUtils::DryRun. The output of the method you call is a representation of a UNIX-style system command, equivalent to what you'd get if you called the same method on FileUtils:

```
>> FileUtils::DryRun.rm_rf("backup")
rm -rf backup
=> nil
>> FileUtils::DryRun.ln_s("backup", "backup_link")
ln -s backup backup_link
=> nil
```

If you want to make sure you don't accidentally delete, overwrite, or move files, you can give your commands to FileUtils::NoWrite, which has the same interface as FileUtils but doesn't perform any disk-writing operations:

```
>> FileUtils::NoWrite.rm("backup/super.rb")
=> nil
>> File.exist?("backup/super.rb")
=> true
```

You'll almost certainly find `FileUtils` useful in many situations. Even if you're not familiar with the UNIX-style commands on which many of `FileUtils`'s method names are based, you'll learn them quickly, and it will save you having to dig deeper into the lower-level I/O and file libraries to get your tasks done.

Next we'll look at another file-related offering from the standard library: the pathname extension.

12.5.2 *The Pathname class*

The `Pathname` class lets you create `Pathname` objects and query and manipulate them so you can determine, for example, the basename and extension of a pathname, or iterate through the path as it ascends the directory structure.

`Pathname` objects also have a large number of methods that are proxied from `File`, `Dir`, `IO`, and other classes. We won't look at those methods here; we'll stick to the ones that are uniquely `Pathname`'s.

First, start with a `Pathname` object:

```
>> require 'pathname'
=> true
>> path = Pathname.new("/Users/dblack/hacking/test1.rb")
=> #<Pathname:/Users/dblack/hacking/test1.rb>
```

When you call methods on a `Pathname` object, you often get back another `Pathname` object. But the new object always has its string representation visible in its own `inspect` string. If you want to see the string on its own, you can use `to_s` or do a `puts` on the pathname.

Here are two ways to examine the basename of the path:

```
>> path.basename
=> #<Pathname:test1.rb>
>> puts path.basename
test1.rb
```

You can also examine the directory that contains the file or directory represented by the pathname:

```
>> path.dirname
=> #<Pathname:/Users/dblack/hacking>
```

If the last segment of the path has an extension, you can get the extension from the `Pathname` object:

```
>> path.extname
=> ".rb"
```

The `Pathname` object can also walk up its file and directory structure, truncating itself from the right on each iteration, using the `ascend` method and a code block:

```
>> path.ascend do |dir|
?>    puts "Next level up: #{dir}"
>> end
```

Here's the output:

```
Next level up: /Users/dblack/hacking/test1.rb
Next level up: /Users/dblack/hacking
Next level up: /Users/dblack
Next level up: /Users
Next level up: /
```

The key behavioral trait of `Pathname` objects is that they return other `Pathname` objects. That means you can extend the logic of your pathname operations without having to convert back and forth from pure strings. By way of illustration, here's the last example again, but altered to take advantage of the fact that what's coming through in the block parameter `dir` on each iteration isn't a string (even though it prints out like one) but a `Pathname` object:

```
>> path = Pathname.new("/Users/dblack/hacking/test1.rb")
=> #<Pathname:/Users/dblack/hacking/test1.rb>
>> path.ascend do |dir|
?>    puts "Ascended to #{dir.basename}"
>> end
```

The output is

```
Ascended to test1.rb
Ascended to hacking
Ascended to dblack
Ascended to Users
Ascended to /
```

The fact that `dir` is always a `Pathname` object means that it's possible to call the basename method on it. It's true that you can always call `File.basename(string)` on any string. But the `Pathname` class pinpoints the particular knowledge that a path might be assumed to encapsulate about itself and makes it available to you via simple method calls.

We'll look next at a different and powerful standard library class: `StringIO`.

12.5.3 *The StringIO class*

The `StringIO` class allows you to treat strings like `IO` objects. You can seek through them, rewind them, and so forth.

The advantage conferred by `StringIO` is that you can write methods that use an `IO` object API, and those methods will be able to handle strings. That can be useful for testing, as well as in a number of real runtime situations.

Let's say, for example, that you have a module that decomments a file: it reads from one file and writes everything that isn't a comment to another file. Here's what such a module might look like:

```
module DeCommenter
  def self.decomment(infile, outfile, comment_re = /\A\s*#/)
    infile.each do |inline|
      outfile.print inline unless inline =~ comment_re
    end
  end
end
```

The `DeCommenter.decomment` method expects two open file handles: one it can read from and one it can write to. It also takes a regular expression, which has a default value. The regular expression determines whether each line in the input is a comment. Every line that does *not* match the regular expression is printed to the output file.

A typical use case for the `DeCommenter` module would look like this:

```
File.open("myprogram.rb") do |inf|
  File.open("myprogram.rb.out", "w") do |outf|
    DeCommenter.decomment(inf, outf)
  end
end
```

In this example, we're taking the comments out of the hypothetical program file myprogram.rb.

What if you want to write a test for the `DeCommenter` module? Testing file transformations can be difficult because you need to maintain the input file as part of the test and also make sure you can write to the output file—which you then have to read back in. `StringIO` makes it easier by allowing all of the code to stay in one place without the need to read or write actual files.

> ### Testing using real files
> If you want to run tests on file input and output using real files, Ruby's `tempfile` class can help you. It's a standard-library feature, so you have to `require 'temp-file'`. Then, you create temporary files with the constructor, passing in a name that Ruby munges into a unique filename. For example:
>
> ```
> tf = Tempfile.new("my_temp_file").
> ```
>
> You can then write to and read from the file using the `File` object `tf`.

To use the decommenter with `StringIO`, save the module to decommenter.rb. Then, create a second file, decomment-demo.rb, in the same directory and with the following contents:

```
require 'stringio'              ❶
require_relative 'decommenter'
string = <<EOM
# This is a comment.
This isn't a comment.           ❷
# This is.
   # So is this.
```

```
This is also not a comment.
EOM                                          ②
infile = StringIO.new(string)            ←  ③
outfile = StringIO.new("")                       ④
DeCommenter.decomment(infile,outfile)        ←
puts "Test succeeded" if outfile.string == <<EOM    ←  ⑤
This isn't a comment.
This is also not a comment.
EOM
```

After loading both the `stringio` library and the decommenter code ❶, the program sets `string` to a five-line string (created using a here-document) containing a mix of comment lines and non-comment lines ❷. Next, two `StringIO` objects are created: one that uses the contents of `string` as its contents, and one that's empty ❸. The empty one represents the output file.

Next comes the call to `DeCommenter.decomment` ❹. The module treats its two arguments as `File` or `IO` objects, reading from one and printing to the other. `StringIO` objects happily behave like `IO` objects, and the filtering takes place between them. When the filtering is done, you can check explicitly to make sure that what was written to the output "file" is what you expected ❺. The original and changed contents are both physically present in the same file, which makes it easier to see what the test is doing and also easier to change it.

Another useful standard library feature is the `open-uri` library.

12.5.4 *The open-uri library*

The `open-uri` standard library package lets you retrieve information from the network using the HTTP and HTTPS protocols as easily as if you were reading local files. All you do is require the library (`require 'open-uri'`) and use the `Kernel#open` method with a URI as the argument. You get back a `StringIO` object containing the results of your request:

```
require 'open-uri'
rubypage = open("http://rubycentral.org")
puts rubypage.gets
```

You get the `doctype` declaration from the Ruby Central homepage—not the most scintillating reading, but it demonstrates the ease with which `open-uri` lets you import networked materials.

12.6 *Summary*

In this chapter you've seen

- I/O (keyboa0rd and screen) and file operations in Ruby
- File objects as enumerables
- The `STDIN`, `STDOUT`, and `STDERR` objects
- The `FileUtils` module
- The `Pathname` module

- The `StringIO` class
- The `open-uri` module

I/O operations are based on the `IO` class, of which `File` is a subclass. Much of what `IO` and `File` objects do consists of wrapped library calls; they're basically API libraries that sit on top of system I/O facilities.

You can iterate through Ruby file handles as if they were arrays, using `each`, `map`, `reject`, and other methods from the `Enumerable` module, and Ruby will take care of the details of the file handling. If and when you need to, you can also address `IO` and `File` objects with lower-level commands.

Some of the standard-library facilities for file manipulation are indispensable, and we looked at several: the `FileUtils` module, which provides an enriched toolkit for file and disk operations; the `StringIO` class, which lets you address a string as if it were an I/O stream; the `Pathname` extension, which allows for easy, extended operations on strings representing file-system paths; and `open-uri`, which makes it easy to "open" documents on the network.

We also looked at keyboard input and screen output, which are handled via `IO` objects—in particular, the standard input, output, and error I/O handles. Ruby lets you reassign these so you can redirect input and output as needed.

With this chapter, we've come to the end of part 2 of the book and thus the end of our survey of Ruby built-in features and classes. We'll turn in part 3 to the broad and deep matter of Ruby dynamics, starting with a look at one of the simplest yet most profound premises of Ruby: the premise that objects, even objects of the same class, can act and react individually.

Part 3

Ruby dynamics

Ruby is dynamic, like human nature.

—Matz, at RubyConf 2001

The phrase *Ruby dynamics* is almost redundant: everything about Ruby is dynamic. Variables don't care what class of object you bind them to, which means you don't have to (indeed, you can't) declare their type in advance. Objects get capabilities from the classes that create them but can also branch away from their classes by having individual methods added to them. Classes and modules can be reopened and modified after their initial definitions. Nothing necessarily stays the same over the life cycle of the running program.

And those examples are just the beginning. In this last part of the book, we'll look more deeply and widely than we yet have at the ways in which Ruby allows you to alter the execution circumstances of your program in your program.

First, in chapter 13, we'll look at *object individuation,* going into the details of how Ruby makes it possible for individual objects to live their own lives and develop their own characteristics and behaviors outside of the class-based characteristics they're "born" with. We'll thus circle back to one of the book's earliest topics: adding methods to individual objects. But here, equipped with the knowledge from the intervening material, we'll zero in much more closely on the underlying mechanisms of object individuation.

Chapter 14 looks at *callable objects*: objects you can execute. You've seen methods already, of course—but you haven't seen method *objects*, which we'll discuss here, as well as anonymous functions in the form of `Proc` objects. Strings aren't callable themselves, but you can evaluate a string at runtime as a piece of Ruby code, and chapter 14 will include that (sometimes questionable) technique. The chapter will also introduce you to Ruby threads, which allow you to run segments of code in parallel.

Finally, chapter 15 looks at the facilities Ruby provides for runtime *reflection*: examining and manipulating the state of your program and your objects while the program is running and the objects exist. Ruby lets you ask your objects for information about themselves, such as what methods they can execute at runtime; and a number of hooks are available, in the form of methods you can write using special reserved names, to intercept runtime events like class inheritance and module inclusion. Here we're entering the territory of dynamic reflection and decision making that gives Ruby its characteristic and striking quality of flexibility and power.

Chapter 13 also includes information—and advice—about the process of making changes to the Ruby core language in your own programs. In fact, this entire part of the book includes many best-practices pointers (and pointers away from some not-so-best practices). That's not surprising, given the kind of ground these chapters cover. This is where your programs can distinguish themselves, for better or worse, as to the nature and quality of their use of Ruby's liberal dynamic-programming toolset. It definitely pays to think through not only the how and why but also the *whether* of some of these powerful techniques in certain circumstances. Used judiciously and advisedly, Ruby's dynamic capabilities can take you to new and fascinating heights.

Object individuation

13

This chapter covers

- Singleton methods and classes
- Class methods
- The `extend` method
- Overriding Ruby core behavior
- The `BasicObject` class

One of the cornerstones of Ruby's design is object individuation—that is, the ability of individual objects to behave differently from other objects of the same class. Every object is a full-fledged citizen of the runtime world of the program and can live the life it needs to.

The freedom of objects to veer away from the conditions of their birth has a kind of philosophical ring to it. On the other hand, it has some important technical implications. A remarkable number of Ruby features and characteristics derive from or converge on the individuality of objects. Much of Ruby is engineered to make object individuation possible. Ultimately, the individuation is more important than the engineering: Matz has said over and over again that the principle of object individuality is what matters, and how Ruby implements it is secondary. Still, the implementation of object individuation has some powerful and useful components.

We'll look in this chapter at how Ruby goes about allowing objects to acquire methods and behaviors on a per-object basis, and how the parts of Ruby that make per-object behavior possible can be used to greatest advantage. We'll start by examining in detail *singleton methods*—methods that belong to individual objects—in the context of *singleton classes*, which is where singleton-method definitions are stored. We'll then discuss class methods, which are at heart singleton methods attached to class objects. Another key technique in crafting per-object behavior is the extend method, which does something similar to module inclusion but for one object at a time. We'll look at how you can use extend to individuate your objects.

Perhaps the most crucial topic connected in any way with object individuation is changing the core behavior of Ruby classes. Adding a method to a class that already exists, such as Array or String, is a form of object individuation, because classes are objects. It's a powerful and risky technique. But there are ways to do it with comparatively little risk—and ways to do it per object (adding a behavior to one string, rather than to the String class)—and we'll walk through the landscape of runtime core changes with an eye to how per-object techniques can help you get the most out of Ruby's sometimes surprisingly open class model.

Finally, we'll renew an earlier acquaintance: the BasicObject class. BasicObject instances provide about the purest laboratory imaginable for creating individual objects, and we'll consider how that class and object individuation complement each other.

13.1   *Where the singleton methods are: The singleton class*

Most of what happens in Ruby involves classes and modules, containing definitions of instance methods

```
class C
  def talk
    puts "Hi!"
  end
end
```

and, subsequently, the instantiation of classes and the calling of those instance methods:

```
c = C.new
c.talk          ⟵┘  Output: Hi!
```

But as you saw earlier (even earlier than you saw instance methods inside classes), you can also define singleton methods directly on individual objects:

```
obj = Object.new
def obj.talk
  puts "Hi!"
end
obj.talk         ⟵┘  Output: Hi!
```

And you've also seen that the most common type of singleton method is the class method—a method added to a `Class` object on an individual basis:

```
class Car
  def self.makes
    %w{ Honda Ford Toyota Chevrolet Volvo }
  end
end
```

But any object can have singleton methods added to it. (Almost any object; see sidebar.) The ability to define behavior on a per-object basis is one of the hallmarks of Ruby's design.

> ### Some objects are more individualizable than others
> Almost every object in Ruby can have methods added to it. The exceptions are instances of certain `Numeric` subclasses, including integer classes and floats, and symbols. If you try this
>
> ```
> def 10.some_method; end
> ```
>
> you'll get a syntax error. If you try this
>
> ```
> class << 10; end
> ```
>
> you'll get a type error and a message saying "Can't define singleton." The same is true, in both cases, of floating-point numbers and symbols.

Instance methods—those available to any and all instances of a given class—live inside a class or module, where they can be found by the objects that are able to call them. But what about singleton methods? Where does a method live, if that method exists only to be called by a single object?

13.1.1 Dual determination through singleton classes

Ruby, true to character, has a simple answer to this tricky question: an object's singleton methods live in the object's *singleton class*. Every object ultimately has two classes:

- The class of which it's an instance
- Its singleton class

An object can call instance methods from its original class, and it can also call methods from its singleton class. It has both. The method-calling capabilities of the object amount, all together, to the sum of all the instance methods defined in these two classes, along with methods available through ancestral classes (the superclass of the object's class, that class's superclass, and so forth) or through any modules that have been mixed in or prepended to any of these classes. You can think of an object's singleton class as an exclusive stash of methods, tailor-made for that object and not shared with other objects—not even with other instances of the object's class.

13.1.2   *Examining and modifying a singleton class directly*

Singleton classes are anonymous: although they're class objects (instances of the class
`Class`), they spring up automatically without being given a name. Nonetheless, you
can open the class-definition body of a singleton class and add instance methods, class
methods, and constants to it, as you would with a regular class.

You do this with a special form of the `class` keyword. Usually, a constant follows
that keyword:

```
class C
  # method and constant definitions here
end
```

But to get inside the definition body of a singleton class, you use a special notation:

```
class << object
  # method and constant definitions here
end
```

The `<< object` notation means the anonymous, singleton class of `object`. When you're
inside the singleton class–definition body, you can define methods—and these methods will be singleton methods of the object whose singleton class you're in.

Consider this program, for example:

```
str = "I am a string"
class << str
  def twice
    self + " " + self
  end
end
puts str.twice
```

The output is

```
I am a string I am a string
```

The method `twice` is a singleton method of the string `str`. It's exactly as if we had
done this:

```
def str.twice
  self + " " + self
end
```

The difference is that we've pried open the singleton class of `str` and defined the
method there.

> ### The difference between def obj.meth and class << obj; def meth
> This question often arises: Is there any difference between defining a method directly
> on an object (using the `def obj.some_method` notation) and adding a method to an
> object's singleton class explicitly (by doing `class << obj; def some_method`)? The
> answer is that there's one difference: constants are resolved differently.

If you have a top-level constant N, you can also define an N inside an object's singleton class:

```
N = 1
obj = Object.new
class << obj
  N = 2
end
```

Given this sequence of instructions, the two ways of adding a singleton method to obj differ in which N is visible from within the method definition:

```
def obj.a_method
  puts N
end
class << obj
  def another_method
    puts N
  end
end
obj.a_method
obj.another_method
```

Output: 1 (outer-level N)

Output: 2 (N belonging to obj's singleton class)

It's relatively unusual for this difference in the visibility of constants to affect your code; in most circumstances, you can regard the two notations for singleton-method definition as interchangeable. But it's worth knowing about the difference, because it may matter in some situations and it may also explain unexpected results.

The class << object notation has a bit of a reputation as cryptic or confusing. It needn't be either. Think of it this way: it's the class keyword, and it's willing to accept either a constant or a << object expression. What's new here is the concept of the singleton class. When you're comfortable with the idea that objects have singleton classes, it makes sense for you to be able to open those classes with the class keyword. The << object notation is the way the concept "singleton class of object" is expressed when class requires it.

By far the most frequent use of the class << object notation for entering a singleton-method class is in connection with class-method definitions.

DEFINING CLASS METHODS WITH CLASS <<

Here's an idiom you'll see often:

```
class Ticket
  class << self
    def most_expensive(*tickets)
      tickets.max_by(&:price)
    end
  end
end
```

This code results in the creation of the class method `Ticket.most_expensive`—much the same method as the one defined in section 3.6.3, but that time around we did this:

```
def Ticket.most_expensive(*tickets)  # etc.
```

In the current version, we're using the `class << object` idiom, opening the singleton class of the object; and in this particular case, the object involved is the class object `Ticket`, which is the value of `self` at the point in the code where `class << self` is invoked. The result of defining the method `most_expensive` inside the class-definition block is that it gets defined as a singleton method on `Ticket`—which is to say, a class method.

The same class method could also be defined like this (assuming this code comes at a point in the program where the `Ticket` class already exists):

```
class << Ticket
  def most_expensive(tickets)
  # etc.
```

Because `self` is `Ticket` inside the class `Ticket` definition body, `class << self` *inside* the body is the same as `class << Ticket` *outside* the body. (Technically, you could even do `class << Ticket` inside the body of class `Ticket`, but in practice you'll usually see `class << self` whenever the object whose singleton class needs opening is `self`.)

The fact that `class << self` shows up frequently in connection with the creation of class methods sometimes leads to the false impression that the `class << object` notation can only be used to create class methods, or that the only expression you can legally put on the right is `self`. In fact, `class << self` inside a class-definition block is just one particular use case for `class << object`. The technique is general: it puts you in a definition block for the singleton class of `object`, whatever `object` may be.

In chapter 4, we looked at the steps an object takes as it looks for a method among those defined in its class, its class's class, and so forth. Now we have a new item on the radar: the singleton class. What's the effect of this extra class on the method-lookup process?

13.1.3 *Singleton classes on the method-lookup path*

Recall that method searching goes up the class-inheritance chain, with detours for any modules that have been mixed in or prepended. When we first discussed this process, we hadn't talked about singleton classes and methods, and they weren't present in the diagram. Now we can revise the diagram to encompass them, as shown in figure 13.1.

The box containing `class << object` represents the singleton class of `object`. In its search for the method `x`, `object` looks first for any modules prepended to its singleton class; then it looks in the singleton class itself. It then looks in any modules that the singleton class has included. (In the diagram, there's one: the module `N`.) Next, the search proceeds up to the object's original class (class `D`), and so forth.

Note in particular that it's possible for a singleton class to prepend or include a module. After all, it's a class.

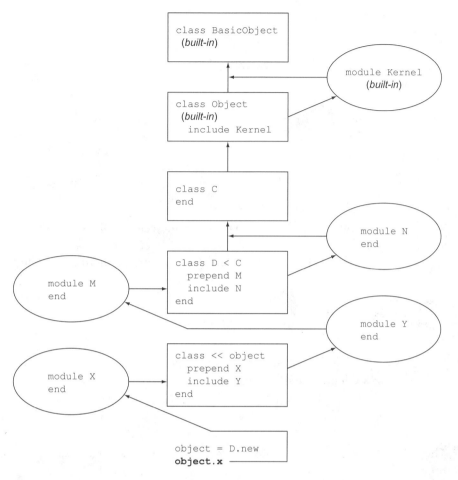

Figure 13.1   Method-search order, revised to include singleton classes

INCLUDING A MODULE IN A SINGLETON CLASS

Let's build a little program that illustrates the effect of including a module in a singleton class. We'll start with a simple `Person` class and a couple of instances of that class:

```
class Person
  attr_accessor :name
end
david = Person.new
david.name = "David"
matz = Person.new
matz.name = "Matz"
ruby = Person.new
ruby.name = "Ruby"
```

Now let's say that some persons—that is, some `Person` objects—don't like to reveal their names. A logical way to add this kind of secrecy to individual objects is to add a singleton version of the `name` method to each of those objects:

```
def david.name
  "[not available]"
end
```

At this point, Matz and Ruby reveal their names, but David is being secretive. When we do a roll call

```
puts "We've got one person named #{matz.name}, "
puts "one named #{david.name},"
puts "and one named #{ruby.name}."
```

we get only two names:

```
We've got one person named Matz,
one named [not available],
and one named Ruby.
```

So far, so good. But what if more than one person decides to be secretive? It would be a nuisance to have to write def person.name... for every such person.

The way around this is to use a module. Here's what the module looks like:

```
module Secretive
  def name
    "[not available]"
  end
end
```

Now let's make Ruby secretive. Instead of using def to define a new version of the name method, we'll include the module in Ruby's singleton class:

```
class << ruby
  include Secretive
end
```

The roll call now shows that Ruby has gone over to the secretive camp; running the previous puts statements again produces the following output:

```
We've got one person named Matz,
one named [not available],
and one named [not available].
```

What happened in Ruby's case? We sent the message "name" to the object ruby. The object set out to find the method. First it looked in its own singleton class, where it didn't find a name method. Then it looked in the modules mixed into its singleton class. The singleton class of ruby mixed in the Secretive module, and, sure enough, that module contains an instance method called name. At that point, the method gets executed.

Given an understanding of the order in which objects search their lookup paths for methods, you can work out which version of a method (that is, which class or module's version of the method) an object will find first. Examples help, too, especially to illustrate the difference between including a module in a singleton class and in a regular class.

SINGLETON MODULE INCLUSION VS. ORIGINAL-CLASS MODULE INCLUSION

When you mix a module into an object's singleton class, you're dealing with that object specifically; the methods it learns from the module take precedence over any methods of the same name in its original class. The following listing shows the mechanics and outcome of doing this kind of include operation.

> **Listing 13.1   Including a module in a singleton class**

```
class C
  def talk
    puts "Hi from original class!"
  end
end
module M
  def talk
    puts "Hello from module!"
  end
end
c = C.new
c.talk                    <--1
class << c
  include M               <--2
end
c.talk                    <--3
```

The output from this listing is as follows:

```
Hi from original class!
Hello from module!
```

The first call to talk ❶ executes the talk instance method defined in c's class, C. Then, we mix the module M, which also defines a method called talk, into c's singleton class ❷. As a result, the next time we call talk on c ❸, the talk that gets executed (the one that c sees first) is the one defined in M.

It's all a matter of how the classes and modules on the object's method lookup path are stacked. Modules included in the singleton class are encountered before the original class and before any modules included in the original class.

You can see this graphically by using the ancestors method, which gives you a list of the classes and modules in the inheritance and inclusion hierarchy of any class or module. Starting from after the class and module definitions in the previous example, try using ancestors to see what the hierarchy looks like:

```
c = C.new
class << c
  include M
  p ancestors
end
```

You get an array of ancestors—essentially, the method-lookup path for instances of this class. Because this is the singleton class of c, looking at its ancestors means looking at the method lookup path for c. Note that c's singleton class comes first in the ancestor list:

```
[#<Class:#<C:0x007fbc8b9129f0>>, M, C, Object, Kernel, BasicObject]
```

Now look what happens when you not only mix M into the singleton class of c but also mix it into c's class (C). Picking up after the previous example,

```
class C
  include M
end
class << c
  p ancestors
end
```

This time you see the following result:

```
[#<Class:#<C:0x007fbc8b9129f0>>, M, C, M, Object, Kernel, BasicObject]
```

The module M appears twice! Two different classes—the singleton class of c and the class C—have mixed it in. Each mix-in is a separate transaction. It's the private business of each class; the classes don't consult with each other. (You could even mix M into Object, and you'd get it three times in the ancestors list.)

You're encouraged to take these examples, modify them, turn them this way and that, and examine the results. Classes are objects, too—so see what happens when you take the singleton class of an object's singleton class. What about mixing modules into other modules? Try some examples with prepend, too. Many permutations are possible; you can learn a lot through experimentation, using what we've covered here as a starting point.

The main lesson is that per-object behavior in Ruby is based on the same principles as regular, class-derived object behavior: the definition of instance methods in classes and modules, the mixing in of modules to classes, and the following of a method-lookup path consisting of classes and modules. If you master these concepts and revert to them whenever something seems fuzzy, your understanding will scale upward successfully.

13.1.4 *The singleton_class method*

To refer directly to the singleton class of an object, use the singleton_class method. This method can save you some class << object roundtrips.

Here's how you'd use this method to get the ancestors of an object's singleton class:

```
string = "a string"
p string.singleton_class.ancestors
```

Now let's go back and look at a special case in the world of singleton methods (special, because it's common and useful): class methods.

13.1.5 *Class methods in (even more) depth*

Class methods are singleton methods defined on objects of class `Class`. In many ways, they behave like any other singleton method:

```
class C
end
def C.a_class_method
  puts "Singleton method defined on C"
end
C.a_class_method
```

Output: Singleton method defined on C

But class methods also exhibit special behavior. Normally, when you define a singleton method on an object, no other object can serve as the receiver in a call to that method. (That's what makes singleton methods singleton, or per-object.) Class methods are slightly different: a method defined as a singleton method of a class object can also be called on subclasses of that class. Given the previous example, with C, you can do this:

```
class D < C
end
D.a_class_method
```

Here's the rather confusing output (confusing because the class object we sent the message to is D, rather than C):

```
Singleton method defined on C
```

You're allowed to call C's singleton methods on a subclass of C in addition to C because of a special setup involving the singleton classes of class objects. In our example, the singleton class of C (where the method a_class_method lives) is considered the superclass of the singleton class of D.

When you send a message to the class object D, the usual lookup path is followed—except that after D's singleton class, the superclass of D's singleton class is searched. That's the singleton class of D's superclass. And there's the method.

Figure 13.2 shows the relationships among classes in an inheritance relationship and their singleton classes.

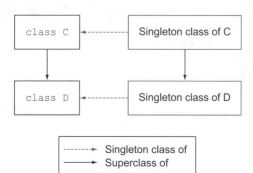

Figure 13.2 Relationships among classes in an inheritance relationship and their singleton classes

As you can see from figure 13.2, the singleton class of C's child, D, is considered a child (a subclass) of the singleton class of C.

Singleton classes of class objects are sometimes called *meta-classes*. You'll sometimes hear the term *meta-class* applied to singleton classes in general, although there's nothing particularly meta about them and singleton class is a more descriptive general term.

You can treat this explanation as a bonus topic. It's unlikely that an urgent need to understand it will arise often. Still, it's a great example of how Ruby's design is based on a relatively small number of rules (such as every object having a singleton class, and the way methods are looked up). Classes are special-cased objects; after all, they're object factories as well as objects in their own right. But there's little in Ruby that doesn't arise naturally from the basic principles of the language's design—even the special cases.

Because Ruby's classes and modules are objects, changes you make to those classes and modules are per-object changes. Thus a discussion of how, when, and whether to make alterations to Ruby's core classes and modules has a place in this discussion of object individuation. We'll explore core changes next.

> **SINGLETON CLASSES AND THE SINGLETON PATTERN** The word "singleton" has a second, different meaning in Ruby (and elsewhere): it refers to the singleton pattern, which describes a class that only has one instance. The Ruby standard library includes an implementation of the singleton pattern (available via the command `require 'singleton'`). Keep in mind that singleton classes aren't directly related to the singleton pattern; the word "singleton" is just a bit overloaded. It's generally clear from the context which meaning is intended.

13.2 *Modifying Ruby's core classes and modules*

The openness of Ruby's classes and modules—the fact that you, the programmer, can get under the hood of the language and change what it does—is one of the most important features of Ruby and also one of the hardest to come to terms with. It's like being able to eat the dishes along with the food at a restaurant. How do you know where one ends and the other begins? How do you know when to stop? Can you eat the tablecloth too?

Learning how to handle Ruby's openness is a bit about programming technique and a lot about best practices. It's not difficult to make modifications to the core language; the hard part is knowing when you should, when you shouldn't, and how to go about it safely.

In this section, we'll look at the landscape of core changes: the how, the what, and the why (and the why not). We'll examine the considerable pitfalls, the possible advantages, and ways to think about objects and their behaviors that allow you to have the best of both worlds: flexibility and safety.

We'll start with a couple of cautionary tales.

13.2.1 *The risks of changing core functionality*

The problem with making changes to the Ruby core classes is that those changes are global: as long as your program is running, the changes you've made will be in effect. If you change how a method works and that method is used somewhere else (inside Ruby itself or in a library you load), you've destabilized the whole interpreter by changing the rules of the game in midstream.

It's tempting, nonetheless, to customize Ruby to your liking by changing core methods globally. After all, you can. But this is the least safe and least advisable approach to customizing core-object behaviors. We're only looking at it so you can get a sense of the nature of the problem.

One commonly cited candidate for ad hoc change is the `Regexp` class.

CHANGING REGEXP#MATCH (AND WHY NOT TO)

As you'll recall from chapter 11, when a match operation using the `match` method fails, you get back `nil`; when it succeeds, you get back a `MatchData` object. This result is irritating because you can't do the same things with `nil` that you can with a `Match-Data` object.

This code, for example, succeeds if a first capture is created by the match:

```
some_regexp.match(some_string)[1]
```

But if there's no match, you get back `nil`—and because `nil` has no `[]` method, you get a fatal `NoMethodError` exception when you try the `[1]` operation:

```
string = "A test string"
re = /A (sample) string/
substring = re.match(string)[1]
```
← NoMethodError: undefined method [ ] for nil:NilClass

It may be tempting to do something like this to avoid the error:

```
class Regexp
  alias __old_match__ match           ⬅─①
  def match(string)
    __old_match__(string) || []
  end
end
```

This code first sets up an alias for `match`, courtesy of the `alias` keyword ①. Then the code redefines `match`. The new `match` hooks into the original version of `match` (through the alias) and then returns either the result of calling the original version or (if that call returns `nil`) an empty array.

> **NOTE** An *alias* is a synonym for a method name. Calling a method by an alias doesn't involve any change of behavior or any alteration of the method-lookup process. The choice of alias name in the previous example is based on a fairly conventional formula: the addition of the word *old* plus the leading and trailing underscores. (A case could be made that the formula is too conventional and that you should create names that are less likely to be chosen by other overriders who also know the convention!)

You can now do this:

```
/abc/.match("X")[1]
```

Even though the match fails, the program won't blow up, because the failed match now returns an empty array rather than nil. The worst you can do with the new match is try to index an empty array, which is legal. (The result of the index operation will be nil, but at least you're not trying to index nil.)

The problem is that the person using your code may depend on the match operation to return nil on failure:

```
if regexp.match(string)
  do something
else
  do something else
end
```

Because an array (even an empty one) is true, whereas nil is false, returning an array for a failed match operation means that the true/false test (as embodied in an if/else statement) always returns true.

Maybe changing Regexp#match so as not to return nil on failure is something your instincts would tell you not to do anyway. And no one advocates doing it; it's more that some new Ruby users don't connect the dots and therefore don't see that changing a core method in one place changes it everywhere.

Another common example, and one that's a little more subtle (both as to what it does and as to why it's not a good idea), involves the String#gsub! method.

THE RETURN VALUE OF STRING#GSUB! AND WHY IT SHOULD STAY THAT WAY

As you'll recall, String#gsub! does a global replace operation on its receiver, saving the changes in the original object:

```
>> string = "Hello there!"
=> "Hello there!"
>> string.gsub!(/e/, "E")        ❶
=> "HEllo thErE!"            ◁──┐
>> string                     ❷
=> "HEllo thErE!"           ◁──┘
```

As you can see, the return value of the call to gsub! is the string object with the changes made ❶. (And examining the object again via the variable string confirms that the changes are indeed permanent ❷.)

Interestingly, though, something different happens when the gsub! operation doesn't result in any changes to the string:

```
>> string = "Hello there!"
=> "Hello there!"
>> string.gsub!(/zzz/, "xxx")
=> nil
>> string
=> "Hello there!"
```

There's no match on /zzz/, so the string isn't changed—and the return value of the call to gsub! is nil.

Like the nil return from a match operation, the nil return from gsub! has the potential to make things blow up when you'd rather they didn't. Specifically, it means you can't use gsub! reliably in a chain of methods:

```
>> string = "Hello there!"
=> "Hello there!"
>> string.gsub!(/e/, "E").reverse!                    ❶
=> "!ErEht ollEH"                                      ◁── ❷
>> string = "Hello there!"
=> "Hello there!"
>> string.gsub!(/zzz/, "xxx").reverse!                                ❸
NoMethodError: undefined method `reverse!' for nil:NilClass          ◁──┘
```

This example does something similar (but not quite the same) twice. The first time through, the chained calls to gsub! and reverse! ❶ return the newly gsub!'d and reversed string ❷. But the second time, the chain of calls results in a fatal error ❸: the gsub! call didn't change the string, so it returned nil—which means we called reverse! on nil rather than on a string.

The tap method

The tap method (callable on any object) performs the somewhat odd but potentially useful task of executing a code block, yielding the receiver to the block, and returning the receiver. It's easier to show this than to describe it:

```
>> "Hello".tap {|string| puts string.upcase }.reverse
HELLO
=> "olleH"
```

Called on the receiver "Hello", the tap method yields that string back to its code block, as confirmed by the printing out of the uppercased version of the string. Then tap returns the entire string—so the reverse operation is performed on the string. If you call gsub! on a string inside a tap block, it doesn't matter whether it returns nil, because tap returns the string. Be careful, though. Using tap to circumvent the nil return of gsub! (or of other similarly behaving bang methods) can introduce complexities of its own, especially if you do multiple chaining where some methods perform in-place operations and others return object copies.

One possible way of handling the inconvenience of having to work around the nil return from gsub! is to take the view that it's not usually appropriate to chain method calls together too much anyway. And you can always avoid chain-related problems if you don't chain:

```
>> string = "Hello there!"
=> "Hello there!"
>> string.gsub!(/zzz/, "xxx")
=> nil
>> string.reverse!
=> "!ereht olleH"
```

Still, a number of Ruby users have been bitten by the nil return value, either because they expected gsub! to behave like gsub (the non-bang version, which always returns its receiver, whether there's been a change or not) or because they didn't anticipate a case where the string wouldn't change. So gsub! and its nil return value became a popular candidate for change.

The change can be accomplished like this:

```
class String
  alias __old_gsub_bang__ gsub!
  def gsub!(*args, &block)
    __old_gsub_bang__(*args, &block)
    self
  end
end
```

First the original gsub! gets an alias; that will enable us to call the original version from inside the new version. The new gsub! takes any number of arguments (the arguments themselves don't matter; we'll pass them along to the old gsub!) and a code block, which will be captured in the variable block. If no block is supplied—and gsub! can be called with or without a block—block is nil.

Now we call the old version of gsub!, passing it the arguments and reusing the code block. Finally, the new gsub! does the thing it's being written to do: it returns self (the string), regardless of whether the call to __old_gsub_bang__ returned the string or nil.

And now, the reasons not to do this.

Changing gsub! this way is probably less likely, as a matter of statistics, to get you in trouble than changing Regexp#match is. Still, it's possible that someone might write code that depends on the documented behavior of gsub!, in particular on the returning of nil when the string doesn't change. Here's an example—and although it's contrived (as most examples of this scenario are bound to be), it's valid Ruby and dependent on the documented behavior of gsub!:

```
>> states = { "NY" => "New York", "NJ" => "New Jersey",
   "ME" => "Maine" }                                              ❶
=> {"NY"=>"New York", "NJ"=>"New Jersey", "ME"=>"Maine"}
>> string = "Eastern states include NY, NJ, and ME."          ❷
=> "Eastern states include NY, NJ, and ME."
>> if string.gsub!(/\b([A-Z]{2})\b/) { states[$1] }           ❸
>>   puts "Substitution occurred"
>> else
?>   puts "String unchanged"
>> end                                ❹
Substitution occurred
```

We start with a hash of state abbreviations and full names ❶. Then comes a string that uses state abbreviations ❷. The goal is to replace the abbreviations with the full names, using a gsub! operation that captures any two consecutive uppercase letters surrounded by word boundaries (\b) and replaces them with the value from the hash corresponding to the two-letter substring ❸. Along the way, we take note of whether any such replacements are made. If any are, gsub! returns the new version of string. If no substitutions are made, gsub! returns nil. The result of the process is printed out at the end ❹.

The damage here is relatively light, but the lesson is clear: don't change the documented behavior of core Ruby methods. Here's another version of the states-hash example, using sub! rather than gsub!. In this version, failure to return nil when the string doesn't change triggers an infinite loop. Assuming we have the states hash and the original version of string, we can do a one-at-a-time substitution where each substitution is reported:

```
>> string = "Eastern states include NY, NJ, and ME."
=> "Eastern states include NY, NJ, and ME."
>> while string.sub!(/\b([A-Z]{2})\b/) { states[$1] }
>>   puts "Replacing #{$1} with #{states[$1]}..."
>> end
Replacing NY with New York...
Replacing NJ with New Jersey...
Replacing ME with Maine...
```

If string.sub! always returns a non-nil value (a string), then the while condition will never fail, and the loop will execute forever.

What you should *not* do, then, is rewrite core methods so that they don't do what others expect them to do. There's no exception to this. It's something you should never do, even though you can.

That leaves us with the question of how to change Ruby core functionality safely. We'll look at four techniques that you can consider. The first three are additive change, hook or pass-through change, and per-object change. Only one of them is truly safe, although all three are safe enough to use in many circumstances. The fourth technique is *refinements*, which are module-scoped changes to classes and which can help you pinpoint your core Ruby changes so that they don't overflow into surrounding code and into Ruby itself.

Along the way, we'll look at custom-made examples as well as some examples from the Active Support library, which is typically used as part of the Rails web application development framework. Active Support provides good examples of the first two kinds of core change: additive and pass-through. We'll start with additive.

13.2.2 Additive changes

The most common category of changes to built-in Ruby classes is the *additive change*: adding a method that doesn't exist. The benefit of additive change is that it doesn't clobber existing Ruby methods. The danger inherent in it is that if two programmers write added methods with the same name, and both get included into the interpreter during execution of a particular library or program, one of the two will clobber the other. There's no way to reduce that risk to zero.

Added methods often serve the purpose of providing functionality that a large number of people want. In other words, they're not all written for specialized use in one program. There's safety in numbers: if people have been discussing a given method for years, and if a de facto implementation of the method is floating around the Ruby world, the chances are good that if you write the method or use an existing implementation, you won't collide with anything that someone else may have written.

The Active Support library, and specifically its core extension sublibrary, adds lots of methods to core Ruby classes. The additions to the String class provide some good examples. Active Support comes with a set of "inflections" on String, with methods like pluralize and titleize. Here are some examples (you'll need to run gem install activesupport to run them, if you don't have the gem installed already):

```
>> require 'active_support/core_ext'
=> true
>> "person".pluralize
=> "people"
>> "little_dorritt".titleize
=> "Little Dorritt"
```

Any time you add new methods to Ruby core classes, you run the risk that someone else will add a method with the same name that behaves somewhat differently. A library like Active Support depends on the good faith of its users and on its own reputation: if you're using Active Support, you presumably know that you're entering into a kind of unwritten contract not to override its methods or load other libraries that do so. In that sense, Active Support is protected by its own reputation and breadth of usage. You can certainly use Active Support if it gives you something you want or need, but don't take it as a signal that it's generally okay to add methods to core classes. You need to be quite circumspect about doing so.

Another way to add functionality to existing Ruby classes and modules is with a passive hooking or pass-through technique.

13.2.3 *Pass-through overrides*

A *pass-through* method change involves overriding an existing method in such a way that the original version of the method ends up getting called along with the new version. The new version does whatever it needs to do and then passes its arguments along to the original version of the method. It relies on the original method to provide a return value. (As you know from the match and gsub! override examples, calling the original version of a method isn't enough if you're going to change the basic interface of the method by changing its return value.)

You can use pass-through overrides for a number of purposes, including logging and debugging:

```
class String
  alias __old_reverse__ reverse
  def reverse
    $stderr.puts "Reversing a string!"
    __old_reverse__
  end
end
puts "David".reverse
```

The output of this snippet is as follows:

```
Reversing a string!
divaD
```

The first line is printed to STDERR, and the second line is printed to STDOUT. The example depends on creating an alias for the original reverse and then calling that alias at the end of the new reverse.

> ### Aliasing and its aliases
>
> In addition to the alias keyword, Ruby has a method called alias_method, which is a private instance method of Module. The upshot is that you can create an alias for a method either like this
>
> ```
> class String
>   alias __old_reverse__ reverse
> end
> ```
>
> or like this:
>
> ```
> class String
>   alias_method :__old_reverse__, :reverse
> end
> ```
>
> Because it's a method and not a keyword, alias_method needs objects rather than bare method names as its arguments. It can take symbols or strings. Note also that the arguments to alias don't have a comma between them. Keywords get to do things like that, but methods don't.

It's possible to write methods that combine the additive and pass-through philosophies. Some examples from Active Support demonstrate how to do this.

ADDITIVE/PASS-THROUGH HYBRIDS

An *additive/pass-through hybrid* is a method that has the same name as an existing core method, calls the old version of the method (so it's not an out-and-out replacement), and adds something to the method's interface. In other words, it's an override that offers a superset of the functionality of the original method.

Active Support features a number of additive/pass-through hybrid methods. A good example is the to_s method of the Time class. Unchanged, Time#to_s provides a nice human-readable string representing the time

```
>> Time.now.to_s
=> "2013-12-31 08:37:32 -0500"
```

Active Support adds to the method so that it can take an argument indicating a specific kind of formatting. For example (assuming you have required active_support) you can format a Time object in a manner suitable for database insertion like this:

```
>> Time.now.to_s(:db)
=> "2013-12-31 08:37:40"
```

If you want the date represented as a number, ask for the `:number` format:

```
>> Time.now.to_s(:number)
=> " 20131231083748 "
```

The `:rfc822` argument nets a time formatted in RFC822 style, the standard date format for dates in email headers. It's similar to the `Time#rfc822` method:

```
>> Time.now.to_s(:rfc822)
=> "Tue, 31 Dec 2013 08:38:00 -0500"
```

The various formats added to `Time#to_s` work by using `strftime`, which wraps the system call of the same name and lets you format times in a large number of ways. So there's nothing in the modified `Time#to_s` that you couldn't do yourself. The optional argument is added for your convenience (and of course the database-friendly `:db` format is of interest mainly if you're using Active Support in conjunction with an object-relational library, such as `ActiveRecord`). The result is a superset of `Time#to_s`. You can ignore the add-ons, and the method will work like it always did.

As with pure method addition (such as `String#pluralize`), the kind of superset-driven override of core methods represented by these examples entails some risk: specifically, the risk of collision. Is it likely that you'll end up loading two libraries that both add an optional `:db` argument to `Time#to_s`? No, it's unlikely—but it's possible. Once again, a library like Active Support is protected by its high profile: if you load it, you're probably familiar with what it does and will know not to override the overrides. Still, it's remotely possible that another library you load might clash with `Active-Support`. As always, it's difficult or impossible to reduce the risk of collision to zero. You need to protect yourself by familiarizing yourself with what every library does and by testing your code sufficiently.

The last major approach to overriding core Ruby behavior we'll look at—and the safest way to do it—is the addition of functionality on a strictly per-object basis, using `Object#extend`.

13.2.4 *Per-object changes with extend*

`Object#extend` is a kind of homecoming in terms of topic flow. We've wandered to the outer reaches of modifying core classes—and `extend` brings us back to the central process at the heart of all such changes: changing the behavior of an individual object. It also brings us back to an earlier topic from this chapter: the mixing of a module into an object's singleton class. That's essentially what `extend` does.

ADDING TO AN OBJECT'S FUNCTIONALITY WITH EXTEND

Have another look at section 13.1.3 and in particular the `Person` example where we mixed the `Secretive` module into the singleton classes of some `Person` objects. As a reminder, the technique was this (where `ruby` is a `Person` instance):

```
class << ruby
  include Secretive
end
```

Here's how the `Person` example would look, using `extend` instead of explicitly opening up the singleton class of the `ruby` object. Let's also use `extend` for `david` (instead of the singleton method definition with `def`):

```
module Secretive
  def name
    "[not available]"
  end
end
class Person
  attr_accessor :name
end
david = Person.new
david.name = "David"
matz = Person.new
matz.name = "Matz"
ruby = Person.new
ruby.name = "Ruby"
david.extend(Secretive)          ◁──❶
ruby.extend(Secretive)
puts "We've got one person named #{matz.name}, " +
     "one named #{david.name}, "                  +
     "and one named #{ruby.name}."
```

Most of this program is the same as the first version, as is the output. The key difference is the use of `extend` ❶, which has the effect of adding the `Secretive` module to the lookup paths of the individual objects `david` and `ruby` by mixing it into their respective singleton classes. That inclusion process happens when you extend a class object, too.

ADDING CLASS METHODS WITH EXTEND

If you write a singleton method on a class object, like so

```
class Car
  def self.makes
    %w{ Honda Ford Toyota Chevrolet Volvo }
  end
end
```

or like so

```
class Car
  class << self
    def makes
      %w{ Honda Ford Toyota Chevrolet Volvo }
    end
  end
end
```

or with any of the other notational variants available, you're adding an instance method to the singleton class of the class object. It follows that you can achieve this, in addition to the other ways, by using `extend`:

```
module Makers
  def makes
    %w{ Honda Ford Toyota Chevrolet Volvo }
  end
end
class Car
  extend Makers
end
```

If it's more appropriate in a given situation, you can extend the class object after it already exists:

```
Car.extend(Makers)
```

Either way, the upshot is that the class object `Car` now has access to the `makes` method.

As with non-class objects, extending a class object with a module means mixing the module into the class's singleton class. You can verify this with the `ancestors` method:

```
p Car.singleton_class.ancestors
```

The output from this snippet is

```
[#<Class:Car>, Makers, #<Class:Object>, #<Class:BasicObject>, Class, Module,
    Object, Kernel, BasicObject]
```

The odd-looking entries in the list are singleton classes. The singleton class of `Car` itself is included; so are the singleton class of `Object` (which is the superclass of the singleton class of `Car`) and the singleton class of `BasicObject` (which is the superclass of the singleton class of `Object`). The main point for our purpose is that `Makers` is included in the list.

Remember too that subclasses have access to their superclass's class methods. If you subclass `Car` and look at the ancestors of the new class's singleton class, you'll see `Makers` in the list.

Our original purpose in looking at `extend` was to explore a way to add to Ruby's core functionality. Let's turn now to that purpose.

MODIFYING CORE BEHAVIOR WITH EXTEND

You've probably put the pieces together by this point. Modules let you define self-contained, reusable collections of methods. `Kernel#extend` lets you give individual objects access to modules, courtesy of the singleton class and the mix-in mechanism. Put it all together, and you have a compact, safe way of adding functionality to core objects.

Let's take another look at the `String#gsub!` conundrum—namely, that it returns nil when the string doesn't change. By defining a module and using `extend`, it's possible to change `gsub!`'s behavior in a limited way, making only the changes you need and no more. Here's how:

```
module GsubBangModifier
  def gsub!(*args, &block)
    super || self                    ⟵❶
  end
```

```
end
str = "Hello there!"
str.extend(GsubBangModifier)         ←──❷
str.gsub!(/zzz/,"abc").reverse!      ←──❸     Output:
puts str                             ←──            !ereht olleH
```

In the module `GsubBangModifier`, we define `gsub!`. Instead of the alias-and-call technique, we call `super`, returning either the value returned by that call or `self`—the latter if the call to `super` returns `nil` ❶. (You'll recall that `super` triggers execution of the next version of the current method up the method-lookup path. Hold that thought....)

Next, we create a string `str` and extend it with `GsubBangModifier` ❷. Calling `str.gsub!` ❸ executes the `gsub!` in `GsubBangModifier`, because `str` encounters `GsubBangModifier` in its method-lookup path before it encounters the class `String`—which, of course, also contains a `gsub!` definition. The call to `super` inside `GsubBangModifier#gsub!` jumps up the path and executes the original method, `String#gsub!`, passing it the original arguments and code block, if any. (That's the effect of calling `super` with no arguments and no empty argument list.) And the result of the call to `super` is either the string itself or `nil`, depending on whether any changes were made to the string.

Thus you can change the behavior of core objects—strings, arrays, hashes, and so forth—without reopening their classes and without introducing changes on a global level. Having calls to `extend` in your code helps show what's going on. Changing a method like `gsub!` inside the `String` class itself has the disadvantage not only of being global but also of being likely to be stashed away in a library file somewhere, making bugs hard to track down for people who get bitten by the global change.

There's one more important piece of the puzzle of how to change core object behaviors: a new feature called *refinements*.

13.2.5 *Using refinements to affect core behavior*

Refinements were added to Ruby 2.0, but were considered "experimental" until the 2.1 release. The idea of a refinement is to make a temporary, limited-scope change to a class (which can, though needn't, be a core class).

Here's an example, in which a `shout` method is introduced to the `String` class but only on a limited basis:

```
module Shout
  refine String do              ←──❶
    def shout
      self.upcase + "!!!"
    end
  end
end

class Person
  attr_accessor :name
                                    ❷
  using Shout               ←──┘
```

```
    def announce
      puts "Announcing #{name.shout}"
    end
end

david = Person.new
david.name = "David"
david.announce
```

Output: Announcing
DAVID!!!

Two different methods appear here, and they work hand in hand: refine ❶ and using ❷. The refine method takes a class name and a code block. Inside the code block you define the behaviors you want the class you're refining to adopt. In our example, we're refining the String class, adding a shout method that returns an upcased version of the string followed by three exclamation points.

The using method flips the switch: once you "use" the module in which you've defined the refinement you want, the target class adopts the new behaviors. In the example, we use the Shout module inside the Person class. That means that for the duration of that class (from the using statement to the end of the class definition), strings will be "refined" so that they have the shout method.

The effect of "using" a refinement comes to an end with the end of the class (or module) definition in which you declare that you're using the refinement. You can actually use using outside of a class or module definition, in which case the effect of the refinement persists to the end of the file in which the call to using occurs.

Refinements can help you make temporary changes to core classes in a relatively safe way. Other program files and libraries your program uses at runtime will not be affected by your refinements.

We'll end this chapter with a look at a slightly oddball topic: the BasicObject class. BasicObject isn't exclusively an object-individuation topic (as you know from having read the introductory material about it in chapter 3). But it pertains to the ancestry of all objects—including those whose behavior branches away from their original classes—and can play an important role in the kind of dynamism that Ruby makes possible.

13.3 *BasicObject as ancestor and class*

BasicObject sits at the top of Ruby's class tree. For any Ruby object *obj*, the following is true:

```
obj.class.ancestors.last == BasicObject
```

In other words, the highest-up ancestor of every class is BasicObject. (Unless you mix a module into BasicObject—but that's a far-fetched scenario.)

As you'll recall from chapter 3, instances of BasicObject have few methods—just a survival kit, so to speak, so they can participate in object-related activities. You'll find it difficult to get a BasicObject instance to tell you what it can do:

```
>> BasicObject.new.methods.sort
NoMethodError: undefined method `methods' for #<BasicObject:0x007fafa308b0d8>
```

But `BasicObject` is a class and behaves like one. You can get information directly from it, using familiar class-level methods:

```
>> BasicObject.instance_methods(false).sort
=> [:!, :!=, :==, :__id__, :__send__, :equal?, :instance_eval,
    :instance_exec]
```

What's the point of `BasicObject`?

13.3.1 *Using BasicObject*

`BasicObject` enables you to create objects that do nothing, which means you can teach them to do everything—without worrying about clashing with existing methods. Typically, this entails heavy use of `method_missing`. By defining `method_missing` for `BasicObject` or a class that you write that inherits from it, you can engineer objects whose behavior you're completely in charge of and that have little or no preconceived sense of how they're supposed to behave.

The best-known example of the use of an object with almost no methods is the `Builder` library by Jim Weirich. Builder is an XML-writing tool that outputs XML tags corresponding to messages you send to an object that recognizes few messages. The magic happens courtesy of `method_missing`.

Here's a simple example of Builder usage (and all Builder usage is simple; that's the point of the library). This example presupposes that you've installed the `builder` gem.

```
require 'builder'
xml = Builder::XmlMarkup.new(:target => STDOUT, :indent => 2)      ←—❶
xml.instruct!                                                       ←—
xml.friends do                                                       ┌—❷
  xml.friend(:source => "college") do
    xml.name("Joe Smith")
    xml.address do
      xml.street("123 Main Street")
      xml.city("Anywhere, USA 00000")
    end
  end
end
```

`xml` is a `Builder::XmlMarkup` object ❶. The object is programmed to send its output to `-STDOUT` and to indent by two spaces. The `instruct!` command ❷ tells the XML builder to start with an XML declaration. All instance methods of `Builder::Xml-Markup` end with a bang (`!`). They don't have non-bang counterparts—which bang methods should have in most cases—but in this case, the bang serves to distinguish these methods from methods with similar names that you may want to use to generate XML tags via `method_missing`. The assumption is that you may want an XML element called `instruct`, but you won't need one called `instruct!`. The bang is thus serving a domain-specific purpose, and it makes sense to depart from the usual Ruby convention for its use.

The output from our `Builder` script is this:

```
<?xml version="1.0" encoding="UTF-8"?>
<friends>
  <friend source="college">
    <name>Joe Smith</name>
    <address>
      <street>123 Main Street</street>
      <city>Anywhere, USA 00000</city>
    </address>
  </friend>
</friends>
```

The various XML tags take their names from the method calls. Every missing method results in a tag, and code blocks represent XML nesting. If you provide a string argument to a missing method, the string will be used as the text context of the element. Attributes are provided in hash arguments.

Builder uses `BasicObject` to do its work. Interestingly, Builder existed before `BasicObject` did. The original versions of Builder used a custom-made class called `BlankSlate`, which probably served as an inspiration for `BasicObject`.

How would you implement a simple `BasicObject`-based class?

13.3.2 *Implementing a subclass of BasicObject*

Simple, in the question just asked, means simpler than `Builder::XmlMarkup` (which makes XML writing simple but is itself fairly complex). Let's write a small library that operates on a similar principle and outputs an indented list of items. We'll avoid having to provide closing tags, which makes things a lot easier.

The `Lister` class, shown in the following listing, will inherit from `BasicObject`. It will define `method_missing` in such a way that every missing method is taken as a heading for the list it's generating. Nested code blocks will govern indentation.

Listing 13.2 `Lister` class: Generates indented lists from a `BasicObject` subclass

```
class Lister < BasicObject
  attr_reader :list
  def initialize                    ◀──❶
    @list = ""
    @level = 0
  end
  def indent(string)                ◀──❷
    " " * @level + string.to_s
  end                           ❸
  def method_missing(m, &block)    ◀──    ❹
    @list << indent(m) + ":"           ◀──
    @list << "\n"                          ❺
    @level += 2                        ◀──    ❻
    @list << indent(yield(self)) if block    ◀──
    @level -= 2
    @list << "\n"
    return ""                      ◀──❼
  end
end
```

On initialization, two instance variables are set ❶: @list will serve as the string accumulator for the entire list, and @level will guide indentation. The indent method ❷ takes a string (or anything that can be converted to a string; it calls to_s on its argument) and returns that string indented to the right by @level spaces.

Most of the action is in method_missing ❸. The symbol m represents the missing method name—presumably corresponding to a header or item for the list. Accordingly, the first step is to add m (indented, and followed by a colon) to @list, along with a newline character ❹. Next we increase the indentation level ❺ and yield ❻. (This step happens only if block isn't nil. Normally, you can test for the presence of a block with block_given?, but BasicObject instances don't have that method!) Yielding may trigger more missing method calls, in which case they're processed and their results added to @list at the new indentation level. After getting the results of the yield, we decrement the indentation level and add another newline to @list.

At the end, method_missing returns an empty string ❼. The goal here is to avoid concatenating @list to itself. If method_missing ended with an expression evaluating to @list (like @list << "\n"), then nested calls to method_missing inside yield instructions would return @list and append it to itself. The empty string breaks the cycle.

Here's an example of Lister in use:

```
lister = Lister.new
lister.groceries do |item|
  item.name { "Apples" }
  item.quantity { 10 }
  item.name { "Sugar" }
  item.quantity { "1 lb" }
end
lister.freeze do |f|
  f.name { "Ice cream" }
end
lister.inspect do |i|
  i.item { "car" }
end
lister.sleep do |s|
  s.hours { 8 }
end
lister.print do |document|
  document.book { "Chapter 13" }
  document.letter { "to editor" }
end
puts lister.list
```

The output from this run is as follows:

```
groceries:
  name:
    Apples
  quantity:
    10
  name:
    Sugar
```

```
   quantity:
     1 lb
freeze:
  name:
     Ice cream
inspect:
   item:
      car
sleep:
   hours:
      8
print:
   book:
      Chapter 13
   letter:
      to editor
```

Admittedly not as gratifying as `Builder`—but you can follow the yields and missing method calls and see how you benefit from a `BasicObject` instance. And if you look at the method names used in the sample code, you'll see some that are built-in methods of (nonbasic) objects. If you don't inherit from `BasicObject`, you'll get an error when you try to call `freeze` or `inspect`. It's also interesting to note that `sleep` and `print`, which are private methods of `Kernel` and therefore not normally callable with an explicit receiver, trigger `method_missing` even though strictly speaking they're private rather than missing.

Our look at `BasicObject` brings us to the end of this survey of object individuation. We'll be moving next to a different topic that's also deeply involved in Ruby dynamics: callable and runnable objects.

13.4   *Summary*

In this chapter, you've seen

- Singleton classes and how to add methods and constants to them
- Class methods
- The `extend` method
- Several approaches to changing Ruby's core behavior
- `BasicObject` and how to leverage it

We've looked at the ways that Ruby objects live up to the philosophy of Ruby, which is that what happens at runtime is all about individual objects and what they can do at any given point. Ruby objects are born into a particular class, but their ability to store individual methods in a dedicated singleton class means that any object can do almost anything.

You've seen how to open singleton class definitions and manipulate the innards of individual objects, including class objects that make heavy use of singleton-method techniques in connection with class methods (which are, essentially, singleton methods on class objects). You've also seen some of the power, as well as the risks, of the ability Ruby gives you to pry open not only your own classes but also Ruby's core classes. This is something you should do sparingly, if at all—and it's also something you should be aware of other people doing, so that you can evaluate the risks of any third-party code you're using that changes core behaviors.

We ended with an examination of `BasicObject`, the ultimate ancestor of all classes and a class you can use in cases where even a vanilla Ruby object isn't vanilla enough.

The next chapter will take us into the area of callable and runnable objects: functions (`Proc` objects), threads, `eval` blocks, and more. The fact that you can create objects that embody runnable code and manipulate those objects as you would any object adds yet another major layer to the overall topic of Ruby dynamics.

Callable and
runnable objects

14

This chapter covers

- `Proc` objects as anonymous functions
- The `lambda` method for generating functions
- Code blocks
- The `Symbol#to_proc` method
- Method objects
- Bindings
- The `eval` family of methods
- Threads
- Executing external programs

In addition to the basic, bread-and-butter method calls that account for most of what happens in your program, Ruby provides an extensive toolkit for making things happen in a variety of ways. You need two or more parts of your code to run in parallel? Create some `Thread` objects and run them as needed. Want to choose from among a set of possible functions to execute, and don't have enough information in advance to write methods for them? Create an array of `Proc` objects—anonymous functions—and call the one you need. You can even isolate methods as objects, or execute dynamically created strings as code.

This chapter is about objects that you can call, execute, or run: threads, anonymous functions, strings, and even methods that have been turned into objects. We'll look at all of these constructs along with some auxiliary tools—keywords, variable bindings, code blocks—that make Ruby's inclusion of callable, runnable objects possible.

Be warned: runnable objects have been at the forefront of difficult and changeable topics in recent versions of Ruby. There's no getting around the fact that there's a lot of disagreement about how they should work, and there's a lot of complexity involved in how they do work. Callable and runnable objects differ from each other, in both syntax and purpose, and grouping them together in one chapter is a bit of an expedient. But it's also an instructive way to view these objects.

14.1 Basic anonymous functions: The Proc class

At its most straightforward, the notion of a *callable object* is embodied in Ruby through objects to which you can send the message `call`, with the expectation that some code associated with the objects will be executed. The main callable objects in Ruby are `Proc` objects, lambdas, and method objects. `Proc` objects are self-contained code sequences that you can create, store, pass around as method arguments, and, when you wish, execute with the `call` method. Lambdas are similar to `Proc` objects. Truth be told, a lambda *is* a `Proc` object, but one with slightly special internal engineering. The differences will emerge as we examine each in turn. Method objects represent methods extracted into objects that you can, similarly, store, pass around, and execute.

We'll start our exploration of callable objects with `Proc` objects.

> **NOTE** For the sake of conciseness, the term *proc* (in regular font) will serve in the text to mean `Proc` object, much as *string* refers to an instance of the class `String`. *Lambda* will mean an instance of the lambda style of `Proc` object. (Don't worry; you'll see what that means soon!) The term *function* is a generic term for standalone units of code that take input and return a value. There's no `Function` class in Ruby. Here, however, you'll sometimes see *function* used to refer to procs and lambdas. It's just another, slightly more abstract way of identifying those objects.

14.1.1 Proc objects

Understanding `Proc` objects thoroughly means being familiar with several things: the basics of creating and using procs; the way procs handle arguments and variable bindings; the role of procs as *closures*; the relationship between procs and code blocks; and the difference between creating procs with `Proc.new`, the `proc` method, the `lambda` method, and the literal lambda constructor `->`. There's a lot going on here, but it all fits together if you take it one layer at a time.

Let's start with the basic callable object: an instance of `Proc`, created with `Proc.new`. You create a `Proc` object by instantiating the `Proc` class, including a code block:

```
pr = Proc.new { puts "Inside a Proc's block" }
```

The code block becomes the body of the proc; when you call the proc, the block you provided is executed. Thus if you call pr

```
pr.call
```

it reports as follows:

```
Inside a Proc's block
```

That's the basic scenario: a code block supplied to a call to Proc.new becomes the body of the Proc object and gets executed when you call that object. Everything else that happens, or that can happen, involves additions to and variations on this theme.

   Remember that procs are objects. That means you can assign them to variables, put them inside arrays, send them around as method arguments, and generally treat them as you would any other object. They have knowledge of a chunk of code (the code block they're created with) and the ability to execute that code when asked to. But they're still objects.

> **The proc method**
>
> The proc method takes a block and returns a Proc object. Thus you can say proc { puts "Hi!" } instead of Proc.new { puts "Hi!" } and get the same result. Proc.new and proc used to be slightly different from each other, with proc serving as a synonym for lambda (see section 14.2) and the proc/lambda methods producing specialized Proc objects that weren't quite the same as what Proc.new produced. Yes, it was confusing. But now, although there are still two variants of the Proc object, Proc.new and proc do the same thing, whereas lambda produces the other variant. At least the naming lines up more predictably.

Perhaps the most important aspect of procs to get a handle on is the relation between procs and code blocks. That relation is intimate and turns out to be an important key to further understanding.

14.1.2 *Procs and blocks and how they differ*

When you create a Proc object, you always supply a code block. But not every code block serves as the basis of a proc. The snippet

```
[1,2,3].each {|x| puts x * 10 }
```

involves a code block but does not create a proc. Yet the plot is a little thicker than that. A method can capture a block, objectified into a proc, using the special parameter syntax that you saw briefly in chapter 9:

```
def call_a_proc(&block)
  block.call
end
call_a_proc { puts "I'm the block...or Proc...or something." }
```

The output isn't surprising:

```
I'm the block...or Proc...or something.
```

But it's also possible for a proc to serve in place of the code block in a method call, using a similar special syntax:

```
p = Proc.new {|x| puts x.upcase }
%w{ David Black }.each(&p)
```

Here's the output from that call to each:

```
DAVID
BLACK
```

But the question remains: exactly what's going on with regard to procs and blocks? Why and how does the presence of (&p) convince each that it doesn't need an actual code block?

To a large extent, the relation between blocks and procs comes down to a matter of syntax versus objects.

SYNTAX (BLOCKS) AND OBJECTS (PROCS)

An important and often misunderstood fact is that a Ruby code block is not an object. This familiar trivial example has a receiver, a dot operator, a method name, and a code block:

```
[1,2,3].each {|x| puts x * 10 }
```

The receiver is an object, but the code block isn't. Rather, the code block is part of the syntax of the method call.

You can put code blocks in context by thinking of the analogy with argument lists. In a method call with arguments

```
puts c2f(100)
```

the arguments are objects but the argument list itself—the whole (100) thing—isn't an object. There's no ArgumentList class, and there's no CodeBlock class.

Things get a little more complex in the case of block syntax than in the case of argument lists, though, because of the way blocks and procs interoperate. An instance of Proc is an object. A code block contains everything that's needed to create a proc. That's why Proc.new takes a code block: that's how it finds out what the proc is supposed to do when it gets called.

One important implication of the fact that the code block is a syntactic construct and not an object is that code blocks aren't method arguments. The matter of providing arguments to a method is independent of whether a code block is present, just as the presence of a block is independent of the presence or absence of an argument list. When you provide a code block, you're not sending the block to the method as an argument; you're providing a code block, and that's a thing unto itself. Let's take another, closer look now at the conversion mechanisms that allow code blocks to be captured as procs, and procs to be pressed into service in place of code blocks.

14.1.3 *Block-proc conversions*

Conversion between blocks and procs is easy—which isn't too surprising, because the purpose of a code block is to be executed, and a proc is an object whose job is to provide execution access to a previously defined code block. We'll look first at block-to-proc conversions and then at the use of procs in place of blocks.

CAPTURING A CODE BLOCK AS A PROC

Let's start with another simple method that captures its code block as a Proc object and subsequently calls that object:

```
def capture_block(&block)
  block.call
end
capture_block { puts "Inside the block" }
```

What happens is a kind of implicit call to Proc.new, using the same block. The proc thus created is bound to the parameter block.

Figure 14.1 provides an artist's rendering of how a code block becomes a proc. The first event (at the bottom of the figure) is the calling of the method capture_block with a code block. Along the way, a new Proc object is created (step 2) using the same block. It's this Proc object to which the variable block is bound, inside the method body (step 3).

The syntactic element (the code block) thus serves as the basis for the creation of an object. The "phantom" step of creating the proc from the block also explains the need for the special &-based syntax. A method call can include both an argument list and a code block. Without a special flag like &, Ruby has no way of knowing that you want to stop binding parameters to regular arguments and instead perform a block-to-proc conversion and save the results.

The & also makes an appearance when you want to do the conversion the other way: use a Proc object instead of a code block.

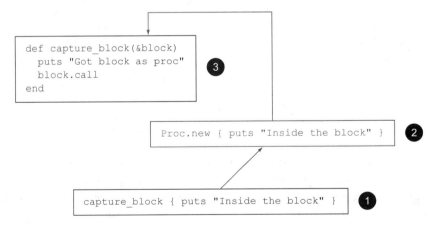

Figure 14.1   A phantom Proc instantiation intervenes between a method call and a method.

USING PROCS FOR BLOCKS

Here's how you might call `capture_block` using a proc instead of a code block:

```
p = Proc.new { puts "This proc argument will serve as a code block." }
capture_block(&p)
```

The output is

```
This proc argument will serve as a code block.
```

The key to using a proc as a block is that you actually use it instead of a block: you send the proc as an argument to the method you're calling. Just as you tag the parameter in the method definition with the & character to indicate that it should convert the block to a proc, so too you use the & on the method-calling side to indicate that the proc should do the job of a code block.

Keep in mind that because the proc tagged with & is serving as the code block, you can't send a code block in the same method call. If you do, you'll get an error. The call

```
capture_block(&p) { puts "This is the explicit block" }
```

results in the error "both block arg and actual block given." Ruby can't decide which entity—the proc or the block—is serving as the block, so you can use only one.

An interesting subplot is going on here. Like many Ruby operators, the & in &p is a wrapper around a method: namely, the method `to_proc`. Calling `to_proc` on a `Proc` object returns the `Proc` object itself, rather like calling `to_s` on a string or `to_i` on an integer.

But note that you still need the &. If you do this

```
capture_block(p)
```

or this

```
capture_block(p.to_proc)
```

the proc serves as a regular argument to the method. You aren't triggering the special behavior whereby a proc argument does the job of a code block.

Thus the & in `capture_block(&p)` does two things: it triggers a call to p's `to_proc` method, and it tells Ruby that the resulting `Proc` object is serving as a code block stand-in. And because `to_proc` is a method, it's possible to use it in a more general way.

GENERALIZING TO_PROC

In theory, you can define `to_proc` in any class or for any object, and the & technique will then work for the affected objects. You probably won't need to do this a lot; the two classes where `to_proc` is most useful are `Proc` (discussed earlier) and `Symbol` (discussed in the next section), and `to_proc` behavior is already built into those classes. But looking at how to roll `to_proc` into your own classes can give you a sense of the dynamic power that lies below the surface of the language.

Here is a rather odd but instructive piece of code:

```
class Person
  attr_accessor :name                        ◁——❶
  def self.to_proc                      ◁┐
    Proc.new {|person| person.name }     │
                                        ❷
  end
end
d = Person.new                 ◁——❸
d.name = "David"
m = Person.new
m.name = "Matz"                      ❹
puts [d,m].map(&Person)          ◁┘
```

The best starting point, if you want to follow the trail of breadcrumbs through this code, is the last line ❹. Here, we have an array of two `Person` objects. We're doing a map operation on the array. As you know, `Array#map` takes a code block. In this case, we're using a `Proc` object instead. That proc is designated in the argument list as `&Person`. Of course, `Person` isn't a proc; it's a class. To make sense of what it sees, Ruby asks `Person` to represent itself as a proc, which means an implicit call to `Person`'s `to_proc` method ❷.

That method, in turn, produces a simple `Proc` object that takes one argument and calls the `name` method on that argument. `Person` objects have `name` attributes ❶. And the `Person` objects created for purposes of trying out the code, sure enough, have names ❸. All of this means that the mapping of the array of `Person` objects (`[d,m]`) will collect the `name` attributes of the objects, and the entire resulting array will be printed out (thanks to `puts`).

It's a long way around. And the design is a bit loose; after all, any method that takes a block could use `&Person`, which might get weird if it involved non-person objects that didn't have a `name` method. But the example shows you that `to_proc` can serve as a powerful conversion hook. And that's what it does in the `Symbol` class, as you'll see next.

14.1.4   *Using Symbol#to_proc for conciseness*

The built-in method `Symbol#to_proc` comes into play in situations like this:

```
%w{ david black }.map(&:capitalize)
```

The result is

```
["David", "Black"]
```

The symbol `:capitalize` is interpreted as a message to be sent to each element of the array in turn. The previous code is thus equivalent to

```
%w{ david black }.map {|str| str.capitalize }
```

but, as you can see, more concise.

If you just saw `&:capitalize` or a similar construct in code, you might think it was cryptic. But knowing how it parses—knowing that `:capitalize` is a symbol and `&` is a `to_proc` trigger—allows you to interpret it correctly and appreciate its expressiveness.

The `Symbol#to_proc` situation lends itself nicely to the elimination of parentheses:

```
%w{ david black }.map &:capitalize
```

By taking off the parentheses, you can make the proc-ified symbol look like it's in code-block position. There's no necessity for this, of course, and you should keep in mind that when you use the `to_proc` & indicator, you're sending the proc as an argument flagged with & and not providing a literal code block.

`Symbol#to_proc` is, among other things, a great example of something that Ruby does for you that you could, if you had to, do easily yourself. Here's how.

IMPLEMENTING SYMBOL#TO_PROC

Here's the `to_proc` case study again:

```
%w{ david black }.map(&:capitalize)
```

We know it's equivalent to this:

```
%w{ david black }.map {|str| str.capitalize }
```

And the same thing could also be written like this:

```
%w{ david black }.map {|str| str.send(:capitalize) }
```

Normally, you wouldn't write it that way, because there's no need to go to the trouble of doing a `send` if you're able to call the method using regular dot syntax. But the send-based version points the way to an implementation of `Symbol#to_proc`. The job of the block in this example is to send the symbol `:capitalize` to each element of the array. That means the `Proc` produced by `:capitalize#to_proc` has to send `:capitalize` to its argument. Generalizing from this, we can come up with this simple (almost anti-climactic, one might say) implementation of `Symbol#to_proc`:

```
class Symbol
  def to_proc
    Proc.new {|obj| obj.send(self) }
  end
end
```

This method returns a `Proc` object that takes one argument and sends `self` (which will be whatever symbol we're using) to that object.

You can try the new implementation in irb. Let's throw in a greeting from the method so it's clear that the version being used is the one we've just defined:

```
class Symbol
  def to_proc
    puts "In the new Symbol#to_proc!"
    Proc.new {|obj| obj.send(self) }
  end
end
```

Save this code to a file called sym2proc.rb, and from the directory to which you've saved it, pull it into irb using the `-I` (include path in load path) flag and the `-r` (require) flag:

```
irb --simple-prompt -I. -r sym2proc
```

Now you'll see the new *to_proc* in action when you use the &:*symbol* technique:

```
>> %w{ david black }.map(&:capitalize)
In the new Symbol#to_proc!
=> ["David", "Black"]
```

You're under no obligation to use the Symbol#to_proc shortcut (let alone implement it), but it's useful to know how it works so you can decide when it's appropriate to use.

One of the most important aspects of Proc objects is their service as *closures*: anonymous functions that preserve the local variable bindings that are in effect when the procs are created. We'll look next at how procs operate as closures.

14.1.5 *Procs as closures*

You've already seen that the local variables you use inside a method body aren't the same as the local variables you use in the scope of the method call:

```
def talk
  a = "Hello"
  puts a
end
a = "Goodbye"           Output:
talk                    Hello        Output:
puts a                               Goodbye
```

The identifier a has been assigned to twice, but the two assignments (the two a variables) are unrelated to each other.

You've also seen that code blocks preserve the variables that were in existence at the time they were created. All code blocks do this:

```
m = 10
[1,2,3].each {|x| puts x * m }
```

This behavior becomes significant when the code block serves as the body of a callable object:

```
def multiply_by(m)
  Proc.new {|x| puts x * m }
end
mult = multiply_by(10)     Ouput:
mult.call(12)              120
```

In this example, the method multiply_by returns a proc that can be called with any argument but that always multiplies by the number sent as an argument to multiply_by. The variable m, whatever its value, is preserved inside the code block passed to Proc.new and therefore serves as the multiplier every time the Proc object returned from multiply_by is called.

Proc objects put a slightly different spin on scope. When you construct the code block for a call to Proc.new, the local variables you've created are still in scope (as with any code block). And those variables remain in scope inside the proc, no matter where or when you call it.

Look at the following listing, and keep your eye on the two variables called a.

```
def call_some_proc(pr)
  a = "irrelevant 'a' in method scope"       ◁—❶
  puts a
  pr.call                                      ◁—❷
end
a = "'a' to be used in Proc block"           ◁—❸
pr = Proc.new { puts a }
pr.call
call_some_proc(pr)
```

As in the previous example, there's an a in the method definition ❶ and an a in the outer (calling) scope ❸. Inside the method is a call to a proc. The code for that proc, we happen to know, consists of `puts a`. Notice that when the proc is called from inside the method ❷, the a that's printed out isn't the a defined in the method; it's the a from the scope where the proc was originally created:

```
'a' to be used in Proc block
irrelevant 'a' in method scope
'a' to be used in Proc block
```

The `Proc` object carries its context around with it. Part of that context is a variable called a to which a particular string is assigned. That variable lives on inside the `Proc`.

A piece of code that carries its creation context around with it like this is called a *closure*. Creating a closure is like packing a suitcase: wherever you open the suitcase, it contains what you put in when you packed it. When you open a closure (by calling it), it contains what you put into it when it was created. Closures are important because they preserve the partial running state of a program. A variable that goes out of scope when a method returns may have something interesting to say later on—and with a closure, you can preserve that variable so it can continue to provide information or calculation results.

The classic closure example is a counter. Here's a method that returns a closure (a proc with the local variable bindings preserved). The proc serves as a counter; it increments its variable every time it's called:

```
def make_counter
  n = 0
  return Proc.new { n += 1 }                  ◁—❶
end
c = make_counter                              ◁—❷
puts c.call
puts c.call
d = make_counter                              ◁—❸
puts d.call
puts c.call                                    ◁—❹
```

The output is

```
1
2
1
3
```

The logic in the proc involves adding 1 to n ❶; so the first time the proc is called, it evaluates to 1; the second time to 2; and so forth. Calling make_counter and then calling the proc it returns confirms this: first 1 is printed, and then 2 ❷. But a new counter starts again from 1; the second call to make_counter ❸ generates a new, local n, which gets preserved in a different proc. The difference between the two counters is made clear by the third call to the first counter, which prints 3 ❹. It picks up where it left off, using the n variable that was preserved inside it at the time of its creation.

Like any code block, the block you provide when you create a Proc object can take arguments. Let's look in detail at how block arguments and parameters work in the course of Proc creation.

14.1.6 *Proc parameters and arguments*

Here's an instantiation of Proc, with a block that takes one argument:

```
pr = Proc.new {|x| puts "Called with argument #{x}" }
pr.call(100)
```

The output is

```
Called with argument 100
```

Procs differ from methods, with respect to argument handling, in that they don't care whether they get the right number of arguments. A one-argument proc, like this

```
>> pr = Proc.new {|x| p x }
=> #<Proc:0x000001029a8960@(irb):1>
```

can be called with any number of arguments, including none. If it's called with no arguments, its single parameter gets set to nil:

```
>> pr.call
nil
```

If it's called with more than one argument, the single parameter is bound to the first argument, and the remaining arguments are discarded:

```
>> pr.call(1,2,3)
1
```

(Remember that the single value printed out is the value of the variable x.)

You can, of course, also use "sponge" arguments and all the rest of the parameter-list paraphernalia you've already learned about. But keep in mind the point that procs are a little less fussy than methods about their argument count—their *arity*. Still, Ruby provides a way to create fussier functions: the lambda method.

14.2 *Creating functions with lambda and ->*

Like Proc.new, the lambda method returns a Proc object, using the provided code block as the function body:

```
>> lam = lambda { puts "A lambda!" }
=> #<Proc:0x0000010299a1d0@(irb):2 (lambda)>
```

```
>> lam.call
A lambda!
```

As the inspect string suggests, the object returned from `lambda` is of class `Proc`. But note the `(lambda)` notation. There's no `Lambda` class, but there is a distinct lambda flavor of the `Proc` class. And lambda-flavored procs are a little different from their vanilla cousins, in three ways.

First, lambdas require explicit creation. Wherever Ruby creates `Proc` objects implicitly, they're regular procs and not lambdas. That means chiefly that when you grab a code block in a method, like this

```
def m(&block)
```

the `Proc` object you've grabbed is a regular proc, not a lambda.

Second, lambdas differ from procs in how they treat the `return` keyword. `return` inside a lambda triggers an exit from the body of the lambda to the code context immediately containing the lambda. `return` inside a proc triggers a return from the method in which the proc is being executed. Here's an illustration of the difference:

```
def return_test
  l = lambda { return }
  l.call                                  ⬅—❶
  puts "Still here!"
  p = Proc.new { return }          ❷
  p.call                            ⬅—┘
  puts "You won't see this message!"      ⬅—❸
end
return_test
```

The output of this snippet is `"Still here!"` You'll never see the second message ❸ printed out because the call to the `Proc` object ❷ triggers a return from the `return_test` method. But the call to the lambda ❶ triggers a return (an exit) from the body of the lambda, and execution of the method continues where it left off.

> **WARNING** Because `return` from inside a (non-lambda-flavored) proc triggers a return from the enclosing method, calling a proc that contains `return` when you're not inside any method produces a fatal error. To see a demo of this error, try it from the command line: `ruby -e 'Proc.new { return }.call'`.

Finally, and most important, lambda-flavored procs don't like being called with the wrong number of arguments. They're fussy:

```
>> lam = lambda {|x| p x }
=> #<Proc:0x000001029901f8@(irb):3 (lambda)>
>> lam.call(1)
1
=> 1
>> lam.call
ArgumentError: wrong number of arguments (0 for 1)
>> lam.call(1,2,3)
ArgumentError: wrong number of arguments (3 for 1)
```

In addition to the lambda method, there's a lambda literal constructor.

THE "STABBY LAMBDA" CONSTRUCTOR, ->

The lambda constructor (nicknamed the "stabby lambda") works like this:

```
>> lam = -> { puts "hi" }
=> #<Proc:0x0000010289f140@(irb):1 (lambda)>
>> lam.call
hi
```

If you want your lambda to take arguments, you need to put your parameters in parentheses after the ->, *not* in vertical pipes inside the code block:

```
>> mult = ->(x,y) { x * y }
=> #<Proc:0x00000101023c38@(irb):7 (lambda)>
>> mult.call(3,4)
=> 12
```

A bit of history: the stabby lambda exists in the first place because older versions of Ruby had trouble parsing method-style argument syntax inside the vertical pipes. For example, in Ruby 1.8 you couldn't use default-argument syntax like this:

```
lambda {|a,b=1| "Doesn't work in Ruby 1.8 -- syntax error!" }
```

The problem was that Ruby didn't know whether the second pipe was a second delimiter or a bitwise OR operator. The stabby lambda was introduced to make it possible to use full-blown method-style arguments with lambdas:

```
->(a, b=1) { "Works in Ruby 1.8!" }
```

Eventually, the parser limitation was overcome; you can now use method-argument syntax, in all its glory, between the vertical pipes in a code block. Strictly speaking, therefore, the stabby lambda is no longer necessary. But it attracted a bit of a following, and you'll see it used fairly widely.

In practice, the things you call most often in Ruby aren't procs or lambdas but methods. So far, we've viewed the calling of methods as something we do at one level of remove: we send messages to objects, and the objects execute the appropriately named method. But it's possible to handle methods as objects, as you'll see next.

14.3   Methods as objects

Methods don't present themselves as objects until you tell them to. Treating methods as objects involves *objectifying* them.

14.3.1   Capturing Method objects

You can get hold of a Method object by using the method method with the name of the method as an argument (in string or symbol form):

```
class C
  def talk
    puts "Method-grabbing test!  self is #{self}."
  end
end
c = C.new
meth = c.method(:talk)
```

At this point, you have a Method object—specifically, a *bound* Method object: it isn't the method `talk` in the abstract, but rather the method `talk` specifically bound to the object `c`. If you send a `call` message to `meth`, it knows to call itself with `c` in the role of `self`:

```
meth.call
```

Here's the output:

```
Method-grabbing test!  self is #<C:0x00000101201a00>.
```

You can also unbind the method from its object and then bind it to another object, as long as that other object is of the same class as the original object (or a subclass):

```
class D < C
end
d = D.new
unbound = meth.unbind
unbound.bind(d).call
```

Here, the output tells you that the method was, indeed, bound to a D object (d) at the time it was executed:

```
Method-grabbing test!  self is #<D:0x000001011d0220>.
```

To get hold of an unbound method object directly without having to call `unbind` on a bound method, you can get it from the class rather than from a specific instance of the class using the `instance_method` method. This single line is equivalent to a `method` call plus an `unbind` call:

```
unbound = C.instance_method(:talk)
```

After you have the unbound method in captivity, so to speak, you can use `bind` to bind it to any instance of either `C` or a `C` subclass like `D`.

But why would you?

14.3.2 *The rationale for methods as objects*

There's no doubt that unbinding and binding methods is a specialized technique, and you're not likely to need more than a reading knowledge of it. But aside from the principle that at least a reading knowledge of anything in Ruby can't be a bad idea, on some occasions the best answer to a "how to" question is, "With unbound methods."

Here's an example. The following question comes up periodically in Ruby forums:

Suppose I've got a class hierarchy where a method gets redefined:

```
class A
  def a_method
    puts "Definition in class A"
  end
end
class B < A
  def a_method
    puts "Definition in class B (subclass of A)"
  end
end
```

```
class C < B
end
```

And I've got an instance of the subclass:

```
c = C.new
```

Is there any way to get that instance of the lowest class to respond to the message (a_method) *by executing the version of the method in the class two classes up the chain?*

By default, of course, the instance doesn't do that; it executes the first matching method it finds as it traverses the method search path:

```
c.a_method
```

The output is

```
Definition in class B (subclass of A)
```

But you can force the issue through an unbind and bind operation:

```
A.instance_method(:a_method).bind(c).call
```

Here the output is

```
Definition in class A
```

You can even stash this behavior inside a method in class C:\

```
class C
  def call_original
    A.instance_method(:a_method).bind(self).call
  end
end
```

and then call `call_original` directly on c.

This is an example of a Ruby technique with a paradoxical status: it's within the realm of things you should understand, as someone gaining mastery of Ruby's dynamics, but it's outside the realm of anything you should probably do. If you find yourself coercing Ruby objects to respond to methods you've already redefined, you should review the design of your program and find a way to get objects to do what you want as a result of and not in spite of the class/module hierarchy you've created.

Still, methods are callable objects, and they can be detached (unbound) from their instances. As a Ruby dynamics inductee, you should at least have recognition-level knowledge of this kind of operation.

We'll linger in the dynamic stratosphere for a while, looking next at the eval family of methods: a small handful of methods with special powers to let you run strings as code and manipulate scope and self in some interesting, use-case-driven ways.

> **Alternative techniques for calling callable objects**
>
> So far we've exclusively used the `call` method to call callable objects. You do, however, have a couple of other options.
>
> One is the square-brackets method/operator, which is a synonym for `call`. You place any arguments inside the brackets:
>
> ```
> mult = lambda {|x,y| x * y }
> twelve = mult[3,4]
> ```
>
> If there are no arguments, leave the brackets empty.
>
> You can also call callable objects using the () method:
>
> ```
> twelve = mult.(3,4)
> ```
>
> Note the dot before the opening parenthesis. The () method has to be called using a dot; you can't just append the parentheses to a `Proc` or `Method` object the way you would with a method name. If there are no arguments, leave the parentheses empty.

14.4　*The eval family of methods*

Like many languages, Ruby has a facility for executing code stored in the form of strings at runtime. In fact, Ruby has a cluster of techniques to do this, each of which serves a particular purpose but all of which operate on a similar principle: that of saying in the middle of a program, "Whatever code strings you might have read from the program file before starting to execute this program, execute *this* code string right now."

　The most straightforward method for evaluating a string as code, and also the most dangerous, is the method `eval`. Other `eval`-family methods are a little softer, not because they don't also evaluate strings as code but because that's not all they do. `instance_eval` brings about a temporary shift in the value of self, and `class_eval` (also known by the synonym `module_eval`) takes you on an ad hoc side trip into the context of a class-definition block. These `eval`-family methods can operate on strings, but they can also be called with a code block; thus they don't always operate as bluntly as `eval`, which executes strings.

　Let's unpack this description with a closer look at `eval` and the other `eval` methods.

14.4.1　*Executing arbitrary strings as code with eval*

`eval` executes the string you give it:

```
>> eval("2+2")
=> 4
```

`eval` is the answer, or at least one answer, to a number of frequently asked questions, such as, "How do I write a method and give it a name someone types in?" You can do so like this:

```
print "Method name: "
m = gets.chomp
eval("def #{m}; puts 'Hi!'; end")
eval(m)
```

This code outputs

```
Hi!
```

A new method is being written. Let's say you run the code and type in abc. The string you subsequently use eval on is

```
def abc; puts 'Hi!'; end
```

After you apply eval to that string, a method called abc exists. The second eval executes the string abc—which, given the creation of the method in the previous line, constitutes a call to abc. When abc is called, "Inside new method!" is printed out.

The Binding class and eval-ing code with a binding

Ruby has a class called Binding whose instances encapsulate the local variable bindings in effect at a given point in execution. And a top-level method called binding returns whatever the current binding is.

The most common use of Binding objects is in the position of second argument to eval. If you provide a binding in that position, the string being eval-ed is executed in the context of the given binding. Any local variables used inside the eval string are interpreted in the context of that binding.

Here's an example. The method use_a_binding takes a Binding object as an argument and uses it as the second argument to a call to eval. The eval operation, therefore, uses the local variable bindings represented by the Binding object:

```
def use_a_binding(b)
  eval("puts str", b)
end
str = "I'm a string in top-level binding!"
use_a_binding(binding)
```

The output of this snippet is "I'm a string in top-level binding!". That string is bound to the top-level variable str. Although str isn't in scope inside the use_a_binding method, it's visible to eval thanks to the fact that eval gets a binding argument of the top-level binding, in which str is defined and bound.

Thus the string "puts str", which otherwise would raise an error (because str isn't defined), can be eval-ed successfully in the context of the given binding.

eval gives you a lot of power, but it also harbors dangers—in some people's opinion, enough danger to rule it out as a usable technique.

14.4.2 *The dangers of eval*

Executing arbitrary strings carries significant danger—especially (though not exclusively) strings that come from users interacting with your program. For example, it would be easy to inject a destructive command, perhaps a system call to rm -rf /*, into the previous example.

eval can be seductive. It's about as dynamic as a dynamic programming technique can get: you're evaluating strings of code that probably didn't even exist when you wrote the program. Anywhere that Ruby puts up a kind of barrier to absolute, easy manipulation of the state of things during the run of a program, eval seems to offer a way to cut through the red tape and do whatever you want.

But as you can see, eval isn't a panacea. If you're running eval on a string you've written, it's generally no less secure than running a program file you've written. But any time an uncertain, dynamically generated string is involved, the dangers mushroom.

In particular, it's difficult to clean up user input (including input from web forms and files) to the point that you can feel safe about running eval on it. Ruby maintains a global variable called $SAFE, which you can set to a high number (on a scale of 0 to 4) to gain protection from dangers like rogue file-writing requests. $SAFE makes life with eval a lot safer. Still, the best habit to get into is the habit of not using eval.

It isn't hard to find experienced and expert Ruby programmers (as well as programmers in other languages) who never use eval and never will. You have to decide how you feel about it, based on your knowledge of the pitfalls.

Let's move now to the wider eval family of methods. These methods can do the same kind of brute-force string evaluation that eval does, but they also have kinder, gentler behaviors that make them usable and useful.

14.4.3 *The instance_eval method*

instance_eval is a specialized cousin of eval. It evaluates the string or code block you give it, changing self to be the receiver of the call to instance_eval:

```
p self
a = []
a.instance_eval { p self }
```

This snippet outputs two different selfs:

```
main
[]
```

instance_eval is mostly useful for breaking into what would normally be another object's private data—particularly instance variables. Here's how to see the value of an instance variable belonging to any old object (in this case, the instance variable of @x of a C object):

```
class C
  def initialize
    @x = 1
  end
end
```

```
c = C.new
c.instance_eval { puts @x }
```

This kind of prying into another object's state is generally considered impolite; if an object wants you to know something about its state, it provides methods through which you can inquire. Nevertheless, because Ruby dynamics are based on the changing identity of self, it's not a bad idea for the language to give us a technique for manipulating self directly.

The instance_exec method

instance_eval has a close cousin called instance_exec. The difference between the two is that instance_exec can take arguments. Any arguments you pass it will be passed, in turn, to the code block.

This enables you to do things like this:

```
string = "A sample string"
string.instance_exec("s") {|delim| self.split(delim) }
```
Output: ["A ", "ample ", "tring"]

(Not that you'd need to, if you already know the delimiter; but that's the basic technique.)

Unfortunately, which method is which—which of the two takes arguments and which doesn't—just has to be memorized. There's nothing in the terms eval or exec to help you out. Still, it's useful to have both on hand.

Perhaps the most common use of instance_eval is in the service of allowing simplified assignment code like this:

```
david = Person.new do
  name "David"
  age 55
end
```

This looks a bit like we're using accessors, except there's no explicit receiver and no equal signs. How would you make this code work?

Here's what the Person class might look like:

```
class Person
  def initialize(&block)
    instance_eval(&block)        ①
  end

  def name(name=nil)             ②
    @name ||= name               ③
  end

  def age(age=nil)
    @age ||= age
  end
end
```

The key here is the call to `instance_eval` ❶, which reuses the code block that has already been passed in to `new`. Because the code block is being `instance_eval`'d on the new person object (the implicit `self` in the definition of `initialize`), the calls to `name` and `age` are resolved within the `Person` class. Those methods, in turn, act as hybrid setter/getters ❷: they take an optional argument, defaulting to `nil`, and set the relevant instance variables, conditionally, to the value of that argument. If you call them without an argument, they just return the current value of their instance variables ❸.

The result is that you can say `name "David"` instead of `person.name = "David"`. Lots of Rubyists find this kind of miniature DSL (domain-specific language) quite pleasingly compact and elegant.

`instance_eval` (and `instance_exec`) will also happily take a string and evaluate it in the switched `self` context. However, this technique has the same pitfalls as evaluating strings with `eval`, and should be used judiciously if at all.

The last member of the `eval` family of methods is `class_eval` (synonym: `module_eval`).

14.4.4 Using class_eval (a.k.a. module_eval)

In essence, `class_eval` puts you inside a class-definition body:

```
c = Class.new
c.class_eval do
  def some_method
    puts "Created in class_eval"
  end
end
c_instance = c.new
c_instance.some_method          Output: Created
                                in class_eval
```

But you can do some things with `class_eval` that you can't do with the regular `class` keyword:

- Evaluate a string in a class-definition context
- Open the class definition of an anonymous class
- Use existing local variables inside a class-definition body

The third item on this list is particularly noteworthy.

When you open a class with the `class` keyword, you start a new local-variable scope. But the block you use with `class_eval` can see the variables created in the scope surrounding it. Look at the difference between the treatment of `var`, an outer-scope local variable, in a regular class-definition body and a block given to `class_eval`:

```
>> var = "initialized variable"
=> "initialized variable"
>> class C
>>   puts var
>> end
```

```
NameError: undefined local variable or method `var' for C:Class
        from (irb):3
>> C.class_eval { puts var }
initialized variable
```

The variable var is out of scope inside the standard class-definition block but still in scope in the code block passed to class_eval.

The plot thickens when you define an instance method inside the class_eval block:

```
>> C.class_eval { def talk; puts var; end }              .
=> nil
>> C.new.talk
NameError: undefined local variable or method `var' for #<C:0x350ba4>
```

Like any def, the def inside the block starts a new scope—so the variable var is no longer visible.

If you want to shoehorn an outer-scope variable into an instance method, you have to use a different technique for creating the method: the method define_method. You hand define_method the name of the method you want to create (as a symbol or a string) and provide a code block; the code block serves as the body of the method.

To get the outer variable var into an instance method of class C, you do this:

```
>> C.class_eval { define_method("talk") { puts var }  }
=> :talk
```

The return value of define_method is a symbol representing the name of the newly defined method.

At this point, the talk instance method of C will have access to the outer-scope variable var:

```
>> C.new.talk
initialized variable
```

You won't see techniques like this used as frequently as the standard class- and method-definition techniques. But when you see them, you'll know that they imply a flattened scope for local variables rather than the new scope triggered by the more common class and def keywords.

define_method is an instance method of the class Module, so you can call it on any instance of Module or Class. You can thus use it inside a regular class-definition body (where the default receiver self is the class object) if you want to sneak a variable local to the body into an instance method. That's not a frequently encountered scenario, but it's not unheard of.

Ruby lets you do lightweight concurrent programming using threads. We'll look at threads next.

14.5 *Parallel execution with threads*

Ruby's threads allow you to do more than one thing at once in your program, through a form of time sharing: one thread executes one or more instructions and then passes control to the next thread, and so forth. Exactly how the simultaneity of threads plays out depends on your system and your Ruby implementation. Ruby will try to use native operating-system threading facilities, but if such facilities aren't available, it will fall back on *green* threads (threads implemented completely inside the interpreter). We'll black-box the green-versus-native thread issue here; our concern will be principally with threading techniques and syntax.

Creating threads in Ruby is easy: you instantiate the `Thread` class. A new thread starts executing immediately, but the execution of the code around the thread doesn't stop. If the program ends while one or more threads are running, those threads are killed.

Here's a kind of inside-out example that will get you started with threads by showing you how they behave when a program ends:

```
Thread.new do
  puts "Starting the thread"
  sleep 1
  puts "At the end of the thread"
end
puts "Outside the thread"
```

`Thread.new` takes a code block, which constitutes the thread's executable code. In this example, the thread prints a message, sleeps for one second, and then prints another message. But outside of the thread, time marches on: the main body of the program prints a message immediately (it's not affected by the `sleep` command inside the thread), and then the program ends. Unless printing a message takes more than a second—in which case you need to get your hardware checked! The second message from the thread will never be seen. You'll only see this:

```
Starting the thread
Outside the thread
```

Now, what if we want to allow the thread to finish executing? To do this, we have to use the instance method `join`. The easiest way to use `join` is to save the thread in a variable and call `join` on the variable. Here's how you can modify the previous example along these lines:

```
t = Thread.new do
  puts "Starting the thread"
  sleep 1
  puts "At the end of the thread"
end
puts "Outside the thread"
t.join
```

This version of the program produces the following output, with a one-second pause between the printing of the first message from the thread and the printing of the last message:

```
Starting the thread
Outside the thread          ⊲──┤  Pause as program
At the end of the thread        waits for thread to
                                finish execution
```

In addition to joining a thread, you can manipulate it in a variety of other ways, including killing it, putting it to sleep, waking it up, and forcing it to pass control to the next thread scheduled for execution.

14.5.1 *Killing, stopping, and starting threads*

To kill a thread, you send it the message `kill`, `exit`, or `terminate`; all three are equivalent. Or, if you're inside the thread, you call `kill` (or one of its synonyms) in classmethod form on Thread itself.

You may want to kill a thread if an exception occurs inside it. Here's an example, admittedly somewhat contrived but brief enough to illustrate the process efficiently. The idea is to read the contents of three files (part00, part01, and part02) into the string `text`. If any of the files isn't found, the thread terminates:

```
puts "Trying to read in some files..."
t = Thread.new do
  (0..2).each do |n|
    begin
      File.open("part0#{n}") do |f|
        text << f.readlines
      end
    rescue Errno::ENOENT
      puts "Message from thread: Failed on n=#{n}"
      Thread.exit
    end
  end
end
t.join
puts "Finished!"
```

The output, assuming part00 exists but part01 doesn't, is this:

```
Trying to read in some files...
Message from thread: Failed on n=1
Finished!
```

You can also stop and start threads and examine their state. A thread can be asleep or awake, and alive or dead. Here's an example that puts a thread through a few of its paces and illustrates some of the available techniques for examining and manipulating thread state:

```
t = Thread.new do
  puts "[Starting thread]"        ◁⎯⎦  [Starting thread]
  Thread.stop
  puts "[Resuming thread]"             Status of thread:
end                                    sleep
puts "Status of thread: #{t.status}"  ◁⎯⎦
puts "Is thread stopped? #{t.stop?}"       Is thread
puts "Is thread alive? #{t.alive?}"  ◁⎯   stopped? true
puts
puts "Waking up thread and joining it..."  Is thread alive?
t.wakeup                                    true
t.join                          ◁⎯⎦  [Resuming thread]
```

```
puts
puts "Is thread alive? #{t.alive?}"          ⟵┘  Is thread alive? false
puts "Inspect string for thread: #{t.inspect}"  ⟵┐  Inspect string for thread:
                                                 │  # <Thread:0x28d20 dead>
```

Fibers: A twist on threads

In addition to threads, Ruby has a `Fiber` class. Fibers are like reentrant code blocks: they can yield back and forth to their calling context multiple times.

A fiber is created with the `Fiber.new` constructor, which takes a code block. Nothing happens until you tell the fiber to `resume`, at which point the code block starts to run. From within the block, you can suspend the fiber, returning control to the calling context, with the class method `Fiber.yield`.

Here's a simple example involving a *talking* fiber that alternates control a couple of times with its calling context:

```
f = Fiber.new do
  puts "Hi."
  Fiber.yield
  puts "Nice day."
  Fiber.yield
  puts "Bye!"
end
f.resume
puts "Back to the fiber:"
f.resume
puts "One last message from the fiber:"
f.resume
puts "That's all!"
```

Here's the output from this snippet:

```
Hi.
Back to the fiber:
Nice day.
One last message from the fiber:
Bye!
That's all!
```

Among other things, fibers are the technical basis of enumerators, which use fibers to implement their own stop and start operations.

Let's continue exploring threads with a couple of networked examples: a date server and, somewhat more ambitiously, a chat server.

14.5.2 A threaded date server

The date server we'll write depends on a Ruby facility that we haven't looked at yet: `TCPServer`. `TCPServer` is a socket-based class that allows you to start up a server almost unbelievably easily: you instantiate the class and pass in a port number. Here's a simple example of `TCPServer` in action, serving the current date to the first person who connects to it:

```
require 'socket'
s = TCPServer.new(3939)
conn = s.accept
conn.puts "Hi. Here's the date."
conn.puts `date`
conn.close
s.close
```

date in backticks executes
the system date command

Put this example in a file called dateserver.rb, and run it from the command line. (If port 3939 isn't available, change the number to something else.) Now, from a different console, connect to the server:

```
telnet localhost 3939
```

You'll see output similar to the following:

```
Trying 127.0.0.1...
Connected to localhost.
Escape character is '^]'.
Hi. Here's the date.
Sat Jan 18 07:29:11 EST 2014
Connection closed by foreign host.
```

The server has fielded the request and responded.

What if you want the server to field multiple requests? Easy: don't close the socket, and keep accepting connections.

```
require 'socket'
s = TCPServer.new(3939)
while true
  conn = s.accept
  conn.puts "Hi. Here's the date."
  conn.puts `date`
  conn.close
end
```

Now you can ask for the date more than once, and you'll get an answer each time.

Things get trickier when you want to send information *to* the server. Making it work for one user is straightforward; the server can accept input by calling gets:

```
require 'socket'
s = TCPServer.new(3939)
while true
  conn = s.accept
  conn.print "Hi. What's your name? "
  name = conn.gets.chomp
  conn.puts "Hi, #{name}. Here's the date."
  conn.puts `date`
  conn.close
end
```

Accepts line of keyboard
input from client

But if a second client connects to the server while the server is still waiting for the first client's input, the second client sees nothing—not even `What's your name?`—because the server is busy.

That's where threading comes in. Here's a threaded date server that accepts input from the client. The threading prevents the entire application from blocking while it waits for a single client to provide input:

```
require 'socket'
s = TCPServer.new(3939)              ①
while (conn = s.accept)
  Thread.new(conn) do |c|            ②
    c.print "Hi. What's your name? "
    name = c.gets.chomp              ③
    c.puts "Hi, #{name}. Here's the date."
    c.puts `date`
    c.close
  end
end
```

In this version, the server listens continuously for connections ①. Each time it gets one, it spawns a new thread ②. The significance of the argument to `Thread.new` is that if you provide such an argument, it's yielded back to you as the block parameter. In this case, that means binding the connection to the parameter c. Although this technique may look odd (sending an argument to a method, only to get it back when the block is called), it ensures that each thread has a reference to its own connection rather than fighting over the variable conn, which lives outside any thread.

Even if a given client waits for several minutes before typing in a name ③, the server is still listening for new connections, and new threads are still spawned. The threading approach thus allows a server to scale while incorporating two-way transmission between itself and one or more clients.

The next level of complexity is the chat server.

14.5.3 *Writing a chat server using sockets and threads*

We'll start code-first this time. Listing 14.2 shows the chat-server code. A lot of what it does is similar to what the date server does. The main difference is that the chat server keeps a list (an array) of all the incoming connections and uses that list to broadcast the incoming chat messages.

Listing 14.2   Chat server using `TCPServer` and threads

```
require 'socket'                                     ①
def welcome(chatter)                                 ②
  chatter.print "Welcome! Please enter your name: "
  chatter.readline.chomp
end
def broadcast(message, chatters)                     ③
  chatters.each do |chatter|
    chatter.puts message
  end
end
```

```
s = TCPServer.new(3939)                                    ◁─┐
  chatters = []                                            ─④
while (chatter = s.accept)                      ◁─⑤
  Thread.new(chatter) do |c|
    name = welcome(chatter)                     ◁─⑥
    broadcast("#{name} has joined", chatters)
    chatters << chatter
    begin                                       ◁─⑦
      loop do
        line = c.readline
        broadcast("#{name}: #{line}", chatters)     ⑧
      end
    rescue EOFError                             ◁─⑨
      c.close
      chatters.delete(c)                            ⑩
      broadcast("#{name} has left", chatters)
    end
  end
end
```

There's a lot of code in this listing, so we'll take it in the order it executes. First comes the mandatory loading of the socket library ❶. The next several lines define some needed helper methods; we'll come back to those after we've seen what they're helping with. The real beginning of the action is the instantiation of TCPServer and the initialization of the array of chatters ❹.

The server goes into a while loop similar to the loop in the date server ❺. When a chatter connects, the server welcomes it (him or her, really, but *it* will do) ❻. The welcome process involves the welcome method ❷, which takes a chatter—a socket object—as its argument, prints a nice welcome message, and returns a line of client input. Now it's time to notify all the current chatters that a new chatter has arrived. This involves the broadcast method ❸, which is the heart of the chat functionality of the program: it's responsible for going through the array of chatters and sending a message to each one. In this case, the message states that the new client has joined the chat.

After being announced, the new chatter is added to the chatters array. That means it will be included in future message broadcasts.

Now comes the chatting part. It consists of an infinite loop wrapped in a begin/rescue clause ❼. The goal is to accept messages from this client forever but to take action if the client socket reports end-of-file. Messages are accepted via readline ❽, which has the advantage over gets (in this situation, anyway) that it raises an exception on end-of-file. If the chatter leaves the chat, then the next attempt to read a line from that chatter raises EOFError. When that happens, control goes to the rescue block ❾, where the departed chatter is removed from the chatters array and an announcement is broadcast to the effect that the chatter has left ❿.

If there's no EOFError, the chatter's message is broadcast to all chatters ❽.

When using threads, it's important to know how the rules of variable scoping and visibility play out inside threads—and in looking at this topic, which we'll do next, you'll also find out about a special category of thread-specific variables.

14.5.4 *Threads and variables*

Threads run using code blocks, and code blocks can see the variables already created in their local scope. If you create a local variable and change it inside a thread's code block, the change will be permanent:

```
>> a = 1
=> 1
>> Thread.new { a = 2 }
=> #<Thread:0x390d8c run>
>> a
=> 2
```

You can see an interesting and instructive effect if you stop a thread before it changes a variable, and then run the thread:

```
>> t = Thread.new { Thread.stop; a = 3 }
=> #<Thread:0x3e443c run>
>> a
=> 2
>> t.run
=> #<Thread:0x3e443c dead>
>> a
=> 3
```

Global variables remain global, for the most part, in the face of threads. That goes for built-in globals, such as $/ (the input record separator), as well as those you create yourself:

```
>> $/
=> "\n"
>> $var = 1
=> 1
>> Thread.new { $var = 2; $/ = "\n\n" }
=> #<Thread:0x38dbb4 run>
>> $/
=> "\n\n"
>> $var
=> 2
```

But some globals are *thread-local globals*—specifically, the $1, $2, …, $n that are assigned the parenthetical capture values from the most recent regular expression–matching operation. You get a different dose of those variables in every thread. Here's a snippet that illustrates the fact that the $n variables in different threads don't collide:

```
/(abc)/.match("abc")
t = Thread.new do
  /(def)/.match("def")
  puts "$1 in thread: #{$1}"      ◁──┐   Output: $1 in
end.join                                 thread: def
puts "$1 outside thread: #{$1}"  ◁──┐   Output: $1 outside
                                         thread: abc
```

The rationale for this behavior is clear: you can't have one thread's idea of $1 overshadowing the $1 from a different thread, or you'll get extremely odd results. The

$n variables aren't really globals once you see them in the context of the language having threads.

In addition to having access to the usual suite of Ruby variables, threads also have their own variable stash—or, more accurately, a built-in hash that lets them associate symbols or strings with values. These thread keys can be useful.

14.5.5   *Manipulating thread keys*

Thread keys are basically a storage hash for thread-specific values. The keys must be symbols or strings. You can get at the keys by indexing the thread object directly with values in square brackets. You can also get a list of all the keys (without their values) using the `keys` method.

Here's a simple set-and-get scenario using a thread key:

```
t = Thread.new do
  Thread.current[:message] = "Hello"
end
t.join
p t.keys
puts t[:message]
```

The output is

```
[:message]
Hello
```

Threads seem to loom large in games, so let's use a game example to explore thread keys further: a threaded, networked rock/paper/scissors (RPS) game. We'll start with the (threadless) RPS logic in an `RPS` class and use the resulting RPS library as the basis for the game code.

A BASIC ROCK/PAPER/SCISSORS LOGIC IMPLEMENTATION

The next listing shows the `RPS` class, which is wrapped in a `Games` module (because RPS sounds like it might collide with another class name). Save this listing to a file called rps.rb.

> **Listing 14.3   RPS game logic embodied in `Games::RPS` class**

```
module Games
  class RPS
    include Comparable            ◄─── ①
    WINS = [%w{ rock scissors },
            %w{ scissors paper },   ②
            %w{ paper rock }]
    attr_accessor :move           ◄─── ③
    def initialize(move)          ◄──┐
      @move = move.to_s             ④
    end
    def <=>(other)                ◄─── ⑤
      if move == other.move
        0
```

```
      elsif WINS.include?([move, other.move])
        1
      elsif WINS.include?([other.move, move])
        -1
      else
        raise ArgumentError, "Something's wrong"
      end
    end
    def play(other)                          <---6
      if self > other
        self
      elsif other > self
        other
      else
        false
      end
    end
  end
end
```

The RPS class includes the Comparable module ❶; this serves as the basis for determining, ultimately, who wins a game. The WINS constant contains all possible winning combinations in three arrays; the first element in each array beats the second element ❷. There's also a move attribute, which stores the move for this instance of RPS ❸. The initialize method ❹ stores the move as a string (in case it comes in as a symbol).

RPS has a spaceship operator (<=>) method definition ❺ that specifies what happens when this instance of RPS is compared to another instance. If the two have equal moves, the result is 0—the signal that the two terms of a spaceship comparison are equal. The rest of the logic looks for winning combinations using the WINS array, returning -1 or 1 depending on whether this instance or the other instance has won. If it doesn't find that either player has a win, and the result isn't a tie, it raises an exception.

Now that RPS objects know how to compare themselves, it's easy to play them against each other, which is what the play method does ❻. It's simple: whichever player is higher is the winner, and if it's a tie, the method returns false.

We're now ready to incorporate the RPS class in a threaded, networked version of the game, thread keys and all.

USING THE RPS CLASS IN A THREADED GAME

The following listing shows the networked RPS program. It waits for two people to join, gets their moves, reports the result, and exits. Not glitzy—but a good way to see how thread keys might help you.

Listing 14.4 Threaded, networked RPS program using thread keys

```
require 'socket'
require_relative 'rps'          ❶
s = TCPServer.new(3939)    <---   ❷
threads = []                     <---
```

```
2.times do |n|                                    ❸
  conn = s.accept
  threads << Thread.new(conn) do |c|         <─┐
    Thread.current[:number] = n + 1            ❹
    Thread.current[:player] = c
    c.puts "Welcome, player #{n+1}!"
    c.print "Your move? (rock, paper, scissors) "
    Thread.current[:move] = c.gets.chomp
    c.puts "Thanks... hang on."
  end
end                              ┌─ Use parallel assignment
a,b = threads              <──── │  syntax to assign two
a.join                           │  variables from an array
b.join
rps1, rps2 = Games::RPS.new(a[:move]), Games::RPS.new(b[:move])  <── ❻
winner = rps1.play(rps2)
if winner
  result = winner.move              ❼
else
  result = "TIE!"
end
threads.each do |t|
  t[:player].puts "The winner is #{result}!"    ❽
end
```

This program loads and uses the `Games::RPS` class, so make sure you have the RPS code in the file rps.rb in the same directory as the program itself.

As in the chat-server example, we start with a server ❶ along with an array in which threads are stored ❷. Rather than loop forever, though, we gather only two threads, courtesy of the `2.times` loop and the server's `accept` method ❸. For each of the two connections, we create a thread ❹.

Now we store some values in the thread's keys: a number for this player (based off the `times` loop, adding 1 so that there's no player 0) and the connection. We then welcome the player and store the move in the `:move` key of the thread.

After both players have played, we grab the two threads in the convenience variables a and b and join both threads ❺. Next, we parlay the two thread objects, which have memory of the players' moves, into two RPS objects ❻. The winner is determined by playing one against the other. The final result of the game is either the winner or, if the game returned false, a tie ❼.

Finally, we report the results to both players ❽. You could get fancier by inputting their names or repeating the game and keeping score. But the main point of this version of the game is to illustrate the usefulness of thread keys. Even after the threads have finished running, they remember information, and that enables us to play an entire game as well as send further messages through the players' sockets.

We're at the end of our look at Ruby threads. It's worth noting that threads are an area that has undergone and continues to undergo a lot of change and development. But whatever happens, you can build on the grounding you've gotten here as you explore and use threads further.

Next on the agenda, and last for this chapter, is the topic of issuing system commands from Ruby.

14.6 *Issuing system commands from inside Ruby programs*

You can issue system commands in several ways in Ruby. We'll look primarily at two of them: the system method and the `` `` `` (backticks) technique. The other ways to communicate with system programs involve somewhat lower-level programming and are more system-dependent and therefore somewhat outside the scope of this book. We'll take a brief look at them nonetheless, and if they seem to be something you need, you can explore them further.

14.6.1 *The system method and backticks*

The system method calls a system program. Backticks (`` `` ``) call a system program and return its output. The choice depends on what you want to do.

EXECUTING SYSTEM PROGRAMS WITH THE SYSTEM METHOD
To use system, send it the name of the program you want to run, with any arguments. The program uses the current STDIN, STDOUT, and STDERR. Here are three simple examples. cat and grep require pressing Ctrl-d (or whatever the "end-of-file" key is on your system) to terminate them and return control to irb. For clarity, Ruby's output is in bold and user input is in regular font:

```
>> system("date")
Sat Jan 18 07:32:11 EST 2014
=> true
>> system("cat")
I'm typing on the screen for the cat command.
I'm typing on the screen for the cat command.
=> true
>> system('grep "D"')
one
two
David
David
```

When you use system, the global variable $? is set to a Process::Status object that contains information about the call: specifically, the process ID of the process you just ran and its exit status. Here's a call to date and one to cat, the latter terminated with Ctrl-c. Each is followed by examination of $?:

```
>> system("date")
Sat Jan 18 07:32:11 EST 2014
=> true
>> $?
=> #<Process::Status: pid 28025 exit 0>
>> system("cat")
^C=> false
>> $?
=> #<Process::Status: pid 28026 SIGINT (signal 2)>
```

And here's a call to a nonexistent program:

```
>> system("datee")
=> nil
>> $?
=> #<Process::Status: pid 28037 exit 127>
```

The $? variable is thread-local: if you call a program in one thread, its return value affects only the $? in that thread:

```
>> system("date")
Sat Jan 18 07:32:11 EST 2014
=> true
>> $?
=> #<Process::Status: pid 28046 exit 0>        ◄─┐   ❶
>> Thread.new { system("datee"); p $? }.join   ◄── ❷
#<Process::Status: pid 28047 exit 127>         ◄─
=> #<Thread:0x3af840 dead>                          ❸
>> $?
=> #<Process::Status: pid 28046 exit 0>        ◄── ❹
```

The `Process::Status` object reporting on the call to date is stored in $? in the main thread ❶. The new thread makes a call to a nonexistent program ❷, and that thread's version of $? reflects the problem ❸. But the main thread's $? is unchanged ❹. The thread-local global variable behavior works much like it does in the case of the $*n* regular-expression capture variables—and for similar reasons. In both cases, you don't want one thread reacting to an error condition that it didn't cause and that doesn't reflect its actual program flow.

The backtick technique is a close relative of system.

CALLING SYSTEM PROGRAMS WITH BACKTICKS

To issue a system command with backticks, put the command between backticks. The main difference between system and backticks is that the return value of the backtick call is the output of the program you run:

```
>> d = `date`
=> "Sat Jan 18 07:32:11 EST 2014\n"
>> puts d
Sat Jan 18 07:32:11 EST 2014
=> nil
>> output = `cat`
I'm typing into cat. Since I'm using backticks,
I won't see each line echoed back as I type it.
Instead, cat's output is going into the
variable output.
=> "I'm typing into cat. Since I'm using backticks,\nI won't etc.
>> puts output
I'm typing into cat. Since I'm using backticks,
I won't see each line echoed back as I type it.
Instead, cat's output is going into the
variable output.
```

The backticks set $? just as system does. A call to a nonexistent method with backticks raises a fatal error:

```
>> `datee`
Errno::ENOENT: No such file or directory - datee
>> $?
=> #<Process::Status: pid 28094 exit 127>
>> `date`
=> "Sat Jan 18 07:35:32 EST 2014\n"
>> $?
=> #<Process::Status: pid 28095 exit 0>
```

> ### Some system command bells and whistles
>
> There's yet another way to execute system commands from within Ruby: the %x operator. %x{date}, for example, will execute the date command. Like the backticks, %x returns the string output of the command. Like its relatives %w and %q (among others), %x allows any delimiter, as long as bracket-style delimiters match: %x{date}, %x-date-, and %x(date) are all synonymous.
>
> Both the backticks and %x allow string interpolation:
>
> ```
> command = "date"
> %x(#{command})
> ```
>
> This can be convenient, although the occasions on which it's a good idea to call dynamically evaluated strings as system commands are, arguably, few.

Backticks are extremely useful for capturing external program output, but they aren't the only way to do it. This brings us to the third way of running programs from within a Ruby program: open and Open.popen3.

14.6.2 Communicating with programs via open and popen3

Using the open family of methods to call external programs is a lot more complex than using system and backticks. We'll look at a few simple examples, but we won't plumb the depths of the topic. These Ruby methods map directly to the underlying system-library calls that support them, and their exact behavior may vary from one system to another more than most Ruby behavior does.

Still—let's have a look. We'll discuss two methods: open and the class method Open.popen3.

TALKING TO EXTERNAL PROGRAMS WITH OPEN

You can use the top-level open method to do two-way communication with an external program. Here's the old standby example of cat:

```
>> d = open("|cat", "w+")        ← ❶
=> #<IO:fd 11>
>> d.puts "Hello to cat"         ← ❷
=> nil
```

```
>> d.gets                        ←┐
=> "Hello to cat\n"               ❸
>> d.close                  ←──❹
=> nil
```

The call to open is generic; it could be any I/O stream, but in this case it's a two-way connection to a system command ❶. The pipe in front of the word cat indicates that we're looking to talk to a program and not open a file. The handle on the external program works much like an I/O socket or file handle. It's open for reading and writing (the w+ mode), so we can write to it ❷ and read from it ❸. Finally, we close it ❹.

It's also possible to take advantage of the block form of open and save the last step:

```
>> open("|cat", "w+") {|p| p.puts("hi"); p.gets }
=> "hi\n"
```

A somewhat more elaborate and powerful way to perform two-way communication between your Ruby program and an external program is the Open3.popen3 method.

TWO-WAY COMMUNICATION WITH OPEN3.POPEN3

The Open3.popen3 method opens communication with an external program and gives you handles on the external program's standard input, standard output, and standard error streams. You can thus write to and read from those handles separately from the analogous streams in your program.

Here's a simple cat-based example of Open.popen3:

```
>> require 'open3'               ←──❶
=> true
>> stdin, stdout, stderr = Open3.popen3("cat")    ←──❷
=> [#<IO:fd 10>, #<IO:fd 11>, #<IO:fd 13>,
   #<Thread:0x000001011356f8 sleep>]              ❸
>> stdin.puts("Hi.\nBye")          ←┐
=> nil                              ❹
>> stdout.gets               ←┐
=> "Hi.\n"                     ❺
>> stdout.gets
=> "Bye\n"
```

After loading the open3 library ❶, we make the call to Open3.popen3, passing it the name of the external program ❷. We get back three I/O handles and a thread ❸. (You can ignore the thread.) These I/O handles go into and out of the external program. Thus we can write to the STDIN handle ❹ and read lines from the STDOUT handle ❺. These handles aren't the same as the STDIN and STDOUT streams of the irb session itself.

The next example shows a slightly more elaborate use of Open.popen3. Be warned: in itself, it's trivial. Its purpose is to illustrate some of the basic mechanics of the technique—and it uses threads, so it reillustrates some thread techniques too. The following listing shows the code.

```ruby
require 'open3'
stdin, stdout, stderr = Open3.popen3("cat")
t = Thread.new do                          ◁——❶
  loop { stdin.puts gets }
end
u = Thread.new do           ◁——❷
  n = 0
  str = ""
  loop do
     str << stdout.gets
     n += 1
     if n % 3 == 0                         ◁——❸
       puts "--------\n"
       puts str
       puts "--------\n"
       str = ""
     end
  end
end
t.join
u.join
```

The program opens a two-way pipe to cat and uses two threads to talk and listen to that pipe. The first thread, t ❶, loops forever, listening to STDIN—your STDIN, not cat's—and writing each line to the STDIN handle on the cat process. The second thread, u ❷, maintains a counter (n) and a string accumulator (str). When the counter hits a multiple of 3, as indicated by the modulo test ❸, the u thread prints out a horizontal line, the three text lines it's accumulated so far, and another horizontal line. It then resets the string accumulator to a blank string and goes back to listening.

If you run this program, remember that it loops forever, so you'll have to interrupt it with Ctrl-c (or whatever your system uses for an interrupt signal). The output is, predictably, somewhat unexciting, but it gives you a good, direct sense of how the threads are interacting with the in and out I/O handles and with each other. In this output, the lines entered by the user are in italics:

```
One
Two
Three
--------
One
Two
Three
--------
Four
Five
Six
--------
Four
Five
Six
--------
```

As stated, we're not going to go into all the details of Open.popen3. But you can and should keep it in mind for situations where you need the most flexibility in reading from and writing to an external program.

14.7   Summary

In this chapter you've seen

- Proc objects
- The lambda "flavor" of process
- Code block-to-proc (and reverse) conversion
- Symbol#to_proc
- Method objects
- Bindings
- eval, instance_eval, and class_eval
- Thread usage and manipulation
- Thread-local "global" variables
- The system method
- Calling system commands with backticks
- The basics of the open and Open.popen3 facilities

Objects in Ruby are products of runtime code execution but can, themselves, have the power to execute code. In this chapter, we've looked at a number of ways in which the general notion of callable and runnable objects plays out. We looked at Proc objects and lambdas, the anonymous functions that lie at the heart of Ruby's block syntax. We also discussed methods as objects and ways of unbinding and binding methods and treating them separately from the objects that call them. The eval family of methods took us into the realm of executing arbitrary strings and also showed some powerful and elegant techniques for runtime manipulation of the program's object and class landscape, using not only eval but, even more, class_eval and instance_eval with their block-wise operations.

Threads figure prominently among Ruby's executable objects; every program runs in a main thread even if it spawns no others. We explored the syntax and semantics of threads and saw how they facilitate projects like multiuser networked communication. Finally, we looked at a variety of ways in which Ruby lets you execute external programs, including the relatively simple system method and backtick technique, and the somewhat more granular and complex open and Open.popen3 facilities.

There's no concrete definition of a callable or runnable object, and this chapter has deliberately taken a fairly fluid approach to understanding the terms. On the one hand, that fluidity results in the juxtaposition of topics that could, imaginably, be handled in separate chapters. (It's hard to argue any direct, close kinship between, say, instance_eval and Open.popen3.) On the other hand, the specifics of Ruby are, to a large extent, manifestations of underlying and supervening principles, and the idea of objects that participate directly in the dynamism of the Ruby landscape is important. Disparate though they may be in some respects, the topics in this chapter all align themselves with that principle; and a good grounding in them will add significantly to your Ruby abilities.

At this point we'll turn to our next—and last—major topic: runtime reflection, introspection, and callbacks.

Callbacks, hooks, *15*
and runtime introspection

In keeping with its dynamic nature and its encouragement of flexible, supple object and program design, Ruby provides a large number of ways to examine what's going on while your program is running and to set up event-based callbacks and hooks—essentially, tripwires that are pulled at specified times and for specific reasons—in the form of methods with special, reserved names for which you can, if you wish, provide definitions. Thus you can rig a module so that a particular method gets called every time a class includes that module, or write a callback method for a class that gets called every time the class is inherited, and so on.

In addition to runtime callbacks, Ruby lets you perform more passive but often critical acts of examination: you can ask objects what methods they can execute (in even more ways than you've seen already) or what instance variables they have. You can query classes and modules for their constants and their instance methods. You can examine a stack trace to determine what method calls got you to a particular point in your program—and you even get access to the filenames and line numbers of all the method calls along the way.

In short, Ruby invites you to the party: you get to see what's going on, in considerable detail, via techniques for runtime introspection; and you can order Ruby to push certain buttons in reaction to runtime events. This chapter, the last in the book, will explore a variety of these introspective and callback techniques and will equip you to take ever greater advantage of the facilities offered by this remarkable, and remarkably dynamic, language.

15.1 Callbacks and hooks

The use of *callbacks* and *hooks* is a fairly common meta-programming technique. These methods are called when a particular event takes place during the run of a Ruby program. An event is something like

- A nonexistent method being called on an object
- A module being mixed in to a class or another module
- An object being extended with a module
- A class being subclassed (inherited from)
- A reference being made to a nonexistent constant
- An instance method being added to a class
- A singleton method being added to an object

For every event in that list, you can (if you choose) write a callback method that will be executed when the event happens. These callback methods are per-object or per-class, not global; if you want a method called when the class `Ticket` gets subclassed, you have to write the appropriate method specifically for class `Ticket`.

What follows are descriptions of each of these runtime event hooks. We'll look at them in the order they're listed above.

15.1.1 Intercepting unrecognized messages with method_missing

Back in chapter 4 (section 4.3) you learned quite a lot about `method_missing`. To summarize: when you send a message to an object, the object executes the first method it finds on its method-lookup path with the same name as the message. If it fails to find any such method, it raises a `NoMethodError` exception—unless you've provided the object with a method called `method_missing`. (Refer back to section 4.3 if you want to refresh your memory on how `method_missing` works.)

Of course, `method_missing` deserves a berth in this chapter too, because it's arguably the most commonly used runtime hook in Ruby. Rather than repeat chapter 4's coverage, though, let's look at a couple of specific `method_missing` nuances. We'll consider using method_missing as a delegation technique; and we'll look at how method_missing works, and what happens when you override it, at the top of the class hierarchy.

DELEGATING WITH METHOD_MISSING

You can use method_missing to bring about an automatic extension of the way your object behaves. For example, let's say you're modeling an object that in some respects is a container but that also has other characteristics—perhaps a cookbook. You want to be able to program your cookbook as a collection of recipes, but it also has certain characteristics (title, author, perhaps a list of people with whom you've shared it or who have contributed to it) that need to be stored and handled separately from the recipes. Thus the cookbook is both a collection and the repository of metadata about the collection.

To do this in a method_missing-based way, you would maintain an array of recipes and then forward any unrecognized messages to that array. A simple implementation might look like this:

```
class Cookbook
  attr_accessor :title, :author
  def initialize
    @recipes = []
  end
  def method_missing(m,*args,&block)
    @recipes.send(m,*args,&block)
  end
end
```

Now we can perform manipulations on the collection of recipes, taking advantage of any array methods we wish. Let's assume there's a Recipe class, separate from the Cookbook class, and we've already created some Recipe objects:

```
cb = Cookbook.new
cb << recipe_for_cake
cb << recipe_for_chicken
beef_dishes = cb.select {|recipes| recipe.main_ingredient == "beef" }
```

The cookbook instance, cb, doesn't have methods called << and select, so those messages are passed along to the @recipes array courtesy of method_missing. We can still define any methods we want directly in the Cookbook class—we can even override array methods, if we want a more cookbook-specific behavior for any of those methods—but method_missing saves us from having to define a parallel set of methods for handling pages as an ordered collection.

Ruby's method-delegating techniques

In this method_missing example, we've *delegated* the processing of messages (the unknown ones) to the array @recipes. Ruby has several mechanisms for delegating actions from one object to another. We won't go into them here, but you may come across both the Delegator class and the SimpleDelegator class in your further encounters with Ruby.

This use of `method_missing` is very straightforward (though you can mix and match it with some of the bells and whistles from chapter 4) but very powerful; it adds a great deal of intelligence to a class in return for little effort. Let's look now at the other end of the spectrum: `method_missing` not in a specific class, but at the top of the class tree and the top level of your code.

THE ORIGINAL: BASICOBJECT#METHOD_MISSING

`method_missing` is one of the few methods defined at the very top of the class tree, in the `BasicObject` class. Thanks to the fact that all classes ultimately derive from `Basic-Object`, all objects have a `method_missing` method.

The default `method_missing` is rather intelligent. Look at the difference between the error messages in these two exchanges with irb:

```
>> a
NameError: undefined local variable or method `a' for main:Object
>> a?
NoMethodError: undefined method `a?' for main:Object
```

The unknown identifer a could be either a method or a variable (if it weren't unknown, that is); and though it gets handled by `method_missing`, the error message reflects the fact that Ruby can't ultimately tell whether you meant it as a method call or a variable reference. The second unknown identifier, a?, can only be a method, because variable names can't end with a question mark. `method_missing` picks up on this and refines the error message (and even the choice of which exception to raise).

It's possible to override the default `method_missing`, in either of two ways. First, you can open the `BasicObject` class and redefine `method_missing`. The second, more common (though, admittedly, not all that common) technique is to define `method_missing` at the top level, thus installing it as a private instance method of `Object`.

If you use this second technique, all objects except actual instances of `BasicObject` itself will find the new version of `method_missing`:

```
>> def method_missing(m,*args,&block)
>>   raise NameError, "What on earth do you mean by #{m}?"
>> end
=> nil
>> a
NameError: What on earth do you mean by a?
        from (irb):2:in `method_missing'
>> BasicObject.new.a
NoMethodError: undefined method `a' for #<BasicObject:0x4103ac>
```

(You can put a super call inside your new version, if you want to bounce it up to the version in `BasicObject`, perhaps after logging the error, instead of raising an exception yourself.)

Remember that if you define your own `method_missing`, you lose the intelligence that can discern variable naming from method naming:

```
>> a?
NameError: What on earth do you mean by a??
```

It probably doesn't matter, especially if you're going to call super anyway—and if you really want to, you can examine the details of the symbol m yourself. But it's an interesting glimpse into the subtleties of the class hierarchy and the semantics of overriding.

METHOD_MISSING, RESPOND_TO?, AND RESPOND_TO_MISSING?

An oft-cited problem with method_missing is that it doesn't align with respond_to?. Consider this example. In the Person class, we intercept messages that start with set_, and transform them into setter methods: set_age(n) becomes age=n and so forth. For example:

```
class Person
  attr_accessor :name, :age
  def initialize(name, age)
    @name, @age = name, age
  end

  def method_missing(m, *args, &block)
    if /set_(.*)/.match(m)
      self.send("#{$1}=", *args)
    else
      super
    end
  end
end
```

So does a person object have a set_age method, or not? Well, you can call that method, but the person object claims it doesn't respond to it:

```
person = Person.new("David", 54)        | 55
person.set_age(55)              ⊲──┘
p person.age
p person.respond_to?(:set_age)      ⊲──┘ false
```

The way to get method_missing and respond_to? to line up with each other is by defining the special method respond_to_missing?. Here's a definition you can add to the preceding Person class:

```
  def respond_to_missing?(m, include_private = false)
    /set_/.match(m) || super
  end
```

Now the new person object will respond differently given the same queries:

```
55
true
```

You can control whether private methods are included by using a second argument to respond_to?. That second argument will be passed along to respond_to_missing?. In the example, it defaults to false.

As a bonus, methods that become visible through respond_to_missing? can also be objectified into method objects using method:

```
person = Person.new("David", 55)     | #<Method:
p person.method(:set_age)        ⊲──┘ Person#set_age>
```

Overall, `method_missing` is a highly useful event-trapping tool. But it's far from the only one.

15.1.2 *Trapping include and prepend operations*

You know how to include a module in a class or other module, and you know how to prepend a module to a class or module. If you want to trap these events—to trigger a callback when the events occur—you can define special methods called `included` and `prepended`. Each of these methods receives the name of the including or prepending class or module as its single argument.

Let's look closely at `included`, knowing that `prepended` works in much the same way. You can do a quick test of `included` by having it trigger a message printout and then perform an `include` operation:

```
module M
  def self.included(c)
    puts "I have just been mixed into #{c}."
  end
end
class C
  include M
end
```

You see the message `"I have just been mixed into C."` as a result of the execution of `M.included` when `M` gets included by (mixed into) `C`. (Because you can also mix modules into modules, the example would also work if `C` were another module.)

When would it be useful for a module to intercept its own inclusion like this? One commonly discussed case revolves around the difference between instance and class methods. When you mix a module into a class, you're ensuring that all the instance methods defined in the module become available to instances of the class. But the class object isn't affected. The following question often arises: What if you want to add class methods to the class by mixing in the module along with adding the instance methods?

Courtesy of `included`, you can trap the `include` operation and use the occasion to add class methods to the class that's doing the including. The following listing shows an example.

Listing 15.1 Using `included` to add a class method as part of a mix-in operation

```
module M
  def self.included(cl)
    def cl.a_class_method
      puts "Now the class has a new class method."
    end
  end
  def an_inst_method
    puts "This module supplies this instance method."
  end
end
```

```
class C
  include M
end
c = C.new
c.an_inst_method
C.a_class_method
```

The output from this listing is

```
This module supplies this instance method.
Now the class has a new class method.
```

When class C includes module M, two things happen. First, an instance method called an_inst_method appears in the lookup path of its instances (such as c). Second, thanks to M's included callback, a class method called a_class_method is defined for the class object C.

Module#included is a useful way to hook into the class/module engineering of your program. Meanwhile, let's look at another callback in the same general area of interest: Module#extended.

15.1.3 *Intercepting extend*

As you know from chapter 13, extending individual objects with modules is one of the most powerful techniques available in Ruby for taking advantage of the flexibility of objects and their ability to be customized. It's also the beneficiary of a runtime hook: using the Module#extended method, you can set up a callback that will be triggered whenever an object performs an extend operation that involves the module in question.

The next listing shows a modified version of listing 15.1 that illustrates the workings of Module#extended.

Listing 15.2   Triggering a callback from an extend event

```
module M
  def self.extended(obj)
    puts "Module #{self} is being used by #{obj}."
  end
  def an_inst_method
    puts "This module supplies this instance method."
  end
end
my_object = Object.new
my_object.extend(M)
my_object.an_inst_method
```

The output from this listing is

```
Module M is being used by #<Object:0x007f8e2a95bae0>.
This module supplies this instance method.
```

It's useful to look at how the included and extended callbacks work in conjunction with singleton classes. There's nothing too surprising here; what you learn is how consistent Ruby's object and class model is.

SINGLETON-CLASS BEHAVIOR WITH EXTENDED AND INCLUDED

In effect, extending an object with a module is the same as including that module in the object's singleton class. Whichever way you describe it, the upshot is that the module is added to the object's method-lookup path, entering the chain right after the object's singleton class.

But the two operations trigger different callbacks: extended and included. The following listing demonstrates the relevant behaviors.

> **Listing 15.3 Extending an object and including it into its singleton class**

```
module M
  def self.included(c)                             ←——❶
    puts "#{self} included by #{c}."
  end
  def self.extended(obj)                           ←——❷
    puts "#{self} extended by #{obj}."
  end
end
obj = Object.new
puts "Including M in object's singleton class:"    ⎫
class << obj                                       ⎬ ❸
  include M
end                                                ⎭
puts
obj = Object.new                                   ⎫
puts "Extending object with M:"                    ⎬ ❹
obj.extend(M)                                      ⎭
```

Both callbacks are defined in the module M: included ❶ and extended ❷. Each callback prints out a report of what it's doing. Starting with a freshly minted, generic object, we include M in the object's singleton class ❸ and then repeat the process, using another new object and extending the object with M directly ❹.

The output from this listing is

```
Including M in object's singleton class:
M included by #<Class:#<Object:0x0000010193c978>>.

Extending object with M:
M extended by #<Object:0x0000010193c310>.
```

Sure enough, the include triggers the included callback, and the extend triggers extended, even though in this particular scenario the results of the two operations are the same: the object in question has M added to its method lookup path. It's a nice illustration of some of the subtlety and precision of Ruby's architecture and a useful reminder that manipulating an object's singleton class directly isn't *quite* identical to doing singleton-level operations directly on the object.

Just as modules can intercept include and extend operations, classes can tell when they're being subclassed.

15.1.4 *Intercepting inheritance with Class#inherited*

You can hook into the subclassing of a class by defining a special class method called inherited for that class. If inherited has been defined for a given class, then when you subclass the class, inherited is called with the name of the new class as its single argument.

Here's a simple example, where the class C reports on the fact that it has been subclassed:

```
class C
  def self.inherited(subclass)
    puts "#{self} just got subclassed by #{subclass}."
  end
end
class D < C
end
```

The subclassing of C by D automatically triggers a call to inherited and produces the following output:

```
C just got subclassed by D.
```

inherited is a class method, so descendants of the class that defines it are also able to call it. The actions you define in inherited cascade: if you inherit from a subclass, that subclass triggers the inherited method, and so on down the chain of inheritance. If you do this

```
class E < D
end
```

you're informed that D just got subclassed by E. You get similar results if you subclass E, and so forth.

The limits of the inherited callback

Everything has its limits, including the inherited callback. When D inherits from C, C is D's superclass; but in addition, C's singleton class is the superclass of D's singleton class. That's how D manages to be able to call C's class methods. But no callback is triggered. Even if you define inherited in C's singleton class, it's never called.

Here's a testbed. Note how inherited is defined inside the singleton class of C. But even when D inherits from C—and even after the explicit creation of D's singleton class—the callback isn't triggered:

```
class C
  class << self
    def self.inherited
      puts "Singleton class of C just got inherited!"
      puts "But you'll never see this message."
    end
  end
end
```

(continued)
```
class D < C
  class << self
    puts "D's singleton class now exists, but no callback!"
  end
end
```

The output from this program is

```
D's singleton class now exists, but no callback!
```

You're extremely unlikely ever to come across a situation where this behavior matters, but it gives you a nice X-ray of how Ruby's class model interoperates with its callback layer.

Let's look now at how to intercept a reference to a nonexistent constant.

15.1.5 The Module#const_missing method

Module#const_missing is another commonly used callback. As the name implies, this method is called whenever an unidentifiable constant is referred to inside a given module or class:

```
class C
  def self.const_missing(const)
    puts "#{const} is undefined—setting it to 1."
    const_set(const,1)
  end
end
puts C::A
puts C::A
```

The output of this code is

```
A is undefined—setting it to 1.
1
1
```

Thanks to the callback, C::A is defined automatically when you use it without defining it. This is taken care of in such a way that puts can print the value of the constant; puts never has to know that the constant wasn't defined in the first place. Then, on the second call to puts, the constant is already defined, and const_missing isn't called.

One of the most powerful event callback facilities in Ruby is method_added, which lets you trigger an event when a new instance method is defined.

15.1.6 The method_added and singleton_method_added methods

If you define method_added as a class method in any class or module, it will be called when any instance method is defined. Here's a basic example:

```
class C
  def self.method_added(m)          ◁──┐   Defines callback
    puts "Method #{m} was just defined."
  end
  def a_new_method          ◁──┐   Triggers it by defining
  end                            │   instance method
end
```

The output from this program is

```
Method a_new_method was just defined.
```

The `singleton_method_added` callback does much the same thing, but for singleton methods. Perhaps surprisingly, it even triggers itself. If you run this snippet

```
class C
  def self.singleton_method_added(m)
    puts "Method #{m} was just defined."
  end
end
```

you'll see that the callback—which is a singleton method on the class object C—triggers its own execution:

```
Method singleton_method_added was just defined.
```

The callback will also be triggered by the definition of another singleton (class) method. Let's expand the previous example to include such a definition:

```
class C
  def self.singleton_method_added(m)
    puts "Method #{m} was just defined."
  end
  def self.new_class_method
  end
end
```

The new output is

```
Method singleton_method_added was just defined.
Method new_class_method was just defined.
```

In most cases, you should use `singleton_method_added` with objects other than class objects. Here's how its use might play out with a generic object:

```
obj = Object.new
def obj.singleton_method_added(m)
  puts "Singleton method #{m} was just defined."
end
def obj.a_new_singleton_method
end
```

The output in this case is

```
Singleton method singleton_method_added was just defined.
Singleton method a_new_singleton_method was just defined.
```

Again, you get the somewhat surprising effect that defining `singleton_method_added` triggers the callback's own execution.

Putting the class-based and object-based approaches together, you can achieve the object-specific effect by defining the relevant methods in the object's singleton class:

```ruby
obj = Object.new
class << obj
  def singleton_method_added(m)
    puts "Singleton method #{m} was just defined."
  end
  def a_new_singleton_method
  end
end
```

The output for this snippet is exactly the same as for the previous example. Finally, coming full circle, you can define `singleton_method_added` as a regular instance method of a class, in which case every instance of that class will follow the rule that the callback will be triggered by the creation of a singleton method:

```ruby
class C
  def singleton_method_added(m)                    ◁─❶
    puts "Singleton method #{m} was just defined."
  end
end
c = C.new
def c.a_singleton_method                           ◁─❷
end
```

Here, the definition of the callback ❶ governs every instance of C. The definition of a singleton method on such an instance ❷ therefore triggers the callback, resulting in this output:

```
Singleton method a_singleton_method was just defined.
```

It's possible that you won't use either `method_added` or `singleton_method_added` often in your Ruby applications. But experimenting with them is a great way to get a deeper feel for how the various parts of the class, instance, and singleton-class pictures fit together.

We'll turn now to the subject of examining object capabilities (`"abc".methods` and friends). The basics of this topic were included in the "Built-in Essentials" survey in chapter 7, and as promised in that chapter, we'll go into them more deeply here.

15.2 *Interpreting object capability queries*

At this point in your work with Ruby, you can set your sights on doing more with lists of objects' methods than examining and discarding them. In this section we'll look at a few examples (and there'll be plenty of room left for you to create more, as your needs and interests demand) of ways in which you might use and interpret the information in method lists. The Ruby you've learned since we last addressed this topic directly will stand you in good stead. You'll also learn a few fine points of the method-querying methods themselves.

Let's start at the most familiar point of departure: listing non-private methods with the methods method.

15.2.1 *Listing an object's non-private methods*

To list the non-private (i.e., public or protected) methods that an object knows about, you use the method methods, which returns an array of symbols. Arrays being arrays, you can perform some useful queries on the results of the initial query. Typically, you'll filter the array in some way so as to get a subset of methods.

Here, for example, is how you might ask a string what methods it knows about that involve modification of case:

```
>> string = "Test string"
=> "Test string"
>> string.methods.grep(/case/).sort
=> [:casecmp, :downcase, :downcase!, :swapcase, :swapcase!, :upcase,
:upcase!]
```

The grep filters out any symbol that doesn't have case in it. (Remember that although they're not strings, symbols exhibit a number of stringlike behaviors, such as being grep-pable.) The sort command at the end is useful for most method-listing operations. It doesn't make much of a difference in this example, because there are only seven methods; but when you get back arrays of 100 or more symbols, sorting them can help a lot.

Grepping for case depends on the assumption, of course, that case-related methods will have case in their names. There's definitely an element of judgment, often along the lines of making educated guesses about what you think you'll find, in many method-capability queries. Things tend to work out, though, as Ruby is more than reasonably consistent and conventional in its choice of method names.

Some of the case methods are also bang (!) methods. Following that thread, let's find out all the bang methods a string has, again using a grep operation:

```
>>string.methods.grep(/.!/).sort
=> [:capitalize!, :chomp!, :chop!, :delete!, :downcase!, :encode!, :gsub!,
    :lstrip!, :next!, :reverse!, :rstrip!, :scrub!, :slice!, :squeeze!,
    :strip!, :sub!, :succ!, :swapcase!, :tr!, :tr_s!, :upcase!]
```

Why the dot before the ! in the regular expression? Its purpose is to ensure that there's at least one character before the ! in the method name, and thus to exclude the !, !=, and !~ methods, which contain ! but aren't bang methods in the usual sense. We want methods that end with a bang, but not those that begin with one.

Let's use methods a little further. Here's a question we can answer by interpreting method query results: do strings have any bang methods that don't have corresponding non-bang methods?

```
string = "Test string"
methods = string.methods                        ❶
bangs = string.methods.grep(/.!/)
```

```
unmatched = bangs.reject do |b|
  methods.include?(b[0..-2].to_sym)                    ❷
end
if unmatched.empty?
  puts "All bang methods are matched by non-bang methods."    ❸
else
  puts "Some bang methods have no non-bang partner: "
  puts unmatched
end
```

> ❸ **Output: All bang methods are matched by non-bang methods.**

The code works by collecting all of a string's public methods and, separately, all of its bang methods ❶. Then, a reject operation filters out all bang method names for which a corresponding non-bang name can be found in the larger method-name list ❷. The [0..-2] index grabs everything but the last character of the symbol—the method name minus the !, in other words—and the call to to_sym converts the resulting string back to a symbol so that the include? test can look for it in the array of methods. If the filtered list is empty, that means that no unmatched bang method names were found. If it isn't empty, then at least one such name was found and can be printed out ❸.

If you run the script as it is, it will always take the first (true) branch of the if statement. If you want to see a list of unmatched bang methods, you can add the following line to the program, just after the first line:

```
def string.surprise!; end
```

When you run the modified version of the script, you'll see this:

```
Some bang methods have no non-bang partner:
surprise!
```

As you've already seen, writing bang methods without non-bang partners is usually bad practice—but it's a good way to see the methods method at work.

You can, of course, ask class and module objects what their methods are. After all, they're just objects. But remember that the methods method always lists the non-private methods of the object itself. In the case of classes and modules, that means you're not getting a list of the methods that instances of the class—or instances of classes that mix in the module—can call. You're getting the methods that the class or module itself knows about. Here's a (partial) result from calling methods on a newly created class object:

```
>> class C; end
=> nil
>> C.methods.sort
=> [:!, :!=, :!~, :<, :<=, :<=>, :==, :===, :=~, :>, :>=, :__id__, :__send__,
    :allocate, :ancestors, :autoload, :autoload?, :class, :class_eval,
    :class_exec, :class_variable_defined?, :class_variable_get,
    :class_variable_set, :class_variables, etc.
```

Class and module objects share some methods with their own instances, because they're all objects and objects in general share certain methods. But the methods you see are those that the class or module itself can call. You can also ask classes and modules about the instance methods they define. We'll return to that technique shortly. First, let's look briefly at the process of listing an object's private and protected methods.

15.2.2 *Listing private and protected methods*

Every object (except instances of `BasicObject`) has a `private_methods` method and a `protected_methods` method. They work as you'd expect; they provide arrays of symbols, but containing private and protected method names, respectively.

Freshly minted Ruby objects have a lot of private methods and no protected methods:

```
$ ruby -e 'o = Object.new; p o.private_methods.size'
72
$ ruby -e 'o = Object.new; p o.protected_methods.size'
0
```

What are those private methods? They're private instance methods defined mostly in the `Kernel` module and secondarily in the `BasicObject` class. Here's how you can track this down:

```
$ ruby -e 'o = Object.new; p o.private_methods -
    BasicObject.private_instance_methods(false) -
    Kernel.private_instance_methods(false)'
[]
```

Note that after you subtract the private methods defined in `Kernel` and `BasicObject`, the original object has no private methods to list. The private methods defined in `Kernel` are the methods we think of as "top-level," like `puts`, `binding`, and `raise`. Play around a little with the method-listing techniques you're learning here and you'll see some familiar methods listed.

Naturally, if you define a private method yourself, it will also appear in the list of private methods. Here's an example: a simple `Person` class in which assigning a name to the person via the `name=` method triggers a name-normalization method that removes everything other than letters and selected punctuation characters from the name. The `normalize_name` method is private:

```
class Person
  attr_reader :name
  def name=(name)              ◁─┐ Defines nondefault
    @name = name                 │ write accessor
    normalize_name           ◁─┐ Normalizes name
  end                          │ when assigned
  private
  def normalize_name          ◁─┐ Removes undesired
    name.gsub!(/[^-a-z'.\s]/i, "")  │ characters from name
  end
end                          Makes sure        Print success message
david = Person.new          normalization works
david.name = "123David!! Bl%a9ck"
raise "Problem" unless david.name == "David Black"  ◁─┘
puts "Name has been normalized."                    ◁──┘  Result of private
p david.private_methods.sort.grep(/normal/)         ◁──┘  method inspection:
                                                          [:normalize_name]
```

Protected methods can be examined in much the same way, using the `protected_` `methods` method.

In addition to asking objects what methods they know about, it's frequently useful to ask classes and modules what methods they provide.

15.2.3 *Getting class and module instance methods*

Classes and modules come with a somewhat souped-up set of method-querying methods. Examining those available in `String` illustrates the complete list. The methods that are specific to classes and modules are in **bold**:

```
>> String.methods.grep(/methods/).sort
=> [:instance_methods, :methods, :private_instance_methods,
:private_methods, :protected_instance_methods, :protected_methods,
    :public_instance_methods, :public_methods, :singleton_methods]
```

The methods shown in bold give you lists of instance methods of various kinds defined in the class or module. The four methods work as follows:

- `instance_methods` returns all public and protected instance methods.
- `public_instance_methods` returns all public instance methods.
- `protected_instance_methods` and `private_instance_methods` return all protected and private instance methods, respectively.

When calling any of these methods, you have the option of passing in an argument. If you pass in the argument `false`, then the list of methods you get back will include only those defined in the class or module you're querying. If you pass in any argument with Boolean truth (anything other than `false` or `nil`), or if you pass in no argument, the list of methods will include those defined in the class or module you're querying and all of its ancestor classes and modules.

For example, you can find out which instance methods the `Range` class defines, like this:

```
>> Range.instance_methods(false).sort
=> [:==, :===, :begin, :bsearch, :cover?, :each, :end, :eql?, :exclude_end?,
    :first, :hash, :include?, :inspect, :last, :max, :member?, :min, :size,
    :step, :to_s]]
```

Going one step further, what if you want to know which of the methods defined in the `Enumerable` module are overridden in `Range`? You can find out by performing an and (`&`) operation on the two lists of instance methods: those defined in `Enumerable` and those defined in `Range`:

```
>> Range.instance_methods(false) & Enumerable.instance_methods(false)
=> [:first, :min, :max, :member?, :include?]
```

As you can see, `Range` redefines five methods that `Enumerable` already defines.

We'll look shortly at the last of the `methods`-style methods, `singleton_methods`. But first, let's create a program that produces a list of all the overrides of all classes that mix in `Enumerable`.

GETTING ALL THE ENUMERABLE OVERRIDES

The strategy here will be to find out which classes mix in `Enumerable` and then perform on each such class an and (`&`) operation like the one in the last example, storing the results and, finally, printing them out. The following listing shows the code.

Listing 15.4   Enumerable descendants' overrides of Enumerable instance methods

```
overrides = {}                                                      ➊
enum_classes = ObjectSpace.each_object(Class).select do |c|
  c.ancestors.include?(Enumerable)                                  ➋
end
enum_classes.sort_by {|c| c.name}.each do |c|
  overrides[c] = c.instance_methods(false) &                       ➌
                 Enumerable.instance_methods(false)
end                                                                 ➍
overrides.delete_if {|c, methods| methods.empty? }
overrides.each do |c,methods|
  puts "Class #{c} overrides: #{methods.join(", ")}"               ➎
end
```

First, we create an empty hash in the variable `overrides` ➊. We then get a list of all classes that mix in `Enumerable`. The technique for getting this list involves the `ObjectSpace` module and its `each_object` method ➋. This method takes a single argument representing the class of the objects you want it to find. In this case, we're interested in objects of class `Class`, and we're only interested in those that have `Enumerable` among their ancestors. The `each_object` method returns an enumerator, and the call to `select` on that enumerator has the desired effect of filtering the list of all classes down to a list of only those that have mixed in `Enumerable`.

Now it's time to populate the `overrides` hash. For each class in `enum_classes` (nicely sorted by class name), we put an entry in `overrides`. The key is the class, and the value is an array of method names—the names of the `Enumerable` methods that this class overrides ➌. After removing any entries representing classes that haven't overridden any `Enumerable` methods ➍, we proceed to print the results, using `sort` and `join` operations to make the output look consistent and clear ➎, as shown here:

```
Class ARGF.class overrides: to_a
Class Array overrides: to_a, to_h, first, reverse_each, find_index, sort,
    collect, map, select, reject, zip, include?, count, cycle, take,
    take_while, drop, drop_while
Class Enumerator overrides: each_with_index, each_with_object
Class Enumerator::Lazy overrides: map, collect, flat_map, collect_concat,
    select, find_all, reject, grep, zip, take, take_while, drop, drop_while,
    lazy, chunk, slice_before
Class Hash overrides: to_h, to_a, select, reject, include?, member?
Class ObjectSpace::WeakMap overrides: include?, member?
Class Range overrides: first, min, max, member?, include?
Class Struct overrides: to_a, to_h, select
```

The first line pertains to the somewhat anomalous object designated as `ARGF.class`, which is a unique, specially engineered object involved in the processing of program input. The other lines pertain to several familiar classes that mix in `Enumerable`. In each case, you see which `Enumerable` methods the class in question has overridden.

Let's look next at how to query an object with regard to its singleton methods.

15.2.4 *Listing objects' singleton methods*

A singleton method, as you know, is a method defined for the sole use of a particular object (or, if the object is a class, for the use of the object and its subclasses) and stored in that object's singleton class. You can use the `singleton_methods` method to list all such methods. Note that `singleton_methods` lists public and protected singleton methods but not private ones. Here's an example:

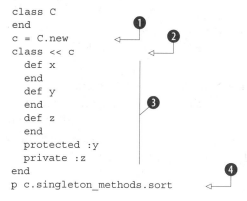

```
class C
end
c = C.new
class << c
  def x
  end
  def y
  end
  def z
  end
  protected :y
  private :z
end
p c.singleton_methods.sort
```

An instance of class `C` is created ❶, and its singleton class is opened ❷. Three methods are defined in the singleton class, one each at the public (`x`), protected (`y`), and private (`z`) levels ❸. The printout of the singleton methods of `c` ❹ looks like this:

```
[:x, :y]
```

Singleton methods are also considered just methods. The methods `:x` and `:y` will show up if you call `c.methods`, too. You can use the class-based method-query methods on the singleton class. Add this code to the end of the last example:

```
class << c
  p private_instance_methods(false)
end
```

When you run it, you'll see this:

```
[:z]
```

The method `:z` is a singleton method of `c`, which means it's an instance method (a private instance method, as it happens) of `c`'s singleton class.

You can ask a class for its singleton methods, and you'll get the singleton methods defined for that class and for all of its ancestors. Here's an irb-based illustration:

```
>> class C; end
=> nil
>> class D < C; end
```

```
=> nil
>> def C.a_class_method_on_C; end
=> nil
>> def D.a_class_method_on_D; end
=> nil
>> D.singleton_methods
=> [:a_class_method_on_D, :a_class_method_on_C]
```

Once you get some practice using the various `methods` methods, you'll find them useful for studying and exploring how and where methods are defined. For example, you can use method queries to examine how the class methods of `File` are composed. To start with, find out which class methods `File` inherits from its ancestors, as opposed to those it defines itself:

```
>> File.singleton_methods - File.singleton_methods(false)
=> [:new, :open, :sysopen, :for_fd, :popen, :foreach, :readlines,
:read, :select, :pipe, :try_convert, :copy_stream]
```

The call to `singleton_methods(false)` provides only the singleton methods defined on `File`. The call without the `false` argument provides all the singleton methods defined on `File` and its ancestors. The difference is the ones defined by the ancestors.

The superclass of `File` is `IO`. Interestingly, although not surprisingly, all 12 of the ancestral singleton methods available to `File` are defined in `IO`. You can confirm this with another query:

```
>> IO.singleton_methods(false)
=> [:new, :open, :sysopen, :for_fd, :popen, :foreach, :readlines,
:read, :select, :pipe, :try_convert, :copy_stream]
```

The relationship among classes—in this case, the fact that `File` is a subclass of `IO` and therefore shares its singleton methods (its class methods)—is directly visible in the method-name arrays. The various `methods` methods allow for almost unlimited inspection and exploration of this kind.

As you can see, the method-querying facilities in Ruby can tell you quite a lot about the objects, class, and modules that you're handling. You just need to connect the dots by applying collection-querying and text-processing techniques to the lists they provide. Interpreting method queries is a nice example of the kind of learning feedback loop that Ruby provides: the more you learn about the language, the more you *can* learn.

We'll turn next to the matter of runtime reflection on variables and constants.

15.3 *Introspection of variables and constants*

Ruby can tell you several things about which variables and constants you have access to at a given point in runtime. You can get a listing of local or global variables, an object's instance variables, the class variables of a class or module, and the constants of a class or module.

15.3.1 *Listing local and global variables*

The local and global variable inspections are straightforward: you use the top-level methods `local_variables` and `global_variables`. In each case, you get back an array of symbols corresponding to the local or global variables currently defined:

```
x = 1
p local_variables
[:x]
p global_variables.sort
[:$!, :$", :$$, :$&, :$', :$*, :$+, :$,, :$-0, :$-F, :$-I, :$-K, :$-W, :$-a,
:$-d, :$-i, :$-l, :$-p, :$-v, :$-w, :$., :$/, :$0, :$1, :$2, :$3, :$4, :$5,
:$6, :$7, :$8, :$9, :$:, :$;, :$<, :$=, :$>, :$?, :$@, :$DEBUG, :$FILENAME,
:$KCODE, :$LOADED_FEATURES, :$LOAD_PATH, :$PROGRAM_NAME, :$SAFE, :$VERBOSE,
:$\, :$_, :$`, :$stderr, :$stdin, :$stdout, :$~]
```

The global variable list includes globals like `$:` (the library load path, also available as `$LOAD_PATH`), `$~` (the global `MatchData` object based on the most recent pattern-matching operation), `$0` (the name of the file in which execution of the current program was initiated), `$FILENAME` (the name of the file currently being executed), and others. The local variable list includes all currently defined local variables.

Note that `local_variables` and `global_variables` don't give you the values of the variables they report on; they just give you the names. The same is true of the `instance_variables` method, which you can call on any object.

15.3.2 *Listing instance variables*

Here's another rendition of a simple `Person` class, which illustrates what's involved in an instance-variable query:

```
class Person
  attr_accessor :name, :age
  def initialize(name)
    @name = name
  end
end
david = Person.new("David")
david.age = 55
p david.instance_variables
```

The output is

```
[:@name, :@age]
```

The object `david` has two instance variables initialized at the time of the query. One of them, `@name`, was assigned a value at the time of the object's creation. The other, `@age`, is present because of the accessor attribute age. Attributes are implemented as read and/or write methods around instance variables, so even though `@age` doesn't appear explicitly anywhere in the program, it gets initialized when the object is assigned an age.

All instance variables begin with the `@` character, and all globals begin with `$`. You might expect Ruby not to bother with those characters when it gives you lists of variable names; but the names you get in the lists do include the beginning characters.

The irb underscore variable

If you run `local_variables` in a new irb session, you'll see an underscore:

```
>> local_variables
=> [:_]
```

The underscore is a special irb variable: it represents the value of the last expression evaluated by irb. You can use it to grab values that otherwise will have disappeared:

```
>> Person.new("David")
=> #<Person:0x000001018ba360 @name="David">
>> david = _
=> #<Person:0x000001018ba360 @name="David">
```

Now the `Person` object is bound to the variable `david`.

Next, we'll look at execution-tracing techniques that help you determine the method-calling history at a given point in runtime.

15.4 *Tracing execution*

No matter where you are in the execution of your program, you got there somehow. Either you're at the top level or you're one or more method calls deep. Ruby provides information about how you got where you are. The chief tool for examining the method-calling history is the top-level method `caller`.

15.4.1 *Examining the stack trace with caller*

The `caller` method provides an array of strings. Each string represents one step in the stack trace: a description of a single method call along the way to where you are now. The strings contain information about the file or program where the method call was made, the line on which the method call occurred, and the method from which the current method was called, if any.

Here's an example. Put these lines in a file called tracedemo.rb:

```
def x
  y
end
def y
  z
end
def z
  puts "Stacktrace: "
  p caller
end
x
```

All this program does is bury itself in a stack of method calls: x calls y, y calls z. Inside z, we get a stack trace, courtesy of `caller`. Here's the output from running tracedemo.rb:

```
Stacktrace:
["tracedemo.rb:6:in `y'", "tracedemo.rb:2:in `x'", "tracedemo.rb:14:in
`<main>'"]
```

Each string in the stack trace array contains one link in the chain of method calls that got us to the point where `caller` was called. The first string represents the most recent call in the history: we were at line 6 of tracedemo.rb, inside the method y. The second string shows that we got to y via x. The third, final string tells us that we were in <main>, which means the call to x was made from the top level rather than from inside a method.

You may recognize the stack trace syntax from the messages you've seen from fatal errors. If you rewrite the z method to look like this

```
def z
  raise
end
```

the output will look like this:

```
tracedemo.rb:10:in `z': unhandled exception
        from tracedemo.rb:6:in `y'
        from tracedemo.rb:2:in `x'
        from tracedemo.rb:13:in `<main>'
```

This is, of course, just a slightly prettified version of the stack trace array we got the first time around from `caller`.

Ruby stack traces are useful, but they're also looked askance at because they consist solely of strings. If you want to do anything with the information a stack trace provides, you have to scan or parse the string and extract the useful information. Another approach is to write a Ruby tool for parsing stack traces and turning them into objects.

15.4.2 *Writing a tool for parsing stack traces*

Given a stack trace—an array of strings—we want to generate an array of objects, each of which has knowledge of a program or filename, a line number, and a method name (or <main>). We'll write a `Call` class, which will represent one stack trace step per object, and a `Stack` class that will represent an entire stack trace, consisting of one or more `Call` objects. To minimize the risk of name clashes, let's put both of these classes inside a module, `CallerTools`. Let's start by describing in more detail what each of the two classes will do.

`CallerTools::Call` will have three reader attributes: `program`, `line`, and `meth`. (It's better to use `meth` than `method` as the name of the third attribute because classes already have a method called `method` and we don't want to override it.) Upon initialization, an object of this class will parse a stack trace string and save the relevant substrings to the appropriate instance variables for later retrieval via the attribute-reader methods.

`CallerTools::Stack` will store one or more `Call` objects in an array, which in turn will be stored in the instance variable `@backtrace`. We'll also write a `report` method, which will produce a (reasonably) pretty printable representation of all the information in this particular stack of calls.

Now, let's write the classes.

THE CALLERTOOLS::CALL CLASS

The following listing shows the Call class along with the first line of the entire program, which wraps everything else in the CallerTools module.

Listing 15.5   Beginning of the `CallerTools` module, including the `Call` class

```
module CallerTools
  class Call
    CALL_RE = /(.*):(\d+):in `(.*)'/            ①
    attr_reader :program, :line, :meth          ②
    def initialize(string)
      @program, @line, @meth = CALL_RE.match(string).captures   ③
    end
    def to_s
      "%30s%5s%15s" % [program, line, meth]      ④
    end
  end
end
```

We need a regular expression with which to parse the stack trace strings; that regular expression is stored in the CALL_RE constant ①. CALL_RE has three parenthetical capture groupings, separated by uncaptured literal substrings. Here's how the regular expression matches up against a typical stack trace string. Bold type shows the substrings that are captured by the corresponding regular expression subpatterns. The nonbold characters aren't included in the captures but are matched literally:

```
myrubyfile.rb:234:in `a_method'
   .*           :\d+:in `  .*     '
```

The class has, as specified, three reader attributes for the three components of the call ②. Initialization requires a string argument, the string is matched against CALL_RE, and the results, available via the captures method of the MatchData object, are placed in the three instance variables corresponding to the attributes, using parallel assignment ③. (We get a fatal error for trying to call captures on nil if there's no match. You can alter the code to handle this condition directly if you wish.)

We also define a to_s method for Call objects ④. This method comes into play in situations where it's useful to print out a report of a particular backtrace element. It involves Ruby's handy % technique. On the left of the % is a sprintf-style formatting string, and on the right is an array of replacement values. You might want to tinker with the lengths of the fields in the replacement string—or, for that matter, write your own to_s method, if you prefer a different style of output.

Now it's time for the Stack class.

THE CALLERTOOLS::STACK CLASS

The Stack class, along with the closing end instruction for the entire CallerTools module, is shown in the following listing.

Listing 15.6 `CallerTools::Stack` **class**

```
class Stack
  def initialize
    stack = caller                        ←①
    stack.shift
    @backtrace = stack.map do |call|      ←②
      Call.new(call)
    end
  end
  def report
    @backtrace.map do |call|              ③
      call.to_s
    end
  end
  def find(&block)                        ←④
    @backtrace.find(&block)
  end
end
```

Upon initialization, a new `Stack` object calls `caller` and saves the resulting array ①. It then shifts that array, removing the first string; that string reports on the call to `Stack.new` itself and is therefore just noise.

The stored `@backtrace` should consist of one `Call` object for each string in the `my_caller` array. That's a job for `map` ②. Note that there's no `backtrace` reader attribute. In this case, all we need is the instance variable for internal use by the object.

Next comes the `report` method, which uses `map` on the `@backtrace` array to generate an array of strings for all the `Call` objects in the stack ③. This report array is suitable for printing or, if need be, for searching and filtering.

The `Stack` class includes one final method: `find` ④. It works by forwarding its code block to the `find` method of the `@backtrace` array. It works a lot like some of the deck-of-cards methods you've seen, which forward a method to an array containing the cards that make up the deck. Techniques like this allow you to fine-tune the interface of your objects, using underlying objects to provide them with exactly the functionality they need. (You'll see the specific usefulness of `find` shortly.)

Now, let's try out `CallerTools`.

USING THE CALLERTOOLS MODULE

You can use a modified version of the "x, y, z" demo from section 15.4.1 to try out `CallerTools`. Put this code in a file called callertest.rb:

```
require_relative 'callertools'
def x
  y
end
def y
  z
end
def z
  stack = CallerTools::Stack.new
```

```
    puts stack.report
end
x
```

When you run the program, you'll see this output:

```
callertest.rb   12                z
callertest.rb   8                 y
callertest.rb   4                 x
callertest.rb   16          <main>
```

Nothing too fancy, but it's a nice programmatic way to address a stack trace rather than having to munge the strings directly every time. (There's a lot of blank space at the beginnings of the lines, but there would be less if the file paths were longer—and of course you can adjust the formatting to taste.)

Next on the agenda, and the last stop for this chapter, is a project that ties together a number of the techniques we've been looking at: stack tracing, method querying, and callbacks, as well as some techniques you know from elsewhere in the book. We'll write a test framework.

15.5   *Callbacks and method inspection in practice*

In this section, we'll implement MicroTest, a tiny test framework. It doesn't have many features, but the ones it has will demonstrate some of the power and expressiveness of the callbacks and inspection techniques you've just learned.

First, a bit of backstory.

15.5.1   *MicroTest background: MiniTest*

Ruby ships with a testing framework called MiniTest. You use MiniTest by writing a class that inherits from the class `MiniTest::Unit::TestCase` and that contains methods whose names begin with the string test. You can then either specify which test methods you want executed, or arrange (as we will below) for every test-named method to be executed automatically when you run the file. Inside those methods, you write *assertions*. The truth or falsehood of your assertions determines whether your tests pass.

The exercise we'll do here is to write a simple testing utility based on some of the same principles as MiniTest. To help you get your bearings, we'll look first at a full example of MiniTest in action and then do the implementation exercise.

We'll test dealing cards. The following listing shows a version of a class for a deck of cards. The deck consists of an array of 52 strings held in the `@cards` instance variable. Dealing one or more cards means popping that many cards off the top of the deck.

> **Listing 15.7   Deck-of-cards implementation with card-dealing capabilities**

```
module PlayingCards
  RANKS = %w{ 2 3 4 5 6 7 8 9 10 J Q K A }
  SUITS = %w{ clubs diamonds hearts spades }
  class Deck
```

```
      def initialize
        @cards = []                        ←┐
        RANKS.each do |r|                    ❶
          SUITS.each do |s|
            @cards << "#{r} of #{s}"
          end
        end
        @cards.shuffle!
      end
      def deal(n=1)                ←—❷
        @cards.pop(n)
      end
      def size
        @cards.size
      end
    end
end
```

Creating a new deck ❶ involves initializing `@cards`, inserting 52 strings into it, and shuffling the array. Each string takes the form "*rank of suit*," where *rank* is one of the ranks in the constant array `RANKS` and *suit* is one of `SUITS`. In dealing from the deck ❷, we return an array of n cards, where n is the number of cards being dealt and defaults to 1.

So far, so good. Now, let's test it. Enter MiniTest. The next listing shows the test code for the cards class. The test code assumes that you've saved the cards code to a separate file called cards.rb in the same directory as the test code file (which you can call cardtest.rb).

Listing 15.8   cardtest.rb: Testing the dealing accuracy of `PlayingCards::Deck`

```
require 'minitest/unit'              ←—❶
require 'minitest/autorun'
require_relative 'cards'                      ❷
class CardTest < MiniTest::Unit::TestCase  ←┘
def setup                             ←┐
    @deck = PlayingCards::Deck.new     ❸
  end
  def test_deal_one              ←—❹
    @deck.deal
    assert_equal(51, @deck.size)    ←—❺
  end
  def test_deal_many                      ←—❻
    @deck.deal(5)
    assert_equal(47, @deck.size)
  end
end
```

The first order of business is to require both the `minitest/unit` library and the cards.rb file ❶. We also require `minitest/autorun`; this feature causes MiniTest to run the test methods it encounters without our having to make explicit method calls. Next, we create a `CardTest` class that inherits from `MiniTest::Unit::TestCase` ❷. In this class, we define three methods. The first is setup ❸. The method name setup is magic to MiniTest; if defined, it's executed before every test method in the test class.

Running the setup method before each test method contributes to keeping the test methods independent of each other, and that independence is an important part of the architecture of test suites.

Now come the two test methods, test_deal_one ❹ and test_deal_many ❻. These methods define the actual tests. In each case, we're dealing from the deck and then making an assertion about the size of the deck subsequent to the dealing. Remember that setup is executed before each test method, which means @deck contains a full 52-card deck for each method.

The assertions are performed using the assert_equal method ❺. This method takes two arguments. If the two are equal (using == to do the comparison behind the scenes), the assertion succeeds. If not, it fails.

Execute cardtest.rb from the command line. Here's what you'll see (probably with a different seed and different time measurements):

```
$ ruby cardtest.rb
Run options: --seed 39562

# Running tests:

. .

Finished tests in 0.000784s, 2551.0204 tests/s, 2551.0204 assertions/s.
2 tests, 2 assertions, 0 failures, 0 errors, 0 skips
```

The last line tells you that there were two methods whose names began with test (2 tests) and a total of two assertions (the two calls to assert_equal). It tells you further that both assertions passed (no failures) and that nothing went drastically wrong (no errors; an error is something unrecoverable like a reference to an unknown variable, whereas a failure is an incorrect assertion). It also reports that no tests were skipped (skipping a test is something you can do explicitly with a call to the skip method).

The most striking thing about running this test file is that at no point do you have to *instantiate* the CardTest class or explicitly call the test methods or the setup method. Thanks to the loading of the autorun feature, MiniTest figures out that it's supposed to run all the methods whose names begin with test, running the setup method before each of them. This automatic execution—or at least a subset of it—is what we'll implement in our exercise.

15.5.2 *Specifying and implementing MicroTest*

Here's what we'll want from our MicroTest utility:

- Automatic execution of the setup method and test methods, based on class inheritance
- A simple assertion method that either succeeds or fails

The first specification will entail most of the work.

We need a class that, upon being inherited, observes the new subclass and executes the methods in that subclass as they're defined. For the sake of (relative!) simplicity, we'll execute them in definition order, which means setup should be defined first.

Here's a more detailed description of the steps needed to implement MicroTest:

1 Define the class `MicroTest`.
2 Define `MicroTest.inherited`.
3 Inside `inherited`, the inheriting class should...
4 Define its own `method_added` callback, which should...
5 Instantiate the class and execute the new method if it starts with `test`, but first...
6 Execute the `setup` method, if there is one.

Here's a nonworking, commented mockup of `MicroTest` in Ruby:

```
class MicroTest
  def self.inherited(c)
    c.class_eval do
      def self.method_added(m)
        # If m starts with "test"
        #   Create an instance of c
        #   If there's a setup method
        #     Execute setup
        #   Execute the method m
      end
    end
  end
end
```

There's a kind of logic cascade here. Inside `MicroTest`, we define `self.inherited`, which receives the inheriting class (the new subclass) as its argument. We then enter into that class's definition scope using `class_eval`. Inside that scope, we implement `method_added`, which will be called every time a new method is defined in the class.

Writing the full code follows directly from the comments inside the code mockup. The following listing shows the full version of micro_test.rb. Put it in the same directory as callertools.rb.

> ### Listing 15.9 `MicroTest`, a testing class that emulates some MiniTest functionality

```
require_relative 'callertools'
class MicroTest
  def self.inherited(c)
    c.class_eval do
      def self.method_added(m)                             ❶
        if m =~ /^test/                             ←
          obj = self.new                            ←  ❷
          if self.instance_methods.include?(:setup) ←
            obj.setup                                  ┐
          end                                          ❸
          obj.send(m)
        end
      end
    end
  end
end
```

```
    def assert(assertion)
      if assertion                           ◀┐
        puts "Assertion passed"               ④
        true
      else
        puts "Assertion failed:"
        stack = CallerTools::Stack.new                        ⑤
        failure = stack.find {|call| call.meth !~ /assert/ }
        puts failure
        false
      end
    end
    def assert_equal(expected, actual)                ◀─⑥
      result = assert(expected == actual)
      puts "(#{actual} is not #{expected})" unless result    ◀─⑦
      result
    end
  end
```

Inside the class definition (class_eval) scope of the new subclass, we define method_added, and that's where most of the action is. If the method being defined starts with test ❶, we create a new instance of the class ❷. If a setup method is defined ❸, we call it on that instance. Then (whether or not there was a setup method; that's optional), we call the newly added method using send because we don't know the method's name.

> **NOTE** As odd as it may seem (in light of the traditional notion of pattern matching, which involves strings), the m in the pattern-matching operation m =~ /^test/ is a symbol, not a string. The ability of symbol objects to match themselves against regular expressions is part of the general move we've already noted toward making symbols more easily interchangeable with strings. Keep in mind, though, the important differences between the two, as explained in chapter 8.

The assert method tests the truth of its single argument ❹. If the argument is true (in the Boolean sense; it doesn't have to be the actual object true), a message is printed out, indicating success. If the assertion fails, the message printing gets a little more intricate. We create a CallerTools::Stack object and pinpoint the first Call object in that stack whose method name doesn't contain the string assert ❺. The purpose is to make sure we don't report the failure as having occurred in the assert method nor in the assert_equal method (described shortly). It's not robust; you might have a method with assert in it that you did want an error reported from. But it illustrates the kind of manipulation that the find method of CallerTools::Stack allows.

The second assertion method, assert_equal, tests for equality between its two arguments ❻. It does this by calling assert on a comparison. If the result isn't true, an error message showing the two compared objects is displayed ❼. Either way—success or failure—the result of the assert call is returned from assert_equal.

To try out `MicroTest`, put the following code in a file called microcardtest.rb, and run it from the command line:

```
require_relative 'microtest'
require_relative 'cards'
class CardTest < MicroTest
  def setup
    @deck = PlayingCards::Deck.new
  end
  def test_deal_one
    @deck.deal
    assert_equal(51, @deck.size)
  end
  def test_deal_many
    @deck.deal(5)
    assert_equal(47, @deck.size)
  end
end
```

As you can see, this code is almost identical to the MiniTest test file we wrote before. The only differences are the names of the test library and parent test class. And when you run the code, you get these somewhat obscure but encouraging results:

```
Assertion passed
Assertion passed
```

If you want to see a failure, change 51 to 50 in `test_deal_one`:

```
Assertion failed:
                microcardtest.rb    11   test_deal_one
(51 is not 50)
Assertion passed
```

MicroTest won't supplant MiniTest any time soon, but it does do a couple of the most magical things that MiniTest does. It's all made possible by Ruby's introspection and callback facilities, techniques that put extraordinary power and flexibility in your hands.

15.6 Summary

In this chapter, you've seen

- Intercepting methods with `method_missing`
- Runtime hooks and callbacks for objects, classes, and modules
- Querying objects about their methods, on various criteria
- Trapping references to unknown constants
- Stack traces
- Writing the MicroTest framework

We've covered a lot of ground in this chapter, and practicing the techniques covered here will contribute greatly to your grounding as a Rubyist. We looked at intercepting unknown messages with `method_missing`, along with other runtime hooks and callbacks like `Module.included`, `Module.extended`, and `Class.inherited`. The chapter also took us into method querying in its various nuances: public, protected, private; class, instance, singleton. You've seen some examples of how this kind of querying can help you derive information about how Ruby does its own class, module, and method organization.

The last overall topic was the handling of stack traces, which we put to use in the `CallerTools` module. The chapter ended with the extended exercise consisting of implementing the `MicroTest` class, which pulled together a number of topics and threads from this chapter and elsewhere.

We've been going through the material methodically and deliberately, as befits a grounding or preparation. But if you look at the results, particularly `MicroTest`, you can see how much power Ruby gives you in exchange for relatively little effort. That's why it pays to know about even what may seem to be the magic or "meta" parts of Ruby. They really aren't—it's all Ruby, and once you internalize the principles of class and object structure and relationships, everything else follows.

And that's that! Enjoy your groundedness as a Rubyist and the many structures you'll build on top of the foundation you've acquired through this book.

index